Student Problem Manual

for use with

Fundamentals of Corporate Finance

Fourth Edition

Stephen A. Ross
Yale University

Randolph W. Westerfield
University of Southern California

Bradford D. Jordan
University of Kentucky

Prepared by
Thomas H. Eyssell
University of Missouri, St. Louis

 **Irwin
McGraw-Hill**

Boston, Massachusetts   Burr Ridge, Illinois   Dubuque, Iowa
Madison, Wisconsin   New York, New York   San Francisco, California   St. Louis, Missouri

Irwin/McGraw-Hill

A Division of The McGraw-Hill Companies

Student Problem Manual for use with
FUNDAMENTALS OF CORPORATE FINANCE

1 2 3 4 5 6 7 8 9 0 BKM/BKM 9 0 9 8 7

ISBN 0-256-27185-2

http://www.mhhe.com

CONTENTS

INTRODUCTION TO CORPORATE FINANCE

CONCEPTS FOR REVIEW

This chapter introduces several new concepts which will be used throughout the text. Two ideas should be kept in mind while you are reading this chapter. First, although we provide a relatively narrow list of individuals we call **financial managers**, virtually *any* individual may, at some point, be charged with the responsibility for making financial decisions. Second, many of the principles and management techniques described in this text can be applied to decisions in other for-profit forms of organization, as well as not-for-profit organizations.

CHAPTER HIGHLIGHTS

Two major issues are addressed in this chapter: (1) What is corporate finance? and (2) What is the goal of the financial manager? The answers to these two questions require an understanding of the forms of business organization. We also explore the agency problem as it relates to financial decision-making and generates costs for securityholders.

I. CORPORATE FINANCE AND THE FINANCIAL MANAGER (p. 2)

<u>**What is Corporate Finance?**</u> (p. 2) The major decisions faced by financial managers are:

1. What long-term investments should be made?
2. What is the best way to raise funds in order to finance these investments?
3. How should the firm manage its short-term assets and liabilities?

<u>**The Financial Manager**</u> (p. 3) *Stockholders* of large corporations are generally not involved in day-to-day operations of the firm. *Managers* are employed to make decisions on behalf of the stockholders. Financial functions of the firm are generally shared by the *treasurer* and *controller*.

<u>**Financial Management Decisions**</u> (p. 4) The first decision is the *capital budgeting* decision, which encompasses planning and managing a firm's investments in long-term assets.

The second decision is the *capital structure* decision. Capital structure refers to the mix of long-term debt and equity utilized by the firm in order to finance investment in fixed assets.

The third decision is the *working capital* decision. Since cash inflows and outflows do not generally coincide, cash flows must be managed by appropriate adjustments of current assets and current liabilities.

II. FORMS OF BUSINESS ORGANIZATION (p. 5)

Businesses take one of three legal forms. These differ with respect to (1) the life of the business, (2) the ability of the business to obtain financing, and (3) the way in which the business is taxed.

Sole Proprietorship (p. 5) A *sole proprietorship* is owned by one person who keeps all the business' profits but has *unlimited liability* for its debts. The life span of the sole proprietorship is limited to that of the proprietor. The unlimited liability aspect makes capital harder to raise, and for tax purposes, no distinction is made between personal and business income.

Partnership (p. 6) A *partnership* has two or more owners, or partners. All partners in a *general partnership* share in gains or losses and all have unlimited liability for debts incurred by the partnership. In a *limited partnership*, one or more general partners run the business, while one or more limited partners do not actively participate. The life of the business is limited to the partners' life spans - when a general partner dies, the partnership is terminated. The amount of equity financing available to the business is limited to the combined partners' personal wealth. And for tax purposes, no distinction is made between personal and business income.

Corporation (p. 6) A corporation is a legal entity and is separate and distinct from its owners. The corporation can incur debts. The liability of the owners of the corporation for these debts is limited to the amount of money they have invested in the business. Formation of a corporation requires the preparation of *articles of incorporation* and *bylaws*. The shareholders of a corporation are its owners. Shareholders elect the *board of directors* who hire (and sometimes fire) the managers who operate the business for the shareholders.

The life of the corporation is not limited to the life of its owners. It is generally easier to raise capital because of the limited liability of the owners. Earnings are subject to *double taxation*.

A Corporation by Another Name (p. 8) The corporate form of organization pervades the industrialized world, although names differ across countries. Table 1.1 lists several international variants.

III. THE GOAL OF FINANCIAL MANAGEMENT (p. 8)

Possible Goals (p. 9) Several possible goals might be followed by financial managers - survival, profit maximization, sales maximization, etc. Unfortunately, none encompass the effects of management decision on both risk and return.

The Goal of Financial Management (p. 9) Since stockholders buy common stock to derive a financial benefit, the decisions of financial managers which are in the best interests of stockholders are those decisions which increase the value of the stock. So, **the goal of financial management in a corporation is to maximize the current price of the existing stock.**

A More General Goal (p. 10) The stock of a corporation represents the *owners' equity* in the firm. Thus, we can generalize and say that, regardless of the organizational form, **the goal of the financial managers is to maximize the value of the owners' equity in the firm.**

IV. THE AGENCY PROBLEM AND CONTROL OF THE CORPORATION (p. 11)

Although we have stated that corporate financial managers should adopt the goal of share price maximization, managers do not always do so. There are inherent conflicts between managers' goals and those of the owners; managers sometimes choose to pursue their own goals at the expense of the owners.

Agency Relationships (p. 11) The relationship between stockholders and management is an *agency relationship*. Instead of managing the firm themselves, principals (shareholders) hire agents (managers) to do so. An *agency problem* exists whenever management goals differ from shareholder goals.

Management Goals (p. 11) Shareholders can encourage managers to perform in a manner consistent with shareholder interests by creating appropriate management incentive contracts and by monitoring management activity. The costs associated with these activities are called *agency costs*. Since agency problems are often costly to resolve, it is unlikely that every action taken by the corporation will be strictly in the best interests of the owners.

Do Managers Act in the Stockholders' Interests? (p. 13) The extent to which management actions are consistent with stockholder goals depends largely on (1) how managers are compensated, and (2) the control of the firm.

Managerial compensation is often related to firm performance. Additionally, promotions and future job opportunities are often related to the manager's success in achieving stockholder goals.

Control mechanisms exist that tend to ensure that management will act in the shareholders' interest. Shareholders elect corporate directors who hire (and fire) management. Shareholders who are dissatisfied with existing management can attempt to remove management by means of a *proxy fight*. And corporate takeovers have been shown to result in the ouster of ineffective managers and directors.

Stakeholders (p. 14) Several parties besides stockholders and bondholders have an interest (or "stake") in the performance of the firm. Suppliers, employees, and customers, to name a few, are potentially affected by managerial decisions.

V. FINANCIAL MARKETS AND THE CORPORATION (p. 14)

The debt and equity securities issued by firms are bought and sold in the financial markets. In this section, we discuss the different kinds of securities that are traded in the financial markets, the manner in which trading is conducted, and the buyers and sellers of different securities.

Cash Flows to and from the Firm (p. 14) The firm acquires funds by issuing securities and selling them to market participants; in turn, it returns cash to them in the form of dividends and interest paid on the stocks and bonds issued, respectively.

Primary versus Secondary Markets (p. 15) The original sale (or issuance) of securities by a governmental body or a corporation is a *primary market* transaction. Any subsequent sale and purchase of a security (i.e., from one investor to another) is a *secondary market* transaction.

KEY TERMS AND CONCEPTS

Agency problem - inherent conflicts of interest between stockholders and management. (p. 11)
Capital budgeting - process of planning and managing a firm's long-term investments. (p. 4)
Capital structure - the mix of debt and equity maintained by the firm. (p. 4)
Corporation - distinct legal entity composed of one or more individuals or entities. (p. 6)
Partnership - a business formed by two or more co-workers. (p. 6)

4

Sole proprietorship - a business owned by a single individual. (p. 5)
Stakeholder - someone other than stockholder or creditor who has a claim on the firm. (p. 14)
Working capital - a firm's short-term assets and liabilities. (p. 4)

CONCEPT TEST

1. Corporate finance is the study of ways to answer three major questions: What fixed assets should the firm buy? What is the best way to raise cash to finance the purchase of fixed assets? How should the firm manage its short-term assets and liabilities? These subjects are referred to as _____ , _____ , and _____ decisions. (p. 2)

2. The _____ (i.e., the owners) of large corporations are generally not involved in the day-to-day operations of the firm. _____ make decisions on their behalf. (p. 3)

3. Officially, the financial functions of the firm are shared by the _____ and the _____ . (p. 3)

4. The three legal forms of business organization are the _____ , the _____ , and the _____ . The forms of organization are distinguished by differences in _____ , _____ , and _____ . (p. 5)

5. In a _____ partnership, all partners have unlimited liability for firm debts. A _____ partnership has two kinds of partners: _____ partners, who have unlimited liability, and _____ partners who have limited liability. (p. 6)

6. The rules and procedures by which a corporation governs itself are contained in the corporate _____ . All corporations must prepare a document called the _____ describing the number of shares to be issued, the business purpose, and other details. (p. 7)

7. The primary goal of the managers in a corporation is the maximization of _____ . (p. 10)

8. If management goals conflict with shareholder goals, a(n) _____ problem exists. _____ are costs of aligning goals. (p. 11)

9. The original sale (or issuance) of securities by a governmental body or a corporation is a _____ transaction. Subsequent sales and purchases (i.e., from one investor to another) is a _____ transaction. (p. 15)

ANSWERS TO CONCEPT TEST

1.   capital budgeting, capital structure, working capital
2.   stockholders; Managers
3.   treasurer, controller
4.   sole proprietorships, partnerships, corporations; life, ability to obtain financing, taxation
5.   general; limited, general, limited
6.   bylaws; articles of incorporation
7.   the current stock price
8.   agency; Agency costs
9.   primary market; secondary market

CHAPTER 2

FINANCIAL STATEMENTS, TAXES, AND CASH FLOW

CONCEPTS FOR REVIEW

In the previous chapter we determined that the overriding goal in financial decision-making is the maximization of shareholder wealth. Now we introduce several determinants of share price and, by implication, shareholder wealth. Financial statements measure firm performance, which is ultimately reflected in the price of the firm's common stock. Crucial to the analysis of the firm's financial statements and to the evaluation of firm performance is the concept of liquidity, the effects of taxes, and the measurement of cash flow. Pay special attention to the latter, as it will turn out to be a crucial determinant of value in many financial decisions.

CHAPTER HIGHLIGHTS

This chapter delves more deeply into two topics introduced in Chapter 1: financial statements and cash flow concepts. We also discuss some important tax considerations. You should understand that financial statements are a key source of information for financial decisions; thus, the chapter emphasizes the **use**, rather than the **preparation** of financial statements. Throughout this chapter, two important distinctions must be kept in mind: (1) the difference between accounting value and market value; and (2) the difference between accounting income and cash flow. These concepts are essential to an understanding of corporate finance.

I. THE BALANCE SHEET (p. 20)

Assets: The Left-Hand Side (p. 20) The balance sheet is a snapshot of a firm's accounting value as of a particular date. **Assets** are listed on the left-hand side, and include both *tangible* assets such as buildings and equipment, and *intangible* assets, such as trademarks.

Liabilities and Owners' Equity: The Right-Hand Side (p. 21) Liabilities are debts owed by the firm, and are classified as *current* (if the maturity is less than one year) or as *long-term* (if the maturity is greater than one year). *Owners' equity* is the difference between assets and liabilities. The *balance sheet equation* is:

$$\text{Assets} = \text{Liabilities} + \text{Shareholders' Equity}.$$

Net Working Capital (p. 22) Net working capital is the difference between a firm's current assets and its current liabilities. Net working capital can be positive or negative, but is usually positive in a healthy firm, since it indicates that more cash will be available than will be paid out over the next 12 months.

Liquidity (p. 22) The financial manager must be especially aware of the following three aspects of the balance sheet: **liquidity, debt versus equity,** and **market value versus book value.** Each of these concepts is related to one of the three basic issues of corporate finance introduced in Chapter 1.

The **liquidity** of an asset is measured by the speed with which it can be converted to cash without significant loss in value. Liquidity is valuable because it increases the firm's ability to meet short-term obligations. However, there is a tradeoff between liquidity and foregone potential returns.

The **liquidity** of an asset is measured by the speed with which it can be converted to cash without significant loss in value. Liquidity is valuable because it increases the firm's ability to meet short-term obligations. However, there is a tradeoff between liquidity and foregone potential returns.

Debt versus Equity (p. 23) Liabilities represent obligations to repay principal and interest to creditors at a specified time. In contrast, equity holders are entitled only to *residual* cash flows and assets; that is, the portion which remains after creditors' claims are satisfied.

Market Value versus Book Value (p. 23) The balance sheet values of a firm's assets (**book values**), generally do not indicate the assets' current worth, or **market values**. Market value is the relevant value for financial decisions, because it is the market value of the firm that is reflected in share prices.

II. THE INCOME STATEMENT (p. 25)

A firm's income statement measures the firm's performance over a specified period of time. The income statement equation is:

$$\text{Revenues - Expenses = Income}$$

Net income (i.e., 'the bottom line') equals revenue less all expenses and taxes. Net income divided by the number of shares of stock outstanding is referred to as **earnings per share** (**EPS**).

GAAP and the Income Statement (p. 26) Generally Accepted Accounting Principles (GAAP) require that revenue be recorded on the income statement when it is earned, or **accrued**, even if the actual cash inflow from payment has not occurred. Costs, as indicated on the income statement, are determined according to the 'matching' principle; that is, costs are matched with the revenues they produce. Thus, revenues and costs recorded for a particular period may not reflect actual cash flows during that period.

Noncash Items (p. 26) The existence of noncash items such as depreciation cause accounting income and cash flow to differ.

III. TAXES (p. 28)

Corporate Tax Rates (p. 28) Table 2.3 in the text indicates current corporate tax rates.

Average versus Marginal Tax Rates (p. 28) An **average tax rate** is equal to total taxes paid divided by total taxable income. A **marginal tax rate** is the tax rate applied to the last dollar earned.

Financial decisions generally involve changes in cash flows from existing levels. Therefore, the marginal tax rate is generally the relevant rate for financial decision-making.

IV. CASH FLOW (p. 30)

The balance sheet equation indicates that the value of a firm's assets is equal to the value of its liabilities plus the value of its equity. Similarly, firm cash flow generated by the use of its assets must be equal to the sum of the cash flow paid to its creditors and the cash flow paid to its stockholders.

Cash Flow from Assets (p. 30) Cash flow from assets has three components: **operating cash flow**, **capital spending** and **additions to net working capital**.

Operating cash flow (OCF) is the cash flow resulting from a firm's day-to-day operations and is equal to revenues minus costs, excluding depreciation and interest.

Capital spending is the net amount spent on fixed assets, or the difference between sales of fixed assets and the acquisition of fixed assets.

A firm invests in current assets as well as fixed assets. Since net working capital is the difference between the level of current assets and the level of current liabilities, the *change in net working capital* is the change in the level of current assets minus the change in the level of current liabilities.

The total *cash flow from the firm's assets* equals operating cash flow, less net capital spending, less the additions to net working capital.

Cash Flow to Creditors and Stockholders (p. 32) Funds not used for expenses and taxes or reinvested in the firm are distributed to the suppliers of capital - the creditors and the stockholders.

The cash flow to creditors (or bondholders) is: interest paid minus net new long-term borrowing.

Cash flow to stockholders equals dividends paid less net new equity financing obtained.

An Example: Cash Flows for Dole Cola (p. 34)

KEY TERMS AND CONCEPTS

Average tax rate - total taxes paid divided by total taxable income. (p. 28)
Balance sheet - financial statement showing a firm's accounting value on a particular date. (p. 20)
Cash flow from assets - the total cash flow to creditors and cash flow to stockholders, consisting of the following: operating cash flow, capital spending, and additions to net working capital. (p. 30)
Cash flow to creditors - interest paid plus repayments of long-term debt, minus new long-term borrowing. (p. 32)
Cash flow to stockholders - dividends paid plus the dollar value of stock repurchased by the firm, minus the proceeds from the sale of new equity. (p. 33)
Generally accepted accounting principles (GAAP) - the common set of standards and procedures by which audited financial statements are prepared. (p. 24)
Income statement - financial statement summarizing firm performance over a period of time. (p. 25)
Marginal tax rate - amount of tax payable on the next dollar earned. (p. 28)
Net Capital Spending - ending fixed assets minus beginning fixed assets, plus depreciation (p. 31)
Net working capital - current assets less current liabilities. (p. 32)
Noncash items - expenses charged against revenues that do not directly affect cash flow. (p. 26)
Operating cash flow - cash generated from a firm's normal business activities. (p. 31)

1. A _____ can be thought of as a snapshot of firm accounting value at a particular date. The value of a firm's assets equals _____ + _____. Alternatively, shareholders' equity = assets - _____. (p. 20, 21)

2. The difference between current assets and current liabilities is called _____, and can be positive or negative. (p. 22)

3. An asset that can be converted to cash quickly and without loss in value is _____. Assets are listed on the balance sheet in order of decreasing _____. Liquid assets generally earn _____ rates of return than fixed assets. (p. 22)

4. _____ are debts, so the firm is obligated to pay creditors principal and interest. Equity holders are entitled only to _____ cash flows and assets. The use of debt financing is referred to as _____. (p. 23)

5. Fixed asset values on the balance sheet are not current market values. Instead, they are shown at _____. The difference between market value and _____ value is generally small for current assets, but can be large for _____ assets. (p. 24)

6. The income statement equation is _____ - _____ = _____. Net income divided by the number of shares outstanding is called _____. (p. 25)

7. For accounting purposes, revenue is shown on the income statement when it _____, not when payment is received. For financial decision-making purposes, accounting income must be distinguished from _____. (p. 26)

8. One of the reasons net income is not the same as cash flow from operations is that some deductions are _____ deductions; the most common of these is _____. In the short run, rent is an example of a _____ cost. (p. 27)

9. A(n) _____ tax rate equals total taxes paid divided by total taxable income, while a(n) _____ tax rate is the rate applied to the last dollar earned. (p. 28)

10. Operating cash flow equals _____ + _____ - _____. Cash flow from assets equals _____ + _____. Cash flow to creditors (debtholders) is _____ + _____ - _____. Cash flow to stockholders is _____ + _____ - _____. (pp. 30-33)

ANSWERS TO CONCEPT TEST

1. balance sheet; liabilities, shareholders' equity; liabilities
2. net working capital
3. liquid; liquidity; lower
4. Liabilities; residual; financial leverage
5. book value or historical cost; book; fixed
6. revenues, expenses, income; earnings per share (EPS)
7. accrues; cash flow

8.   noncash; depreciation; fixed
9.   average; marginal;
10.   earnings before interest and taxes, depreciation, taxes; cash flow to creditors, cash flow to stockholders; interest, repayments of long-term debt, proceeds from new long-term debt; dividends, stock repurchased, stock issued

PROBLEMS

1. During the year 1997, the Terri-Yung Company had sales of $1,000, cost of goods sold of $400, depreciation of $100, and interest paid of $150. If the tax rate is 34% and all taxes are paid currently, what is net income?

2. Refer to Problem 1 above. Assume the Terri-Yung Company has 100 shares of common stock outstanding at the end of 1997. Total dividends paid were $120. Compute earnings per share (EPS) and dividends per share (DPS).

3. At year-end 1996, Terri-Yung had notes payable of $1,200, accounts payable of $2,400, and long-term debt of $3,000. Corresponding entries for 1997: $1,600, $2,000, and $2,800. Assets for 1996 and 1997 are:

Current Assets	1996	1997
Cash	$ 800	$ 500
Marketable Securities	400	300
Accounts Receivable	900	800
Inventory	1,800	2,000
Fixed Assets		
Net Plant and Equipment	$6,000	$8,000

Prepare the company's balance sheets for the end of 1996 and 1997, respectively.

4. Based on the information in Problem 1, what is Terri-Yung's operating cash flow for 1997?

5. During the year 1997 Terri-Yung sold $300 of fixed assets and $2,400 worth of stock, and used the entire proceeds to buy fixed assets. Compute net capital spending.

6. Based on the balance sheets for Terri-Yung, what was net working capital for 1996? For 1997? What must additions to net working capital have been?

7. What was Terri-Yung's total cash flow to the firm in 1997?

8. What was Terri-Yung's cash flow to long-term creditors in 1997?

9. What was Terri-Yung's cash flow to shareholders in 1997?

10. The K&M Corporation had taxable income of $200,000. What is the total tax bill for K&M? What is K&M's average tax rate? What is the marginal tax rate?

11. Suppose that K&M had taxable income of $1,000,000. What are the total taxes paid, the average tax rate and the marginal tax rate?

CHAPTER 3

WORKING WITH FINANCIAL STATEMENTS

CONCEPTS FOR REVIEW

Because investors base their buying and selling decisions on information about the firm, the role of information is crucial in determining firm value. Information is available from many sources, not the least of which are the firm's financial statements. To analyze financial statements in a systematic manner, we measure five dimensions of firm performance: liquidity, long-term solvency, asset management, profitability, and measures based on market values. Each captures a different aspect of managerial performance, and will be of greater or lesser importance to the analyst, depending on his or her purposes.

CHAPTER HIGHLIGHTS

In this chapter we examine more closely the financial statements discussed in Chapter 2. It is important to remember that, under ideal circumstances, financial decisions are based on market value information rather than accounting data; however, in many situations, accounting statements provide the best information available.

I. CASH FLOW AND FINANCIAL STATEMENTS: A CLOSER LOOK (p. 47)

From Chapter 2, we know that: Cash flow from assets = Cash flow to creditors + Cash flow to owners In this section, we analyze more closely the cash flow impacts of firm transactions.

Sources and Uses of Cash (p. 47) Transactions which create cash inflows for the firm are referred to as **sources of cash,** and transactions which create cash outflows are **uses of cash.** Transactions which increase (decrease) asset accounts represent uses (sources) of cash, while transactions which increase (decrease) liability accounts or equity account represent sources (uses) of cash.

The Statement of Cash Flows (p. 49) In order to summarize the transactions which affect the firm's sources and uses of cash over a given period, we construct a **statement of cash flows.** This statement organizes the sources and uses of cash into three categories: operating activities, investing activities, and financing activities.

Learning Tip: An easy way to remember sources and uses is to keep in mind that there are five of each, and that, for the first four items in the list below, the use is just the opposite of the source.

Sources	*Uses*
Net income	*Net loss*
Decrease in assets	*Increase in assets*
Increase in liabilities	*Decrease in liabilities*
Increase in common stock	*Decrease in common stock*
Depreciation	*Payment of Dividends*

Notice that both net income and depreciation are shown on the statement of cash flows for the firm. The latter is included as a source because it is deducted as an expense in computing taxable income and reduces the firm's tax liability.

II. STANDARDIZED FINANCIAL STATEMENTS (p. 50)

In making financial decisions, it is often helpful to compare a firm's financial statements with those of companies in the same industry. However, companies in the same industry can differ substantially in size, thus making comparisons of financial statement data difficult. A similar problem arises when a firm chooses to compare its current financial statements to those of preceding years; if the company has grown significantly, comparisons based on dollar values may not be meaningful. Two approaches to standardizing financial statements to make comparisons more useful are described in this section.

Common-Size Statements (p. 51) **Common-size statements** are standardized by presenting balance sheet accounts as a percentage of total assets and income statement data as a percentage of sales. Because common-size statements represent financial statement values as ratios with a common denominator (i.e., sales or total assets), the effects of size differences across firms are removed.

Common-Base Year Financial Statements: Trend Analysis (p. 53) A second approach to standardizing financial statements is the use of **common-base year financial statements.** For these statements, a base year is selected and each financial statement item for the base year is assigned a value of 1.00. Then for subsequent years, each item is assigned a value which reflects the increase or decrease in the item. By looking at the values on the statement for the latest period, we can determine whether and by how much they have changed since the base year.

Combined Common-Size and Base-Year Analysis (p. 53) By combining these two approaches, one can analyze changes over time, with the effects of size differences removed.

III. RATIO ANALYSIS (p. 54)

In order to make comparisons over time, or with similar firms, financial statement analysis is often based on ratios of various balance sheet and income statement items, rather than on dollar values. Accounting data for firms of vastly different size, or for a firm which grows over time, cannot otherwise be reasonably compared.

The following five categories of financial ratios are discussed in this section:

1. Short-term solvency or liquidity ratios.
2. Long-term solvency or financial leverage ratios.
3. Asset management or turnover ratios.
4. Profitability ratios.
5. Market value ratios.

Learning Tip: Many students find that the easiest way to learn the ratios is to learn the five categories first; then learn the ratios in each. Doing so emphasizes the fact that all of the ratios in a given category are related, and makes them easier to remember.

Short-term Solvency or Liquidity Measures (p. 55) These ratios measure the firm's short-term liquidity; emphasis is placed on the firm's ability to meet short-term obligations. The *current ratio* is:

Current Assets/Current Liabilities

Deterioration of this ratio through time may indicate a worsening liquidity position.

The *quick ratio* or *acid-test ratio* is similar to the current ratio, except that inventory is not included in the numerator:

$$(Current\ Assets\ -\ Inventory)/Current\ Liabilities$$

Inventory is subtracted from current assets in computing the quick ratio because inventory is usually the least liquid current asset.

Three additional measures of liquidity are:

1) The *cash ratio*:
$$Cash/Current\ Liabilities$$

(2) The *NWC to total assets ratio*:

$$Net\ Working\ Capital/Total\ Assets$$

(3) The *interval measure*:

$$Current\ Assets/Average\ Daily\ Operating\ Costs$$

Long-Term Solvency Measures (p. 58) Long-term solvency measures gauge the extent to which a firm uses debt financing rather than equity financing. All else equal, an increase in the level of debt increases the probability of default, so these ratios can also be considered to be indicators of default risk.

The *total debt ratio* measures the proportion of assets acquired with borrowed money:

$$(Total\ Assets\ -\ Total\ Equity)/Total\ Assets$$

The *debt/equity ratio* measures the relative capital contributions of creditors and stockholders:

$$Total\ Debt/Total\ Equity$$

The *equity multiplier* is computed as follows:

$$Total\ Assets/Total\ Equity$$

Since it is sometimes appropriate to focus on long-term debt, rather than total debt, the *long-term debt ratio* is often useful:

$$Long\text{-}Term\ Debt/(Long\text{-}Term\ Debt\ +\ Total\ Equity)$$

The *times interest earned ratio* (sometimes called the "interest coverage" ratio) measures the firm's ability to meet its interest obligations. It is calculated as follows:

$$EBIT/Interest$$

Deterioration in this ratio over time may signal that the firm is more likely to encounter financial distress.

A meaningful modification of the times interest earned ratio is the *cash coverage ratio*:

$$EBIT/Interest$$

The cash coverage ratio is often considered more meaningful than the times interest earned ratio because the firm's ability to meet its interest obligations is more closely related to its cash flow than its earnings.

Asset Management or Turnover Measures (p. 59) These ratios measure how effectively the firm uses its assets, and are sometimes referred to as *asset utilization ratios*.

Inventory turnover measures how quickly inventory is produced and sold, and is calculated as follows:

$$Cost\ of\ Goods\ Sold/Inventory$$

A high level of the inventory turnover ratio, relative to that of similar firms, may indicate that the firm is efficient in its inventory management. We can also compute the *days sales in inventory* as follows:

$$365/Inventory\ Turnover$$

The *receivables turnover* measures the firm's ability to manage collections of accounts from customers. The receivables turnover ratio is equal to:

$$Sales/Accounts\ Receivable$$

The *days sales in receivables* is computed from the receivables turnover as follows:

$$365/Receivables\ Turnover$$

Days sales in receivables is also referred to as the *average collection period (ACP)*.

Three additional turnover ratios are:

(1) The *NWC turnover*:
$$Sales/Net\ Working\ Capital$$

(2) The *fixed asset turnover*:
$$Sales/Net\ Fixed\ Assets$$

(3) The *total asset turnover*:
$$Sales/Total\ Assets$$

The fixed asset and total asset turnover ratios indicate how effectively the firm utilizes its assets to generate sales revenues. A low value may indicate that assets are not being used as efficiently as possible; either the firm should be able to generate more sales revenue from the given level of assets, or the firm should reduce the level of assets for the given level of sales.

Profitability Measures (p. 62) These ratios measure management's ability to control expenses and, as a result, generate income from sales. The *profit margin* is computed as follows:

$$Net\ Income/Sales$$

It might seem reasonable to conclude that a higher profit margin is preferable to a lower profit margin. However, a firm may elect a marketing strategy which emphasizes relatively low prices, and, consequently, low profit margins, in order to increase sales and total profits.

Return on assets (ROA) is a commonly reported measure of performance. This ratio is defined as follows:

$$Net\ Income/Total\ Assets$$

Return on equity (ROE) is a measure of the return to the firm's stockholders. ROE is defined as:

$$Net\ Income/Total\ Equity$$

Market Value Measures (p. 63) Financial statements provide little information about market values, so it is often useful to combine accounting and market values when analyzing financial statements.

The *price/earnings (P/E) ratio* is a widely quoted ratio in financial analysis. The price/earnings ratio is:

$$Price\ per\ Share/Earnings\ per\ Share$$

where *Earnings per Share* is equal to

$$Net\ Income/Number\ of\ Shares\ Outstanding$$

The P/E ratio is actually a multiple which tells how much investors will pay to buy $1 of earnings.

The *market-to-book ratio* is the market price per share divided by the book value per share:

$$Price\ per\ Share/Book\ Value\ per\ Share$$

where book value per share equals total equity divided by the number of shares outstanding.

IV. THE DU PONT IDENTITY (p. 65)

The Du Pont identity is a means of decomposing ROE into its component parts. It suggests that ROE is a function of those decisions which impact profitability, asset utilization, and financial leverage.

$$Net\ Income/Sales \times Sales/Total\ Assets \times Total\ Assets/Equity$$

V. USING FINANCIAL STATEMENT INFORMATION (p. 67)

In this section we discuss three issues associated with using financial statement information: reasons for evaluating financial statements; appropriate benchmarks; and problems encountered in the analysis.

Why Evaluate Financial Statements? (p. 75) Financial statement analysis has both internal and external uses. Internal uses include: performance evaluation, and planning for the future. External uses include: analysis performed by creditors and potential investors, evaluation of competitors, and the assessment of a potential acquisition of another firm.

Learning Tip: The previous section organized financial ratios into five categories. You might find it useful to think of these categories as financial 'dimensions' of the firm, analogous to the physical dimensions of an object, such as of length, width, and height. As such, financial dimensions are used to 'describe' a firm, where physical dimensions are used to describe an object. Thus, one of the most important aspects of financial ratio analysis is that it provides us with a systematic means of describing, in a relatively simple manner, something which might otherwise seem fairly complicated.

Choosing a Benchmark (p. 68) The two basic forms of comparison when evaluating financial statement information are time-trend analysis and peer group analysis. For time trend analysis, the analysis is based on comparison of current data with historical data. Peer group analysis is the comparison of firms which are similar to the firm being evaluated.

Problems with Financial Statement Analysis (p. 72) Unfortunately, there are no clear guidelines regarding the determination of optimal values for the ratios discussed in the preceding section. Other problems are associated with: (1) identification of comparable peer groups; (2) differences in accounting procedures; (3) differences in fiscal years for financial statements; and, (4) unusual events which have an impact on reported financial results.

KEY TERMS AND CONCEPTS

Common-size statement - standardized financial statement presenting items in percentage terms. (p. 51)
Common-base-year statement - standardized financial statement presenting all items relative to a certain base-year amount. (p. 53)
Du Pont identity - a financial ratio which illustrates the combined effect of profitability, total asset turnover, and leverage on return on equity (ROE). (p. 65)
Financial ratios - relationships determined from firm financial information and used for comparison and evaluation purposes. (p. 54)
Sources of cash - firm activities that generate cash. (p. 47)
Standard industry classification (SIC) code - U.S. government code to classify a firm by its type of business operations. (p. 68)
Statement of cash flows - financial statement that summarizes the firm's sources and uses of cash over a specified period. (p. 49)
Uses of cash - firm activities in which cash is spent. Also "applications" of cash. (p. 47)

CONCEPT TEST

1. Transactions which create cash inflows are referred to as _____ of cash, and transactions which create cash outflows are _____ of cash. An increase in an asset account represents a _____ of cash. A decrease in a liability or equity account is a _____ of cash, while an increase in a liability or equity account is a _____ of cash. (p. 47)

2. The statement of cash flows organizes sources and uses of cash into three categories: _____ , _____ , and _____ activities. Depreciation reduces the firm's tax liability; it appears as a _____ of cash, while dividends paid are a _____ of cash. (p. 49)

3. Common-size statements are standardized by presenting balance sheet accounts as a percentage of _____ and income statement data as a percentage of _____ . Common-base-year financial statements are standardized by comparing each statement item to its corresponding value during a _____ year. Each financial statement item for the base year is assigned a value of _____ , then for subsequent years, each item is assigned a value which reflects the increase in the item. (p. 51)

4. Ratios intended to measure the firm's short-term liquidity are referred to as _____ ratios or _____ . Some important ratios in this category are:
Current ratio = _____ / _____
Quick ratio = _____ / _____
Cash ratio = _____ / _____
Net working capital to total assets = _____ / _____
Interval measure = _____ / _____ (p. 55)

5. Ratios which gauge the extent to which a firm uses debt rather than equity financing are called _____ ratios or _____ ratios. Important ratios include:
Total debt ratio = _____ / _____
Debt/equity ratio = _____ / _____
Equity multiplier = _____ / _____
Long-term debt ratio = _____ / _____
Times interest earned ratio = _____ / _____
Cash coverage ratio = _____ / _____ (p. 58)

6. Ratios designed to measure how effectively the firm uses its assets are called _____ ratios or _____ measures; these ratios are also referred to as _____ ratios. Some important ratios in this category are:
Inventory turnover = _____ / _____
Days sales in inventory = _____ / _____
Receivables turnover = _____ / _____
Days sales in receivables = _____ / _____
NWC turnover = _____ / _____
Fixed asset turnover = _____ / _____
Total asset turnover = _____ / _____ (p. 59)

7. Ratios designed to measure a firm's profitability are _____ ratios. Some important ratios in this category are:
Profit margin = _____ / _____
Return on assets = _____ / _____
Return on equity = _____ / _____ (p. 62)

8. Ratios based on market values are called _____ ratios. These include:
    P/E ratio = _____/_____
    Market-to-book ratio = _____/_____ (p. 63)

9. The Du Pont identity expresses ROE as a function of _____,
    _____, and _____ . (p. 65)

ANSWERS TO CONCEPT TEST

1. sources; uses; use; use; source
2. operating; financing; investment; source; use
3. total assets; sales; base; 1.00;
4. short-term solvency; liquidity; current assets; current liabilities; current assets less inventory; current liabilities; cash; current liabilities; net working capital; total assets; current assets; average daily operating costs
5. long-term solvency; financial leverage; total assets less total equity; total assets; total debt; total equity; total assets; total equity; long-term debt; long-term debt plus total equity; earnings before interest and taxes; interest; EBIT plus depreciation; interest
6. asset management; turnover; asset utilization; cost of goods sold; inventory; 365 days; inventory turnover; sales; accounts receivable; 365 days; receivables turnover; sales; net working capital; sales; net fixed assets; sales; total assets
7. profitability; net income; sales; net income; total assets; net income; total equity
8. market value; price per share; earnings per share; market value per share; book value per share
9. profitability; asset utilization; financial leverage;

PROBLEMS

Use the following financial statements to solve Problems 1 through 15:

COOGAN DEVELOPMENT CO., INC.
1997 Income Statement

Sales	$25,000
Cost of goods sold	16,000
Depreciation	3,000
Earnings before interest and taxes	$ 6,000
Interest paid	2,000
Taxable income	$ 4,000
Taxes (34%)	1,360
Net income	$ 2,640
Retained earnings	$ 1,584
Dividends	1,056

COOGAN DEVELOPMENT CO., INC.
Balance Sheets as of December 31, 1996 and 1997

		1996	1997
Assets			
Current Assets			
	Cash	$ 4,000	$ 3,000
	Accounts Receivable	9,000	11,000
	Inventory	5,000	4,500
Total		$18,000	$18,500
Fixed assets			
	Net plant and equipment	30,000	31,500
Total assets		$48,000	$50,000
Liabilities and Owners' Equity			
Current liabilities			
	Accounts payable	$ 3,000	$ 2,500
	Notes payable	6,000	6,416
Total		$9,000	$ 8,916
Long-term debt		$15,000	$13,000
Owners' equity			
	Common stock and		
	paid-in surplus	14,000	16,500
Retained earnings		10,000	11,584
Total		$24,000	$28,084
Total liabilities and equity		$48,000	$50,000

1. Compute changes in the above balance sheet accounts, and compute the sources and uses of cash.

2. Prepare a statement of cash flows for Coogan Development.

3. Prepare a sources and uses of cash statement for Coogan Development.

4. Prepare common-size balance sheets for Coogan Development.

5. Prepare a common-size income statement for Coogan Development.

6. Compute the measures of short-term solvency, using the 1997 financial statement data.

7. Compute the measures of long-term solvency, using the 1997 financial statement data.

8. Compute the asset management measures using the 1997 financial statement data.

9. Compute the profitability measures using the 1997 balance sheet and income statement data.

10. Use the Du Pont identity to compute return on equity and return on assets for Coogan Development.

11. Suppose that Coogan Development has 1,000 shares of common stock outstanding, and that the market price per share is $40. Compute EPS, the P/E ratio, and the market-to-book ratio.

12. Suppose the firm decides to reduce its total debt ratio to 0.20 from 0.44 by selling new common stock and using the proceeds to repay principal on some outstanding long-term debt. Compute each of following: debt/equity ratio, equity multiplier, and return on equity. Also, how much equity financing will Coogan have to obtain in order to accomplish this reduction in the total debt ratio?

13. Suppose Coogan Development decides to increase its total debt ratio to 0.80 by borrowing additional long-term funds and using the proceeds to buy some of its outstanding common stock. Compute the following: debt/equity ratio, equity multiplier, and return on equity. Also, how much long-term debt financing will Coogan have to obtain in order to accomplish this increase in the total debt ratio?

14. Suppose the firm decides to reduce its average collection period (ACP) to 120 days from 161 days. How much of its currently outstanding accounts receivable must be collected to accomplish this reduction? If collected funds were held as cash, how would this affect the firm's current and quick ratios? If the collected funds were used to repay notes payable, how would this affect the current and quick ratios?

CHAPTER 4

LONG-TERM FINANCIAL PLANNING AND GROWTH

CONCEPTS FOR REVIEW

Chapter 3 described a conceptual framework with which we can analyze the firm's historical performance in five dimensions: liquidity, long-term solvency, asset management, profitability, and market value. This chapter extends our analysis to the *future* performance of the firm, and illustrates the interrelationships between growth and the firm's operating, investment, and financing decisions.

CHAPTER HIGHLIGHTS

This chapter is primarily concerned with long-term financial planning and financial planning models. The guidelines established as part of the financial planning process should identify the firm's financial goals, analyze the difference between the firm's current status and the established goals, and identify the actions required to achieve those goals.

The basic policy elements which must be established in order to develop a financial plan are:

1. The firm's needed investment in new assets.
2. The degree of financial leverage the firm elects to employ.
3. The dividend payment to stockholders.
4. The firm's liquidity and working capital requirements.

These four areas represent, respectively, the firm's capital budgeting decisions, capital structure policy, dividend policy, and net working capital decision. These decisions affect the firm's future profitability, need for external financing, and growth opportunities.

I. WHAT IS FINANCIAL PLANNING? (p. 83)

A financial plan identifies the method for achieving financial goals. Since the implementation of a financial decision can require several years, financial planning is required to achieve the firm's goals.

Growth as a Financial Management Goal (p. 83) The appropriate goal for the financial manager is the maximization of the value of the firm's common stock. We discuss growth as a component of the financial planning process. Thus, growth is a *result* of financial decision-making, not a goal in itself.

Dimensions of Financial Planning (p. 84) A financial plan has two dimensions: The **planning horizon** and a level of **aggregation**. A *long-term* plan usually covers two to five years; the short-run is generally considered to be the next 12 months. In this chapter, we are primarily concerned with a long-run planning horizon. The creation of a financial plan typically involves combining smaller investment proposals into larger units, so we treat the sum of these smaller proposals as if they were one larger investment. This process is called **aggregation**.

What Can Planning Accomplish? (p. 85) The planning process is useful in several ways. First, a financial plan makes explicit the linkage between proposed investment or growth and the financing required to implement the proposals. Second, a plan allows the firm to evaluate different investment and financing options, and their long-run impact on profitability, cash flow, and value. Third, a financial plan lends itself to the identification and evaluation of possible future events; this process helps the firm to avoid unpleasant surprises and to prepare contingency plans. Finally, a financial plan establishes whether courses of action are feasible and consistent with corporate objectives of maximizing shareholder wealth.

II. FINANCIAL PLANNING MODELS: A FIRST LOOK (p. 86)

The exact form and level of detail in a financial plan varies from firm to firm. In this section we describe some of the common elements of a financial plan.

A Financial Planning Model: The Ingredients (p. 86) Most financial planning models include at least six components: (1) the sales forecast, (2) pro forma statements, (3) asset requirements, (4) financial requirements, (5) a "plug" figure, and (6) the economic assumptions employed.

A Simple Financial Planning Model (p. 86) A simple financial planning model is described in this section. It illustrates the procedure and the interrelationships mentioned earlier.

III. THE PERCENTAGE OF SALES APPROACH (p. 89)

The simple financial planning model described previously is based on the assumption that all income statement and balance sheet items increase proportionately with sales. In the *percentage of sales* approach to financial modelling, we exploit the fact that some accounting statement data are likely to increase with sales. A detailed example of this technique appears in this section of the text.

IV. EXTERNAL FINANCING AND GROWTH (p. 94)

Growth and external financing needed (EFN) are positively related; that is, the higher the rate of growth in sales (and, therefore, assets), the greater the need for external financing.

EFN and Growth (p. 94) The relationship between EFN and projected sales growth is illustrated in this section. More rapid rates of projected sales growth are associated with both greater retained earnings and greater asset needs. Since asset needs grow more rapidly than retained earnings, funds needed outstrip funds available, and the firm requires external financing.

Financial Policy and Growth (p. 97) The discussion above suggests that financial managers must be aware of the relationship between projected sales growth and the level of funds available from internal sources (i.e., retained earnings). The *internal growth rate* is the maximum growth rate the firm can achieve without obtaining external financing and is equal to

$$(ROA \times b)/(1 - ROA \times b)$$

where ROA is the return on assets as described in Chapter 3, and b is the plowback ratio.

The *sustainable growth rate* is the growth rate the firm can achieve without issuing new equity, while maintaining the current debt/equity ratio. The SGR is a function of the firm's return on equity and plowback ratio:

$$SGR = (ROE \times b)/(1 - ROE \times b).$$

Determinants of Growth: The Du Pont identity developed in Chapter 3 specifies that return on equity (ROE) can be written:

$$\text{ROE} = \text{Profit margin} \times \text{Total asset turnover} \times \text{Equity multiplier}$$

Since ROE is a determinant of the sustainable growth rate, the three determinants of ROE are also determinants of the SGR. In this form, it is clear that the sustainable growth rate is positively related to profit margin, asset turnover, and the debt-to-equity ratio, and inversely related to dividend payout, all else equal. This view of the sustainable growth rate clarifies the relationship among the four aspects of financial decision making and their respective effects on the firm's ability to grow.

V. SOME CAVEATS OF FINANCIAL PLANNING MODELS (p. 101)

Financial planning models do not identify optimal financial policies. Rather, they are useful for pointing out inconsistencies between firm goals and available resources. Financial planning should be viewed as both a learning process and an iterative process. Planning forces decision-makers to formulate their assumptions more precisely and subject them to the scrutiny of others, and in most cases, requires ongoing revision to those assumptions.

CONCEPT TEST

1. The basic policy elements which must be established by management in order to develop a financial plan are:

   1. The firm's needed investment in new assets.
   2. The degree of financial leverage the firm elects to employ.
   3. The dividend payment to stockholders.
   4. The firm's liquidity and working capital requirements.

   These four areas represent the firm's _____ decisions, _____ policy, _____ policy, and _____ decisions. (p. 83)

2. A universal requirement for financial planning is the _____ forecast. Projected or forecasted accounting statements are called _____ statements. The financial plan describes projected capital expenditures and working capital needs; these are _____ requirements. The firm's financial requirements detail the manner in which required financing will be obtained; the firm's _____ policy and _____ are also relevant here because of their impact on required financing. The projected growth rates in sales, assets, and financial requirements are generally not compatible without some adjustment; the amount of external financing required in order to finance the projected increase in assets is the _____ . Assumptions about variables such as interest rates and the general state of the economy must be explicitly stated; these are called _____ assumptions. (p. 86)

3. The financial planning model which is based on the assumption that some, but not all, accounting statement data increase proportionately with sales is called the _____ approach. Using this approach, we assume that costs, as a percentage of sales, (do/do not) remain constant;

a consequence of this assumption is that the profit margin (does/does not) remain constant. If in preparing the pro forma income statement, we assume that the dividend payout ratio is constant, this (is/is not) equivalent to assuming that the retention ratio is constant. (p. 89)

4. For the financial planning model described above, it is generally assumed that assets (do/do not) increase proportionately with sales. It is also assumed that liabilities (other than accounts payable) and owners' equity (do/do not) increase proportionately with sales. The addition to retained earnings figure from the _____ statement is added to the current balance sheet retained earnings figure. All other balance sheet accounts remain constant, and external financing needed is the _____ figure. The pro forma balance sheet is complete when the source(s) of external financing are determined. Possible sources of financing are: _____ debt, _____ debt and _____ . (p. 91)

5. The _____ growth rate is the rate which allows the firm to grow indefinitely without external financing. Since all internal financing is derived from _____ and the firm obtains no new external debt financing, the debt/equity ratio will (increase/decrease) over time. The growth rate which the firm could maintain without issuing new equity, while maintaining the current debt/equity ratio, is the _____ . (p. 97)

6. The Du Pont identity specifies that return on equity can be written:
ROE = _____ × _____ × _____ .
Thus, the sustainable growth rate depends on four factors: (1) An increase in the profit margin (increases/decreases) the firm's ability to generate internal financing, and (increases/decreases) the firm's SGR. (2) An increase in the retention ratio (increases/decreases) retained earnings and, (increases/decreases) SGR. (3) An increase in the debt/equity ratio (increases/decreases) financial leverage, and thereby makes additional debt financing available and (increases/decreases) the SGR. (4) An increase in total asset turnover (increases/decreases) the need for financing of new assets and consequently (increases/decreases) the SGR. (p. 98)

ANSWERS TO CONCEPT TEST

1. capital budgeting; capital structure; dividend; net working capital
2. sales; pro forma; asset; debt; dividend; plug; economic
3. percentage of sales; do; does; is
4. do; do not; pro forma income; plug; short-term; long-term; new equity financing
5. internal; retained earnings; decrease; sustainable growth rate
6. Profit margin, Total asset turnover, Equity multiplier; increases; increases; increases; increases; increases; increases; decreases; increases

KEY TERMS AND CONCEPTS

Capital intensity ratio - assets divided by sales; level of assets needed to generate $1 in sales. (p. 90)
Dividend payout ratio - amount of cash paid out to shareholders divided by net income. (p. 90)
Internal growth rate - minimum growth rate achievable without external financing of any kind. (p. 97)
Percentage of sales approach - financial planning method in which accounts are varied depending on a firm's predicted sales level. (p. 89)
Retention (plowback) ratio - addition to retained earnings divided by net income. (p. 90)

Sustainable growth rate - the maximum growth rate a firm can achieve without external equity financing while maintaining a constant debt/equity ratio. (p. 97)

PROBLEMS

1. Below are the most recent financial statements for the G. T. Seaver Corporation:

G. T. SEAVER CORPORATION
Financial Statements
Income Statement

Sales	$80,000
Costs	56,000
Net Income	$24,000

Balance Sheet

Current assets	$ 15,000	Current liabilities	$ 10,000
Fixed assets	85,000	Long-term debt	25,000
		Equity	65,000
Total	$100,000	Total	$100,000

Seaver expects sales to increase by 15% in the coming year. Assume that all variables will grow at the same rate as sales. Prepare the pro forma income statement and balance sheet. Reconcile these statements using dividends as the "plug" figure.

2. Reconcile the pro forma statements in the solution to Problem 1, using long-term debt as the "plug" figure, under the assumption that Seaver Corporation pays no dividends.

3. Reconcile the pro forma statements in the solution to Problem 1, using long-term debt as the "plug" figure, under the assumption that Seaver Corporation has a payout ratio of 80%.

4. The most recent balance sheet and income statement for Grote & Co., Inc., are presented here:

GROTE & CO., INC.
Balance Sheet

Current assets			Current liabilities		
Cash	$ 3,000	(15%)	Accounts payable	$ 6,000	(30%)
Accounts			Notes payable	3,000	(n/a)
receivable	5,000	(25%)			
Inventory	7,000	(35%)			
Total	$15,000	(75%)	Total	$ 9,000	(n/a)
			Long-term debt	$15,000	(n/a)
Fixed assets			Owners' equity		
Net plant and			Common stock and		
equipment	$30,000	(150%)	paid-in surplus	$13,000	(n/a)
			Retained earnings	8,000	(n/a)
			Total	$21,000	(n/a)
Total assets	$45,000	(225%)	Total liabilities	$45,000	(n/a)

Income Statement

Sales	$20,000
- Costs	17,000
Taxable income	$ 3,000
- Taxes (34%)	1,020
Net income	$ 1,980
Retained earnings	$ 1,188
Dividends	$ 792

For each balance sheet item, the percentage in parentheses represents the given item as a percentage of annual sales; those items not expected to increase proportionately with sales are identified by "n/a," indicating that the percentage calculation is not applicable. Grote & Co. has projected a 25% increase in sales. The dividend payout ratio is expected to remain constant. Use the percentage of sales approach to prepare the pro forma statements and to compute the external financing needed (EFN).

5. The most recent income statement and balance sheet for the T. McGraw Corporation are as follows:

T. MCGRAW CORPORATION
Financial Statements
Income Statement

Sales	$10,000
- Costs	7,500
Taxable income	$ 2,500
- Taxes (34%)	850
Net income	$ 1,650
Retained earnings	$ 660
Dividends	$ 990

Balance Sheet

Current assets	$ 5,000	Total debt	$ 6,000
Fixed assets	10,000	Owner's equity	9,000
Total	$15,000	Total	$15,000

McGraw is forecasting a 20% increase in sales for the coming year; assets vary directly with sales, while liabilities and equity do not. Compute the following for McGraw: profit margin (PM), retention ratio (R), return on assets (ROA), return on equity (ROE) and debt/equity ratio (D/E).

6. Use the ratios computed in the solution to Problem 5 to calculate the EFN for by T. McGraw Co.

7. Use pro forma statements to verify the results in the solution to Problem 6.

T. MCGRAW CORPORATION
Pro Forma Income Statement

Sales	$12,000
- Costs	9,000
Taxable income	$ 3,000
-Taxes (34%)	1,020
Net income	$ 1,980
Retained earnings	$ 792
Dividends	$ 1,188

Pro Forma Balance Sheet

Current assets	$ 6,000	Total debt	$ 6,000
Fixed assets	12,000	Owner's equity	9,792
Total	$18,000	Total	$15,792
		External funds needed	$ 2,208

8. Use the solution to Problem 6 to determine the growth rate McGraw can maintain if no external financing is used.

9. Use the data from the solution to Problem 5 to determine the sustainable growth rate for McGraw.

10. Use the Du Pont identity to verify the calculations in the solution to Problem 9.

11. Verify the results in the solutions to Problems 9 and 10 by preparing the pro forma income statement and balance sheet for McGraw, using the 7.914% sustainable growth rate.

Use the following information to solve problem 12.

RYAN & CO.
Income Statement

Sales	$2,000
- Costs	1,800
Taxable income	$ 200
- Taxes (34%)	68
Net income	$ 132
Retained earnings	$ 88
Dividends	$ 44

Balance Sheet

Current assets	$ 500	Current Liabilities	$ 165
Fixed assets	1,150	Long-term debt	535
Total	$ 1,650	Equity	950
		Total	$ 1,650

12. Ryan & Co. forecasts that sales next year will be $2,200. Costs, assets and current liabilities increase proportionately with sales, and the retention ratio remains constant. Compute external financing needed.

CHAPTER 5

INTRODUCTION TO VALUATION:

THE TIME VALUE OF MONEY

CONCEPTS FOR REVIEW

Finance is sometimes called the "science of valuation" because virtually every decision faced by the financial manager ultimately comes down to how firm value will be affected. The core of the valuation process is the time-value model, which describes how cash flows to be paid or received at various points in time are valued. After reading this chapter, you will understand two concepts crucial to any valuation problem you will ever face: *present value* and *future value*.

CHAPTER HIGHLIGHTS

In this chapter and the next we discuss several basic financial calculations. When you understand the concepts in these chapters, you will be able to solve many of the 'mysteries' of everyday financial life. Therefore, in addition to providing the foundation for financial decision-making for corporate managers, the material in these chapters also has important applications in the financial life of every consumer who makes a bank deposit or an investment, buys life insurance, or takes out an automobile or mortgage loan.

*Learning Tip: A thorough knowledge of this chapter is **essential** to an understanding of the material which follows. This is one of the most important topics you will cover in this course. Furthermore, since the topics in the chapter are developed sequentially, it is crucial that each subject in the chapter be understood before moving to the next.*

I. FUTURE VALUE AND COMPOUNDING (p. 113)

Investing for a Single Period (p. 113) A *future value* is the amount to which an initial dollar deposit (the *principal*) will grow when interest is compounded at a specified interest rate for a specified number of years. In general, the future value (FV), for an investment over a one-year period, can be determined from the following equation:

$FV = P \times (1 + r)$, where P is the original principal and r is the annual interest rate.

Investing for More than One Period (p. 113) If the principal is left on deposit for, say, two years, the future value depends on whether or not the interest earned during the first year is left on deposit during the second year. If not, then the deposit earns *simple interest* on original principal each year; that is, the interest received each year does not earn interest during any subsequent year. If, on the other hand, the first year's interest is left on deposit to earn interest, then the interest earned in the second year will include interest on both the original principal and on the first year's interest. Since the depositor earns interest on the previous year's interest, this is referred to as *compound interest*, or the process of *compounding interest*.

In general, the future value (FV) of an original principal P, invested for any given number of years t, at an interest rate r, is given by:
$$FV_t = P \times (1 + r)^t$$

The expression $[(1 + r)^t]$ is called the *future value interest factor*, or simply *future value factor*, and is sometimes abbreviated as FVIF(r,t). Future value interest factors appear in Appendix Table 1.

A Note on Compound Growth (p. 117) The compounding equation is also useful for computing the periodic rate of growth. In a growth problem, r represents the growth rate.

II. PRESENT VALUE AND DISCOUNTING (p. 118)

In this section we ask the following question: What deposit P is required today, in an account paying r% interest, in order to have $X t years from now? P is the *present value* (henceforth *PV*) of $X to be received t years from now, when the appropriate interest rate is r%.

The Single-Period Case (p. 119) The process of computing a PV is *discounting*, and the interest rate in a PV calculation is the *discount rate*. The PV of a single cash flow can be found as follows:

$$PV = FV/(1+r).$$

Present Values for Multiple Periods (p. 199) The PV of dollars to be paid or received in t periods is

$$PV = FV \times [1/(1+r)^t] = FV/(1+r)^t.$$

The term $[1/(1 + r)^t]$ in the above formula is the *present value interest factor*, and is abbreviated PVIF(r,t). Calculating a PV is called discounting, so we refer to the term $[1/(1 + r)^t]$ as the *discount factor*. The process of computing a present value is referred to as *discounted cash flow (DCF)* valuation.

III. MORE ON PRESENT AND FUTURE VALUES (p. 122)

In this section, we discuss further the relationship between present values and future values; we also analyze some additional aspects of these concepts.

Present versus Future Value (p. 122) The basic equations developed above are, in fact, two algebraically equivalent versions of the same equation. That is, given the FV equation

$$FV_t = PV \times FVIF(r,t),$$

the corresponding PV equation is

$$PV = FV_t/FVIF(r,t) = FV_t \times 1/FVIF(r,t) = FV_t \times PVIF(r,t).$$

Determining the Discount Rate (p. 123) It is often useful to solve for r. Consider the following.

In 1987, Vincent Van Gogh's "Sunflowers" sold for $36 million. The painting had first sold in 1889 for $125. Suppose a relative of yours had made the initial purchase and you were the recent seller. What was the average annually compounded on the $125 investment? Set this up as a future value problem:

$$FV_t = PV \times FVIF(r,t)$$
$$\$36 \text{ million} = \$125 \times FVIF(r,98)$$
$$\$36 \text{ million}/\$125 \text{ million} = 288{,}000 = (1 + r)^{98}$$

Solve for r:

$$288,000^{1/98} = 1 + r$$
$$r = .13686 = 13.69\%.$$

Most people look at the two initial values ($125 and $36 million) and assume that the rate of return will be very large. In actuality, it's close to the annual return on common stocks over the last seven decades.

APPENDIX 5: USING YOUR CALCULATOR

Financial mathematics deals with relationships between PV, FV, Payment, Interest Rate and Time. If you know any three of these variables, it's possible to solve for the fourth. Although the basic equations governing transformations between present and future values have been known for centuries, the advent of the electronic calculator has alleviated much of the tedium and imprecision associated with former methods. This appendix provides an introduction to basic problem-solving using the time value of money (TVM) registers on a financial calculator.

I. HOW TO SOLVE FINANCIAL PROBLEMS

Beginning finance students sometimes freeze up on learning that they will be expected to solve "story problems." Fortunately, there are a few tricks you can employ to get a handle on most financial story problems. The first involves drawing a time line, or cash flow diagram.

Cash Flow Diagrams Cash flow diagrams are useful analytical tools because they allow you to determine at a glance whether money is coming or going and at which points in time (Figure 5A-1).

Figure 5A-1. A Cash Flow Diagram

```
                           FV = ?
                             |
                             |
       0----1----2----3----4----5
       |                        r = 10%
       |                        t = 5
  PV = $250
```

A few observations about cash flow diagrams are in order. They are usually drawn beginning at t = 0, your present position in time. Cash outflows are indicated by vertical lines going down, while cash inflows are shown as vertical lines going up. It is good practice to label the axis and to note the interest rate prevailing over the period in question. Unknowns are indicated by variable names or by question marks. In Figure 5A-1, a cash outflow of $250 is made *today* and an unspecified cash inflow resulting from the compounding process is expected 5 periods in the future. The rate is 10 percent per period.

Identifying Variables and Writing Equations The second step is to identify the known and unknown variables and to write the appropriate equations. The cash flow diagram makes this a simple exercise.

Source: Mark White, **Financial Analysis with an Electronic Calculator**, Second Edition, © 1995.

Computing present values and future values requires that we set up an equation which includes the cash flow(s) picture in the cash flow diagram, and the appropriate present or future value factors. The factors, in turn, can be obtained either by referring to Tables 1 through 4 of the appendix, or by computing them using your calculator. Below are examples illustrating the use of three popular calculators in solving time value problems.

1. Determine the present value interest factor (PVIF) for ten periods at 8 percent.

HP-10B	**EL-733A**	**BA II Plus**
1.0000 [FV]	1.0000 [FV]	1.0000 [FV]
10.0000 [N]	10.0000 [n]	10.0000 [N]
8.0000 [I/YR]	8.0000 [i]	8.0000 [I/Y]
[PV] -0.4632	[COMP] [PV] -0.4632	[CPT] [PV] -0.4632

$$PVIF(8\%,10) = 0.4632$$

Future Value of a Present Sum

In a "future value" problem, you're trying to determine the value of an amount of money at some period in the future based upon a known sum at $t = 0$. Note that $t = 0$ does not necessarily mean *today*. For instance, problem 2 is a popular way of illustrating the impact of compound interest:

2. In 1626, Peter Minuit supposedly purchased Manhattan Island from the Canarsee Indians for 60 guilders, or about $24. Suppose the Indians had invested their proceeds from the sale at a 5 percent annual interest rate. How much would they have accumulated by 1995, 369 years later?

Step 1. Construct a cash flow diagram indicating the direction of each cash flow and the known and unknown variables.

```
                                              FV = ?
                                                |
                                                |
                                                |
      0----1----2----3----4----5----6----7---- ... ---369
      |                                     r = 5%
      |                                     t = 369
      |
   PV = $24
```

Step 2. Write the appropriate equation describing this problem.

$$FV = \$24(1+.05)^{369} \quad \textbf{or} \quad FV = \$24 \cdot FVIF(5\%,369)$$

Step 3. Enter the data into the registers. Be sure to CLEAR them first and change signs where necessary!

HP-10B	**EL-733A**	**BA II Plus**
-24 [PV]	-24 [PV]	-24 [PV]
367 [N]	367 [n]	367 [N]
5 [I/YR]	5 [i]	5 [I/Y]
[FV] ≈ $1.58 bil.	[COMP] [FV] ≈ $1.58 bil.	[CPT] [FV] ≈ $1.58 bil.

At an annual interest rate of 5 percent, the FV of $24 compounded for 369 years = $1,581,476,000 or about $1.58 billion!

In this case, $t = 0$ refers to the year 1626. The original payment of $24 represents a cash outflow (deposit) from the Indians' point of view and is entered as a negative number. The $1.58 billion is what the Canarsee would have hypothetically received 369 years in the future. You could also diagram this problem from the bank's point of view, treating the $24 deposit as a cash inflow and the accrued interest and principal as a cash outflow. (Try it! If the $24 initial deposit is positive, the FV will be negative).

Present Value of a Future Sum Present value problems are concerned with how much money you need now in order to achieve some goal in the future. They bear a strong relationship to future value problems, and you've probably already noticed that the PVIF and FVIF factors are reciprocals. Problem 3 illustrates a typical present value problem and the steps in its solution.

3. Grandfather White is very proud of his new granddaughter, Katie. He's figured out that she will need approximately $100,000 to attend college when she's eighteen, and he would like to give her a gift to ensure she achieves this goal. Ignoring taxes and inflation, and assuming Katie will be able to earn a constant 6 percent interest rate over the next 18 years, how much money should he give to Katie *now*?

Step 1. Construct a cash flow diagram

```
                              FV = $100,000
                                  |
                                  |
     0----1----2----3----4----5----6----7-- ... --18
     |                           r =  6%
     |                           t = 18
   PV = ?
```

Step 2. Write the appropriate equation

$$PV = \$100,000/(1.06)^{18} \text{ or } PV = \$100,000 \times PVIF(6\%,18)$$

Step 3. Enter the data into the appropriate registers

HP-10B	EL-733A	BA II Plus
100,000 [FV]	100,000 [FV]	100,000 [FV]
18 [N]	18 [n]	18 [N]
6 [I/YR]	6 [i]	6 [I/Y]
[PV] -35,034	[COMP] [PV] -35'034	[CPT] [PV] -35,034

Grandfather White should write a check for $35,034 so Katie will have $100,000 for college in 18 years. If you are just beginning to use your calculator, you might want to check the calculator's solution against the present value/future value tables. (It's also useful to know how to use the tables in case your calculator suddenly goes dead in the middle of a test!) According to Appendix Table 2, the PVIF at 6 percent for 18 years is 0.3503. Multiplying this figure by $100,000 equals $35,030. The difference between this answer and the calculator's is due to rounding error.

Solving for an Unknown Number of Periods Sometimes it is important to know how long it will take for a sum to reach some future amount, or how many payments are remaining on an outstanding loan.

4. Overpopulation is believed to be a significant factor leading to the degradation of Earth's environmental resources. The world population in 1991 was approximately 5.4 billion and was increasing at a rate of 1.7 percent per year. Some experts have estimated that the Earth can support no more than 8 billion people assuming current technology and patterns of resource utilization. If population growth rates are not slowed, when will this figure be achieved?

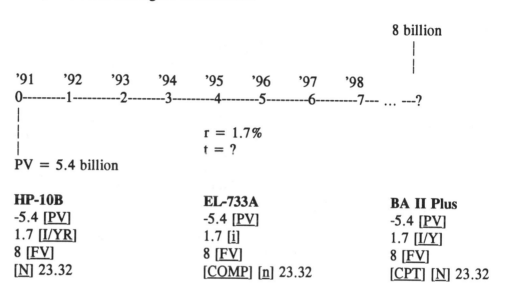

HP-10B	EL-733A	BA II Plus
-5.4 [PV]	-5.4 [PV]	-5.4 [PV]
1.7 [I/YR]	1.7 [i]	1.7 [I/Y]
8 [FV]	8 [FV]	8 [FV]
[N] 23.32	[COMP] [n] 23.32	[CPT] [N] 23.32

If population growth remains unchecked, the Earth's human population will reach 8 billion 23.32 years from 1991, i.e., in the year 2014.

Besides providing food for thought, this illustrates the usefulness of exponential functions in other disciplines. Populations grow in exactly the same fashion as interest. An early economist, Thomas Malthus (1766-1834) made just this point. He predicted that humanity was doomed to extinction since population increased at an exponential rate while food supplies and arable land increased at an arithmetic rate. (Malthus was wrong, partly because he failed to account for improvements in technology.)

Multiperiod Compounding Before leaving the time value of money, a few words on interest rates are in order. In finance, payments are computed using either *simple interest* or *compound interest*. Under simple interest, a fixed percentage of the *original* principal is added to your account at the end of each period. Because simple interest is relatively easy to determine and because few institutions price their financial products in simple interest terms, it is mostly ignored in finance textbooks. All the examples up to now have dealt with *compound interest*, i.e., the situation in which interest accrues on the sum of principal and previously paid interest. Thus far, however, we have assumed that interest is compounded only once per period. This is not the general case. As noted above, interest can be compounded multiple times per period. Built-in functions on the HP-10B, EL-733A and BA II Plus quickly convert between nominal and effective rates.

The above material is from: Mark White, **Financial Analysis with an Electronic Calculator**, Second Edition, © 1995.

KEY TERMS AND CONCEPTS

Compound interest - interest earned on both the initial principal and the interest reinvested from prior periods. (p. 113)

Discount - to calculate the present value of some future amount. (p. 119)

Discount rate - the rate used to calculate the present value of future cash flows. (p. 120)

Future value - the value of an investment after one or more periods. (Also *compound value*.) (p. 113)

Present value - the current value of future cash flows discounted at the appropriate discount rate. (p. 119)

Simple interest - interest earned only on the original principal amount invested. (p. 113)

CONCEPT TEST

1. When a deposit or investment earns interest on interest previously received, it is said to be earning _____; this process is referred to as _____. A _____ is the amount to which an initial deposit, called the _____, will grow when interest is compounded at a specified interest rate for a specified number of years. The future value (FV_t) of an initial deposit (PV) which earns interest at the rate r for t years is given by the following formula: $FV_t =$ _____ . The expression _____ is referred to as the future value interest factor, and is abbreviated as _____ . (p. 113)

2. A present value is the amount which must be invested today, at a specified _____, to grow to a specified _____, at a specified _____. The PV is dependent on three values: the _____, the amount of the _____, and the _____. Computing a PV is called _____. The rate used in the calculation is called the _____. (p. 119)

3. A PV can be calculated by substituting known values of the _____, the _____, and the _____ into the basic PV equation as follows: PV = _____ . Alternatively, we can rearrange the basic PV equation so that the PV is determined by multiplying the future value (FV) times the _____ of the FV interest factor: PV = _____ . The term _____ is called the present value interest factor (PVIF) and is abbreviated _____ . The PVIF can be determined from tables. The PVIF is also called the _____ and computing a PV is also referred to as _____ valuation. (p. 119)

ANSWERS TO CONCEPT TEST

1. compound interest; compounding; future value; principal; $[PV \times (1+r)^t]$; $[(1+r)^t]$; FVIF(r,t)
2. interest rate; amount; future date; interest rate; future payment; time; discounting; discount rate
3. interest rate; future payment; time period; $[FV_t/(1+r)^t]$; reciprocal; $FV_t \times [1/(1+r)^t]$; $[1/(1+r)^t]$; PVIF(r,t); discount factor; discounted cash flow

PROBLEMS

1. If you deposit $10,000 today in a bank account paying 10.38%, how much will you have in one year? If you need $12,000 in one year, how much do you have to deposit today?

2. An art collector has the opportunity to invest in paintings; the investment requires an outlay of $2 million. He is certain that he will be able to sell the paintings for $2.18 million in one year. He also has the opportunity to invest in certificates of deposit (CDs) which pay 10% per year. What is the FV of the $2 million if the collector purchases the CDs? Is the investment in the paintings a good investment?

3. In Problem 2, what is the rate of return for the investment in paintings?

4. For the paintings described in Problem 2, what is the PV of the future cash flow the collector would receive if he sold the paintings one year from now? What is the value of the paintings to the collector?

5. Calculate the present value for each of the following cash flows to be received one year hence:

Future cash flow	Interest rate	Present value
$ 10,000	10%	
153,200	13%	
153,200	10%	
2,567,450	5%	
120,600	9%	

6. As a newly-minted MBA embarking on a career in investment banking, you naturally must own a BMW 325is immediately. The car costs $28,320. You also have to spend $3,248 on blue pin-stripe suits. Your salary this year is $42,000, and next year it will be $46,000. Your routine living expenses this year will be $34,000. You plan to make up the difference between current income and current consumption by borrowing; the interest rate for the loan is 14% and you intend to repay the loan, plus interest, in one year. How much will you have left to spend next year?

7. An individual has the opportunity to invest $1,000 today to acquire an asset which will generate $300 in income one year from today and which can be sold for $900 at that time. Determine the minimum level of the market interest rate for which this investment would be attractive.

8. An investment requires an initial outlay of $195. The cash inflow from this investment will be $114 one year from today (year 1) and $144 two years from today (year 2). The market rate of interest is 20%. Find the present value for this investment. Is the investment acceptable?

9. An entrepreneur has purchased an asset for $200,000 which will produce a cash inflow of $300,000 in one year. He plans to issue 100 shares of common stock to himself and sell 900 shares to the public. His business consists entirely of this one asset and will close after one year. The market rate of interest is 20%, and the future cash inflow to the firm is guaranteed. At what price per share should the entrepreneur sell the common stock? What gain will the entrepreneur realize?

10. What is the present value of $145 to be received in 5 years if the market interest rate is 8%?

11. What is the future value of $235 invested at 12% for 4 years?

12. For each of the following, compute the present value:

Future value	Years	Interest rate	Present value
$ 498	7	13%	
1,033	13	6	
14,784	23	4	
898,156	4	31	

13. For each of the following, compute the future value:

Present value	Years	Interest rate	Future value
$ 123	13	13%	
4,555	8	8	
74,484	5	10	
167,332	9	1	

14. Solve for the unknown time period in each of the following:

Present value	Future value	Interest rate	Time (years)
$ 100	$ 348	12%	
123	$ 351	10%	
4,100	$ 8,523	5%	
10,543	$26,783	6%	

15. Solve for the unknown interest rate in each of the following:

Present value	Future value	Interest rate	Time (years)
$ 100	$ 466		20
123	$ 218		6
4,100	$ 9,064		7
10,543	$21,215		12

CHAPTER 6

DISCOUNTED CASH FLOW VALUATION

CONCEPTS FOR REVIEW

As noted in the previous chapter, corporate finance is sometimes called the "science of valuation" because most of the decisions faced by financial managers boil down to how firm value will be affected. We considered the valuation of single cash flows to be paid or received at different points in time. Here we take the next logical step - we learn to value *streams of cash flows*.

CHAPTER HIGHLIGHTS

The material in this chapter builds on that in Chapter 5. Before you get deeply into this chapter, be sure that you understand the concepts described there. Additionally, keep in mind that most of the valuation problems faced by either professional financial managers or by individual consumers involve streams of cash flows, rather than single cash flows, making the concepts below even more important..

*Learning Tip: We feel strongly enough about it that we reiterate a point made in the previous chapter: A thorough knowledge of this chapter is **essential** to an understanding of business finance.*

I. FUTURE AND PRESENT VALUES OF MULTIPLE CASH FLOWS (p. 132)

Future Value with Multiple Cash Flows (p. 132) In this section we describe how to compute the balance in an account when several deposits are made over a period of years. One approach is to compute the ending balance at the end of the first year using the appropriate FVIF(r,t), add the second deposit, compute the balance at the end of the second year, and continue to do so as long as necessary. Alternatively, we can use the compounding formula to obtain the future value of each deposit at year t and sum these future values. The result will be the same as that obtained using the first approach.

Present Value with Multiple Cash Flows (p. 135) Similarly, there are two techniques which can be used to determine the present value of multiple cash flows: first, we can discount future payments year-by-year; or, we can separately compute the present value of each future cash flow and then sum the separate present values to determine the total present value for all the cash flows. As before, the two approaches are mathematically equivalent.

A Note on Cash Flow Timing (p. 138) Whether we are computing future values or present values, we must specify exactly *when* cash flows occur; we generally assume that cash flows occur at the *end* of a time period. More on this later.

II. VALUING LEVEL CASH FLOWS: ANNUITIES AND PERPETUITIES (p. 139)

An *annuity* is a series of equal cash flows that occur at regular intervals for a fixed number of time periods. If the payments occur at the end of each time period, the annuity is an *ordinary annuity* or a *regular annuity*. If payments are at the beginning of each time period, we call the annuity a *deferred annuity* or *annuity due*. A *perpetuity* is a perpetual annuity; that is, cash flows go on forever.

Present Value for Annuity Cash Flows (p. 139) When the series of cash flows is an ordinary annuity we can greatly simplify the computation by finding the sum of the individual present value factors and multiplying by the cash flow amount (C). We denote the sum of the present value factors as PVIFA(r,t), which stands for present value interest factor for an annuity, and the present value is equal to

$$PV = C \times PVIFA(r,t)$$

where C is the constant annuity payment. Values of PVIFA(r,t) can be found in the text Appendix. Alternatively, one can compute PVIFA(r,t) by using the following formula:

$$PVIFA(r,t) = (1 - [1/(1 + r)^t])/r = (1 - [PVIF(r,t)])/r.$$

Future Value for Annuities (p. 143) We can employ a similar approach to find the future value of an annuity. From Table A.4 we obtain the *future value interest factor for an annuity* [FVIFA(r,t)]. This factor, which is the sum of the individual future value interest factors for each payment in an annuity, is then multiplied by the constant payment to determine the future value. Or FVIFA(r,t) can be computed from a formula, indicated below, and is then multiplied by the constant payment, C, to calculate the future value of the annuity. The FVIFA(r,t) formula is:

$$FVIFA(r,t) = ([(1 + r)^t] - 1)/r = ([FVIF(r,t)] - 1)/r.$$

And the future value of an annuity, FV, equals $C \times FVIFA(r,t)$.

A Note on Annuities Due (p. 144) Previously it was pointed out that we generally assume that cash flows occur at the end of each period. However, there are instances in which cash flows occur at the beginning of each period (for example, an apartment lease). We define an *annuity due* as an annuity for which the cash flows occur at the beginning of each period. To value an annuity due, make the following adjustment to the ordinary annuity formula:

$$Annuity\ due\ value = Ordinary\ annuity\ value \times (1 + r).$$

Perpetuities (p. 144) A perpetuity (or perpetual annuity) is a series of equal cash flows, occurring at regular intervals, which continues forever. The present value of a perpetuity is

$$PV = C/r = C \times (1/r).$$

III. COMPARING RATES: THE EFFECT OF COMPOUNDING (p. 146)

The preceding discussion of future-value and present-value analysis has been based on the assumption that interest rates are compounded annually. However, financial institutions often compound interest more frequently. In this section, we see how different compounding periods affect financial calculations.

Effective Annual Rates and Compounding (p. 146) Consider a bank which pays 12% interest per year, compounded quarterly; this is equivalent to 3% interest each quarter. The 12% rate in this example is sometimes referred to as the *stated interest rate*, the *quoted rate* or the *nominal rate*. However, when interest is compounded more than once a year, the actual rate the depositor receives is greater than the quoted rate. The true rate is often called the *effective annual interest rate* or the *effective annual yield*.

Calculating and Comparing Effective Annual Rates (p. 146) In general, the relationship between the quoted interest rate and the effective annual rate (EAR) is as follows:

$$EAR = (1 + q/m)^m - 1$$

where m is the number of times per year interest is compounded and q is the quoted interest rate. In the context of present and future values, the formula for compounding m times per year over t years is

$$FV = PV \times (1 + r/m)^{mt}.$$

EARs and APRs (p. 148) We define EAR as the interest rate expressed as if it were compounded once a year. The *APR* or *annual percentage rate* is defined as the interest rate charged per period multiplied by the number of periods per year. Thus, the relationship between EAR and APR is as follows:

$$EAR = (1 + APR/12)^{12} - 1.$$

TAKING IT TO THE LIMIT: A NOTE ON CONTINUOUS COMPOUNDING (p. 149) At the limit, m approaches infinity; this is called continuous compounding, which is equivalent to compounding over the smallest possible period of time. It can be shown that, in the case of continuous compounding, the future value is equal to:

$$FV = PV \times (e^{qt})$$

where e is a constant whose value is approximately 2.718 and q is the quoted interest rate. Alternatively, we can obtain the continuously compounded EAR:

$$\text{effective annual interest rate} = EAR = e^q - 1$$

where q is the quoted interest rate.

IV. LOAN TYPES AND LOAN AMORTIZATION (p. 151)

The three basic forms of loans are: pure-discount loans, interest-only loans, and amortized loans. Below we discuss the application of present value principles to these three kinds of loans.

Pure Discount Loans (p. 151) A *pure-discount loan* is a loan which is repaid in a single payment; the single payment therefore represents principal plus interest for the period of the loan. The mathematics of pure-discount loans is simply the mathematics of single cash flows.

Interest Only Loans (p. 151) *Interest-only loans* require payment of interest each year and repayment of the principal at a later date.

Amortized Loans (p. 151) An *amortized loan* requires that the lender make periodic payments which include interest plus repayment of a portion of the principal. A table showing which describes the periodic payments, as well as the interest and principal portion of each payment, is called an *amortization schedule*.

APPENDIX 6: USING YOUR CALCULATOR

As we noted in the previous appendix, financial mathematics deals with relationships between Present Value, Future Value, Payment, Interest Rate and Time. If you know any three of these variables, it's possible to solve for a fourth. This appendix concludes our introduction to basic problem-solving using the financial calculator by considering problems with multiple cash flows. Below are more examples illustrating the use of three popular calculators in solving time value problems.

1. What is the future value interest factor of an annuity (FVIFA) of 6.5 percent for nine periods?

HP-10B	EL-733A	BA II Plus
1.000 [PMT]	1.000 [PMT]	1.000 [PMT]
9.000 [N]	9.000 [n]	9.000 [N]
6.500 [I/YR]	6.500 [i]	6.500 [I/Y]
[FV] -11.732	[COMP] [FV] -11.732	[CPT] [FV] -11.732

FVIFA(6.5%,9) = 11.732

Before checking the answer against the tables, let's see if it agrees with our intuition. We know that the FV of the annuity must be at least 9, because that would be true at an interest rate of zero percent. A FVIFA of 11.732 seems reasonable, and indeed lies between the FVIFA factors for 6 percent and 7 percent in the tables. By the way, the answers appear as *negative* numbers because the present value was *positive*. Entering a negative present value will yield a positive future value.

Future Value of an Ordinary Annuity Solving for the future value of an ordinary annuity allows you to determine how much money has accumulated as the result of a series of periodic payments. As mentioned earlier, ordinary annuities assume payments are at the end of a period, while annuities due assume payment are at the beginning.

2. John wants to buy a car when he gets his drivers' license in 2 years. He's just taken a job that will allow him to save $50 per month for the next 24 months. His money is deposited in the Shoreham National Bank earning 6 percent compounded monthly (r = 0.5 percent per month). How much money will he have in the account when he turns 16?

Step 1. Construct a cash flow diagram

```
                                         FV = ?
    r = .5%                               |
    t = 24                                |
                                          |
              0----1----2----3----4----5----6----7--- ... --24

              50  50  50  50  50  50  50        50
```

Adapted from: Mark White, **Financial Analysis with an Electronic Calculator**, Second Edition, © 1995.

Step 2. *Write the proper equation.*

$$FV = \$50 \times [(1+.005)^{24}-1]/.005 \text{ or } FV = \$50 \cdot FVIFA(0.5\%,24)$$

Step 3. *Enter the data into the appropriate registers.*

HP-10B	**EL-733A**	**BA II Plus**
-50.00 [PMT]	-50.00 [PMT]	-50.00 [PMT]
24.00 [N]	24.00 [n]	24.00 [N]
0.50 [I/YR]	0.50 [i]	0.5 [I/Y]
[FV] 1,271.60	[COMP] [FV] 1'271.60	[CPT] [FV] 1,271.60

John will have $1,271.60 in his account when he turns 16.

In problem 2 the periods were defined as months, which required you to use a *monthly* interest rate. The HP-10B and the BA II Plus are able to solve this problem in a more direct fashion using multiperiod compounding, which will be discussed later in this chapter.

Annuities Due Annuities due were defined previously as annuities for which cash flows occur at the beginning of each period. Problem 3 illustrates the difference in timing between cash flows at the beginning and end of periods.

3. It is New Year's Day and Zoe has resolved to keep better control of her finances during the coming year. Tomorrow morning she plans to open a holiday savings account with an initial deposit of $150. She plans to make **ten** more monthly deposits and withdraw her money on December 2nd for holiday shopping. If she earns interest at the rate of 1 percent per month, how much will she be able to spend?

Step 1. *Construct a cash flow diagram*

```
                                                                  FV = ?
                                                                   |
                                                                   |
   JAN    FEB    MAR    APR    MAY   JUN    JUL    AUG         NOV   DEC
    0----------1---------2--------3---------4--------5-------6----------7------...---------10------11

   150    150    150    150    150   150    150    150         150
```

$$r = 1\%$$
$$t = 11$$

Source: Mark White, **Financial Analysis with an Electronic Calculator**, Second Edition, ©1995.

Step 2. *Set BEGIN mode and enter the data into the appropriate registers*

HP-10B	**EL-733A**	**BA II Plus**
		[2nd] {BGN}
		[2nd] {SET}
[_] {BEG/END}	[BGN]	[2nd] {QUIT}
-150.00 [PMT]	-150.00 [PMT]	-150.00 [PMT]
11.00 [N]	11.00 [n]	11.00 [N]
1.00 [I/YR]	1.00 [i]	1.00 [I/Y]
[FV] 1,752.38	[COMP] [FV] 1'752.38	[CPT] [FV] 1,752.38

Zoe will be able to spend $1,752.38 on holiday presents.

The annuity due equations have been omitted for brevity. Note that the payment stream begins at $t = 0$ and concludes one period *before* the FV is computed. The *number* of payments is still 11, even though the last payment occurs at $t = 10$. In contrast to ordinary annuities, the last payment of an annuity due *is* compounded.

Present Value of an Ordinary Annuity Present value of annuity problems are familiar to anyone who has ever taken out a loan which had to be repaid in a fixed number of payments. Problem 4 shows how to determine the size of the payments.

4. Newlyweds Clayton and Deirdre are interested in financing a new car. At present, only Clayton has been able to find a job and the couple is experiencing some monetary constraints. Consequently, they are concerned about the size of the monthly payment. The automobile dealer has proposed two alternatives to finance a $12,000 purchase: 1) 36 months at 6 percent interest or 2) 48 months at 12 percent interest. Assume monthly compounding. Which alternative offers the lower monthly payment?

Step 1. *Construct a cash flow diagram*

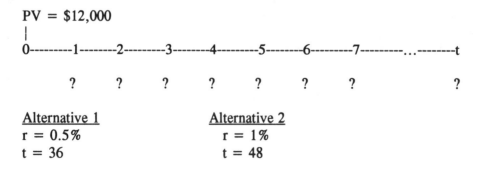

```
PV = $12,000
|
0---------1--------2---------3--------4---------5-------6---------7---------...-------t

          ?        ?        ?        ?        ?        ?        ?                  ?

Alternative 1              Alternative 2
r = 0.5%                   r = 1%
t = 36                     t = 48
```

Source: Mark White, **Financial Analysis with an Electronic Calculator**, Second Edition, © 1995.

Step 2. Write the proper equations.

Alternative 1: $12,000 = PMT \times \{1-1/(1+0.005)^{36}\}/.005$ or $12,000 = PMT \times PVIFA(0.5\%,36)$

Alternative 2: $12,000 = PMT \times \{1-1/(1+0.01)^{48}\}/.01$ or $12,000 = PMT \times PVIFA(1\%,48)$

Step 3. Enter the data into the appropriate registers.

Alternative 1:

HP-10B	**EL-733A**	**BA II Plus**
12,000.00 [PV]	12'000.00 [PV]	12,000.00 [PV]
36.00 [N]	36.00 [n]	36.00 [N]
0.50 [I/YR]	0.50 [i]	0.50 [I/Y]
[PMT] -365.06	[COMP] [PMT] -365.06	[CPT] [PMT] -365.06

Alternative 2:

HP-10B	**EL-733A**	**BA II Plus**
12,000.00 [PV]	12'000.00 [PV]	12,000.00 [PV]
48.00 [N]	48.00 [n]	48.00 [N]
1.00 [I/YR]	1.00 [i]	1.00 [I/Y]
[PMT] -316.01	[COMP] [PMT] -316.01	[CPT] [PMT] -316.01

Alternative 1 has monthly payments of $365.06 and Alternative 2 has monthly payments of $316.01. Focusing only on payment size, Clayton and Deirdre should choose Alternative 2.

Solving for an Unknown Interest Rate The superiority of financial calculators over present value/future value tables is most easily demonstrated when solving for unknown interest rates and unknown periods.

5. Ben's Pawn Shop makes 12-month loans in amounts up to $2,000. Ben requires equal monthly payments of one-tenth of the original loan amount. What monthly interest rate is Ben charging?

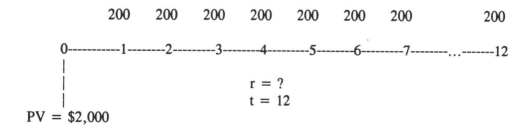

Source: Mark White, **Financial Analysis with an Electronic Calculator**, Second Edition, © 1995.

HP-10B	EL-733A	BA II Plus
-2,000.00 [PV]	-2'000.00 [PV]	-2,000.00 [PV]
12.00 [N]	12.00 [n]	12.00 [N]
200.00 [PMT]	200.00 [PMT]	200.00 [PMT]
[I/YR] 2.92	[COMP] [i] 2.92	[CPT] [I/Y] 2.92

Ben charges a rather high monthly interest rate of 2.92 percent.

The answer to problem 5 is independent of the amount borrowed. To see this, try it again using a loan amount of $1,000 and $100 payments. Also, it is perfectly normal for display screens on the EL-733A and BA II Plus to go blank for 10-20 seconds while these calculators are "thinking." The length of time serves as an indication of the difficulty involved in solving these problems manually.

Source: Mark White, **Financial Analysis with an Electronic Calculator**, Second Edition, ©1995.

KEY TERMS AND CONCEPTS

Annual percentage rate (APR) - the interest rate per period times number of periods per year. (p. 146)

Annuity - a level stream of cash flows for a fixed period of time. (p. 139)

Annuity due - an annuity for which the cash flows occur at the beginning of the period. (p. 144)

Effective annual interest rate (EAR) - the interest rate expressed as if compounded annually (p. 146)

Ordinary annuity - an annuity for which the cash flows occur at the end of the period. (p. 139)

Perpetuity - an annuity in which the cash flows continue forever. (p. 144)

Stated interest rate - the interest rate expressed in terms of the interest payment each period. Also *quoted rate* or *nominal rate*. (p. 146)

CONCEPT TEST

1. A FV with multiple cash flows can be computed by finding the _____ of each deposit and then summing the separate _____. A PV with multiple cash flows can be calculated by separately computing the _____ of each cash flow and then summing the separate _____. (p. 132)

2. An annuity is a series of _____ cash flows that occur at _____ intervals for a _____ number of periods. When the payments occur at the end of the time period, the annuity is referred to as an _____ annuity or a _____ annuity. If payments are at the beginning of the time period, we call the annuity an _____ . (p. 139)

3. The present value of an annuity formula is: PV = _____ , where PV is the present value of the annuity, C is the _____ , and PVIFA(r,t) is the _____. PVIFA(r,t) can be determined either from a table or from the following formula: PVIFA(r,t) = _____ . (p. 139)

4. The future value of an annuity formula is: FV = _____ where FV is the future value of the annuity, C is the _____ , and FVIFA(r,t) is the _____. FVIFA(r,t) can be determined either from a table or from the following formula: FVIFA(r,t) = _____ . (p. 143)

5. A perpetuity is a perpetual series of _____ cash flows, occurring at _____ intervals. The PV of a perpetuity formula is: PV = _____ . The formula can also be solved for C, and written as: C = _____ . It can also be solved for r: r = _____ . (p. 144)

6. A quoted interest rate is also called a _____ interest rate or a _____ interest rate. When interest is compounded more than once a year, the actual interest rate is _____ than the quoted interest rate. The actual interest rate is often called the effective annual interest rate or _____ . The effective annual rate (EAR) is computed as follows: EAR = _____ where m is the number of times per year interest is compounded and q is the quoted interest rate. When interest is compounded m times per year, the future value is equal to _____ . (p. 146)

50

7. The three basic forms of loans are: pure-discount loans, interest-only loans, and amortized loans. A pure-discount loan is a loan which is repaid in a _____ which includes _____ plus _____ for the loan period. Interest-only loans require payment of _____ each year, and repayment of _____ later. An amortized loan requires that the lender make periodic payments which include _____ plus repayment of a portion of the _____. Two common forms of amortized loans are: a loan payment schedule which requires periodic repayment of a fixed portion of the _____ plus _____; and, a loan payment which is constant over the life of the loan, so that successive payments repay progressively _____ portions of the principal and correspondingly _____ interest payments. (p. 151)

ANSWERS TO CONCEPT TEST

1. future value; future values; present value; present values
2. equal; regular; fixed; ordinary; regular; annuity due
3. $[C \times PVIFA(r,t)]$; constant payment; present value interest factor for an annuity; $\{1-[1/(1+r)^t]\}/r$
4. $[C \times FVIFA(r,t)]$; constant payment; future value interest factor for an annuity; $[(1+r)^t-1]/r$
5. equal; regular; (C/r); $(PV \times r)$; (C/PV)
6. stated; nominal; greater; effective annual yield; $\{[1+(q/m)^m]-1\}$; $\{PV \times [1+(r/m)]^{mt}\}$
7. single payment; interest; principal; interest; principal; interest; principal; larger; smaller

PROBLEMS

1. Compute the present values of the following ordinary annuities:

Payment	Years	Interest rate	Present value
$678.09	7	13%	
7,968.26	13	6	
20,322.93	23	4	
69,712.54	4	31	

2. Compute the future values of the following ordinary annuities:

Payment	Years	Interest rate	Future value
$ 123	13	13%	
4,555	8	8	
74,484	5	10	
167,332	9	1	

3. A local bank is offering 9% interest, compounded monthly, on savings accounts. If you deposit $700 today, how much will you have in 2 years? How much will you have in 2.5 years?

4. For each of the following, calculate the effective annual rate (EAR):

Stated rate	Number of times compounded	Effective rate
5%	semiannually	
11%	quarterly	
16%	daily	

5. You have just joined the investment banking firm of Knot, Wirthem, et al. They have offered you two different salary arrangements. You can have $50,000 per year for the next 3 years or $25,000 per year for the next 3 years, along with a $50,000 signing bonus today. If the market interest rate is 16%, which salary arrangement do you prefer?

6. A bank pays interest compounded monthly; the EAR is 8%. What is the quoted rate?

7. A local loan shark offers 'four for five on payday,' this means you borrow $4 today and you must repay $5 in 6 days, when you get your paycheck. What is the effective annual interest rate for this loan?

8. You expect to receive an annuity of $1000 per year for the next five years. The market rate of interest is 12%. Assuming that you do not spend any of the income at any other time, what is the most you can spend from these payments at the end of five years? What is the most you can spend today?

9. An investment will increase in value by 270% over the next 17 years. What is the annual interest rate which, when compounded quarterly, provides this return?

10. Consider a perpetuity which pays $100 per year; the market rate of interest is 10%. What is the PV of the perpetuity? What is the PV of the perpetuity three years from now? What is the present value of the perpetuity n years from now? Under what circumstances does the value of a perpetuity change?

11. A firm invests $3 million in a project which will yield a perpetuity of $1 million per year. What is the discount rate r for which this project's present value is $4.5 million?

CHAPTER 7

INTEREST RATES AND BOND VALUATION

CONCEPTS FOR REVIEW

It's now time to apply what you know about the time value of money to some important valuation problems in finance. Managers should make decisions that will maximize security values; putting this rule into practice requires that we understand how market values are determined. The model we use to value bonds in this chapter and stocks in the next are variants of the time value models discussed previously.

CHAPTER HIGHLIGHTS

In order to value financial instruments it is necessary to understand the basic features of securities; these features are introduced early in the chapter; further details are provided in later sections.

I. BONDS AND BOND VALUATION (p. 169)

Bonds are long-term debt securities issued by corporations and by federal, state, and local governments. Although bonds can take many different forms, the basic form discussed in this section is the *level-coupon* bond, which pays the holder interest on a periodic basis.

Bond Features and Prices (p. 169) A *level-coupon bond* promises regular interest payments (either annually or semi-annually), as well as a specified principal payment, or *face value*, at the *maturity date*. The annual interest payment is called the bond's *coupon interest payment*, or simply *coupon* for short. The face value is also referred to as the *par value* or *maturity value* of the bond. The *coupon interest rate*, or *coupon rate*, indicates the annual coupon interest payment to the holder of the bond; the coupon interest rate times the face value of the bond is equal to the coupon payment. The *maturity date* is the date of the principal payment to the owner of the bond, and is also the date of the last coupon payment.

Bond Values and Yields (p. 169) The value of any bond is the present value of the future coupon payments plus the present value of the principal payment, discounted at the appropriate opportunity cost for bonds of similar characteristics. The *opportunity cost* is the rate of return available on other corporate bonds with about the same term to maturity and risk. The bond pricing equation takes the following form:

$$PV = C/(1+r)^1 + C/(1+r)^2 + \ldots C/(1+r)^t + \$1,000/(1+r)^t$$

where C is the semi-annual coupon payment, t is the number of semi-annual time periods to the maturity date, r is the appropriate semi-annual opportunity cost, and $1,000 is the principal payment at maturity. Since the coupon payments are in the form of an annuity, the above equation can be rewritten as:

$$PV = [C \times PVIFA(r,t)] + [F \times PVIF(r,t)]$$

where F is the face value (usually $1,000 for a corporate bond).

The model above suggests two additional aspects of bond valuation: the relationship between interest rates and bond prices, and the concept of a bond's yield to maturity, which is the rate of return for a bond. Mathematically, the value of the bond decreases when the market rate of interest increases because the interest rate is in the denominator of the present value formula; an increase in the denominator reduces the present value. Similarly, a decrease in the market rate of interest increases the value of the bond.

When a bond sells for more than its $1,000 face value, it is said to be selling at a *premium* and is referred to as a *premium bond*; a bond which sells for less than face value is selling at a *discount* and is called a *discount bond*. When the market rate of interest is equal to the bond's coupon rate, the bond's market value is equal to its face value and is said to be a *par* bond.

Interest Rate Risk (p. 173) Bond price changes attributable to changes in market interest rates constitute *interest rate risk*. The interest rate risk of a given bond is positively related to its time to maturity and negatively related to its coupon rate. Thus, the market price of a long-term bond will change more with a given change in market interest rates than the market price of a short-term bond. Similarly, the market price of a bond with a low coupon will change more, for a given change in market interest rates, than will the price of a bond with a higher coupon.

Finding the Yield to Maturity: More Trial and Error (p. 175) An understanding of the relationship between interest rates and bond values is essential in determining the rate of return, or *yield to maturity*, for a given bond. The yield to maturity is the discount rate which equates the present value of the future cash flows and the current market price.

II. MORE ON BOND FEATURES (p. 177)

A bond is a promise to repay *principal* (the original amount of the loan) plus *interest*, at a specified time to the lender (or *creditor*). The firm is the *debtor* or *borrower*, and the debt owed is a liability.

Debt securities are often classified according to the *maturity* of the debt. Short-term debt has a maturity of less than one year, while long-term securities have maturities greater than one year. Typically, corporate debt securities are either *notes*, *debentures*, or *bonds*. Strictly speaking, a bond is secured by a mortgage on specific property, whereas a debenture is unsecured; however, the word 'bond' is often used generically. A note matures in less than ten years.

Is it Debt or Equity? (p. 177) From a financial point of view, three features distinguish debt from equity: (1) debt does not represent an ownership interest in the firm; (2) interest paid on debt is tax-deductible while dividends paid on common stock are not; and, (3) failure to pay creditors can result in bankruptcy.

Long-term Debt: The Basics (p. 178) Debt securities are often classified according to the *maturity* of the debt. Short-term debt has a maturity of less than one year, while long-term securities have maturities greater than one year. Typically, corporate debt securities are either **notes**, **debentures**, or **bonds**. Strictly speaking, a bond is secured by a mortgage on specific property, whereas a debenture is unsecured; however, the word 'bond' is often used generically. A note matures in less than ten years.

A **public issue** is a debt issue which is sold to the general public. In a **private issue**, terms are negotiated directly between the borrower and the lender, and the security is issued directly to the lender.

The Indenture (p. 179) The **indenture** is the written agreement between the firm and the bondholders. It sets forth the *terms* of the loan and identifies all **protective covenants** which restrict actions by the firm. The indenture also identifies the **trustee**, who is appointed by the firm to represent the bondholders.

Long-term corporate debt is generally in the form of a bond which has a **principal** or **face value** of $1,000. Annual interest on corporate bonds is generally specified as a **coupon rate** equal to a specified percentage of face value; interest payments are made semi-annually. Principal, along with the last interest payment, is repaid to the bondholder on the **maturity date**.

Bonds can be either **registered** or **bearer bonds**. The company's appointed registrar mails interest payments directly to owners of registered bonds. Bearer bonds have dated coupons attached. Every six months, the bondholder detaches a coupon and mails it to the firm, which then makes the payment.

Debt securities differ with regard to the collateral pledged as **security** for the payment of debt. **Mortgage securities** are secured by a mortgage on real property, usually real estate. A **debenture** is not secured by specific property.

Seniority governs priority of payment to creditors in the event of bankruptcy. Some debt is **subordinated**, which means that other creditors must be repaid first in the event of bankruptcy.

Most corporate bonds are repaid prior to maturity. For public issues, repayment takes place through the use of a sinking fund and a call provision. A **sinking fund** requires the corporation to make annual payments to the bond trustee, who then repurchases bonds. Bonds may be either repurchased in the open market or selected by lottery and redeemed at a specified price.

A **call provision** allows the company to repurchase (i.e., call), the debt issue prior to maturity at a specified price. Almost all debentures are callable. The **call price** equals face value plus a **call premium**. The call premium might equal one year's interest initially and decrease every year as maturity nears. Often, bonds cannot be called for a number of years (a **deferred call**) and are said to be **call-protected**.

A **protective covenant** restricts actions of the company. A **negative covenant** disallows certain actions. A **positive covenant** requires that certain actions be taken by the firm.

III. BOND RATINGS (p. 182)

Firms often pay to have a credit rating assigned to their bonds. Moody's Investors Services and Standard & Poor's Corporation (S&P) are the two largest rating agencies. Bonds are rated according to the likelihood of default and the protection afforded bondholders in the event of default. The highest ratings (AAA, AA for S&P, Aaa, Aa for Moody's) indicate a very low probability of default. Bonds rated at least BBB (S&P) or Baa (Moody's) are considered *investment grade*, while lower-rated bonds are referred to as *low-grade, high-yield, or junk* bonds. A table defining all of the ratings issued by Standard & Poor's and Moody's appears in this section of the text.

IV. SOME DIFFERENT TYPES OF BONDS (p. 184)

Government Bonds (p. 184) The federal government borrows by issuing Treasury notes and bonds. Both are coupon issues, and have maturities ranging from 2 to 30 years. (Treasury *bills* are discount instruments with maturities of up to one year.) Treasury issues have no default risk (we hope!)

State and local governments borrow by issuing municipal bonds ("munis") of various types. Default risk varies widely; most notable is the fact that munis are exempt from federal income taxation.

Zero Coupon Bonds (p. 185) A **zero-coupon bond** (or **pure-discount bond**) pays no annual coupon interest; principal and all interest are paid at maturity, and the bond is issued at a price below face value. The difference between the face value and the original issue price bond constitutes the interest paid.

Floating-Rate Bonds (p. 187) The coupon payments on a **floating-rate** bond are adjusted as interest rates change. Most 'floaters' have a 'put' provision which gives the holder the option to redeem the bond at face value; the put provision takes effect following a specified period after issuance. Most floaters also have a floor-and-ceiling provision, specifying minimum and maximum coupon rates over the bond's life.

Other Types of Bonds (p. 187) As with most securities, the number of features and variants found in bonds is limited only by investment bankers' and financial officers' imaginations The coupon payment for an **income bond** is made only if income is sufficient, so it is not necessarily in default when a payment is omitted. **Convertible bonds** can be exchanged for a specified number of the issuing firm's common stock at the bondholder's option. Put bonds can be sold back to the issuer at a specified price, again at the bondholder's option.

V. BOND MARKETS (p. 188)

How Bonds are Bought and Sold (p. 188) Most bond transactions take place *over the counter* (i.e., not on the floor of an organized exchange). While the amount of bonds outstanding is huge, corporate bonds trade less frequently than common stocks. As a result, obtaining up-to-date bond values can be difficult.

Bond Price Reporting (p. 189) Market prices for the bonds of many of the largest corporations can be found in *The Wall Street Journal*. The format of the listing is shown in Figure 7.3 in the text.

Similarly, Figure 7.4 is a set of sample *Wall Street Journal* Treasury note and bond quotations.

VI. INFLATION AND INTEREST RATES (p. 192)

Real versus Nominal Returns. (p. 193) Suppose the rate of return on an investment is 10% and the rate of inflation is 5%. If one invests $1 at the 10% rate of return, he will have $1.10 at the end of one year; this is a nominal amount, because it is measured in actual dollars. It does not reflect the change in one's purchasing power, however. If an item costs $1 at the beginning of the year, then $1 will buy one item. If during the year the cost of the item increases by 5% due to inflation, $1.10 will buy ($1.10/$1.05) = 1.048 units of the same item. Consequently, one's purchasing power has increased by only 4.8%, rather than by the 10% earned on the investment.

The Fisher Effect. (p. 193) In the above example, the **nominal rate of return** is 10%, but the **real rate of return** is only 4.8%; the real rate indicates the actual change in purchasing power. The nominal rate is about equal to $R \approx r + h$, where r and h represent the real rate and the inflation rate, respectively.

VII. DETERMINANTS OF BOND YIELDS (p. 194)

The Term Structure of Interest Rates (p. 195) Bond yields reflect the required rates of return existing in the economy at a point in time. The **term structure of interest rates** is the relationship between nominal short-and long-term interest rates for debt issues which have no default risk. The nominal rates reflected in the term structure (or in its graphical representation, the **yield curve**) impound (a) the real rate of interest, (b) an inflation premium, and (c) an interest rate risk premium.

Bond Yields and the Yield Curve: Putting it all Together (p. 197) The required return on corporate bonds includes not only the three components mentioned above, but also premiums for default risk, taxability, and illiquidity.

KEY TERMS AND CONCEPTS

Asked price - the price a dealer is willing to take for a security. (p. 191)

Bearer form - bond is issued without record of the owner's name; payments to owner of record. (p. 180)

Bid-ask spread - the difference between the bid price and the asked price. (p. 192)

Bid price - the price a dealer is willing to pay for a security. (p. 191)

Bond rating - independent measure of bond issue's risk of default. (p. 182)

Call premium - amount by which the call price exceeds the par value of the bond. (p. 181)

Call protected - bond during period in which it cannot be redeemed by the issuer. (p. 181)

Call provision - gives the firm the option to redeem the bond at specified price before maturity. (p. 181)

Call premium - amount by which call price exceeds par value. (p. 156)

Coupon - the stated interest payments made on a bond. (p. 170)

Coupon rate - a bond's coupon payment divided by its face value. (p. 170)

Current yield - coupon payment divided by closing price. (p. 189)

Debenture - unsecured debt, usually with a maturity of 10 years or more. (p. 180)

Default risk premium - compensation investors demand for bearing default risk. (p. 198)

Deferred call provision - form of call provision prohibiting issuer from redeeming bond prior to a specified date. (p. 181)

Face value - the principal amount of a bond that is repaid at the end of the term. (p. 170)

Fisher effect - the relationship between nominal returns, real returns, and inflation. (p. 193)

Indenture - written agreement between issuer and lender detailing the terms of the debt issue. (p. 170)

Inflation premium - compensation investors demand for risk of expected future inflation. (p. 196)

Interest rate risk premium - compensation investors demand for bearing interest rate risk. (p. 196)

Liquidity premium - compensation investors demand for bearing liquidity risk. (p. 198)

Nominal rates - rates that have not been adjusted for inflation. (p. 193)

Note - unsecured debt, usually with a maturity under 10 years. (p. 180)

Par value - see face value.

Protective covenant - indenture provision limiting transactions, to protect the lender's interest. (p. 181)

Real rates - rates that have been adjusted for inflation. (p. 193)

Registered form - registrar records ownership of each bond; payment made to owner of record. (p. 180)

Sinking fund - account managed by the bond trustee for early bond redemption. (p. 181)

58

Straight voting - shareholder may cast all votes for each member of the board (p. 168)
Taxability premium - compensation investors demand for unfavorable tax status. (p. 198)
Term structure of interest rates - relationship between nominal interest rates on default-free, pure discount securities and time to maturity. (p. 195)
Treasury yield curve - plot of the yields on Treasury notes and bonds, relative to maturity. (p. 197)
Yield to maturity - the rate required in the market on a bond. (p. 170)
Zero coupon bond - bond that makes no coupon payments and is issued at a discount to par. (p. 185)

CONCEPT TEST

1. A long-term debt instrument issued by a corporation is a _____. A long-term debt instrument which promises interest payments and a principal payment at a specified date is a _____ . The interest payment is the _____ and the principal payment is the _____ value, _____, or _____ value. The principal for most corporates is _____. (p. 170)

2. The value of a bond (or of any asset) equals the _____ of the future _____ to the holder. Bond valuation requires that we determine the relevant future _____ and the appropriate market rate of interest, or _____ for the bond; then the _____ of the future _____ is calculated using the appropriate opportunity cost, or _____ rate. (p. 171)

3. Bond prices and interest rates are inversely related: when the relevant market interest rate for a particular bond increases, the market price of the bond _____, and when the market rate decreases, the bond price _____. This relationship can be understood mathematically by noting that the interest rate is in the _____ of the basic present value equation, so that when the interest rate increases (or decreases), the size of the denominator _____ (or _____), resulting in a(n) _____ (or _____) in the PV of the bond. Intuitively, this result means that an investor is willing to pay less (or more) for a bond with a fixed annual payment, when the level of interest rates available on comparable investments _____ (or _____). (p. 173)

4. All other things being equal, the longer the time to maturity, the (greater/lesser) the interest rate risk. All other things being equal, the lower the coupon rate, the (greater/lesser) the interest rate risk. (p. 173)

5. The yield to maturity for a bond is the bond's _____. Unless the market value of the bond is equal to its _____, the yield to maturity is determined by using a _____ approach. (p. 175)

6. Debt (is/is not) an ownership interest in the firm. The payment of interest on debt (is/is not) a tax deductible expense for the issuing firm; the payment of dividends on common stock (is/is not) a tax-deductible expense for the firm. _____ is a residual claim on the firm; i.e., there is no upper limit to the potential reward for the securityholder. (p. 177)

7. Long-term corporate debt is usually in the form of a bond which has a principal or face value of _____. Annual interest on bonds is specified as a _____ equal

to a percentage of _____. Principal, along with the last interest payment, is repaid to the bondholder on a specified date, called the _____. (p. 179)

8. If a bond is _____, the company's registrar mails the interest payment to the owner of record. _____ bonds have dated coupons attached; every six months, the bondholder detaches a coupon and mails it to the firm which then makes the interest payment to the bondholder. The ownership of a _____ bond is not recorded with the company. (p. 180)

9. _____ governs priority of payment to creditors in the event of bankruptcy. Some debt is _____ which means that other creditors must be repaid first. (p. 180)

10. A _____ provision allows the company to repurchase the entire debt issue prior to maturity. The call price equals the _____ of the bond plus a _____. Often, bonds cannot be called for a number of years after issue; this is a _____ call, and the bonds are _____ during this period. (p. 181)

11. A _____ restricts actions of the issuer. A _____ disallows certain actions. A _____ requires that certain actions be taken by the corporation. (p. 181)

12. Bonds are rated according to the likelihood of _____ and the protection afforded the bondholders in the event of _____. High ratings indicate _____ probability of default. (p. 182)

13. _____ bonds have no default risk. _____ bonds are exempt from federal income taxation. _____ make no coupon payments, and are initially priced at a deep discount from par. _____ bonds have adjustable coupon payments, which are tied to a specified index. The coupon payments of _____ bonds are paid only if the firm's income is sufficient to do so. A _____ bond can be swapped for a fixed number of shares of stock. (p. 184)

14. Most bond trading takes place _____. As a result, it is difficult to obtain data on bond prices and volume. Thus, it is said that the bond market is not _____. A bond's _____ is equal to the coupon payment divided by the bond's current price. The _____ is the price a bond dealer is willing to pay for a security; the _____ is the price a bond dealer is willing to take for a security. (p. 189)

15. _____ rates are "observed" rates, since they are what we observe in the financial markets. Nominal rates (are/are not) adjusted for inflation. _____ rates are rates that have been adjusted for inflation. The _____ describes the relationship between nominal returns, real returns, and inflation. (p. 193)

16. The observed relationship between short- and long-term interest rates is known as the _____; it is depicted graphically as the _____. (p. 195)

17. The _____ is the portion of a nominal rate that represents compensation for unfavorable tax status. The _____ is the portion of a nominal rate that represents compensation for default risk. The _____ is the portion of a nominal rate that represents compensation for illiquidity. (p. 198)

ANSWERS TO CONCEPT TEST

1. bond; level-coupon bond; coupon interest; face; par; maturity; $1,000
2. present value; cash payments; cash payments; opportunity cost; present value; cash payments; discount
3. decreases; increases; denominator; increases; decreases; decrease; increase; increases; decreases
4. greater; greater
5. rate of return; face value; trial-and-error
6. is not; is, is not; Equity
7. $1,000; coupon interest rate; face value; maturity date
8. registered; Bearer; bearer
9. Seniority; subordinated
10. call; face value; call premium; deferred; call-protected
11. protective covenant; negative covenant; positive covenant
12. default; default; low
13. Treasury; Municipal; Zero-coupon; Floating-rate; income; convertible
14. over the counter; transparent; current yield; bid price, ask price
15. Nominal; are not; Real; Fisher effect
16. term structure of interest rates, yield curve
17. taxability premium; default premium; liquidity premium

PROBLEMS

1. Verbrugge Company has a level-coupon bond outstanding that pays coupon interest of $120 per year and has 10 years to maturity. The face value of the bond is $1,000. If the yield for similar bonds is currently 14%, what is the bond's current market value?

2. For the Verbrugge Company bond described in Problem 1, find the bond's value if the yield for similar bonds decreases to 12%.

3. For the Verbrugge Company bond described in Problem 1, find the bond's value if the yield for similar bonds decreases to 9%.

4. Suppose the Verbrugge bond paid interest semiannually. What would its value be if the yield is 14%?

5. Sasha Company has a level-coupon bond with a 9% coupon rate; interest is paid annually. The bond has 20 years to maturity and a face value of $1,000; similar bonds currently yield 7%. By prior agreement the company will skip the coupon interest payments in years 8, 9, and 10. These payments will be repaid, without interest, at maturity. What is the bond's value?

6. A firm issues a bond today with a $1,000 face value, an 8% coupon interest rate, and 25-year maturity. An investor purchases the bond for $1,000. What is the yield to maturity (YTM)?

7. Suppose the investor bought the bond described in the previous problem for $900. What is the YTM?

8. Suppose the bond described in the previous two problems has a price of $1,100 five years after it is issued. What is the YTM at that time?

9. If the real rate is 4% and the inflation rate is 10%, what is the nominal return for a one-year T-bill?

10. If the real return is 2% and the inflation rate is 5%, what is the nominal return for a one-year T- bill?

11. If the one-year T-bill rate is 8% and the expected inflation rate is 3% during the next year, what real rate of return does the investor expect?

12. Suppose the investor described in the previous problem purchases the one-year T-bill, then finds that after one year, the actual inflation rate was 10%. What real return did the investor earn during the year?

13. Consider the AMR bond reported in Figure 7.3 of the text. Assume the par value is $1,000 and the bond will mature in 20 years. What is the current market price (in dollars) of the bond? How much is the annual coupon payment (in dollars)? Assuming semiannual coupon payments, what is the AMR bond's yield-to-maturity?

CHAPTER 8

STOCK VALUATION

CONCEPTS FOR REVIEW

In the last chapter we learned to value bonds. In this chapter we extend our analysis to the valuation of stocks; we will find that, although we again use a variant of the time value model, stocks pose some special challenges.

CHAPTER HIGHLIGHTS

It is important to remember that, once we have identified the variables that drive stock price changes, we can better apply the fundamental rule of financial management: *Maximize shareholder wealth*.

I. COMMON STOCK VALUATION (p. 206)

The valuation of common stocks is based on the same present value principles applied earlier to the valuation of bonds. However, three factors complicate the valuation of common stocks relative to bonds.

First, bondholders receive coupon interest payments while stockholders receive dividend payments. Coupon payments are specified contractually, so the promised amounts and timing of these payments are known with some degree of certainty. The stockholder has no such contractual basis for his dividend payments, which can, and often do, vary substantially from one year to the next. Second, the face value and the maturity date for a bond are also specified contractually; a share of common stock has neither a maturity date nor a maturity value. And third, it is difficult to obtain an appropriate opportunity rate for a given stock, since doing so requires us to compare the risk of its future cash flows with that of another firm's stock whose cash flows are also difficult to estimate. This topic is covered later in the text.

Cash Flows (p. 206) Investors purchase common stock expecting returns in the form of dividends and/or future price appreciation. Thus, an investor who plans to hold a share of stock for t years would compute the current value of a share as the present value of the expected dividends to be received over the next t years plus the present value of the selling price at that time.

Some Special Cases (p. 208) Because of the difficulties associated with the estimation of future dividends, we find it useful to make one of three simplifying assumptions regarding the pattern of future payments. They are: (1) zero growth in dividends, or constant dividends; (2) constant rate of growth in dividends; and, (3) a nonconstant rate of growth in dividends.

A stock with constant dividends is a perpetuity. Previously we noted that the present value of a perpetuity, PV, equals C/r. Since, for a *zero-growth stock*, D = C, the value of a share of stock which pays a constant dividend is $P_0 = PV = D/r$.

A growing perpetuity is a series of cash flows, occurring at regular intervals, which grows perpetually at a constant rate. The series of dividend payments for a share of common stock can be considered a growing perpetuity as long as the dividend payment increases at the same rate each year. Let D_t be the dividend paid in year t, and let g be the annual growth rate in dividends. The dividend at any future date (D_t) is:

$$D_t = D_0 \times (1 + g)^t .$$

64

It can be shown algebraically that, as long as r is greater than g, the present value of an infinite stream of cash flows which are changing at constant rate is equal to

$$P_0 = PV = [D_0 \times (1+g)]/(r - g) = D_1/(r - g).$$

Learning Tip: The constant-growth model is nothing more than a modified version of the ordinary annuity model described previously. As such, it assumes that payments occur at the end of each period. In turn, we can use it to find the price of the stock at any point in time:

$$P_t = (D_t+1)/(r - g).$$

The assumption of nonconstant growth is more realistic for many firms. The hallmark of this model is the assumption that dividends change at different rates in different periods, until, at a specified future date, the growth rate settles at some constant equilibrium rate. Fortunately, no new formulas are required to value such a stock. In order to use the **nonconstant** or **supernormal growth model** we simply:

1. Compute the FV of each dividend in the nonconstant growth period, using the assumed growth rate.
2. Compute the present value of the abovementioned dividends discounted at r.
3. Use the constant-growth model to compute the present value of all of the remaining dividends which, by assumption, are expected to grow at a constant rate forever.
4. Sum the present values obtained in steps 2 and 4; this is the present value of all future dividends, which is P_0.

Components of the Required Return (p. 214) Previously it was stated that investors purchase stock in the hope of earning returns in the form of dividends and capital gains. Given a constant growth rate, we can obtain the components of return by solving the constant-growth formula for r:

$$r = D_1/P_0 + g.$$

Thus, the rate of return for a constant growth stock consists of two components: the **dividend yield** and the **capital gains yield**. The former can be thought of as the rate of return for a stock whose dividend is constant; an investor who purchased a share of common stock for a price P_0, and who received a constant dividend of D_1, would be receiving a perpetuity whose yield is equal to D_1/P_0. The capital gains yield represents the expected annual increase in the price of the stock. Given the assumption that annual cash flows are growing at a constant rate forever, it is not surprising that the capital gains yield is the same as the dividend growth rate g.

II. SOME FEATURES OF COMMON AND PREFERRED STOCKS (p. 214)

Common Stock Features (p. 216) Shareholders control the corporation by electing directors who then hire management. Some directors are elected each year at the annual shareholders meeting. The voting mechanism is either **straight voting** or **cumulative voting**. With the former, each share entitles the shareholder to one vote and each director is elected separately. With cumulative voting, the directors are elected simultaneously and the number of votes a shareholder may cast is equal to the number of shares owned multiplied by the number of directors to be elected. Cumulative voting makes it easier for minority shareholders to achieve representation on the board.

A shareholder may cast his votes in person at the annual meeting, or by **proxy**, which grants to another party the authority to vote the shares. When a group of dissatisfied shareholders seek to obtain enough proxy votes to elect board members who will replace current management, a **proxy fight** ensues.

Corporations may have different **classes** of common stock with different voting rights. The usual reason for multiple classes of stock is to allow one group of shareholders to control the corporation by granting a majority of the voting rights to one class of stock held by that group. This class of stock is often held by corporate management or founding shareholders.

Shareholders also generally have rights to:

1. Share proportionally in dividends paid
2. Share proportionally in assets remaining after liquidation
3. Vote on stockholder matters

Corporations, at the discretion of the board of directors, pay cash dividends to shareholders, but are not legally obligated to do so. Dividends, once declared, are liabilities of the firm. Dividends are not deductible for tax purposes.

Preferred Stock Features (p. 219) **Preferred stock** differs from common stock in that preferred shareholders must be paid a dividend before dividends are paid to common shareholders, and preferred shareholders have preference over common shareholders to the residual value of assets following liquidation of the firm. Preferred shares normally have a liquidation value of $100 per share, and dividends may be stated as a percentage of this value.

A corporation is not legally obligated to pay dividends on preferred stock. If dividends are **cumulative**, then any dividends not paid are accumulated, and the entire amount must be paid before any dividends on common stock can be paid.

Although preferred stock has many of the features of debt, the fact that the dividend is not deductible creates a tax disadvantage relative to debt for the issuer. To some extent, this disadvantage is offset by the fact that corporate investors are willing to accept a lower return on preferred stock because of the 70% dividend exclusion. However, the result of these two tax effects is a net disadvantage to issuers of preferred stock. Three reasons are commonly cited for the issuance of preferred stock. First, the largest issuers of preferred stock are regulated public utilities, and the nature of utility regulation is such that the additional cost of the preferred stock, to the issuer, is passed on to the consumer. Second, preferred stock does not subject the issuer to the threat of potential bankruptcy. Finally, preferred stockholders do not have voting rights, so a firm which issues preferred stock raises equity financing without affecting control of the corporation.

III. THE STOCK MARKETS (p. 220)

Dealers and Brokers (p. 220) The **primary market** is the market in which new securities are sold to investors for the first time; the **secondary market** is the market in which previously issued securities are traded among investors. A **dealer** maintains an inventory of securities and stands ready to buy and sell at any time. A **broker** is simply an agent who arranges security transactions among investors.

Organization of the NYSE (p. 221) Approximately 1,400 **members** own **seats** on the NYSE. **Commission brokers** are members who execute customer orders to buy and sell stock on the floor of the exchange. **Specialists** (or **market makers**) deal in a few securities from **posts** on the exchange floor. **Floor brokers** are members who execute orders for commission brokers in return for a fee. **Floor traders** trade independently for their own accounts.

Orders are also transmitted to the exchange floor electronically via the **SuperDOT** system. **Order flow** is the flow of customer orders to buy and sell securities.

NASDAQ Operations (p. 223) Approximately 5,000 securities are traded on Nasdaq. All Nasdaq trading is done through dealers. The key differences between the NYSE and Nasdaq are: (1) Nasdaq is an electronic network with no single physical exchange floor, and (2) Nasdaq is a system of multiple market makers.

Stock Market Reporting (p. 224) Figure 8.2 reproduces stock listings from *The Wall Street Journal*.

KEY TERMS AND CONCEPTS

Broker - an agent who arranges security transactions among investors. (p. 220)
Capital gains yield - the rate at which the value of an investment grows. (p. 214)
Common stock - equity without priority for dividends or in bankruptcy. (p. 216)
Cumulative voting - shareholder may cast all votes for one member of the board. (p. 216)
Dealer - agent who buys and sells securities from inventory. (p. 220)
Dividend yield - a stock's expected cash dividend divided by its current price. (p. 214)
Dividend growth model - model that determines the current price of a stock as its dividend next period divided by the discount rate less the dividend growth rate. (p. 210)
Dividends - payment by corporation to shareholders, made either in cash or stock. (p. 218)
Floor brokers - NYSE members who execute orders for commission brokers on a fee basis. (p. 221)
Floor traders - NYSE members who trade for their own accounts. (p. 222)
Inside quotes - highest bid quotes and lowest ask quotes for a security. (p. 224)
Member - owner of a seat on the NYSE. (p. 221)
Order flow - flow of customer orders to buy and sell securities. (p. 222)
Preferred stock - stock with dividend priority over common stock, with a fixed dividend rate, sometimes without voting rights. (p. 219)
Primary market - the market in which new securities are originally sold to investors. (p. 220)
Proxy - grant of authority by shareholder allowing another individual to vote his or her shares. (p. 217)
Secondary market - market in which previously issued securities are traded among investors. (p. 220)
Specialist - NYSE member acting as a dealer in a few securities on the floor of the exchange. (p. 221)
Specialist's post - fixed place on the exchange floor where the specialist operates. (p. 222)
Straight voting - shareholder may cast all votes for each member of the board (p. 216)
SuperDOT system - electronic system allowing orders to be transmitted directly to specialists. (p. 221)

CONCEPT TEST

1. The value of a share of common stock equals the _____ of the future _____ to the holder. The relevant cash flows for common stock are future _____ and the future _____ value of a share. (p. 206)

2. Three alternative simplifying assumptions which are sometimes made for the purpose of common stock valuation are: (1) zero growth in dividends, or _____ dividends; (2) constant _____ in dividends; and, (3) _____ in dividends. The mathematics of a zero-growth stock is summarized by the equation: $D =$ _____. Or, this equation can be expressed as $P_0 = PV =$ _____, or $r =$ _____. The value of a constant-growth stock is: $P_0 = PV =$ _____. The case of nonconstant growth requires the calculation of the _____ of several initial dividend payments and then the application of the formula for _____ to subsequent dividend payments. (p. 208)

3. The rate of return for a share of stock has two components: the dividend yield and the capital gains yield. The former equals _____ and the latter equals the _____. The capital gains yield equals the _____ because the rate at which the _____ of a constant growth stock increases equals the dividend growth rate (p. 214)

4. _____ control the firm by electing directors, who hire _____. Directors are elected using either _____ voting or _____ voting. (p. 216)

5. Stockholders have the right to share proportionately in _____ paid, in distributions following _____, and to vote on important issues. In some cases, stockholders also have the right to share proportionately in the purchase of new stock issued by the corporation; this is called the _____. Corporations pay cash dividends at the discretion of the _____. The corporation (is/is not) legally obligated to declare dividends. Dividends (are/are not) tax-deductible for the corporation. (p. 216)

6. Shareholders generally have rights to:

   1. Share proportionally in _____ .
   2. Share proportionally in _____ .
   3. Vote on _____ . (p. 218)

7. Preferred shareholders must be paid a _____ dividend before _____ can be paid to _____ shareholders, and preferred shareholders have preference over _____ shareholders to the _____ value of assets following _____ of the firm. A firm (is/is not) legally obligated to pay dividends on preferred stock. If dividends are _____, then any dividends not paid are accumulated, and all must be paid before any dividends on common stock can be paid. (p. 219)

8. The _____ is the market in which new securities are sold to investors for the first time; the _____ is the market in which previously issued securities are traded among investors. A _____ maintains an inventory of securities and stands ready to buy and sell at any time. A _____ is an agent who arranges security transactions among investors. (p. 220)

9. Approximately 1,400 **members** own _____ on the NYSE. _____ are members who execute customer orders to buy and sell stock on the floor of the exchange. _____ (or **market makers**) deal in a few securities from **posts** on the exchange floor. _____ are members who execute orders for commission brokers in return for a fee. _____ trade independently for their own accounts. (p. 221)

ANSWERS TO CONCEPT TEST

1. present value; cash payments; dividends; market
2. constant; growth; nonconstant growth; $(PV \times r)$; (D/r); (D/PV); $[D_1/(r-g)]$; PV; constant growth
3. (D_1/P_0); dividend growth rate; dividend growth rate; price
4. Shareholders; management; straight; cumulative
5. dividends; liquidation; preemptive right; board of directors; is not; are not
6. dividends paid; in assets remaining after liquidation; stockholder matters
7. stated; dividends; common; common; residual; liquidation; is not; cumulative
8. primary market; secondary market; dealer; broker
9. seats; Commission brokers; Specialists; Floor brokers; Floor traders

PROBLEMS

1. A security analyst has forecast the dividends of Hodges Enterprises for the next three years. His forecast is: $D_1 = \$1.50$; $D_2 = \$1.75$; $D_3 = \$2.20$. He has also forecast a price in three years of $48.50. The rate of return for similar-risk common stock is 14%. What is the value of Hodges common stock?

2. TTK Corp. preferred stock pays a $10 annual dividend per share. What is the price of a share of TTK preferred if similar-risk preferred yields 8%? What is the price if comparable preferred yields 11%?

3. A share of preferred stock with a $12 annual dividend is selling for $75. What is the required rate of return for the preferred stock?

4. Hilliard, Inc., just paid a $2 annual dividend on its common stock. The dividend is expected to increase at 8% per year indefinitely. If the required rate of return is 16%, what is the stock's value?

5. The dividend paid this year (D_0) on a share of common stock is $10. If dividends grow at a 5% rate for the foreseeable future, and the required return is 10%, what is the value of the stock today? Last year (date $t = -1$)? Next year (date $t = 1$)?

6. The current price of a stock (P_0) is $20 and last year's price (P_{-1}) was $18.87. The latest dividend (D_0) is $2. Assume a constant growth rate (g) in dividends and stock price. What is the stock's return for the coming year?

7. The current year's dividend (D_0) for a share of common stock is $2 and the current price (P_0) of the stock is $30. Dividends are expected to grow at 5% forever. What is the rate of return for this stock?

8. Pettway Corporation's next annual dividend (D_1) is expected to be $4. The growth rate in dividends over the following three years is forecasted at 15%. After that, Pettway's growth rate is expected to equal the industry average of 5%. If the required return is 18%, what is the current value of the stock?

9. A company pays a current dividend (D_0) of $1.20 per share on its common stock. The annual dividend will increase by 3%, 4% and 5%, respectively, over the next three years, and by 6% per year thereafter. The appropriate discount rate is 12%. What is P_0?

CHAPTER 9

NET PRESENT VALUE AND OTHER INVESTMENT CRITERIA

CONCEPTS FOR REVIEW

This chapter extends our discussion of valuation techniques to nonfinancial assets. Although some new terminology is introduced, the underlying idea remains: good managers will invest only in those assets which will increase the value of the firm and, therefore, the current price of its common stock.

CHAPTER HIGHLIGHTS

In this chapter we examine six of the most commonly used criteria for making capital budgeting decisions: (1) net present value, (2) payback period, (3) discounted payback period, (4) average accounting return, (5) internal rate of return, and (6) the profitability index. Our major conclusion is that the net present value rule is the most appropriate criterion for capital budgeting decisions.

I. NET PRESENT VALUE (p. 233)

The net present value concept is of primary to decision-makers because it results in capital budgeting decisions which maximize the current price of the firm's common stock.

The Basic Idea (p. 233) An investment is "good" if it creates value for its owners. The net present value (NPV) approach measures *how much* value a given investment creates. Consider the following example.

Example. Suppose you are considering the formation of a corporation with a one-year life. It is being formed in order to acquire an asset which costs $200,000 and which, you are certain, can be sold one year from now for $250,000. You would like to convince each of 100 investors (including yourself) to purchase a share in this corporation for $2000. Since each investor is a 1% owner, each investor would then receive 1% of $250,000, or $2500, one year from now. Assume the market rate of interest is 8%. Is this investment opportunity attractive to potential investors?

If the corporation purchases this asset today, the present value of $250,000 to be received next year is $250,000/1.08 = $231,481.48. In well-functioning financial markets, investors would be willing to pay as much as $231,481.48 to receive $250,000 in one year. Since the cost of the asset is $200,000, the difference between the asset's current market value and its cost is $250,000 - 231,481.48 = $18,518.52. This difference is the **Net Present Value (NPV)**.

Since the entire corporation consists of one asset, this present value is the value of the corporation once the asset is purchased. An investor who purchases one share for $2,000 and then wishes to immediately sell his 1% share in the financial market will be able to sell it for $2,314.81 (= .01 × $231,481.48).

Further, the NPV of an investor's share is $314.81. This can be viewed as 1% of the NPV of the firm (i.e., 1% of the difference between $231,481.48 and $200,000) or as the difference between the present value of one share ($2,314.81) and the cost of one share ($2,000). Consequently, an investor who chooses to sell his share immediately will realize a net gain equal to 1% of the NPV of the corporation.

The above example illustrates several points. First, an investment with a positive NPV provides a net benefit to the investor equal to the NPV; thus, an investment with a negative NPV should be rejected.

Second, the NPV not only provides a criterion for determining whether an investment is acceptable, but is also an unambiguous measure of the value of the investment. Third, a corporate investment with a positive NPV provides a net benefit to the shareholder equal to his proportionate share of the NPV of the corporate investment. Fourth, the management of the firm can determine whether an investment is acceptable to the stockholders without regard for the preferences of individual stockholders; i.e., the NPV is the net gain to the stockholder, regardless of whether he intends to keep his share or to sell it immediately. Finally, the results suggest the **NPV rule: Management must accept investments with positive NPVs since such investments provide value to the stockholders, and they must reject investments with negative NPVs because such investments destroy stockholder value.**

<u>Estimating Net Present Value</u> (p. 234) The formula for computing the NPV of an investment is:

$$NPV = -C_0 + C_1/(1+r)^1 + C_2/(1+r)^2 + \ldots C_t/(1+r)^t$$

where t represents the last period during which a payment is received, C_0 is the initial outlay, C_1 is the payment one year from now, and r is the market interest rate.

II. THE PAYBACK RULE (p. 236)

The **payback period** is the time required to recover the initial investment for a capital budgeting project from the subsequent cash inflows produced by the project. Unfortunately, it has several major deficiencies which generally make it an inappropriate criterion for capital budgeting decisions.

<u>Defining the Rule</u> (p. 236) The **payback period rule** specifies that an investment is acceptable if the sum of its undiscounted cash flows equals the initial investment before some specified cutoff time period.

<u>Analyzing the Rule</u> (p. 238) The deficiencies of the payback rule are:

1. The timing of cash flows within the payback period is ignored, thereby treating these cash flows as equally valuable; in contrast, the net present value properly discounts these cash flows.
2. All cash flows after the cutoff date are ignored, while the net present value discounts all cash flows.
3. There is no objective criterion for choosing an optimal cutoff time period.

<u>Redeeming Qualities of the Rule</u> (p. 239)

1. It is quickly and easily applied; thus, it is appropriate for frequent, small-scale decisions that don't warrant extensive analysis.
2. It is biased toward liquidity.
3. It (crudely) adjusts for risk in later cash flows (by ignoring them).

III. THE DISCOUNTED PAYBACK (p. 240)

The **discounted payback period** rule specifies that a project is acceptable if the sum of the discounted cash flows equals the initial investment before a specified cutoff time period. Mechanically, it is the Payback Period method with discounted cash flows.

IV. THE AVERAGE ACCOUNTING RETURN (p. 243)

The **average accounting return (AAR)** equals the average net income of an investment divided by its average book value. The **average accounting return rule** specifies that an investment is acceptable if its average accounting return exceeds a specified target level.

The AAR rule has several serious deficiencies. First, it uses accounting income and book value data, which generally are not closely related to cash flows, the relevant data for financial decision-making. Second, it ignores the time value of money. And third, the target AAR must be arbitrarily specified because it is not a rate of return in the financial market sense.

V. THE INTERNAL RATE OF RETURN (p. 245)

The **internal rate of return (IRR)** is the rate of return (or discount rate) which equates the PV of the cash inflows with the cash cost of the investment; alternatively, the IRR is defined as the rate of return for an investment. Algebraically, the IRR is the solution for the discount rate r in the following equation:

$$C_0 = C_1/(1+r) + C_2/(1+r)^2 + \ldots C_T/(1+r)^T$$

where C_i is the cash flow for year i. The right side of the above equation is the present value of all cash inflows expected for the project under consideration; C_T is the cash inflow expected at the end of year T, which is the last year that cash inflows are expected from the project.

Learning Tip: Solving this equation for r is equivalent to solving for the yield to maturity of a level coupon bond, as discussed in the chapter on bond valuation. Therefore, the value of r can be determined by either trial-and-error or with a financial calculator. For either approach, the solution technique is analogous to the corresponding solution of the yield to maturity problem presented previously.

The IRR can also be interpreted as the annually compounded rate of return on the initial outlay (assuming we are using annual time periods). Hence the IRR decision rule: **An investment project is acceptable if the IRR is greater than the rate of return which could be earned in the financial markets on investments of equal risk; an investment project is unacceptable if the IRR is less than the relevant rate of return in the financial markets.**

The relationship between discount rates, NPVs, and IRR are apparent in the **NPV profile**, which is a graph of the NPVs of a given investment computed using several discount rates. NPV profiles have the following characteristics:

1. As the discount rate increases, the NPV decreases; i.e., NPV and r are inversely related.
2. The slope of the NPV profile is an indication of the sensitivity of the investment's NPV to the discount rate - the steeper the slope, the more sensitive the NPV.
3. The IRR is found at the point where the NPV profile intersects the X-axis (i.e., where NPV = 0).

Problems with the IRR (p. 248) The problems which arise in applying the internal rate of return criterion occur when we have nonconventional cash flows and/or mutually exclusive investments.

A **conventional** cash flow pattern consists of a cash outlay followed by a series of inflows. A **nonconventional** series of cash flows includes more than one net outflow. As a result, there may exist more than one rate that equates the PV of the inflows and the PV of the outlays; i.e., multiple IRRs. Since there is no basis for choosing either rate as the relevant IRR, it is impossible to apply the IRR criterion when cash flows change sign more than once.

An **independent investment project** is an investment whose acceptance or rejection does not affect, and is not affected by, the acceptance or rejection of any other projects. **Mutually exclusive investment projects** are those projects for which acceptance of any one project implies the rejection of another.

Learning Tip: *Independent projects can be evaluated on a "stand-alone" basis. Mutually exclusive projects, on the other hand, must be evaluated simultaneously. Not doing so exposes the decision-maker to the risk of accepting a good project but foregoing the ability to accept its better substitute later.*

The difficulties encountered in applying the IRR criterion to mutually exclusive projects arise when the projects being compared differ with respect to either scale or timing. In the former case, there are differences in the size of the initial outlay for the projects under consideration; in the latter case, the differences are generally between one project whose cash flows are concentrated in the early years of the project's life and another project whose cash flows are concentrated in the later years. In either case, it is possible that the NPV of one project is higher than that of its mutually exclusive substitute, while its IRR is lower. In this case, we return to our primary goal: maximize firm value, which suggests that, all else equal, we should select the project with the highest NPV.

VI. THE PROFITABILITY INDEX (p. 253)

The **profitability index (PI)** equals the PV of the future cash flows divided by the initial investment. If this ratio exceeds 1.0, the project's NPV exceeds zero, and the investment is desirable.

The PI is useful when a firm is subject to **capital rationing** during the current time period. Capital rationing occurs when, for whatever reason, the amount of investable funds is limited and a firm has more positive NPV projects than can currently be undertaken. The proposed solution is to rank the projects by profitability index, and accept those with the highest values.

VII. THE PRACTICE OF CAPITAL BUDGETING (p. 254)

In surveys of large corporations, discounted cash flow (DCF) approaches such as NPV, IRR, and PI, are the most commonly used capital budgeting techniques. It appears that 80% or more use discounted cash flow, but not necessarily to the exclusion of other procedures.

KEY TERMS AND CONCEPTS

Average accounting return - investment's average net income divided by average book value. (p. 243)
Discounted payback period - time for investment's discounted cash flows to equal its cost. (p. 240)
Internal rate of return - the discount rate that makes the NPV of an investment zero. (p. 2245)
Multiple rates of return - one potential problem in using the IRR method if more than one discount rate makes the NPV of an investment zero. (p. 248)
Mutually exclusive investments - two investments which accomplish the same purpose. (p. 253)
Net present value - the difference between an investment's market value and its cost. (p. 233)
Net present value profile - a graphical representation of the relationship between an investment's NPVs and various discount rates. (p. 252)

74

Payback period - time required for an investment's cash flows to equal its initial cost. (p. 236)
Profitability index - the present value of an investment's future cash flows divided by its cost. (p. 253)

CONCEPT TEST

1. PV analysis of an investment opportunity specifies that it is _____ if the PV of the future cash inflows is _____ the cash outlay; the investment is _____ if the PV of future cash inflows is _____ the cash outlay. (p. 233)

2. The NPV of an asset equals the difference between the PV of the future _____ produced by the asset and the _____ of the asset. An investment is acceptable if its NPV is _____ . An investment is unacceptable if its NPV is _____ . The NPV of an asset measures the _____ which accrues to the _____ of the firm if the asset is acquired. Thus, the use of the NPV criterion is consistent with the financial manager's goal of maximizing the _____ of the firm's common stock. (p. 233)

3. The payback period is the amount of time required to recover the _____ for a capital budgeting project from the future _____ produced by the project. The payback period rule specifies that an investment is _____ if the payback period is less than a specified _____ . Deficiencies of the rule include: the _____ of cash flows within the payback period is ignored, thereby treating these cash flows as _____ ; all cash flows after the _____ are ignored; and, there is no objective criterion for choosing the optimal _____ . The primary advantage of the payback rule is its _____ . (p. 236)

4. The discounted payback period for an asset is the time required for the sum of the discounted future _____ to equal the _____ for the asset. The discounted payback period rule specifies that a project is _____ if the discounted payback period is less than a specified _____ . Deficiencies of the discounted payback rule include: cash flows after the _____ are ignored; and, there is no objective criterion for choosing the optimal _____ . (p. 240)

5. The average accounting return for an investment project equals _____ attributed to the asset divided by _____ of the asset. The AAR rule specifies that an investment is _____ if its average accounting return exceeds a _____ . Deficiencies of the AAR are: the method uses _____ income and _____ value data, rather than _____ ; the AAR ignores the _____ ; and, the _____ must be arbitrarily specified. (p. 243)

6. The IRR is the rate of return (or discount rate) which equates the _____ of the future _____ for an investment with its _____ . The IRR can be defined as the rate of return which equates the NPV of an investment to _____ . An investment is _____ if the IRR exceeds the rate of return that could be earned in the financial markets on investments of equal risk; an investment project is _____ if the IRR is less than the relevant rate of return in the financial markets. (p. 245)

7. The IRR criterion may not correctly indicate whether an investment is acceptable. The problems which arise in applying the IRR criterion are associated with the following situations: _____ cash flows and _____ investments. (p. 248)

8. A conventional cash flow for a capital budgeting project has a _____ cash flow followed by _____ cash flows. A _____ series of cash flows changes sign more than once, and may have more than one IRR. (p. 248)

9. An _____ investment project is an investment whose acceptance or rejection does not affect, and is not affected by, the acceptance or rejection of any other projects. A mutually exclusive projects is a project for which acceptance implies _____ of another. The difficulties encountered in applying the IRR criterion to mutually exclusive projects arise when the projects being compared differ with respect to either _____ or _____. Incorrect decisions are avoided by: (1) applying the _____ criterion; or, (2) applying the IRR criterion to the _____ cash flows. (p. 250)

10. The profitability index is defined as the _____ of the future _____ divided by _____. If the PI exceeds _____, the investment is _____, because the PV of the future cash inflows exceeds the _____. Any _____ investment acceptable by the PI criterion is also acceptable by the NPV criterion. Problems may arise in applying the PI to _____ investment projects. Incorrect decisions are avoided by: (1) applying the _____ criterion; (2) applying the criterion to the _____ cash flows. (p. 253)

ANSWERS TO CONCEPT TEST

1. acceptable; greater than; unacceptable; less than
2. cash inflows; cost; positive; negative; value; owners; price
3. initial investment; cash inflows; acceptable; cutoff time period; timing; equally valuable; cutoff time period; cutoff time period; simplicity
4. cash inflows; initial outlay; acceptable; cutoff time period; cutoff time period; cutoff time period
5. average net income; average book value; acceptable; specified target level; accounting; book; cash flows; time value of money; target AAR
6. present value; cash inflows; cost; zero; acceptable; unacceptable
7. nonconventional; mutually exclusive
8. negative; positive; nonconventional;
9. independent; rejection; scale; timing; net present value; incremental
10. present value; cash inflows; initial investment; one; acceptable; initial investment; independent; mutually exclusive; net present value; incremental

PROBLEMS

For Problems 1-6, use the following cash flows for projects A and B:

A: (-$2000, $500, $600, $700, $800)
B: (-$2000, $950, $850, $400, $300)

1. Calculate the payback period for projects A and B.

2. If the discount rate is 12%, what is the discounted payback period for project A? For B?

3. Calculate the internal rate of return for projects A and B.

4. If A and B are mutually exclusive and the required rate of return is 5%, which should be accepted?

5. If the discount rate is 12%, and A and B are mutually exclusive, which project should be accepted?

6. At what discount rate will we be indifferent between A and B?

7. Compute the IRR for investments with the following cash flows in years 0, 1 and 2: (-$60, $155, -$100) and ($60, -$155, $100). How do you interpret the results in terms of the IRR criterion?

8. You have been asked to analyze an investment with the following cash flows in years 0, 1 and 2, respectively: (-$51, $100, -$50). Compute the IRR. Is the investment acceptable? The required return is unknown.

9. Consider the following abbreviated financial statements for a proposed investment:

Year	0	1	2	3	4
Gross Book Value	$160	$160	$160	$160	$160
Accumulated Dep.		40	80	120	160
Net Book Value	$160	$120	$80	$40	$0
Sales		$95	$90	$97	$80
Costs		33	30	25	10
Depreciation		40	40	40	40
Taxes (50%)		$11	$10	$16	$15
Net Income		$11	$10	$16	$15

What is the average accounting return (AAR) for the proposed investment?

10. What is the internal rate of return for the investment described in Problem 9?

11. Calculate the IRR of an investment with these cash flows in years 0, 1 and 2: ($792, -$1780, $1000).

12. For the investment identified in Problem 11, determine the acceptability of the investment when the required return is 10%; when the required rate of return is 12%; and when the required return is 14%.

13. You can borrow $8000, to be repaid in installments of $2,200 at the end of each of the next 5 years. Use the IRR to determine whether this loan is preferable to borrowing at the market rate of 11.5%.

14. A firm is considering the following mutually exclusive investment projects. Project A requires an initial outlay of $500 and will return $120 per year for the next seven years. Project B requires an initial outlay of $5,000 and will return $1,350 per year for the next five years. The required rate of return is 10%. Use the net present value criterion to determine which investment is preferable.

15. Calculate the internal rate of return for each of the projects described in Problem 14.

16. Calculate the profitability index for each of the investment projects described in Problem 14.

CHAPTER 10

MAKING CAPITAL INVESTMENT DECISIONS

CONCEPTS FOR REVIEW

The focus of the preceding chapter was on a set of techniques used to distinguish "good" investments from "bad" ones. In this chapter, we examine more closely project cash flows and their underlying components. We find that value is dependent on cash flows at the project level, as well as the firm level.

CHAPTER HIGHLIGHTS

The major emphasis of this chapter is on the identification of the *relevant* cash flows for NPV analysis of a capital budgeting problem. Although financial managers use accounting data in their decision-making, financial decisions must be based on cash flows rather than accounting income. Consequently, it is important to correctly interpret accounting data in order to identify relevant cash flows.

I. PROJECT CASH FLOWS: A FIRST LOOK (p. 265)

By undertaking a capital budgeting project, a firm changes current and future cash flows. Capital investment decision-making requires that financial managers determine whether changes in cash flows which result from undertaking a particular project add value to the firm.

Relevant Cash Flows (p. 266) The relevant cash flows for the analysis of a capital budgeting project are the **incremental cash flows** associated with the project, which consist of any and all changes in the firm's cash flows that are a *direct consequence* of accepting the project.

The Stand-Alone Principle (p. 266) Since a particular project can be viewed as having its own cash flows, we employ the **stand-alone principle**, which specifies that the financial manager can view the incremental cash flows from the perspective of the project, rather than from the perspective of the firm.

II. INCREMENTAL CASH FLOWS (p. 266)

Three of the most frequently encountered complications relate to the interpretation of the following concepts: sunk costs, opportunity costs, side effects, net working capital, and financing costs.

Sunk Costs (p. 267) A **sunk cost** is money the firm has already spent, or is committed to spend, regardless of whether it accepts the project under consideration. Since sunk costs are not incremental to the project, they are not relevant to the capital budgeting decision.

Opportunity Costs (p. 267) Opportunity costs are cash flows foregone as a result of the decision to invest in a project. Thus, opportunity costs are relevant to the capital budgeting decision.

Side Effects (p. 267) The introduction of a new product may reduce sales of some of the firm's existing products (this is called **erosion**). The resulting reduction in cash flow to other product lines is a **side-effect** of the new product; the reduction is an incremental cost to the project under consideration.

Net Working Capital (p. 268) Net working capital is the difference between current assets and current liabilities. A capital budgeting project often requires an increase in net working capital during the life of the project. This investment in net working capital is an incremental cash outflow. At the termination of a project, this outflow is typically recovered, and is therefore an inflow at that time.

Financing Costs (p. 268) Financing costs are not included in the computation of incremental cash flows because they do not represent cash flows from the assets acquired. Rather, financing costs are included in the computation of the appropriate discount rate.

Other Issues (p. 269) Two additional issues are: first, cash flows are measured when they occur, not when they accrue in the accounting sense; and, second, since taxes are clearly cash outflows, we are concerned with *after-tax* incremental cash flows.

III. PRO FORMA FINANCIAL STATEMENTS AND PROJECT CASH FLOWS (p. 269)

Getting Started: Pro Forma Financial Statements (p. 269) For a typical capital budgeting project, a current cash outflow is followed by future inflows. Thus it is necessary to *forecast* incremental cash inflows. Projected inflows for a project are derived from **pro forma financial statements**; these are projected financial statements for future time periods. We apply definitions of firm cash flow from Chapter 2 to individual projects.

Project Cash Flows (p. 270) Project cash flow equals:

Project operating cash flow - Project additions to net working capital - Project capital spending,

where project operating cash flow = project EBIT + project depreciation - project taxes.

IV. MORE ON PROJECT CASH FLOW (p. 272)

A Closer Look at Net Working Capital (p. 272) Generally Accepted Accounting Principles (GAAP) require that revenue is recorded on the income statement when it is accrued; furthermore, for income statement purposes, costs are determined according to the 'matching' principle, which requires that expenses are recognized at the time of the sale. Neither of these accounting principles is consistent with the cash flow concepts we have studied in this chapter. We have also observed that NPV analysis of a capital budgeting project requires that we identify the size, **and** the timing of cash inflows and outflows. Consequently, it is important to adjust accounting information, which is reported on an accrual basis, in such a way that it reflects the actual timing of cash flows.

Depreciation (p. 275) Depreciation is a non-cash expense; it is relevant to the computation of incremental cash flows only because it affects taxes. Computation of depreciation expenses for tax purposes is specified in the 1986 Tax Reform Act. Annual depreciation rates under the Modified Accelerated Cost Recovery System (MACRS) appear in the text.

Depreciation affects taxes (and cash flow) in two ways: first, depreciation expense affects operating cash flow, since it reduces taxable income; and, second, depreciation affects the book value of an asset, and the difference between book value and market value has tax implications when an asset is sold.

An Example: The Majestic Mulch and Compost Company (MMCC) (p. 278) This section contains an extended cash flow analysis example.

V. ALTERNATIVE DEFINITIONS OF OPERATING CASH FLOW (p. 284)

Previously we computed project operating cash flow as EBIT plus depreciation minus taxes. Below are three alternative, but equivalent, approaches to computing operating cash flow.

The Bottom-Up Approach (p. 285) The **bottom-up approach** accentuates the relationship between net income and operating cash flow.

$$OCF = \text{Net income} + \text{Depreciation}$$

The Top-Down Approach (p. 285) The top-down approach defines operating cash flow as follows:

$$OCF = \text{Sales} - \text{Costs} - \text{Taxes}$$

This perspective emphasizes the fact that operating cash flow is equal to sales minus expenses (including taxes, but excluding non-cash expenses such as depreciation).

The Tax Shield Approach (p. 285) The **tax shield** approach to defining operating cash flow emphasizes the role of depreciation - depreciation serves as a tax shield which increases OCF.

$$OCF = (\text{Sales} - \text{Costs}) \times (1 - T_c) + \text{Depreciation} \times T_c$$

VI. SOME SPECIAL CASES OF DISCOUNTED CASH FLOW ANALYSIS (p. 286)

Three particularly useful applications of DCF analysis are (1) the evaluation of cost-cutting proposals, (2) setting the bid price, and (3) evaluating equipment with different lives.

Evaluating Cost-Cutting Proposals. (p. 286) A common purpose of capital expenditure is cost reduction. The NPV is the difference between the present value of the projected cost savings and the initial outlay.

Setting the Bid Price (p. 288) Under certain circumstances, a supplier of a product or service submits a bid price to a prospective customer who then purchases the product or service from the supplier who has submitted the lowest bid. From the supplier's viewpoint, the lowest acceptable bid is that which results in operating cash flows associated with a zero NPV.

Evaluating Equipment Options with Different Lives (p. 290) A special capital budgeting problem arises when we compare two different machines that provide the same essential service, but differ with respect to useful life. If two machines have different operating lives **and** if we will be replacing the selected machine at the end of its useful life, then some allowance for the different lives must be made. This problem is resolved by the use of either matching replacement cycles in the present value comparison or the **equivalent annual cost (EAC)** method. The EAC answers the question: what constant dollar amount, paid each year, has exactly the same present value as the machine's purchase price plus operating costs?

KEY TERMS AND CONCEPTS

Accelerated Cost Recovery System (ACRS) - depreciation method under U.S. tax law allowing for the accelerated write-off of property under various classifications. (p. 275)
Depreciation tax shield - tax saving that results from the depreciation deduction, calculated as depreciation multiplied by the corporate tax rate. (p. 286)

Equivalent annual cost - the present value of a project's costs calculated on an annual basis. (p. 291)
Erosion - cash flows of a new project that come at the expense of a firm's existing projects. (p. 268)
Incremental cash flows - difference between firm's future cash flows with a project or without. (p. 266)
Opportunity cost - most valuable alternative given up if a particular investment is undertaken. (p. 267)
Pro forma financial statements - financial statements projecting future years' operations. (p. 269)
Stand-alone principle - evaluation of a project based on the project's incremental cash flows. (p. 266)
Sunk cost - a cost that has already been incurred, cannot be recovered, and should not be considered in an investment decision. (p. 267)

CONCEPT TEST

1. In the evaluation of a capital budgeting project, relevant cash flows are the incremental cash flows, which consist of all _____ in the firm's cash flows that are a direct consequence of _____ the project. The incremental cash flows for a project can be defined as the firm's cash flows if the project is undertaken minus _____. The _____ principle specifies that incremental cash flows can be analyzed from the perspective of the _____, rather than from the perspective of the _____. (p. 266)

2. A sunk cost for a capital budgeting project is money the firm has already _____, or is _____, regardless of whether it accepts the project under consideration. A sunk cost (is/is not) incremental to a capital budgeting project, and therefore (is/is not) relevant to the capital budgeting decision. (p. 267)

3. An opportunity cost for a particular capital budgeting project is a benefit which the firm would _____ if it _____ the project. An opportunity cost (is/is not) an incremental cost for a capital budgeting project. (p. 267)

4. A _____ is the impact which a given capital budgeting project might have on cash flows in another area of the firm. These changes in cash flows (are/are not) incremental cash flows for the project under consideration. (p. 267)

5. Net working capital equals _____ minus _____. A project typically requires a(n) _____ in net working capital during the life of the project. This investment is an incremental cash _____. At the termination of a project, this investment is typically recovered, and is therefore an incremental _____ at that time. This treatment of changes in net working capital adjusts accounting data to a cash flow basis. Generally Accepted Accounting Principles require that revenue is recorded on the income statement when it _____, and that costs are determined according to the _____ principle. Consequently, it is essential to adjust accounting information, which is reported on an _____ basis, to reflect the actual timing of _____. (p. 268)

6. Depreciation is a _____ expense; it is relevant to the computation of incremental cash flows only because it affects _____. Depreciation affects cash flow calculations in two ways: first, depreciation expenses affect operating cash flows since the deduction of depreciation expense reduces _____; and, second, depreciation affects the _____ value of an asset, and the difference between _____ value and _____ value has tax implications when an asset is sold. There are tax implications associated with the sale of an asset whenever the asset is sold for a price which differs from its _____ value at the time of the sale. When the asset is sold for more than its _____ value, a tax obligation is created; when the asset is sold for less than its _____ value, the difference is a _____ for the firm. (p. 268)

7. Projected cash flows for a project are derived from _____ financial statements, which are projected financial statements for future periods. Operating cash flow (OCF) equals _____ + _____ - _____. Interest is not deducted because it is not a(n) _____ expense; financing costs impact our NPV analysis since these costs determine the appropriate _____. We do not deduct depreciation in computing OCF because depreciation is a(n) _____ expense. (p. 270)

8. The tax shield approach to defining OCF emphasizes the manner in which _____ affects cash flow. The tax shield approach defines OCF as follows: OCF = _____ + _____. The first term is the project's _____ in the absence of _____. The second term is the _____. (p. 285)

9. The bottom-up approach accentuates the relationship between _____ and OCF. This approach defines OCF as follows: OCF = _____ + _____. (p. 285)

10. The top-down approach defines operating cash flow as follows: OCF = _____ - _____ - _____. (p. 285)

11. In a bidding situation, the problem for the supplier is to set the bid price at the _____ price which still provides the _____. To derive this price, the supplier solves the capital budgeting problem 'backwards.' The supplier first determines the annual OCF which makes the NPV equal to _____; this OCF would provide the supplier with the _____. The supplier then determines the level of _____ and the price per unit which would provide the required OCF. This price per unit is the supplier's _____. (p. 288)

ANSWERS TO CONCEPT TEST

1. changes; accepting; firm cash flows if the project is not undertaken; stand-alone; project; entire firm
2. spent; committed to spend; is not; is not
3. forego; accepts; is
4. side effect; are
5. current assets; current liabilities; increase; outflow; inflow; accrues; matching; accrual; cash flows
6. non-cash; taxes; taxes; book; book; market; book; book; book; tax deduction
7. pro forma; earnings before interest and taxes; depreciation; taxes; operating; discount rate; non-cash
8. depreciation; (Sales-Costs)$\times$(1-T$_c$); Depreciation$\times$T$_c$; cash flow; depreciation; depreciation tax shield

9. net income; net income; depreciation
10. Sales; costs; taxes;
11. lowest; required rate of return; zero; required rate of return; sales; bid price

PROBLEMS

Use the following information to solve Problems 1-8:

Aunt Sally's Sauces, Inc., is considering expansion into a new line of all-natural, cholesterol-free, sodium-free, fat-free, low-calorie tomato sauces. Sally has paid $50,000 for a marketing study which indicates that the new product line would have sales of $650,000 per year for each of the next six years. Manufacturing plant and equipment would cost $500,000, and will be depreciated according to ACRS as a five-year asset. The fixed assets will have no market value at the end of six years. Annual fixed costs are projected at $80,000 and variable costs are projected at 60% of sales. Net working capital requirements are $75,000 for the six-year life of the project; the outlay for working capital will be recovered at the end of six years. Aunt Sally's tax rate is 34% and the firm requires a 16% return.

1. Compute the annual depreciation and the ending book value for the fixed assets.

2. Prepare pro forma income statements for the project for years 1 through 6.

3. Compute operating cash flow for the project for years 1 through 6.

4. Compute total projected cash flows for years 0 through 6 for the project.

5. Compute the net present value and the internal rate of return for the new product line.

6. Use the tax-shield approach to compute the operating cash flow for years 1 through 6.

7. Use the 'bottom-up' approach to compute the operating cash flow for years 1 through 6.

8. Use the 'top-down' approach to compute the operating cash flow for years 1 through 6.

9. A company is considering the acquisition of production equipment which will reduce both labor and materials costs. The cost is $100,000 and it will be depreciated on a straight-line basis over a four-year period. However, the useful life of the equipment is five years, and it will have a $20,000 salvage value at the end of five years. Operating costs will be reduced by $30,000 in the first year and the savings will increase by $5,000 per year for years 2, 3 and 4. Due to increased maintenance costs, savings in year 5 will be $10,000 less than the year 4 savings. The equipment will also reduce net working capital by $5,000 throughout the life of the project. The firm's tax rate is 35% and the firm requires a 16% return. Compute operating cash flow for the project for years 1 through 5.

10. Compute total projected cash flows for years 0 through 5 for the project.

11. Compute the net present value and the internal rate of return for the production equipment.

12. A firm is considering the purchase of either Machine A or Machine B. The two machines provide the same benefit to the company and the machine selected will be replaced at the end of its useful life. The lives and annual costs for each are:

Year	Machine A	Machine B
0	$5,000	$4,000
1	800	1,200
2	800	1,200
3	800	1,200
4	800	1,200
5	800	

The opportunity cost is 12%. Given no taxes, which machine should be selected? (Hint: Compute EACs.)

13. Suppose that, in the previous problem, all costs are before-tax costs and the tax rate is 35%; the company will depreciate either machine using straight-line depreciation over the life of the asset, and the salvage value of both is zero at the end of their lives. Compute the EAC for each. Which is preferable?

14. A firm is considering the purchase of either Machine X or Machine Y. The two machines provide the same benefit to the company and the machine selected will be replaced at the end of its useful life. The lives and annual costs for each are:

Year	Machine X	Machine Y
0	$800	$600
1	150	200
2	150	200
3	150	200
4	150	

The opportunity cost is 15%. Given no taxes, which machine should be selected? (Hint: Compute EACs.)

15. A tool manufacturer plans to submit a bid to supply hammers to the U.S. Department of Defense (DOD). The DOD will buy 1000 hammers per year for the next three years. To supply the hammers, the manufacturer must acquire equipment at a cost of $150,000. It has a five-year life and will be depreciated on a straight-line basis. The manufacturer plans to sell the equipment after three years; it is expected to have a market value of $50,000. Additional fixed costs will total $38,000 per year and variable costs will be $2 per hammer. An additional investment of $25,000 in net working capital will be required; this investment will be recovered at the end of three years. The tax rate is 35% and the required return is 18%. What is the lowest price the manufacturer can charge for the hammers?

CHAPTER 11

PROJECT ANALYSIS AND EVALUATION

CONCEPTS FOR REVIEW

It will become apparent as you learn more about the field of finance that the evaluation of risk is crucial to most financial decisions. This chapter provides deeper insight into process of estimating risky **project cash flows**. Keep in mind the alternative definitions of OCF while studying this chapter.

CHAPTER HIGHLIGHTS

In this chapter we recognize the fact that project cash flows, as well as the resulting net present value calculations, are *estimates* which must be evaluated more closely. Therefore, the emphasis here is on procedures for assessing these forecasts and estimates.

I. EVALUATING NPV ESTIMATES (p. 302)

The Basic Problem (p. 302) How good is the NPV we have estimated? If we overestimate project NPVs, we run the risk of investing in bad projects. If we underestimate project NPVs, we forego some projects we should have invested in. In either case, we have failed to maximize firm value.

Forecasting Risk (p. 303) The accuracy of estimated NPVs is largely dependent on the accuracy of our cash flow estimates. **Forecasting risk** is the risk that the financial manager makes an incorrect decision because of errors in forecasting future cash flows.

Sources of Value (p. 303) Positive NPVs represent unexploited opportunities. Apple Computer grabbed the personal computer market in the mid-1970s; Netscape grabbed the web browser market in the mid-1990s. Notice, however, that in both cases, the excess returns generated attracted other competitors (Compaq and IBM, among others in the former case; Microsoft in the latter).

II. SCENARIO AND OTHER "WHAT IF" ANALYSES (p. 304)

Getting Started (p. 304) If our *assumptions* about future cash flows are incorrect, our NPV estimates are likely to be incorrect too. **Scenario analysis, sensitivity analysis,** and **simulation analysis** are commonly used techniques for evaluating the critical assumptions of net present value calculations.

Scenario Analysis (p. 305) By employing a "base case" and best/worst case situations, **scenario analysis** examines the effect on all variables, and consequently on NPV, of a hypothetical sequence of events.

Sensitivity Analysis (p. 305) **Sensitivity analysis** is a variant of scenario analysis in which each scenario represents a change in only one variable, rather than a number of variables.

Simulation Analysis (p. 307) **Simulation analysis** is another variant of scenario analysis in which we consider a large number of different combinations of the forecasted variables.

III. BREAK-EVEN ANALYSIS (p. 308)

The goal of break-even analysis is to identify the level of *sales* below which the project is unacceptable.

Fixed and Variable Costs (p. 309) Break-even analysis requires that we first distinguish between fixed and variable costs. **Variable costs** are costs that vary directly with production. Total variable costs (VC) equal variable cost per unit of output (v) times the number of units of output (Q). I.e., $VC = v \times Q$.

Fixed costs (FC) do not change over a specified time interval and must be paid regardless of output level. **Total costs** (TC) are the sum of the variable and fixed costs: $TC = VC + FC = (v \times Q) + FC$.

Accounting Break-Even (p. 312) The **accounting break-even** point is the sales level at which a project's *net income is zero*. The accounting break-even equals

$$Q = (\text{Total fixed costs} + \text{Depreciation})/(\text{Unit price - Unit variable cost}) = (FC + D)/(P - v)$$

Note that a project whose sales level exceeds accounting break-even may not have a positive NPV.

Uses for the Accounting Break-Even (p. 314) This measure is useful because it:

1. is easy to calculate and understand;
2. measures the contribution to accounting income; and
3. reflects the project's impact on out-of-pocket (but not opportunity) costs.

IV. OPERATING CASH FLOW, SALES, VOLUME, AND BREAK-EVEN (p. 315)

Accounting Break-Even and Cash Flow (p. 315) Recall that OCF equals net income plus depreciation. At the break-even sales level, net income is zero, so OCF equals annual depreciation expense. If sales remain at the break-even level over the life of the project, then the IRR is zero, and the project's payback period is equal to its life. And, at any positive discount rate, the NPV of such a project is negative.

Sales Volume and Operating Cash Flow (p. 315) Ignoring taxes, OCF is defined as follows:

$$OCF = EBIT + D = (S - C - D) + D$$

Since $EBIT = [(P - v) \times Q] - FC - D$, OCF is equal to $= [(P - v) \times Q] - FC$.

Cash Flow, Accounting, and Financial Break-Even Points (p. 317) The **cash break-even** point equals

$$Q = FC/(P - v)$$

The most significant break-even point for the financial manager is the **financial break-even**, which is the level of sales such that *the NPV of the project is zero*. To compute the financial break-even,

1. Identifying the level of operating cash flow (OCF) for which net present value is zero.
2. Substitute this value of OCF into the accounting break-even equation and solve for Q. This is the sales level that results in a zero NPV.

V. OPERATING LEVERAGE (p. 320)

The level of fixed costs for a capital budgeting project, or for a company as a whole, has an important impact on the break-even concepts developed in the previous section.

The Basic Idea (p. 320) **Operating leverage** is the extent to which a capital budgeting project, or a firm, relies on fixed production costs. A high level of fixed costs is associated with a relatively large investment in plant and equipment; such a situation is said to be capital-intensive.

Implications of Operating Leverage (p. 320) Fixed costs magnify the effect of a change in operating revenue on operating cash flow and NPV. The higher the degree of operating leverage, the greater the danger from forecasting risk.

Measuring Operating Leverage (p. 320) The **degree of operating leverage** (DOL) is defined below:

$$DOL = (\text{Percentage change in OCF})/(\text{Percentage change in Q})$$

DOL = 1 + FC/OCF. The key insight is that OCF and NPV increase (decrease) more rapidly with an increase (decrease) in sales for capital-intensive firms than for labor-intensive firms, all else equal.

VI. ADDITIONAL CONSIDERATIONS IN CAPITAL BUDGETING (p. 323)

Managerial Options (p. 323) Capital investment decisions entail **managerial options** during the life of the project; these options include numerous alternative courses of action available to management. After a project is implemented, management can change the product price, expand production, modify the production process, or even abandon a project which proves to be unsuccessful. Capital budgeting analysis which ignores the value of such managerial options underestimates the true NPV of a project.

Capital Rationing (p. 326) **Capital rationing** exists if a firm, (or a division), has identified positive NPV capital budgeting projects but is unable to obtain financing for the projects. **Soft rationing** occurs when funds are limited from within the firm. **Hard rationing** occurs financing is unavailable from any source. A solution to rationing is to accept the set of projects which maximizes the NPV with the funds available. This is generally equivalent to accepting those projects with the highest profitability index.

KEY TERMS AND CONCEPTS

Accounting break-even - the sales level that results in zero project net income. (p. 312)
Capital rationing - when a firm has positive NPV projects but cannot obtain financing. (p. 326)
Cash break-even - the sales level where operating cash flow is equal to zero. (p. 318)
Contingency planning - taking into account the managerial options that are implicit in a project. (p. 324)
Degree of operating leverage - % change in OCF divided by % change in quantity sold. (p. 320)
Financial break-even - the sales level that results in a zero NPV. (p. 318)
Fixed costs - costs that do not change when the quantity of output changes during a period. (p. 310)
Forecasting risk - the possibility that error in projected cash flows lead to incorrect decisions. (p. 303)
Hard rationing - when a business cannot raise financing for a project under any circumstances. (p. 327)
Managerial options - opportunities managers can exploit if certain things happen in the future. (p. 324)
Marginal or incremental cost - change in costs that occurs given a small change in output. (p. 311)
Marginal or incremental revenue - the change in revenue given a small change in output. (p. 311)
Operating leverage - the degree to which a firm or project relies on fixed costs. (p. 320)
Scenario analysis - determination of what happens to NPV estimates when we ask what-if? (p. 305)
Sensitivity analysis - investigation of what happens to NPV when only one variable is changed. (p. 307)
Simulation analysis - a combination of scenario and sensitivity analyses. (p. 308)

Soft rationing - the situation that occurs when units in a business are allocated a certain amount of financing for capital budgeting. (p. 326)

Strategic options - options for future, related business products or strategies. (p. 326)

Variable costs - costs that change when the quantity of output changes. (p. 309)

CONCEPT TEST

1. The risk that a financial manager makes an incorrect decision because of errors in forecasting future cash flows is called _____. Several forms of "what if" analysis are used to evaluate cash flow forecasts in capital budgeting. An analysis of the effect on all forecasted variables and on NPV, of a hypothetical sequence of events is referred to as _____. An assessment of the sensitivity of one variable to changes in another variable is called _____. In capital budgeting, we are concerned about the sensitivity of _____ to variation in the level of a forecasted variable. For example, the financial manager would evaluate the change in _____ which results if actual sales are at the lower bound of a forecasted range, while all other variables are held at their base case levels. The process of analyzing the impact of a large number of different combinations of the forecasted variables on the acceptability of a capital budgeting project is called _____; the combinations of variables are not selected with an hypothesized scenario in mind, but rather are selected _____ . (p. 303)

2. Variable costs are costs that vary with the level of _____ and are generally assumed to be proportional to the level of _____. Total variable costs (VC) equal _____ multiplied by _____. This relationship is summarized algebraically as: VC = _____ . Costs which do not change over a specified interval and must be paid regardless of production levels are called _____. Total costs (TC) for a given level of output in a given period are defined as the sum of _____ and _____. Algebraically, TC = _____ . (p. 309)

3. The accounting break-even point is the sales level at which a project's _____ is equal to _____. The accounting break-even point is: Q = _____. If sales are equal to the accounting break-even point, then both _____ and _____ are equal to zero. The "bottom-up" approach defines OCF as _____ + _____. At the break-even sales level, OCF equals _____ . If sales remain at the break-even level throughout the life of a project, then the IRR is equal to _____ . Therefore, at any positive discount rate, the net present value of such a project is _____ . (p. 312)

4. In the absence of corporate income taxes, the level of output (Q) required to achieve a given level of OCF can be written as: Q = _____ . The cash break-even point is the level of sales for which the _____ equals _____. The formula for the cash break-even point is derived from the previous equation by substituting _____ = _____, resulting in the following: Q = _____ . A project with sales equal to the cash break-even level throughout the life of the project has an IRR equal to _____ because the initial outlay produces no cash inflow. (p. 315)

5. The most significant break-even point for the financial manager is the financial break-even point, which is the level of sales such that the _____ of the project equals _____ . (p. 318)

6. The extent to which a capital budgeting project, or a firm as a whole, relies on fixed production costs is called _____. A firm or project with a relatively high level of fixed costs is said to have high _____. A high level of fixed costs is associated with a large investment in plant and equipment; this situation is said to be _____. Degree of operating leverage (DOL) is: DOL = _____. This definition is algebraically equivalent to: DOL = _____. (p. 320)

7. For a given level of output, DOL (increases/decreases/remains constant) as the size of the increase in Q increases. When the base level of Q increases, the DOL (increases/decreases/remains constant). A capital-intensive production process has a (higher/lower) DOL than a less capital-intensive process, so that OCF and NPV increase (more/less) rapidly with an increase in sales; if sales are below the forecasted level, then NPV decreases (more/less) rapidly for the capital-intensive process. (p. 321)

8. If capital budgeting analysis ignores managerial options, then computed NPV may be _____. (p. 323)

9. If a firm, or a unit of a corporation, has identified positive NPV capital budgeting projects but is unable to obtain financing for the projects, then _____ exists. One approach to resolving such a problem is to accept the set of projects which maximizes the _____ with the funds available. This is generally equivalent to accepting those projects with the highest _____. (p. 326)

ANSWERS TO CONCEPT TEST

1. forecasting risk; scenario analysis; sensitivity analysis; net present value; net present value; simulation analysis; randomly
2. production; production; variable costs per unit of output; number of units of output; $(v \times Q)$; fixed costs; total variable costs; fixed costs; (VC+FC) or $[(v \times Q)+FC]$
3. net income; zero; $[(FC+D)/(P-v)]$; EBIT; net income; net income; annual depreciation expense; annual depreciation expense; zero; negative
4. $[(FC+OCF)]/(P-v)]$; operating cash flow; zero; OCF; zero; $[FC/(P-v)]$; -100%
5. net present value; zero;
6. operating leverage; operating leverage; capital intensive; $[(\% \text{ change in OCF})/(\% \text{ change in Q})]$; $[1+(FC/OCF)]$
7. remains constant; decreases; higher; more; more
8. underestimated
9. capital rationing; net present value; profitability index

PROBLEMS

Use the following information to solve Problems 1 - 13.

D. Newcombe & Associates, Inc., is considering the introduction of a new product. Production of the new product requires an investment of $140,000 in equipment which has a five-year life. The equipment has no salvage value at the end of five years and will be depreciated on a straight-line basis. Newcombe's required return is 15% and the tax rate is 34%. The firm has made the following forecasts:

	Base case	Lower bound	Upper bound
Unit sales	2,000	1,800	2,200
Price per unit	$ 55	$ 50	$ 60
Variable costs per unit	$ 22	$ 21	$ 23
Fixed costs per year	$10,000	$ 9,500	$10,500

1. Compute the annual OCF for the project, using the base case forecast for each variable.

2. Compute the NPV for the project, using the base case forecast for each variable.

3. Compute the NPV and the IRR for the project under the best case and worst case scenarios.

4. Assume that all variables, except unit sales, take on their base case levels. What is the effect on NPV and IRR if unit sales are at their lower bound? Also, compute NPV and IRR under the assumption that unit sales are at their upper bound.

5. Assume that all variables, except price per unit, take on their base case levels. What is the effect on NPV and IRR if price per unit is at its lower bound? Also, compute NPV and IRR under the assumption that price per unit is at the upper bound.

6. Assume that all variables, except variable costs per unit, take on their base case levels. What is the effect on NPV and IRR if variable costs per unit are at their upper bound? Also, compute NPV and IRR under the assumption that variable costs per unit are at their lower bound.

7. Assume that all variables, except fixed costs, take on their base case levels. What is the effect on NPV and IRR if fixed costs are at their upper bound? Also, compute NPV and IRR under the assumption that fixed costs are at their lower bound.

8. Assume the base-case forecasts for the Newcombe project; compute the accounting break-even point.

9. Assume the base-case forecasts and no taxes for the project; compute the cash break-even point.

10. Assume the base-case forecasts and no taxes for the project; compute the financial break-even point.

11. Suppose that sales for the project under consideration by Newcombe increase from 2,000 units to 2,200 units per year. Compute the DOL for the project at sales of 2,000 units. Use both the definition of the DOL and its algebraic equivalent. Assume Newcombe pays no taxes on this project.

12. Suppose that sales for the project under consideration by Newcombe decrease from 2,000 units to 1,600 units per year. Compute the DOL for the project using the definition of DOL. Assume Newcombe pays no taxes on this project.

13. Assume that sales increase from 1,600 units to 2,000 units for the project. Compute DOL for the project at sales of 1,600 units. Use both the definition of DOL and its algebraic equivalent. Assume Newcombe pays no taxes on this project.

14. The following data have been computed for a firm: when output is 20,000 units, OCF is $50,000 and operating leverage is 2.5. Suppose output increases to 23,000 units; what is the new level of OCF?

15. For the data in Problem 14, compute the firm's fixed costs.

16. Suppose that an investor is considering buying property to use as a parking lot; it costs $10,000. He expects the value of the property to remain constant for the foreseeable future; no depreciation expense will be taken. He also expects that, for the foreseeable future, 6,000 cars per year will use the parking lot at a daily rate of $3 per car. Variable costs are zero, but an attendant must be paid $16,000 per year. Assume the required return is 25% and there are no taxes. Compute the NPV. Is the project acceptable?

17. Suppose that, in the previous problem, the investor intends to re-evaluate his forecast at the end of the first year. He believes that usage of the parking lot during the first year will be either 5500 or 6500 cars per year, and that the volume of business during the first year will indicate which of these figures will continue beyond the first year. In addition, he believes that each of these figures is equally likely. Compute the NPV. Is the project acceptable?

CHAPTER 12

SOME LESSONS FROM CAPITAL MARKET HISTORY

CONCEPTS FOR REVIEW

When determining how much to pay for a given security, investors consider the uncertainty of its cash flows; the result is that discount rates are positively related to risk. The effect of risk on market values is clear when we recall the bond and stock valuation formulas. All else equal, higher discount rates decrease market values. As you read this chapter, keep the security valuation formulas in mind.

CHAPTER HIGHLIGHTS

The process of asset valuation generally involves risky cash flows, so it is necessary to identify an appropriate risk-adjusted rate with which to discount them. In this chapter we begin the task of identifying the appropriate opportunity cost for risky assets. This process requires that we learn how to measure returns and risk, and that we understand the relationship between risk and return in the financial markets.

I. RETURNS (p. 337)

Dollar Returns (p. 337) The return on an investment comes in either or both of two general forms; the **income component**, and the **capital gain** or **capital loss** which reflects the change in value of the asset.

For common stock, return takes two forms: **dividends** and **capital gains**. The total *dollar* return is:

$$\text{Dividend income + Capital gain (or loss)}$$

Percentage Returns (p. 339) For financial decision-making, it is often more convenient to think of percentage returns because the results apply regardless of the dollar amount invested in a particular asset. The total *percentage* return on an investment in stock is:

$$\text{(Dividend income + Capital gain (or loss))/Initial investment}$$

Notice that the total return is comprised of the **dividend yield** plus the **percentage capital gain** (or **capital gains yield**). That is,

$$\text{Total return} = D_{t+1}/P_t + P_{t+1} - P_t/P_t = (D_{t+1} + P_{t+1} - P_t)/P_t$$

where P_t is the price of the stock at the beginning of the year, D_{t+1} is the dividend paid during the year, and P_{t+1} is the price at the end of the year.

II. THE HISTORICAL RECORD (p. 341)

A First Look (p. 342) Historical evidence indicates a positive relationship between return and risk. In descending order of both return and risk, lower returns have been observed for (1) all common stocks, (2) long-term corporate bonds, (3) long-term government bonds, and (4) U.S. Treasury bills.

A Closer Look (p. 342) In general, the variability of historical returns is positively related to the magnitude of the returns.

III. AVERAGE RETURNS: THE FIRST LESSON (p. 344)

Average Returns: The First Lesson (p. 344) To use the history of stock market returns for financial decision-making, it is necessary to summarize percentage return data for an individual stock and for the stock market as a whole.

Calculating Average Returns (p. 347) The **average (or mean) rate of return** is simply the arithmetic average: total returns divided by the number of observations. The average return is also the best guess of what returns will be in any given future year.

Average Returns: The Historical Record (p. 347) For the securities considered, historical average annual returns have been the lowest for U.S. Treasury bills, and highest for small firm common stocks.

Risk Premiums (p. 347) A common benchmark used in comparing returns is the return on securities issued by the U.S. government. Since the U.S. government can always raise taxes in order to repay its debts, and because their maturities are relatively short, we consider U.S. *Treasury bills* to be virtually risk-free; hence, we refer to the T-bill rate as the **risk-free rate of return**.

From 1926 to 1990, the average return on T-bills was 3.7% per year. During this period, the common stocks of the 500 largest companies in the United States had an average return of 12.1%. The difference between these returns is the **excess return** or **risk premium** for the risky asset (stocks).

The First Lesson (p. 348) The empirical evidence indicates there is a reward for bearing risk.

IV. THE VARIABILITY OF RETURNS: THE SECOND LESSON (p. 350)

Frequency Distributions and Variability (p. 350) Frequency distributions are often used to describe the changes in a variable. The *variability* of those changes is indicated by the spread of the distribution, which is often measured by its variance or standard deviation.

The Historical Variance and Standard Deviation (p. 351) Financial economists equate risk with the statistical concept of variability. In a financial context, the greater the deviations from the average return, the more variable the rate of return and the higher the level of risk. The variance is equal to

$$\text{Var(R)} = \sigma^2 = [(R_1 - \bar{R})^2 + (R_2 - \bar{R})^2 + \ldots + (R_T - \bar{R})^2]/(T - 1)$$

Note that when we compute the variance for historical data we divide by $(T - 1)$; for a strict average, we divide by T, the number of observations.

Historical Record (p. 353) The standard deviation of returns is positively related to historical returns.

Normal Distribution (p. 353) For many random events, the **normal distribution** (or "bell curve") is useful for deriving the probability that the value of a variable falls within a certain range. Stock returns have been shown to be approximately normally distributed.

The Second Lesson (p. 355) Historically, those securities which have displayed the greatest variability have, on average, earned the greatest historical returns over the 1926-1996 period. The second lesson is: *the greater the risk, the greater the return.*

Using Capital Market History (p. 355) Suppose we are interested in evaluating an investment that is about as risky as the stock market overall. What discount rate should we use for our present value analysis? The appropriate discount rate for evaluating a risky investment is the sum of the risk-free rate plus a risk premium. From 1926-1996, the historic risk premium for the stock market was 8.5%. If T-bills are currently yielding 7%, then the appropriate discount rate would be (7% + 8.5%) = 15.5%.

Not all risky investments have the same risk level as the 500-stock portfolio, so we cannot use the above procedure for evaluating all risky investments. It is necessary to determine the appropriate measure of risk, and to quantify the risk-return relationship. We complete this discussion in the next chapter.

V. CAPITAL MARKET EFFICIENCY (p. 356)

The financial markets in the U. S. have low trading costs, and many buyers and sellers, all of whom have ready access to relevant information. In such a market, all transactions have exactly zero NPV: assets are worth exactly what they cost. This is the basis for the notion that financial markets are *efficient*.

Price Behavior in an Efficient Market (p. 356) An **efficient capital market** is a market in which all transactions have a NPV equal to zero. Alternatively, it can be said that the rate of return for an investment is equal to the equilibrium rate of return for a given level of risk. *In an efficient market, current prices reflect all available information.*

The Efficient Markets Hypothesis (p. 358) The **efficient markets hypothesis (EMH)** asserts that U.S. capital markets are efficient with respect to information. This implies that no investment strategy based on current or historical information produces extraordinarily large profits, and that the adjustment of prices to new information is almost instantaneous.

Two important implications of market efficiency are: (1) investors buying stocks and bonds should expect to earn an equilibrium rate of return commensurate with the level of risk they assume, and (2) firms issuing securities will receive a price equal to the present value of the securities' expected cash flows.

Some Common Misconceptions About the EMH (p. 358) First, note that daily fluctuation in security prices is not consistent with market efficiency. Since new information ("news") arrives daily, the EMH predicts that prices adjust daily. (Recall that market prices depend on expected future cash flows.) It is the expectations of these future cash flows that change when new information arrives. Second, the hypothesis does not imply that we should select stocks randomly: the result could be an undiversified portfolio with an undesirable level of risk. Finally, the EMH does *not* imply that investors are uninformed. To the contrary, it assumes that investors are rational, and not easily fooled or manipulated.

The Forms of Market Efficiency (p. 359) Financial economists generally identify three forms of market efficiency. A market is **weak-form efficient** if current security prices completely incorporate the information contained in past prices. A great deal of evidence indicates that financial markets are weak-form efficient. A market is **semistrong-form efficient** if current prices incorporate all **publicly** available information. Finally, a market is **strong-form efficient** if current prices reflect **all** information, including

inside information; inside information is information about a firm which is available only to "insiders," (e.g., corporate executives and major stockholders). Markets do not appear to be strong-form efficient; available evidence seems to indicate that valuable inside information does exist.

KEY TERMS AND CONCEPTS

Efficient capital market - a market in which security prices reflect available information. (p. 356)
Efficient markets hypothesis (EMH) - the hypothesis that actual capital markets are efficient. (p. 358)
Normal distribution - bell-shaped frequency distribution defined by mean and variance. (p. 353)
Risk premium - the excess return required from investment in a risky asset over a risk-free asset (p. 347)
Standard deviation - the positive square root of the variance. (p. 351)
Variance - the average squared deviation between the actual return and the average return. (p. 351)

CONCEPT TEST

1. The return on an investment comes in either or both of two general forms: the _____ component, and the _____ gain or loss. The return on investment in common stock comes in two forms: _____ and _____ gains. _____ are cash payments by a corporation to its shareholders and represent the income component of the return. _____ gains (or losses) for an investment in common stock result from _____ (or _____) in the value of the stock. (p. 337)

2. The total return for an investment in common stock is the sum of the _____ yield and the percentage _____ gain (or _____ gains yield). The _____ yield is defined algebraically as _____. The _____ gains yield is equal to _____ . (p. 338)

3. The _____ return is the best guess of the annual return selected at random from a set of historical returns. (p. 347)

4. Treasury bills are virtually _____, so the T-bill rate is often called the _____ . The difference between the rate of return for a risky investment and the return on T-bills is the _____ (or _____) for the risky asset. (p. 347)

5. Financial economists equate risk with the statistical concept of _____, which is commonly measured by the variance or the standard deviation. The variance is the average of the _____ deviations from the _____ rate of return. The variance formula is: $\text{Var}(R) = \sigma^2 = $ _____ , where $\text{Var}(R)$ and σ^2 are alternative notations for variance, R_1, R_2, and R_T are the returns for each year, and T is the number of observations. The _____ is the square root of the variance, and is denoted _____ or _____ . (p. 351)

6. For many random events, the _____ distribution is useful for deriving the probability that the value of a variable falls within a certain range. If returns have this distribution, the probability that the return in a given year is within one σ of the mean is _____ . (p. 354)

7. An efficient capital market is one in which all transactions have an NPV equal to _____.
In an efficient market, prices reflect _____. If a market is efficient with respect to
some piece of information, then that information cannot be used to identify an investment with a
_____. The adjustment of prices to new information is _____ . (p. 356)

8. We identified three forms of market efficiency. A market is _____-form efficient if
current security prices completely incorporate the information contained in past prices. A market is
_____-form efficient if current prices incorporate all publicly available information.
A market is _____-form efficient if current prices reflect all information, including
inside information. Evidence indicates that valuable inside information exists, so financial markets
(are/are not) strong-form efficient. Markets (are/are not) weak-form efficient. (p. 359)

ANSWERS TO CONCEPT TEST

1. income; capital; dividends; capital; dividends; capital; increases; decreases
2. dividend; capital; capital; dividend; (D_{t+1}/P_t); capital; $[(P_{t+1}-P_t)/P_t]$
3. average
4. risk-free; risk-free rate of return; excess return; risk premium
5. variability; squared; mean; $[(R_1 - \bar{R})^2 + (R_2 - \bar{R})^2 + \ldots + (R_T - \bar{R})^2]/(T - 1)$;   SD(R); σ
6. normal; about 68%
7. zero; available information; positive NPV; almost instantaneous
8. weak; semistrong; strong; are not; are

PROBLEMS

1. A year ago you bought 100 shares of Bradley Corp. common stock for $32 per share. During the year, you received dividends of $2.50 per share. The stock is currently selling for $33.50 per share. What was your total dividend income during the year? How much was your capital gain? Your total dollar return?

2. For the Bradley common stock investment in Problem 1, compute the dividend yield, the capital gains yield, and the total percentage return on a per share basis.

3. Suppose that, one year from today, you expect the Bradley Corporation common stock in Problem 1 to be selling for $33 per share, and that during the coming year, you expect to receive dividends of $2 per share. What is the total dividend income expected during the year? What is the total capital gain expected during the year? What is the total dollar return expected during the year?

4. For the investment described in Problem 3, compute the dividend yield, the capital gains yield, and the total percentage return on a per share basis.

Use the information in the table to solve Problems 5-9.

Suppose the following information represents the return for General Motors (GM) and American Telephone & Telegraph (ATT) common stocks over a five-year period:

Year	Returns	
	GM	ATT
1	10%	12%
2	4	6
3	-9	-10
4	20	22
5	5	5

5. What is the mean return for GM common stock? For ATT common stock?

6. What is the variance of the return for GM common stock? For ATT common stock?

7. What is the standard deviation of the return for GM common stock? For ATT common stock?

8. Suppose the returns for GM and ATT have normally distributed returns with means and standard deviations (SDs) calculated in Problems 6 and 7, respectively. For each stock, determine the range of returns within one SD of the mean and the range within two SDs of the mean. Interpret the results.

9. Given the data from Problems 5, 7 and 8, what is the probability that, in any given year, the return for GM common stock will be negative? What is the probability that the ATT return will be negative?

CHAPTER 13

RETURN, RISK, AND THE SECURITY MARKET LINE

CONCEPTS FOR REVIEW

We extend our use of statistical tools in order to quantify risk in this chapter. Expected value, variance, and standard deviation lead to the decomposition of total risk into systematic and unsystematic elements, which leads, in turn, to the development of the beta coefficient and the Capital Asset Pricing Model.

CHAPTER HIGHLIGHTS

We previously established that investments with greater risk provide, on average, higher returns. In this chapter we establish a rigorous description of the relationship between risk and return in the securities markets. By doing so, we obtain the means with which to compute the required returns (and therefore equilibrium values) of both financial and physical assets.

I. EXPECTED RETURNS AND VARIANCES (p. 367)

Expected Return (p. 367) Given all possible outcomes for a particular investment, the average rate of return is called the **expected return**. The actual return can differ from the expected return.

The expected return is a weighted average of the possible rates of return:

$$E(R) = (Pr_1 \times R_1) + (Pr_2 \times R_2) + (Pr_3 \times R_3) + \cdots + (Pr_T \times R_T)$$

where T is the number of possible states of the economy, Pr_1, Pr_2, Pr_3, and Pr_T are the probabilities of the respective states of the economy, and R_1, R_2, R_3, and R_T are the possible rates of return. We define the *risk premium* as the expected return - risk-free rate.

Calculating the Variance (p. 369) The variance of the expected return on an asset equals the sum of the products of the squared deviations from the expected return, weighted by their probabilities.

II. PORTFOLIOS (p. 370)

An investor's **portfolio** is the combination of assets he owns. Rational investors are more concerned about the characteristics of the portfolio than with the characteristics of the individual assets themselves.

Portfolio Weights (p. 370) The respective percentages of a portfolio's total value invested in each of the assets in the portfolio are referred to as the **portfolio weights**.

Portfolio Expected Returns (p. 370) The expected return for a portfolio is the weighted average of the expected returns of the securities which comprise the portfolio.

$$E(R_P) = [x_1 \times E(R_1)] + [x_2 \times E(R_2)] + [x_3 \times E(R_3)] + \cdots + [x_n \times E(R_n)]$$

where n is the number of assets in the portfolio, x_1, x_2, x_3, and x_n are the portfolio weights, and $E(R_1)$, $E(R_2)$, $E(R_3)$, and $E(R_n)$ are the expected returns.

Portfolio Variance (p. 370) Unlike the expected return, the variance and standard deviation of a portfolio are not equal to the weighted average of the corresponding characteristics of the individual securities. The portfolio standard deviation is virtually always less than the weighted average of the standard deviations of the securities in the portfolio.

III. ANNOUNCEMENTS, SURPRISES, AND EXPECTED RETURNS (p. 373)

Our measurement of risk is based on the size of the differences between actual returns, R, and expected returns, E(R). In this section, we discuss the reasons why differences between R and E(R) exist.

Expected and Unexpected Returns (p. 374) The actual return on a security consists of two parts: the normal (or expected) return, which is the part of the return predicted or expected by participants in the financial markets; and, a "surprise," or unexpected, part. Alternatively, the difference between the actual and expected returns is due to surprises which are reflected in the unexpected return.

Announcements and News (p. 374) An announcement has two components: the expected part and the surprise. In the language of Wall Street, the market has already 'discounted' the expected part; thus market prices already reflect a part of the announcement because it was anticipated by investors.

*Learning Tip: This seemingly simple idea has profound implications. For example, it helps explain how a company's stock price could **fall** upon the announcement of a dividend **increase** (normally a "good news" event). If shareholders are anticipating a 10% increase in the dividend but the company announces a 8% increase, the surprise is negative; many shareholders will sell their shares and the price may fall.*

IV. RISK: SYSTEMATIC AND UNSYSTEMATIC (p. 376)

The risk of owning a risky asset such as common stock emanates from unexpected events. We identify two categories of risk: systematic risk and unsystematic risk.

Systematic and Unsystematic Risk (p. 376) A **systematic** (or **market**) risk factor affects a large number of assets. An **unsystematic** risk factor affects only a single asset or a small group of assets.

Systematic and Unsystematic Components of Return (p. 376) Previously we noted that R is the sum of expected and unexpected returns. Since the latter is influenced by two kinds of risk, we contend that the unexpected return has systematic and unsystematic portions. By definition, the unsystematic risk of one asset is unrelated to the unsystematic risk of another.

V. DIVERSIFICATION AND PORTFOLIO RISK (p. 377)

The Effect of Diversification: Another Lesson from Market History (p. 377) **Diversification** is the process of combining assets to reduce risk. Studies of common stocks listed on the New York Stock Exchange (NYSE) demonstrate that the standard deviation of a portfolio decreases as the number of securities in the portfolio increases, albeit at a decreasing rate. The risk eliminated by diversification is called *diversifiable risk*. That portion of risk which cannot be eliminated by diversification is called *nondiversifiable risk*.

The Principle of Diversification (p. 378) Spreading an investment across a number of assets will eliminate some, but not all, of the risk.

Diversification and Unsystematic Risk (p. 379) In a large portfolio of common stocks, the unsystematic risk associated with one stock typically has no impact on the unsystematic risk associated with any other stock; this conclusion is derived from the definition of an unsystematic risk. Consequently, the portion of the return on a stock which arises from the unsystematic risk would tend to offset the portion which arises from the unsystematic risk for another stock in the portfolio. In a portfolio of thirty or more stocks, it would be reasonable to expect that the effects of unsystematic risk on various stocks would offset each other, thereby eliminating the risk arising from this source. This is the risk we identified in the preceding section as diversifiable risk; thus, *diversifiable risk and unsystematic risk are synonymous*.

Diversification and Systematic Risk (p. 380) Systematic risk has an impact on all the stocks in a portfolio. It cannot be diversified away; hence, *systematic risk and nondiversifiable risk are synonymous*.

Learning Tip: The discussion above suggests that there are two types of risk that we must be concerned with. It will be useful to remember the following equation:

   Total risk = nondiversifiable risk + diversifiable risk = systematic risk + unsystematic risk.

VI. SYSTEMATIC RISK AND BETA (p. 380)

The Systematic Risk Principle (p. 380) The **systematic risk principle** states that the reward for bearing risk (i.e., the expected return) depends only on the systematic risk of an investment.

Measuring Systematic Risk (p. 381) The systematic risk of an asset is measured by its **beta coefficient** (β), which measures the amount of systematic risk for a particular asset relative to the amount of systematic risk for the average asset. Since systematic risk is the relevant risk for an investor, the expected return is dependent on β. *This is true regardless of the standard deviation for a stock.*

Portfolio Betas (p. 382) The beta of a portfolio (β_P) is a weighted-average of the betas of the securities which comprise the portfolio:

$$\beta_P = (x_1 \times \beta_1) + (x_2 \times \beta_2) + (x_3 \times \beta_3) + \cdots + (x_n \times \beta_n)$$

where n is the number of assets in the portfolio, x_1, x_2, x_3, and x_n are the portfolio weights, and β_1, β_2, β_3, and β_n are the betas of the assets in the portfolio.

VII. THE SECURITY MARKET LINE (p. 383)

We now develop the relationship between systematic risk and expected return. This relationship is described both graphically and algebraically; the graphic representation is called the *security market line (SML)* and the algebraic representation is called the *capital asset pricing model (CAPM)*.

Beta and the Risk Premium (p. 383) The relationship between a portfolio's expected return, $E(R_P)$, and its systematic risk, β_P, is linear. The slope of the line is the reward-to-risk ratio, which indicates what an investor's compensation would be for taking on risk. The reward-to-risk ratio for a given asset is equal to its risk premium divided by its beta.

The Security Market Line (p. 388) In equilibrium, the above result must hold for any asset; thus, all assets will plot on a straight line which relates risk and return. This line is the **security market line or SML**. The equation for the SML is:

$$E(R_i) = R_f + [E(R_M) - R_f] \times \beta_i$$

where $E(R_i)$ and β_i are the expected return and beta, respectively, for any asset. This equation is referred to as the **Capital Asset Pricing Model (CAPM)**, and indicates the expected return for any asset for a given level of systematic risk.

VIII. THE SML AND THE COST OF CAPITAL: A PREVIEW (p. 391)

The Basic Idea (p. 391) The SML describes investors' opportunities in the financial markets in terms of systematic risk (i.e., β) and expected rate of return. A capital budgeting project. for example, must provide an expected return to shareholders which exceeds that available for investments of comparable risk in the financial markets. The **cost of capital** associated with a capital budgeting project is the minimum required return for the investment. Since this minimum is the expected return available in the financial markets for investments with a specified risk level, it is also the shareholders' opportunity cost.

KEY TERMS AND CONCEPTS

Beta coefficient - measure of systematic risk in a risky asset relative to an average risky asset. (p. 381)
Capital asset pricing model (CAPM) - SML equation showing the relationship between expected return and beta. (p. 389)
Cost of capital - the minimum required return on a new investment. (p. 391)
Expected return - return on a risky asset expected in the future. (p. 367)
Market risk premium - slope of the SML; expected return on the market less the risk-free rate. (p. 388)
Portfolio - group of assets such as stocks and bonds held by an investor. (p. 370)
Portfolio weight - percentage of a portfolio's total value in a particular asset. (p. 370)
Principle of diversification - combining investments to reduce risk. (p. 378)
Security market line - linear relationship between expected return and beta. (p. 388)
Systematic risk - a risk that influences a large number of assets. Also *market risk*. (p. 379)
Systematic risk principle - expected return on a risky asset depends only on its systematic risk. (p. 381)
Total risk - variability of possible outcomes, measured by variance or standard deviation. (p. 369)
Unsystematic risk - risk that affects, at most, a small number of assets. (p. 380)

CONCEPT TEST

1.   The expected return is the _____ of possible returns for an investment. (p. 367)

2.   The portfolio variance is a weighted average of the _____, that is, $Var(R) = \sigma^2 =$ _____ . (p. 372)

3. An investor's portfolio is the _____ the investor owns. The percentages of a portfolio's total value invested in each asset are the _____. (p. 372)

4. The expected return for a portfolio is a weighted average of the _____ of the securities which comprise the portfolio: $E(R_p) =$ _____, where n is the number of assets in the portfolio, x_1, x_2, and x_n are the _____ for the assets, and $E(R_1)$, $E(R_2)$, and $E(R_n)$ are the _____ for the assets. (p. 372)

5. The variance and standard deviation of a portfolio (are/are not) equal to weighted averages of the corresponding characteristics of the individual securities. For most portfolios, the standard deviation is generally (greater than/less than/equal to) the weighted average of the standard deviations of the securities in the portfolio. (p. 373)

6. The actual return on a security consists of two parts: _____ return, which is the part of the return expected by participants in the financial markets; and the _____ part which is not. The risk of an asset comes from the _____ part. (p. 374)

7. A _____ risk factor tends to affect a large number of assets to a greater or lesser degree; this kind of risk is also called a _____ risk factor. An _____ risk factor affects only a single or small group of assets. (p. 376)

8. The process of investing in a portfolio of several assets to reduce risk is called _____. The standard deviation of a portfolio decreases as the number of securities in the portfolio (increases/decreases). As the number of common stocks in a portfolio increases from one to approximately ten, significant (increases/decreases) in standard deviation occur. (p. 378)

9. Risk that is eliminated by diversification is _____ risk. However, there is a minimum level of risk in a portfolio of common stocks which cannot be eliminated by diversification; this minimum level is referred to as _____ risk. (p. 380)

10. In a large portfolio of common stocks the _____ risk associated with one stock typically has no impact on the _____ risk associated with any other. In a portfolio of thirty or more stocks, it would be reasonable to expect that the effects of _____ risk on various stocks would offset each other, thereby eliminating the risk to the investor arising from this source. This source of risk is synonymous with _____ risk. _____ risk has an impact on all the stocks in a portfolio, and cannot be diversified away; so terms _____ risk and _____ risk are synonymous. (p. 381)

11. Financial markets do not reward investors for taking on risks which can be eliminated by _____ . Investors are not rewarded for taking _____ risk, because this risk is _____ . The *systematic risk principle* states that the reward for bearing risk depends only on _____ risk. Consequently, the expected return for an asset depends on its _____ risk. (p. 381)

12. Beta measures the amount of an asset's systematic risk relative to the _____ risk for the average asset. The average stock has a beta of _____ . (p. 381)

13. The portfolio beta (β_P) is a weighted-average of the _____ of the securities in the portfolio: β_P = _____, where n is the number of assets in the portfolio, x_1, x_2, and x_n are the _____, and β_1, β_2, and β_n are the betas of the assets in the portfolio. (p. 382)

14. For portfolios comprised of a risk-free asset and a risky asset, the relationship between $E(R_P)$ and β_P is a straight line. The slope of the line is called the _____ ratio. (p. 384)

15. In equilibrium, points representing expected return and β for all assets fall on a straight line called the _____ . The portfolio of all assets in the market is the _____ portfolio. Its beta equals the beta for the _____ security, which is _____. The slope of the SML is _____ . Since this slope is the excess return on the market over the risk-free rate, it is called the _____ . (p. 388)

ANSWERS TO CONCEPT TEST

1. average
2. squared deviations; ; $[Pr_1 \times (R_1 - \overline{R})^2] + [Pr_2 \times (R_2 - \overline{R})^2] + \cdots + [Pr_T \times (R_T - \overline{R})^2]$
3. combination of assets; portfolio weights
4. expected returns; $[x_1 \times E(R_1)] + [x_2 \times E(R_2)] + \cdots + [x_n \times E(R_n)]$; portfolio weights; expected returns
5. are not; less than
6. expected; unexpected; unexpected
7. systematic; market; unsystematic
8. diversification; increases; decreases
9. diversifiable; nondiversifiable
10. unsystematic; unsystematic; unsystematic; diversifiable; systematic; nondiversifiable; systematic
11. diversification; unsystematic; diversifiable; systematic; systematic
12. systematic; 1.0
13. betas; $(x_1 \times \beta_1) + (x_2 \times \beta_2) + \cdots + (x_n \times \beta_n)$; portfolio weights
14. reward-to-risk
15. SML; market; average; 1.0; $[E(R_M) - R_f]$; market risk premium

PROBLEMS

Suppose the following information represents possible future returns for ATT stock next year:

State of economy	Probability of state of economy	Rate of return if state occurs
1	.20	12%
2	.20	6
3	.20	-10
4	.20	22
5	.20	5
	1.00	

Use the information in the table to solve Problems 1-3.

1. What is the expected rate of return for ATT common stock?

2. What is the variance of the return for ATT common stock?

3. What is the standard deviation of the return for ATT common stock?

4. The probability that the economy will experience a recession next year is .3, while the probabilities of moderate growth or rapid expansion are .5 and .2, respectively. The stock of Firm A is expected to return 5%, 15% or 20%, depending on whether the economy experiences a recession, moderate growth or rapid expansion, respectively. The returns for Firm B are expected to be 0%, 16% or 30%, respectively. Calculate the expected returns for each firm's common stock.

5. What is the variance of the rate of return for Firm A common stock? For Firm B common stock?

6. What is the standard deviation of the return for Firm A common stock? For Firm B common stock?

Use the following information for Stock K and Stock M to solve Problems 7-12.

State of economy	Probability of state of economy	Rate of return if state occurs K	M
Boom	.10	.25	.18
Growth	.20	.10	.20
Normal	.50	.15	.04
Recession	.20	-.12	.00

7. What is the expected return for Stock K? For Stock M?

8. What is the variance for Stock K? For Stock M?

9. What is the standard deviation for Stock K? For Stock M?

10. An individual plans to invest $5,000: $3,000 in Stock K and $2,000 in Stock M. What are the portfolio weights for this portfolio?

11. Using the portfolio weights computed in Problem 10, what is the expected return for the portfolio?

12. Given the weights from Problem 10, compute the variance and standard deviation of the portfolio.

13. An individual plans to invest in Stock A and/or Stock B. The expected returns are 9% and 10% for A and B, respectively. The betas are 0.95 and 1.25 for Stocks A and B, respectively. Find the expected return and beta for the portfolio if she invests 75% of her funds in Stock A.

14. Suppose that the investor in Problem 13 wants to construct a portfolio with expected return equal to 9.5%. What are the portfolio weights for this portfolio? What is the beta for this portfolio?

15. Suppose the investor described in Problem 13 forms a portfolio consisting of three assets: 10% invested in Stock A, 30% invested in Stock B and 60% invested in a risk-free asset with a return of 6%. What is the expected return for this portfolio? What is the beta?

16. Use the following information to compute the reward-to-risk ratio for Stocks A, B and C:

	Expected return	Beta
Stock A	10.5%	0.90
Stock B	13.0%	1.15
Stock C	14.5%	1.20
Risk-free	6.0%	0.00

For Problems 17-21, assume the risk-free return is 6% and the expected return for the market is 14%.

17. Write the equation for the CAPM. What is the intercept of the CAPM? What is the slope? What is the market risk premium?

18. Speiss Corporation has a beta of 2. What is its expected return?

19. Suppose an individual invests $4,000 in a portfolio as follows: $2,800 invested in Speiss common stock and $1,200 invested in the risk-free asset. What are the portfolio weights? What is the expected return for the portfolio? What is the beta for the portfolio?

20. What are the portfolio weights for a portfolio comprised of Speiss common stock and the risk-free asset if the portfolio beta equals 1.5. What is the expected return for this portfolio?

21. Dorigan Corporation has a beta of 1.45 and an expected return of 15%. Given the CAPM equation of Problem 17, is Dorigan common stock correctly priced?

22. Assume that the three stocks listed below plot on the SML. What is the equation for the SML? Fill in the missing numbers in the table.

Security	$E(R_i)$	$Var(R_i)$	β_i
1	.07	.0225	?
2	.14	.0400	.8
3	.10	.1225	?
4	.07	.0000	?

Use the information in the table below to solve problems 23-25.

State of economy	Probability of state	Rate of return if state occurs	
		X	M
1	.20	.03	.09
2	.20	.17	.16
3	.30	.28	.10
4	.20	.05	.02
5	.10	-.04	.16

23. Calculate the expected return for asset X and for asset M.

24. What is the standard deviation for asset X? For asset M?

25. Assume Asset M is the market portfolio, and Asset X is a capital budgeting project under consideration. If Asset X is to be financed with equity and β_X is equal to 1.25, what is the required return for Asset X, according to the CAPM? (The risk-free rate is 6%.)

CHAPTER 14

COST OF CAPITAL

CONCEPTS FOR REVIEW

Previously we discussed the use of the CAPM as a method for measuring the cost of equity. The current chapter extends the discussion to the measurement of the costs of preferred equity and debt.

CHAPTER HIGHLIGHTS

The appropriate discount rate for evaluating a capital budgeting project depends on project risk. In this chapter we establish the relationship between the risk of a capital budgeting project, the relevant discount rate for the project, and for the firm as a whole; the latter is the **weighted average cost of capital**.

I. THE COST OF CAPITAL: SOME PRELIMINARIES (p. 403)

Required Return versus the Cost of Capital (p. 403) The security market line (SML) and the capital asset pricing model (CAPM) developed previously describe the relationship between systematic risk and expected return in the financial markets. This relationship allows us to identify the relevant opportunity cost for investment in a capital budgeting project. For a specified ß, the CAPM indicates the expected return available in the financial markets. A capital budgeting project under consideration by management must provide an expected rate of return greater than that available in the financial markets for investments with the same ß; otherwise, stockholders do not benefit from the project and would prefer an investment in the financial markets.

Financial Policy and the Cost of Capital (p. 403) The expected return available in the financial markets is the stockholders' *opportunity cost* and is the relevant cost of capital for the firm considering a capital budgeting project. Since the cost of capital specifies the minimum acceptable rate of return for a capital budgeting project, it is also referred to as the *required return*. A key point is that the use of investors' opportunity cost as the cost of capital implies that it is dependent on how the firm *invests* funds, rather than how it *obtains* funds.

II. THE COST OF EQUITY (p. 404)

Two alternative approaches to computing the cost of equity capital are developed in this section: the dividend growth model approach and the security market line approach.

The Dividend Growth Model Approach (p. 404) We solve the dividend growth model for R_E, the required return on equity:

$$R_E = D_1/P_0 + g$$

where P_0 is the current price of the firm's stock, D_1 is next year's project dividend, and g is the expected growth rate of dividends. Of the required data, only g is not directly observable. The deficiencies of this approach are: (1) it assumes constant growth in dividends; (2) the value of g must be estimated, and forecasting errors impact the value of R_E; and, (3) it does not explicitly consider risk.

The SML Approach (p. 406) The expected or required return for a share of stock is indicated by the security market line (SML), and can be determined as follows:

$$E(R_i) = R_f + ß_i \times [E(R_M) - R_f]$$

where $E(R_i)$ and $ß_i$ are the expected return and beta, respectively, for the ith asset. Assuming the required return (R_E) is the same as the expected return $[E(R_i)]$, the above equation can be written:

$$R_E = R_f + ß_E \times [R_M - R_f]$$

The advantages of this approach to computing the cost of equity capital are: (1) it explicitly adjusts for risk; and, (2) it is applicable to any firm for which the value of ß can be determined. However, this approach requires that both ß and the market risk premium $[R_M - R_f]$ be determined.

III. THE COSTS OF DEBT AND PREFERRED STOCK (p. 408)

The Cost of Debt (p. 408) The cost of debt financing (R_D) is the interest rate that the firm must pay on new debt. If the company has other bond issues currently outstanding, the interest rate investors expect on the new bond issue can be determined by computing the yield to maturity for the company's currently outstanding bonds. If the firm does not have bonds currently outstanding, it is still possible to determine the cost of new debt financing by observing the yield in the financial markets for bonds with risk similar to that of the bonds the firm would issue.

The Cost of Preferred Stock (p. 409) The cost of preferred stock financing (R_P) can also be observed in the financial markets. A firm which expects to issue preferred stock would compute the yield for either its own currently outstanding preferred stock issue or for preferred stock issued by other firms with ratings similar to that to be issued. Since the dividend paid on preferred stock is a perpetuity, the dividend yield can be computed directly using procedures described previously:

$$R_P = D/P_0$$

where D is the constant annual dividend payment and P_0 is the current price of the preferred stock.

IV. THE WEIGHTED AVERAGE COST OF CAPITAL (p. 409)

The Capital Structure Weights (p. 410) For a firm that uses both debt and equity financing, the average cost of capital is the total amount the firm expects to pay to stockholders and bondholders per dollar of financing obtained.

Taxes and the Weighted Average Cost of Capital (p. 410) Interest is a tax-deductible expense, while dividends paid to stockholders are not. So the cost of capital calculation must be adjusted to reflect this difference in tax treatment. The after-tax cost of debt is $[R_D \times (1 - T_C)]$, and the WACC is equal to:

$$WACC = (E/V) \times R_E + (D/V) \times [R_D \times (1 - T_C)]$$

where E and D represent the market values of equity and debt, respectively; V equals the market value of the firm ($V = E + D$), and E/V and D/V are the capital structure of debt and equity, respectively.

Learning Tip: The WACC is the return the firm must earn on its investments in order to be able to compensate the debt-holders and equity-holders who provide the financial to the firm. Therefore, it is the required return on the firm's investments, and is the appropriate discount rate for the present value analysis of a capital-budgeting project which has the same risk as the rest of the firm's operations.

Calculating the WACC for Eastman Chemical (p. 412) This section contains an extended numerical example describing the calculation of the cost of capital for a real firm.

Solving the Warehouse Problem and Similar Capital Budgeting Problems (p. 413) The example illustrated in this section reiterates a key result of the cost of capital discussion: the appropriate required return for a given project depends on whether that project is more risky, less risky, or of equivalent risk as the firm.

Performance Evaluation: Another Use of the WACC (p. 415) The cost of capital is a benchmark or minimum standard for the evaluation of investment results. The EVA approach, for example, translates cost of capital into financing cash flows, and compares the cash flow from assets to the cash outflows to financing.

V. DIVISIONAL AND PROJECT COSTS OF CAPITAL (p. 416)

When the risk of a proposed investment is different from the firm's risk, we determine the expected return on financial market investments of the same risk as the proposed investment and use it to discount the project's cash flows. Comparable conclusions apply to firms which have divisions engaged in different businesses with significantly different risk levels. In this case, the relevant cost of capital for each division depends on the risk of the division. The overall WACC for this firm would be too low for the evaluation of a project in a high-risk division and too high for a project in a low-risk division.

The SML and the WACC (p. 416) Key insight: the WACC is appropriate only for projects of equivalent risk as the firm; riskier (less risky) projects should be evaluated against higher (lower) capital costs.

Divisional Cost of Capital (p. 416) As noted above, the WACC for a multidivisional firm equals the average of divisional costs of capital. Unfortunately, the appropriate divisional cost of capital may be difficult to obtain, since the securities of individual divisions are not traded in the financial markets. The next two sections describe approaches to handle this situation.

The Pure Play Approach (p. 417) Since we cannot observe the prices (and, therefore, the required returns) on the securities of the division being analyzed, we attempt to find a free-standing firm with publicly traded securities to use as a 'proxy'. Of course, the difficulty is in finding a firm that is not only in the same line of business, but also has the same (or similar) capital structure.

The Subjective Approach (p. 418) A cruder (albeit simpler) approach is to group projects into risk classes and apply a single cost of capital (sometimes called a 'hurdle rate' in this context) to all projects in a given risk class. This approach not as desirable as obtaining a required return for each project, but more desirable than applying a single WACC to all projects regardless of risk.

VI. FLOTATION COSTS AND THE WEIGHTED AVERAGE COST OF CAPITAL (p. 420)

The Basic Approach (p. 420) If a company is considering a capital budgeting project which would require that new securities be issued to obtain the required financing, the flotation costs are incremental costs associated with the project and must be considered in the NPV analysis. Doing so requires the following. Assume the project is approximately as risky as the firm. First compute the weighted average flotation cost (f_A) as follows:

$$f_A = E/V \times f_E + D/V \times f_D$$

where f_E and f_D are the flotation costs for equity and debt, respectively.

Flotation Costs and NPV (p. 422) If we include flotation costs, the total amount of funds needed equals the project cost plus the flotation costs. This "total cost" figure is

$$\text{Project cost}/(1 - f_A).$$

The NPV of the project is then computed in the standard manner, except that the initial outlay is the total cost figure computed above.

KEY TERMS AND CONCEPTS

Cost of debt - the return that lenders require on the firm's debt. (p. 408)
Cost of equity - the return that equity investors require on their investment in the firm. (p. 404)
Pure play approach - use of a WACC unique to a particular project, based on similar firms. (p. 417)
Weighted average cost of capital (WACC) - weighted average of the after-tax costs of debt and equity, based on market values of debt and equity. (p. 411)

CONCEPT TEST

1. For a given ß, the CAPM specifies the _____ in the financial markets. Since the cost of capital specifies the minimum acceptable return for a capital project, it is also called the _____ . The overall cost of capital is the _____ . (p. 406)

2. The dividend growth model specifies that share price (P_0) is given by the following: $P_0 =$ _____ . $R_E =$ _____ . Only _____ is not directly observable. Deficiencies of this approach to computing the cost of equity capital are: (1) it is based on an assumption of _____; (2) the value of _____ must be estimated; and, (3) the model does not explicitly consider _____ . (p. 404)

3. The expected or required return for a share of stock is indicated by the security market line (SML). $E(R_i) =$ _____ . To compute the cost of equity using the CAPM, we assume the required return (R_E) equals the expected return [$E(R_i)$], so $R_E =$ _____ . The advantages of the SML approach to computing the cost of equity capital are: (1) it explicitly adjusts for _____; and, (2) it is applicable to any firm for which the value of _____ can be determined. (p. 407)

4. The interest rate investors expect on a new bond issue can be determined by computing the _____ for the company's _____ . Alternatively, it is possible to determine the cost of new debt financing by computing the _____ for bonds with _____ similar to that of the bonds to be issued. (p. 408)

5. A firm which issues preferred stock computes the yield for either _____ or for _____ . Since the dividend on preferred stock is a _____ , the dividend yield equals _____ . (p. 409)

6. The firm's overall measure of the cost of capital is the _____ . The dollar cost of debt is _____ . The dollar cost of equity is _____ . The overall firm average cost of capital is the cost of equity plus the cost of debt, divided by _____ . (p. 410)

7. Interest (is/is not) a tax-deductible expense, and dividends paid to stockholders (are/are not). The payment of interest reduces the firm's taxes by _____ . The after-tax cost of debt in dollars equals _____ . The after-tax cost of debt in percentage terms is _____ . WACC = _____ . (p. 411)

8. The calculation of the costs of debt and equity assumes the risk of a proposed capital-budgeting project is the same as the _____ . The appropriate discount rate to use in computing project NPV depends on the _____ . (p. 416)

9. When the risk of a proposed investment is different from overall firm risk, we determine the expected return on financial market investments of the same _____ as the proposed investment and use that rate to discount project cash flows. A new investment's return must be at least as great as that for other investments of _____ . (p. 417)

10. If a company is considering a capital budgeting project which would require that new securities be issued, the flotation costs (are/are not) incremental costs associated with the project and (are/are not) considered in the present value analysis. For a firm with debt and equity financing, the weighted-average flotation cost equals: $f_A =$ _____ . (p. 420)

ANSWERS TO CONCEPT TEST

1. expected rate of return; required rate of return; WACC

2. $D_1/(R_E-g)$; $D_1/P_0 + g$; g, the dividend growth rate; constant growth in dividends; g; risk

3. $R_f + \beta_i \times [R_M - R_f]$; $R_f + \beta_E \times [R_M - R_f]$; risk; β

4. yield to maturity; outstanding bonds; yield to maturity; risk level

5. its own outstanding preferred stock; preferred stock of similar firms; perpetuity; D/P_0

6. WACC; $D \times R_D$; $E \times R_E$; total value of the firm's capital

7. is; are not; $D \times R_D \times T_C$; $D \times R_D \times (1 - T_C)$; $R_D \times (1 - T_C)$; $E/V \times R_E + D/V \times R_D \times (1 - T_C)$

8. risk of the firm; risk of the project

9. risk; similar risk

10. are; are; $E/V \times f_E + D/V \times f_D$

PROBLEMS

1. Suppose today is January 1, 1997; on January 1, 1987, MAM Industries issued a 30-year bond with a 9% coupon and a $1,000 face value, payable on January 1, 2017. The bond now sells for $915. Use this bond to determine the firm's after-tax cost of debt. (Assume a 34% tax rate.)

2. Suppose MAM Industries (see Problem 1) also issued a 30-year bond five years ago; it has a $1,000 face value and a 10% coupon. If the bond currently sells for $1,000, what is the after-tax cost of debt capital, as indicated by the market value of this outstanding bond?

3. Suppose five years from now the MAM bond described in the Problem 2 has a market price of $1,100. What is the after-tax cost of debt capital at that time?

4. MAM Industries just declared a dividend of $3.50 per share of common stock. The current stock price is $25 per share, and the dividend is expected to increase at a rate of 4% per year for the foreseeable future. Use the dividend growth model approach to compute the cost of equity capital.

5. Suppose the market risk premium is 8.5%, the risk-free rate is 7.0%, and MAM Industries has ß equal to 1.35. Use the SML to compute the firm's cost of equity capital.

6. Assume the debt-equity ratio for MAM is .50. Use the data of Problems 1 through 5 to compute the WACC for MAM Industries.

7.   Suppose MAM Industries is considering an expansion of its facilities; this expansion requires that MAM obtain $690,000. Flotation costs for debt and equity are 6 percent and 9 percent, respectively. If flotation costs are considered, what is the true cost of the expansion?

8.   MAM Industries has a preferred stock issue outstanding which pays an annual dividend of $3.25 per share and currently has a market price of $25 per share. Compute the cost of preferred stock.

9.   Suppose MAM's capital structure is 30% debt, 10% preferred stock and 60% equity. Assume all other data as presented in Problems 1 through 8; compute the WACC.

10.   As of November, 1997, Illinois Power had several outstanding issues of preferred stock listed on the NYSE. On November 19, 1997, one issue of Illinois Power preferred was priced at $39-5/8 and paid an annual dividend of $4. On this date, two other issues of Illinois Power preferred had prices of $21-1/4 and $39-7/8, respectively, and paid annual dividends of $2.13 and $4.12, respectively. What is Illinois Power's cost of preferred stock financing on November 19?

Use the following information for Problems 11-14:

Margo Corporation is a major producer of lawn care products. Its stock currently sells for $80 per share; there are 10.5 million shares outstanding. Margo also has debt outstanding with a book value of $400 million. Margo bonds currently yield 10% and trade at 90% of face value. The risk-free rate is 8%, the market risk premium is 9%, and Margo has ß equal to 2. The corporate tax rate is 34%.

11. Margo is considering expansion of its facilities. Use the SML to determine the cost of equity.

12. Compute the weighted average cost of capital for Margo.

13. The project under consideration by Margo requires an outlay of $1,000,000 and will produce incremental after-tax cash inflows of $350,000 annually for five years. Compute the NPV.

14. Flotation costs are 5% of the amount of common stock issued and 2% of the amount of debt issued. Using the data from the previous problems, compute the weighted average flotation cost for Margo. Also, compute the NPV of the investment when flotation costs are taken into account.

RAISING CAPITAL

CONCEPTS FOR REVIEW

Previously we examined the features and the risk/return characteristics of debt and equity. These attributes should be kept in mind as you study the process by which securities are issued to the public.

CHAPTER HIGHLIGHTS

The sale of securities to the investing public is an essential source of long-term financing. This chapter describes the means by which firms issue new debt and equity, as well as the roles played by investment bankers and venture capital firms in the financing process.

I. THE FINANCING LIFE CYCLE OF A FIRM: EARLY-STAGE FINANCING AND VENTURE CAPITAL (p. 431)

Start-up companies often find it difficult to raise the funds necessary to get the firm off the ground. In this section we describe the role of *venture capital* firms and the venture capital market in providing financing for new firms.

Venture Capital (p. 432) "Venture capital" is defined as financing for new, high-risk enterprises. Funds are obtained from institutional investors such as pension funds, as well as from individuals. Some venture capitalists provide **first-stage financing**, which allows the new firm's founders to get a prototype product built. Venture capitalists also provide **second-stage financing** to begin manufacturing and selling the product. Finally, suppliers of venture capital also are often actively involved in the operations of the firm, since they typically have a substantial amount of business experience, where the founders may not. It is not surprising, therefore, that venture capitalists often obtain a substantial ownership share in the new firm in return for their services.

Some Venture Capital Realities (p. 432) Suppliers of venture capital must sift through numerous proposals and select those which appear to have the greatest chance of success. Investment opportunities are often discovered via the venture capitalist's network of contacts with inventors, lawyers, accountants, and other venture capital suppliers.

Choosing a Venture Capitalist (p. 433) The following are some relevant facts managers of firms seeking venture capital should consider.

1. Financial strength - adequate financial reserves should additional financing be needed.
2. Management style - How involved will the venture capitalist be in the day-to-day operations of the business?
3. References - How successful has the venture capitalist been in previous business deals?
4. Contacts - Does the venture capitalist know of others (e.g., suppliers, potential customers) that could help ensure the success of the new firm?
5. Exit strategy - How and under what circumstances will the venture capitalist cash out of the business?

126

II. SELLING SECURITIES TO THE PUBLIC: THE BASIC PROCEDURE (p. 434)

The Securities and Exchange Commission (SEC) is responsible for administering the Securities Act of 1933, which governs new interstate issues of securities, and the Securities Exchange Act of 1934, which governs securities already outstanding.

Once the board of directors approves a new issue, the firm must prepare and file with the SEC a **registration statement** - a detailed financial disclosure. Under **Regulation A**, issues of less than $1.5 million require only an abbreviated statement; this is the 'small-issues' exemption. Debt securities maturing in less than 9 months are also exempt from registration.

The SEC studies the registration statement during a twenty-day waiting period, during which the firm may provide potential investors with a **preliminary prospectus**, which contains much of the information in the registration statement. The issue is advertised in the financial press during and after the waiting period. The advertisements are placed by **underwriters** or **investment bankers**, who purchase the securities from the issuing firm and then resell them to the investing public. The ads are called *tombstones* and are comprised largely of the names of the investment banking firms which are underwriting the issue.

The registration becomes effective in twenty days, unless the SEC issues a 'letter of comment' specifying changes in the registration statement. After the changes are made, another twenty-day waiting period begins. Securities may not be sold during the waiting period. When the registration becomes effective, the security's price is determined and the sale to the public commences. A final prospectus must accompany the delivery of securities or the confirmation of sale, whichever comes first.

III. ALTERNATIVE ISSUE METHODS (p. 436)

An issue sold to fewer than 35 investors is a **private issue** and SEC registration is not required. A public offering of a new issue may be a **general cash offer** or a **rights offering**. Most offerings in this country are cash offers. A rights offering is an offer to sell common stock to the firm's existing stockholders. Underwriters are generally employed for the former, but not the latter.

A company's first public offering of equity securities is an **initial public offering (IPO)** or **unseasoned new issue** - an offering by a company that has previously issued securities.

IV. UNDERWRITERS (p. 437)

In a cash offer underwriters formulate the method used to issue the securities, price the securities, and sell the securities to the public. The underwriter normally buys the securities from the firm and offers them to the public at a higher price, the difference being the **spread** or **discount**. For large issues, the risk associated with selling the securities to the public is shared by forming a **syndicate**.

<u>Choosing an Underwriter</u> (p. 437) The issuer selects an investment banker via either a **competitive offer** or a **negotiated offer**. In the former, the issuing firm selects the underwriter who submitted the highest bid for the securities. A negotiated offer involves negotiations between the issuer and one underwriter.

Types of Underwriting (p. 438) If the underwriter purchases the entire issue, then the issuing firm receives a fixed price for the securities and all the risk associated with the sale is transferred to the underwriter. This is a *firm-commitment* **underwriting**.

In a **best-efforts offering**, the underwriter simply acts as an agent and receives a commission for each share sold. The investment bank must make its 'best effort' to sell the shares at the agreed upon offering price, and the issuing firm bears the risk that the securities cannot be sold at that price.

The Aftermarket (p. 438) The time period immediately after the sale is called the **aftermarket**, during which the principal underwriter is allowed to buy shares to 'support' or stabilize the price.

The Green Shoe Provision (p. 438) Underwriting contracts often contain a **Green Shoe provision** allowing the syndicate to purchase additional shares at the offering price.

V. IPOs AND UNDERPRICING (p. 439)

New issues are typically "underpriced" (i.e., the market price quickly rises above the offering price) which is beneficial to new shareholders but detrimental to existing shareholders; existing shareholders are, in effect, selling a portion of the firm which they own at a price below its market value. The degree of underpricing varies considerably, but the tendency toward underpricing is greater for smaller issues.

Evidence on Underpricing (p. 441) Underpricing has been observed in varying degrees for nearly four decades. There are pronounced cycles in the amount of underpricing

Why does Underpricing Exist? (p. 442) Although there is currently no universally accepted reason for the persistence of underpricing, the evidence suggests that the following factors are associated with it:

1. Risk of the issuing firm - underpricing is more prevalent in smaller, speculative issues;
2. Demand for the issue - underpriced issues tend to be allocated by brokers to larger customers;
3. Insurance - underpricing may help to ensure that fewer customers will suffer losses after buying new issues, reducing the likelihood of lawsuits against the investment bankers.

VI. NEW EQUITY SALES AND THE VALUE OF THE FIRM (p. 445)

The announcement of a new issue is often regarded as a negative signal to securities markets participants because (1) superior information in the hands of management may result in the issuing of new shares at a time when the firm's stock is overvalued, and (2) firms needing new equity may have excess debt.

VII. THE COSTS OF ISSUING SECURITIES (p. 446)

Issuers incur *flotation costs* which include the spread, other direct expenses (such as legal fees), indirect costs (such as management time), abnormal returns (the decrease in value of existing shares), costs to existing shareholders of underpricing, and the Green Shoe option. Based on actual issuer experience, five conclusions about flotation costs can be drawn: (1) as a percentage of proceeds, flotation costs are smaller for larger issues; (2) flotation costs are higher for best-efforts underwriting; (3) costs of underpricing can be substantial, especially for smaller issues and best-efforts underwriting; (4) underpricing for best-efforts offers is much greater than for firm-commitment offers; and (5) flotation costs are higher for IPOs than for seasoned offerings.

VIII. RIGHTS (p. 448)

A firm's articles of incorporation may contain a **preemptive right**, which specifies that any new issue of common stock must be first offered to existing stockholders, and gives shareholders the opportunity to maintain their percentage ownership of the firm when new securities are sold. As noted above, a stock issue offered to existing shareholders is a **rights offering** or a **privileged subscription**. A shareholder receives one right for each share owned. A specified number of rights gives the shareholder the option to buy a new share at a fixed price, called the **subscription price**, during a specified time period, after which the rights expire. Shareholders can exercise their rights by purchasing the stock, or sell the rights.

The Mechanics of a Rights Offering (p. 449) The financial manager determines each of the following for a rights offering: (1) subscription price; (2) number of shares to be sold; (3) number of rights required to purchase a new share; and, (4) impact of the rights offering on the value of the existing common stock.

Number of Rights Needed to Purchase a Share (p. 450) The subscription price must be set below the market price in order for the rights offering to succeed. The number of new shares to be issued equals

Total funds to be raised/Subscription price.

The number of rights needed to buy one new share is equal to

Number of old shares/Number of new shares.

The Value of a Right (p. 451) The rights holder has the right to purchase new shares at the subscription price, which is below the current market price, so the value of a right equals the value of a share prior to the offering less the value of a share subsequent to the offering.

Ex Rights (p. 452) The firm establishes a **holder-of-record date**; an investor who is a 'holder-of-record' on that date receives one right for each share owned. The **ex-rights date** is four business days prior to the holder-of-record date.

The Underwriting Arrangements (p. 453) A rights offering often involves **standby underwriting** - the underwriter is paid a **standby fee** and agrees to purchase any unsubscribed shares. Shareholders are usually given an **oversubscription privilege**, i.e., an option to buy additional shares at the subscription price, if available.

Rights Offerings: The Case of Time-Warner (p. 454) This section describes several recent rights offerings in the United States and abroad.

Effects on Shareholders (p. 454) As long as shareholders either exercise or sell their rights, they are not harmed by the rights offering and the subsequent decline in stock price. However, if the investor allows her rights to expire, she suffers a loss equal to the decline in the value of the stock.

The Rights Offerings Puzzle (p. 455) Pure rights offerings (i.e., those without standby underwriting) are less expensive for the issuing firm than other forms of equity offerings; in addition, pure rights offerings permit shareholders to maintain their proportionate ownership of the firm. Despite these advantages of rights offerings, underwritten cash offerings are the dominant form of new equity issues.

IX. DILUTION (p. 456)

Dilution of Proportionate Ownership (p. 456) **Dilution** is a decrease in the value of the common stockholders' position due to the issue of new common stock. **Dilution of proportionate ownership** occurs when the shareholder does not purchase any of the new shares, his proportional share of ownership will decrease.

Dilution of Value: Book versus Market Values (p. 457) **Dilution of value** occurs when new shares are sold below book value and the firm's ROE falls. This is sometimes called **accounting dilution. Market value dilution** is a decrease in the market value per share of the firm's stock following the issue of new shares of common stock and occurs if the funds are used to invest in negative NPV projects.

X. ISSUING LONG-TERM DEBT (p. 459)

A public issue of bonds requires that the issuing firm register the issue with the SEC in a process similar to that required for a common stock issue. However, more than 50% of all debt is **directly placed**, either in the form of **term loans** or **private placements**. A term loan is a direct business loan which is amortized over a period of one to five years. The major lenders are commercial banks and insurance companies. A private placement is similar to a term loan except that the maturity is generally longer.

XI. SHELF REGISTRATION (p. 460)

In 1983, the SEC permanently adopted **Rule 415**, which permits a corporation to register an offering it expects to sell within the next two years. This **shelf registration** procedure permits the corporation to sell a portion of the issue at any time during the two-year period. To qualify for shelf registration, a corporation must be rated investment grade, must not have defaulted on its debt or violated the Securities Act in the past three years, and must have equity market value in excess of $150 million.

KEY TERMS AND CONCEPTS

Best efforts underwriting - underwriter sells as much of the issue as possible, but can return any unsold shares to the issuer without financial responsibility. (p.438)
Dilution - loss to existing shareholders of ownership, market value, book value, or EPS. (p. 456)
Ex-rights date - beginning of the period when stock is sold without a recently declared right, normally two trading days before the holder-of-record date. (p. 452)
Firm commitment underwriting - underwriter buys the entire issue, assuming full financial responsibility for any unsold shares. (p. 438)
General cash offer - issue of securities offered for sale to the general public on a cash basis. (p. 436)
Green Shoe provision - contract provision giving the underwriter the option to purchase additional shares at the offering price. (p. 438)
Holder-of-record date - date on which existing shareholders on company records are designated as the recipients of stock rights. (p. 452)
Initial public offering (IPO) - a company's first public equity issue. (p. 436)

Oversubscription privilege - allows shareholder to purchase unsubscribed shares in a rights offering at the subscription price. (p. 453)

Private placements - loans provided directly by a limited number of investors. (p. 459)

Prospectus - legal document describing details of the issuer and offering to potential investors. (p. 434)

Red herring - preliminary prospectus distributed to prospective investors in a new issue. (p. 434)

Registration statement - SEC filing that discloses all material information concerning the firm making a public offering. (p. 459)

Regulation A - regulation exempting small public issues from most registration requirements. (p. 434)

Rights offer - public issue of securities where securities are first offered to existing shareholders. (p. 436)

Seasoned equity offering - equity issue by a firm that has previously sold securities publicly. (p. 436)

Shelf registration - Rule 415 allowing registration of all issues expected to sell within two years. (p. 460)

Spread - difference between the underwriter's buying price and the offering price. (p. 437)

Standby fee - amount paid to underwriter participating in standby underwriting agreement. (p. 453)

Standby underwriting - agreement where underwriter agrees to purchase the unsubscribed portion of the issue. (p. 453)

Syndicate - a group of underwriters formed to reduce risk and facilitate sale of issue. (p. 437)

Term loan - direct business loans amortized over one to five years. (p. 459)

Tombstone - an advertisement announcing a public offering. (p. 434)

Underwriters - investment firms that act as intermediaries between the issuer and the public. (p. 437)

Venture capital - financing for new, often high-risk ventures. (p. 432)

CONCEPT TEST

1. _____ is defined as financing for new, high-risk enterprises. Funds are obtained from institutional investors such as pension funds, as well as from individuals. Some venture capitalists provide _____, which allows the new firm's founders to get a prototype product built. Venture capitalists also provide _____ to begin manufacturing and selling the product. Venture capitalists often obtain a substantial _____ in the new firm in return for their services. (p. 432)

2. When a firm sells a new issue of securities, the firm must file a _____ statement with the _____ . The SEC studies the registration statement during a 20 day period called the _____ . The securities buyer must receive a _____, which contains much of the information in the registration statement. (p. 434)

3. A public offering of a new issue may be either a _____ offer or a _____ offer. In this country, most securities are sold through a _____ offer, which is an offer to sell securities to the general public. A _____ offering is an offer to sell common stock to the firm's existing stockholders. A company's first public offering of equity securities is called a(n) _____ offering or _____ . A _____ new issue is a new issue by a company that has previously issued securities. (p. 436)

4. For a cash offer, the underwriter, or _____, normally buys the securities from the firm and offers them to the public at a higher price. The difference between the underwriter's buying price and the selling price to the public is the _____ or _____.
If the underwriter purchases the entire issue, then the issuing firm receives a fixed price for the securities, and the risk associated with the sale of the securities is transferred to the _____. This procedure is called _____ underwriting. For a _____ offering, the underwriter acts as an agent and receives a commission. The _____ bears the risk that securities cannot be sold at the specified price. (p. 437)

5. One of the most difficult tasks for an investment banker is the pricing of an IPO. If the price is set too low, the firm's existing shareholders incur a(n) _____ loss; if set too high, the issue _____. New issues are typically _____, which is beneficial to new shareholders, but detrimental to existing shareholders. (p. 439)

6. A firm's _____ may contain a preemptive right, which specifies that any new issue of common stock must be first offered to existing stockholders. That issue is a _____ offering or _____ subscription. A specified number of rights gives the shareholder the option to buy a new share at the _____ price during a specified period, after which rights _____. (p. 448)

7. In order for a rights offering to succeed, the subscription price must be set below the _____. The number of new shares to be issued equals _____.
The value of a right equals _____ minus the _____. (p. 450)

8. For a rights offering, an investor who is a 'holder-of-record' on the record date receives _____ right(s) for each share owned. The _____ date is four business days prior to the holder-of-record date. An investor must purchase the stock prior to the _____ date in order to be considered the owner of the stock on the holder-of-record date. At the close of trading on the fifth day prior to the holder-of-record date, the stock goes _____ so that any subsequent purchaser does not receive the right. (p. 451)

9. As long as shareholders either _____ or _____ their rights, they are not harmed by the rights offering and the subsequent decline in stock price. If the investor allows a right to expire, she suffers a loss equal to _____. (p. 454)

10. Dilution of voting rights (does/does not) occur if the new issue is a rights offering. If the new issue is a public offering, and if an existing stockholder does not purchase any of the new shares, dilution of voting rights (does/does not) occur. (p. 455)

11. Accounting dilution is reduction in both _____ per share and _____. Whether a new stock issue results in accounting dilution depends on the _____ and the firm's _____. Market value dilution is a decrease in the _____ of the firm's stock following the issue of new shares of common stock. Market value dilution (does/does not) occur if the funds obtained are used to finance a negative-NPV project. (p. 458)

12. A public issue of bonds requires that the issuer file a _____ statement with the SEC. More than 50% of all debt is directly placed, either as _____ loans or _____ placements. A _____ loan is a direct business loan that is normally amortized over a period of one to five years. A _____ placement is similar to a term loan except that the _____ . (p. 459)

13. A corporation may register with the SEC an offering it expects to sell within the next two years. This _____ procedure permits the firm to sell a portion of the issue any time during the two-year period. (p. 460)

ANSWERS TO CONCEPT TEST

1. Venture capital; first-stage financing; second-stage financing; ownership share
2. registration; Securities and Exchange Commission; waiting period; prospectus
3. cash; rights; cash; rights; initial public; unseasoned new issue; seasoned
4. investment bank; spread; discount; underwriter; firm-commitment; best-efforts; issuing firm
5. opportunity; fails to sell; underpriced
6. articles of incorporation; rights; privileged; subscription; expire
7. market price; funds to be raised/subscription price; price per share before the rights offering, price per share after the rights are exercised
8. one; ex-rights; ex-rights; ex-rights
9. exercise; sell; the value of a right
10. does not; does
11. book value; EPS; selling price; return on equity; market value; does
12. registration; term; private; term; private; maturity is longer
13. shelf registration

PROBLEMS

1. Yul Company has just floated an IPO. Under a firm-commitment underwriting agreement, Yul received $10 for each of the 1 million shares sold. The initial offering price was $11 per share, and the price rose to $14 in the first few minutes of trading. Yul paid $60,000 in direct legal and other costs; indirect costs were $40,000. What was the flotation cost as a percentage of funds raised?

2. A company requires $15 million in equity financing. Direct costs of a cash offering (including the spread, but excluding underpricing) equal 12% of the financing obtained. How large must the issue be to provide the firm with the required financing? How much are the dollar flotation costs for this offering?

3. Firms A and B have announced IPOs; each firm's stock will be sold for $10 per share. One of these issues is undervalued by $1, while the other is overvalued by $.50, but you are unable to determine which is undervalued and which is overvalued. You plan to buy 100 shares of each. If an issue is rationed, you will be able to purchase only half of your order. If you are able to buy 100 shares of each firm's stock, what is your profit? What profit do you actually expect?

Use the following information to solve Problems 4-7:

Ebbets Manufacturing Co. has been experiencing financial difficulties since its major customer moved to Chavez Ravine. However, Ebbets is considering expansion into a new line of business. The expansion requires $4,500,000 of financing, which will be obtained through a cash offering of common stock. Ebbets currently has 5,000,000 shares of common stock outstanding and no debt. The firm's book value is $60,000,000 and net income is currently $7,500,000. Ebbets common stock currently sells for $9.

4. Calculate each of the following for Ebbets, without the expansion: book value per share (BPS), earnings per share (EPS), price earnings (P/E) ratio, return on equity (ROE), market-to-book ratio.

5. Assume the firm's P/E ratio and ROE remain constant. Calculate each of the following for Ebbets, after the expansion: book value per share, EPS, market price per share, market-to-book ratio.

6. What is the net present value of the expansion under consideration by Ebbets?

7. Suppose the NPV of the expansion is $1,000,000. What is the market value of the common stock after the expansion?

8. Emery Enterprises has announced a rights offering to obtain $10 million of equity financing for a new publishing project. The stock currently sells for $80 per share; there are 2 million shares outstanding. If Emery sets the subscription price at $20 per share, how many shares must be sold? How many rights are required in order to buy one share?

9. For the offering described in Problem 8, what is the ex-rights price? What is the value of a right?

10. Suppose an investor who owns 100 shares of Emery common stock intends to sell her rights, rather than purchase additional shares. Demonstrate that she is not harmed by the rights offering.

11. Suppose that the investor described in the previous problem decides to exercise, rather than sell, her rights. How does this course of action affect her total wealth?

12. Suppose the rights described in Problems 8 and 9 are trading for $10. How will this affect the investor who owns 100 shares of Emery common stock? What action would you recommend to an investor who does not own Emery common stock?

13. Suppose the rights described in Problems 8 and 9 are trading for $13. How will this affect the investor who owns 100 shares of Emery common stock? Now what action would you recommend to an investor who does not own Emery common stock?

CHAPTER 16

FINANCIAL LEVERAGE AND CAPITAL STRUCTURE POLICY

CONCEPTS FOR REVIEW

Previous chapters discussed **how** firms issue various securities to raise funds. In this chapter we address the more complicated question of **why** a given mix of equity and debt may be preferred to another.

CHAPTER HIGHLIGHTS

The appropriate objective for capital structure decisions is to maximize the equity value by minimizing the WACC. Unfortunately, exactly how this goal is to be achieved remains an unsettled issue in Finance. Many of the factors affecting this decision are well understood and are discussed in this chapter; however, the interplay among these factors is complex and less well understood. To comprehend the issues involved in the capital structure decision, it is essential to remember the key point: whether the way a firm chooses to finance its assets make any economic difference.

I. THE CAPITAL STRUCTURE QUESTION (p. 468)

The relevant issues for capital structure decisions are: First, should stockholders be concerned about maximizing the value of the entire firm, rather than maximizing the value of the firm's equity? And, second, what is the ratio of debt to equity that maximizes shareholder wealth?

Firm Value and Stock Value: An Example (p. 468) It can be shown that maximizing the value of the firm's equity is equivalent to maximizing firm value. Thus, financial managers should choose the capital structure which maximizes firm value. This debt-equity mix is the **optimal (or target)** capital structure.

Capital Structure and the Cost of Capital (p. 469) Previously, we established that firm value equals the present value of the firm's cash flows, discounted at the WACC. If capital structure decisions have an impact on the WACC, then these decisions affect the value of the firm. Thus, the capital structure which minimizes the WACC is the capital structure which maximizes the value of the firm.

II. THE EFFECT OF FINANCIAL LEVERAGE (p. 469)

Financial leverage is the extent to which a firm uses debt rather than equity financing. We investigate the relationship between financial leverage and the returns to the firm's stockholders.

The Basics of Financial Leverage (p. 470) All else equal, increasing debt increases the variability of returns to stockholders. Since leverage magnifies gains and losses, we conclude that leverage has a beneficial impact on stockholders when earnings are rising and a detrimental impact when earnings are falling. The reason for this result is the fixed interest cost of debt financing.

Corporate Borrowing and Homemade Leverage (p. 473) The preceding discussion seems to suggest that the firm's capital structure is necessarily important to its stockholders; this is incorrect. Shareholders can adjust the amount of leverage they incur by borrowing or lending on their own, thereby creating **homemade leverage**. Since an investor can duplicate any desired capital structure, she will be indifferent to the firm's capital structure decisions. Thus she will pay no more for the shares of a levered firm than an unlevered firm, and vice-versa.

III. CAPITAL STRUCTURE AND THE COST OF EQUITY CAPITAL (p. 475)

The conclusion of the previous section was initially derived by Modigliani and Miller (M&M) in 1958; hence, we refer to this result as **M&M Proposition I**. This result is based on assumptions that there are no taxes and that investors can borrow on their own account at the same rate the firm pays on its debt.

M&M Proposition I: The Pie Model (p. 475) The value of the firm (V) can be viewed as a pie, and the firm's capital structure is represented by the way in which the pie is sliced - into an equity portion and a debt portion. By Proposition I, the size of the pie is unaffected by the manner in which it is sliced; i.e., the total value of the firm's assets is unaffected by the manner in which financing is obtained. It is the assets of a firm that generate cash flow. The firm's capital structure is simply a way of packaging those cash flows and selling them in financial markets.

The Cost of Equity and Financial Leverage: M&M Proposition II (P. 475) **M&M Proposition II** establishes a positive relationship between leverage and the expected return on equity: the risk of a firm's equity increases as the degree of leverage increases. Algebraically,

$$R_E = R_A + (R_A - R_D) \times (D/E)$$

where R_E, R_A, and R_D reflect the returns on the firm's equity, assets, and debt, respectively. Note that the required return on equity is a linear function of the debt/equity ratio. Proposition I states that the value of the firm is not affected by changes in the debt/equity ratio, so it must also be true that the firm's overall cost of capital R_A does not change with changes in the firm's financial structure. Also, if R_A is greater than R_D, then R_E increases with the debt/equity ratio.

Business and Financial Risk (p. 478) The cost of equity consists of two components: the required return on the firm's assets (R_A), and the return determined by the firm's financial structure: $(R_A - R_D) \times D/E$. The required return on the firm's assets is based on the risk of the assets, or the **business risk** of the firm. Risk that arises due to the firm's financial decisions is called the **financial risk** of the firm.

IV. M&M PROPOSITIONS I & II WITH CORPORATE TAXES (p. 478)

The conclusions of the previous section are derived under a set of assumptions which are inconsistent with the behavior of most corporations, whose debt-equity ratios seem to vary with industry characteristics. These observations make it necessary to assess the validity of the M&M conclusions under more realistic assumptions. In this section we consider how *corporate taxes* affect the M&M propositions.

The Interest Tax Shield (p. 479) A key difference between debt and equity is that the interest on debt is tax-deductible, whereas dividends are not. This *tax subsidy* on interest increases the relative attractiveness of debt and is called the **interest tax shield**.

Taxes and M&M Proposition I (p. 479) If we assume that debt is perpetual, the interest tax shield will be generated every year forever. Thus, the value of the interest tax shield is computed as follows:

$$\text{Value of the interest tax shield} = (T_C \times R_D \times D)/R_D = T_C \times D$$

The value of a levered firm exceeds that of an unlevered firm by the interest tax shield; i.e.,

$$V_L = V_U + T_C \times D.$$

And the value of the unlevered firm, V_U, equals the PV of the future cash flows to its shareholders,

$$V_U = EBIT(1 - T_C)/R_U$$

where R_U is the **unlevered cost of capital** - the cost of capital the firm would have if it had no debt.

The formulas suggest that, in a world with corporate taxes, the firm has an incentive to increase its debt/equity ratio because a higher debt/equity ratio lowers taxes and increases the total value of the firm. In fact, the above results indicate that a firm should move as close as possible to an all-debt capital structure. This is unrealistic; firms do not choose all-debt capital structures. However, this conclusion is derived under the assumption that there are no bankruptcy costs, which are discussed subsequently.

Taxes, the WACC, and Proposition II (p.481) Previously we stated that M&M Proposition II (no taxes) states the following relationship between the debt/equity ratio and the cost of equity capital:

$$R_E = R_A + (R_A - R_D) \times (D/E)$$

M&M demonstrate that, in a world **with** corporate taxes, the following equation describes the relationship between the debt/equity ratio and the cost of equity capital:

$$R_E = R_U + (R_U - R_D) \times (D/E) \times (1 - T_C)$$

This result is known as **M&M Proposition II (with corporate taxes)**. It indicates a positive relationship between expected return on equity and the debt-equity ratio; it also implies that the firm's overall cost of capital decreases as the amount of debt increases, which leads to the conclusion that a capital structure of 100% debt is optimal. This is the same conclusion implied by Proposition I (with corporate taxes).

V. BANKRUPTCY COSTS (p. 484)

Most firms are not as highly levered as the above propositions might suggest. In part, this is because the theory of the previous section ignores the costs of bankruptcy, which increase with the firm's level of debt. In this section, we discuss the impact of bankruptcy costs on the M&M conclusions.

The obligation to pay principal and interest on debt puts pressure on the firm since failure to meet the obligation results in some form of financial distress; the ultimate financial distress is bankruptcy, in which case ownership of the firm's assets is transferred to the bondholders. Costs of financial distress offset the advantages of debt under certain circumstances.

Direct Bankruptcy Costs (p. 484) The *economic* interpretation of bankruptcy is the condition whereby the value of a firm's assets is equal to or less than the value of its debt. The *legal* interpretation of bankruptcy is the process whereby the firm's assets are turned over to the firm's bondholders. This process involves **direct bankruptcy costs**, which include attorneys' fees and administrative and accounting fees. These costs represent a disincentive to debt financing, which offset the debt-tax shield.

Indirect Bankruptcy Costs (p. 485) Bankruptcy often results in an impaired ability to conduct business. Customers question the ability of the firm to provide service subsequent to a purchase, and are less likely to buy from a firm in bankruptcy. Costs such as this are difficult to estimate; nonetheless, they are generally thought to be much greater than the direct costs cited above.

VI. OPTIMAL CAPITAL STRUCTURE (p. 486)

Financial distress costs are insignificant for a firm with little or no debt, so if an unlevered firm adds a small amount of debt to its capital structure, it derives the benefit of the tax shield on debt without incurring significant costs of financial distress. As a firm uses more and more debt, the tax savings are eventually offset by the increased likelihood that financial distress costs will be incurred. The point where these two factors exactly offset each other is where firm value is maximized.

The Static Theory of Capital Structure (p. 486) The **static theory of capital structure** states that a firm uses additional debt financial up to the point where the tax benefit derived from an additional dollar of debt exactly offsets the cost associated with an increased likelihood of financial distress. An optimal (or target) capital structure one for which the benefit of another dollar of debt is balanced by the increased likelihood of financial distress. The optimal capital structure is that which maximizes firm value; it is also that which is associated with the minimum WACC.

Optimal Capital Structure and the Cost of Capital (p. 487) The optimal capital structure is that which minimizes the firm's WACC. According to the static theory, this point is reached somewhere between the no-debt and total debt levels.

Optimal Capital Structure: A Recap (p. 488) The argument for the existence of an optimal capital structure rests on three cases. The no-tax, no-bankruptcy case indicates that the firm's capital structure is irrelevant to its cost of capital. In Case II we add corporate taxes and find that the optimal capital structure is that for which debt is maximized. Under Case III managers should continue to borrow until the benefit of debt (the interest tax shield) is exactly offset by the increased costs of financial distress.

Capital Structure: Some Managerial Recommendations (p. 488) The static theory of capital structure suggests the following. First, firms with higher tax rates should borrow more, as long as they don't have other tax shields (such as depreciation) with which to offset their tax liabilities. Second, firms with higher risk of distress (perhaps due to higher operating risks) should borrow less. Third, firms for which the cost of financial distress is higher should also borrow less.

VII.   THE PIE AGAIN (p. 490)

The Extended Pie Model (p. 490) We initially viewed the value of the firm as equal to the value of the stock plus the value of the debt. We should now recognize that the "pie" representing the firm is actually comprised of much more than just the debt and equity portions. The government takes a substantial slice in the form of taxes; in the event of bankruptcy, many other parties will take a slice. So, many different types of claims to the firm's cash flow may exist at any time. This is the **extended pie model**:

CF =   Payments to stockholders + Payments to bondholders + Payments to
        government + Payments to bankruptcy courts + Payments to others,

where CF represents firm cash flows. Thus, the key to M&M's theory is this: The value of the firm depends on the total firm cash flow. The capital structure cuts that cash flow up into slices without altering the total. But, stockholders and bondholders may not be the only ones who claim a slice.

Marketed Claims versus Nonmarketed Claims (p. 491) The extended pie model also suggests that all claims to the firm's cash flow can be divided into **marketed claims** (debt and equity) and **nonmarketed claims**. Marketed claims can be bought and sold in the financial markets while nonmarketed claims cannot. The essence of this model is that the firm value (which must equal the total value of all claims against it) is unaffected by capital structure changes, although capital structure changes may affect the *relative* values of the marketed and non-marketed claims. The optimal capital structure maximizes the value of marketed claims, or, equivalently, minimizes the value of nonmarketed claims.

VIII.   OBSERVED CAPITAL STRUCTURES (p. 492)

Although capital structure theory provides a starting point for analysis, real-world complexities make it difficult to identify the optimal capital structure for any given firm. For example, firms in similar industries tend to have similar capital structures, but capital structures appear to vary widely across industries. This suggests that capital structure is influenced by additional factors, such as the nature of a firm's assets and the volatility of its earnings.

IX.   A QUICK LOOK AT THE BANKRUPTCY PROCESS (p. 493)

The use of debt increases the possibility of financial distress, which includes the following situations:

1.   **Business failure** is the termination of a business, which results in a loss to the firm's creditors.
2.   **Legal bankruptcy** is a legal proceeding resulting in the liquidation or reorganization of the firm.
3.   **Technical insolvency** results from a firm's default on a legal obligation to pay a debt.
4.   **Accounting insolvency** - when the firm's liabilities exceed the value of its assets, and net worth is negative.

Liquidation and Reorganization (p. 493) Liquidation and reorganization are the two possible outcomes of a legal bankruptcy. **Liquidation** is the termination of the firm following a bankruptcy proceeding; the firm's assets are sold and the proceeds of the sale are distributed to claimants, including employees, consumers, governments, creditors and stockholders. **Reorganization** is a plan that allows the firm to continue to operate, but requires a restructuring of the firm's debts; the restructuring includes payments to creditors and stockholders, and often includes the issuance of new securities to replace existing ones.

Bankruptcy Liquidation (p. 494) Chapter 7 of the Federal Bankruptcy Reform Act of 1978 governs bankruptcy liquidations. Creditors' claims are generally ranked for payment in the order specified by the **absolute priority rule**.

Bankruptcy Reorganization (p. 494) Reorganization is a plan that allows the firm to continue to operate, but requires a restructuring of the firm's debts; the restructuring includes payments to creditors and stockholders, and often includes the issuance of new securities to replace existing securities. Bankruptcy reorganizations are governed by Chapter 11 of the abovementioned Act.

Financial Management and the Bankruptcy Process (p. 495) The right to go bankrupt is valuable because it freezes the actions of creditors and gives management time to evaluate various courses of action. Bankruptcy has also been used as a strategic tool to forestall lawsuits and restructure the firm.

KEY TERMS AND CONCEPTS

Absolute priority rule - rule establishing priority of claims in liquidation. (p. 494)

Bankruptcy - legal proceeding for liquidating or reorganizing a business. Also, the transfer of some or all of a firm's assets to its creditors. (p. 493)

Business risk - the equity risk that comes from the nature of the firm's operating activities. (p. 478)

Direct bankruptcy costs - costs explicitly related to bankruptcy, e.g., legal expenses. (p. 485)

Financial distress costs - direct and indirect costs associated with going bankrupt or experiencing financial distress. (p. 485)

Financial risk - equity risk that comes from the financial policy of the firm. (p. 478)

Homemade leverage - the use of personal borrowing to change the overall amount of financial leverage to which the individual is exposed. (p. 473)

Indirect bankruptcy costs - difficulties of running a business experiencing financial distress. (p. 485)

Interest tax shield - the tax saving attained by a firm from interest expense. (p. 479)

Liquidation - termination of the firm as a going concern. (p. 493)

M&M Proposition I - the value of the firm is independent of its capital structure. (p. 475)

M&M Proposition II - cost of equity capital is a positive linear function of its capital structure. (p. 476)

Reorganization - financial restructuring of a failing firm to continue operations (p. 493)

Static theory of capital structure - theory that a firm borrows up to the point where the tax benefit from an extra dollar in debt equals the cost of the increased probability of financial distress. (p. 486)

Unlevered cost of capital - the cost of capital of a firm that has no debt. (p. 481)

CONCEPT TEST

1. In making capital structure decisions, the firm considers whether the way it chooses to _____ its assets make any economic difference. Shareholders benefit from financial restructuring only if _____ . This occurs because any increase in firm value due to restructuring accrues to _____ . Consequently, maximizing the value of the shareholders' position is equivalent to maximizing _____ . (p. 468)

2. Firm value is the _____ of the firm's cash flows, discounted at the WACC. The capital structure which maximizes firm value also minimizes the _____ . Financial leverage is the extent to which a firm uses _____ financing. Leverage has a beneficial impact on stockholders when EBIT is (high/low) and a detrimental impact when EBIT is (high/low). Financial leverage _____ both the benefits and the losses to shareholders. Variability in the return to stockholders is (greater/less) for a firm that uses debt financial than for an all-equity firm. Variability in stockholder returns (increases/decreases) with increases in financial leverage. (p. 470)

3. The firm's capital structure (is/is not) important to the stockholders, who can adjust the amount of leverage in their position by _____ or _____ on their own, thereby creating _____ . A stockholder who prefers a capital structure with more leverage can duplicate the preferred structure by _____ an amount sufficient to create a personal debt/equity ratio equal to that of the desired structure. So under certain circumstances, the price of a firm's common stock (is/is not) dependent on the firm's capital structure. This is called _____ . It is based on these assumptions: _____ ; and, investors can borrow at the _____ . (p. 473)

4. According to the pie model, the value of the firm can be viewed as a pie, and the firm's capital structure is represented by _____. M&M Proposition I states that the size of the pie is not affected by the manner in which the pie is sliced; that is, the total value of the firm's assets is not affected by the manner in which _____. The firm's cash flow is generated by its _____; the firm's capital structure is a way of packaging those cash flows and selling them in financial markets. (p. 475)

5. M&M Proposition II addresses the relationship between the firm's debt/equity ratio and the firm's _____. It establishes a positive relationship between leverage and the _____. M&M Proposition II (no taxes) states: R_E = _____. The required return on equity is a linear function of the _____. As the debt/equity ratio increases, the cost of equity rises in a linear fashion, but the increased cost of equity is exactly offset by the _____. The overall cost of capital (does/does not) change as the value of the debt/equity ratio changes. Thus, firm value (is/is not) affected by changes in the capital structure. (p. 475)

6. A primary difference between debt and equity is that interest (is/is not) tax-deductible, whereas dividends (are/are not). The tax subsidy on interest (increases/decreases) the attractiveness of debt. The capital structure (does/does not) have an impact on the firm's cash flows. The interest expense on debt generates a tax saving equal to the _____ multiplied by the _____. This tax saving is the _____, and has a value of: _____ = _____. (p. 479)

7. The after-tax cash flow to the stockholders of an unlevered firm equals _____. If we assume that all cash flows are perpetual and constant, the value of an unlevered firm is: V_U = _____. M&M Proposition I (with corporate taxes) states that the value of a levered firm, V_L, equals the value of the _____ plus the value of the _____ i.e., V_L = _____ + _____. Thus, in a world with corporate taxes, the firm should (increase/decrease) its debt/equity ratio, which (increases/decreases) taxes and (increases/decreases) firm value. This indicates that a firm should move as close as possible to _____. This conclusion requires the assumption of no _____. (p. 480)

8. The ultimate financial distress is _____, in which ownership of the firm's assets is transferred to the _____. The legal bankruptcy process involves expenses called _____, which include legal and accounting fees. Bankruptcy often results in impaired ability to do business; the associated costs are _____. (p. 484)

9. The _____ theory of capital structure states that a firm uses additional debt financing to the point where the _____ benefit derived from additional debt exactly offsets the costs associated with the increased likelihood of _____. A(n) _____ capital structure occurs when the PV value of the tax saving from additional debt equals the increase in the PV of expected bankruptcy costs; at this point, firm is _____. (p. 486)

142

10. All claims to firm cash flows can be divided into two groups; the debt and equity are _____ claims and rest are _____ claims. The capital structure issue is really the question of whether the total value of the _____ claims can be increased by decreasing the size of the _____ claims. (p. 490)

11. _____ is the termination of a business resulting in a loss to the creditors. _____ is a legal proceeding which results in firm liquidation or reorganization. _____ results from default on a legal obligation to pay a debt. _____ is a condition in which the firm's liabilities exceed the firm's assets, so that net worth is negative. _____ is the termination of a firm following a bankruptcy proceeding. _____ is a plan that allows the firm to continue to operate. (p. 493)

ANSWERS TO CONCEPT TEST

1. finance; value of the firm increases; stockholders; value of the firm
2. PV; WACC; debt; high; low; magnifies; greater; increases
3. is not; borrowing; lending; homemade leverage; borrowing; lending; is not; M&M Proposition I (no taxes); no taxes; same rate the firm pays on its debt
4. the way in which the pie is sliced; financing is obtained; assets
5. cost of equity; required return on equity; $R_A + (R_A - R_D) \times (D/E)$; debt-to-equity ratio; increased use of cheaper debt; does not; is not
6. is; are not; increases; does; interest payment; corporate tax rate; interest tax shield; $(T_C \times R_D \times D)/R_D$; $(T_C \times D)$
7. EBIT $\times (1-T_C)$; [EBIT $\times (1-T_C)]/R_U$; unlevered firm; interest tax shield; $V_U + (T_C \times D)$; increase; decreases; increases; an all-debt capital structure; bankruptcy costs
8. bankruptcy; creditors; direct bankruptcy costs; indirect bankruptcy costs
9. static; tax; financial distress; optimal; maximized
10. marketed; nonmarketed; marketed; nonmarketed
11. Failure; Bankruptcy; Technical insolvency; Accounting insolvency; Liquidation; Reorganization

PROBLEMS

Use the information below to solve Problems 1 through 9:

Maxlever and Nolever are identical firms in all ways except that Maxlever employs debt in its capital structure and Nolever does not. Earnings before interest and taxes (EBIT) for each firm are expected to be $10,000. The value of the equity if Maxlever is $40,000, and the value of the equity in Nolever is $80,000. Maxlever has 1,000 shares outstanding and Nolever has 2,000 shares outstanding. Maxlever's bonds have a market value and a face value of $40,000. The interest rate is 10% and there are no taxes.

1. Compute EPS, ROE, and share price for Nolever and for Maxlever.

2. In a recession, both Maxlever and Nolever will have EBIT equal to $5,000; EBIT will be $20,000 in the event of an expansion. Compute EPS and ROE for each firm under each scenario.

3. Compute the level of EBIT such that Maxlever and Nolever have the same earnings per share.

4. Suppose that an investor purchased 200 shares of Maxlever. Compute the cost of this investment and the earnings for this position under each of the three scenarios described in Problems 1 and 2.

5. Explain how the investor described in Problem 4 can duplicate the earnings from the investment in Maxlever by borrowing and investing in the shares of Nolever.

6. Suppose that higher leverage increased firm value, so the market value of Maxlever is $90,000, while the value of Nolever remains at $80,000. How would the investor in Problems 4 and 5 react to this?

7. Suppose an investor purchased 200 shares of Nolever. Compute the cost of this investment and the earnings for this position under each of the three scenarios in Problems 1 and 2.

8. Explain how the investor in Problem 7 can duplicate the earnings from the investment in Nolever by lending and investing in the shares of Maxlever.

9. Suppose that increased leverage decreased firm value, so that the market value of Maxlever is $70,000, while the value of Nolever remains at $80,000. How would the investor in Problems 7 and 8 react?

Use the information below to solve Problems 10 through 13:

The North Company, a major manufacturer of document shredders, has a perpetual expected EBIT of $200. The interest rate for North's debt is 12%.

10. Assuming there are no taxes or bankruptcy costs, what is the value of North Co. if its debt to equity ratio is .25 and its WACC is 16%? What is the value of North's equity? What is the value of its debt?

11. What is the cost of equity capital for North Company?

12. Suppose the corporate tax rate is 30%, there are no personal taxes or bankruptcy costs, and North has $400 in debt outstanding. If the unlevered cost of equity is 20%, what is the value of North Company? What is the value of the firm's equity?

13. What is the weighted average cost of capital for North Company?

Use the following information to solve Problems 14 through 18.

14. Merrick Motors is an all-equity firm with earnings expected to be $450,000 forever. The firm has 100,000 shares outstanding. The WACC is 15%. MM is considering a major expansion of its facilities which will require an initial outlay of $400,000 and which is expected to produce additional annual earnings of $150,000 per year forever. Management considers the expansion to have the same risk as the firm's existing assets. Assume that there are no taxes and no costs of bankruptcy.

15. Suppose Merrick plans to finance the expansion by issuing common stock. How many shares must be issued? What is the value of the equity after the stock issue? What is the price per share of the stock?

16. Suppose Merrick plans to finance the expansion by issuing bonds with an interest rate of 10%. What is firm value after the bond issue? What is the value of the equity? What is the price per share?

17. Calculate the expected yearly income after interest for the equityholders. Use the expected yearly income to calculate the expected return for the equityholders.

18. Use M&M Proposition II (no taxes) to determine the expected return for the equityholders.

CHAPTER 17

DIVIDENDS AND DIVIDEND POLICY

CONCEPTS FOR REVIEW

Previously we asked whether a firm's financing decisions can affect firm value and shareholder wealth. Now we ask an equally complex question: Can a firm's *dividend policy* affect shareholder wealth? We find that real-world complexities make it difficult to arrive at a definitive answer to the question.

CHAPTER HIGHLIGHTS

Intuition suggests that dividend policy should be irrelevant. Investors wishing a cash payout from their stock portfolios can simply sell some stock and pay themselves a cash "dividend." Investors who do not want a cash dividend can simply reinvest dividends received. However, several factors complicate this simple argument. As a result, financial managers find that there are logical arguments which favor a high dividend payout and equally logical arguments which support a low dividend payout. Still other arguments indicate that dividend policy is irrelevant. All three points of view are addressed in this chapter.

I. CASH DIVIDENDS AND DIVIDEND PAYMENT (p. 503)

A **dividend** is a cash payment made to stockholders from earnings. If the payment is from sources other than current earnings, it is a **distribution** or a liquidating dividend.

<u>Cash Dividends</u> (p. 503) **Regular cash dividends** are paid four times a year. An **extra cash dividend** may also be paid periodically. Such a dividend is identified as "extra" to communicate to stockholders that the payment may not be repeated. A **special dividend** is a unique event which will not be repeated. A **liquidating dividend** results from the liquidation of part or all of the corporation.

<u>Standard Method of Cash Dividend Payment</u> (p. 503) A cash dividend can be expressed as dollars per share (**dividends per share**), a percentage of market price (**dividend yield**), or as a percentage of EPS (**dividend payout**). A dividend becomes a liability of the firm once declared by the board of directors.

<u>Dividend Payment: A Chronology</u> (p. 504) On the **declaration date**, the board of directors announces the amount of the dividend and the **date of record**. Shares purchased on or after the **ex-dividend date** are sold without the dividend, thus, the price of the stock by approximately the amount of the dividend on that date. The dividend is paid to shareholders who are holders of record as of the date of record. Dividend checks are mailed on the **payment date**.

<u>More on the Ex-Dividend Date</u> (p. 505) The ex-dividend date is two <u>business</u> days prior to the record date. In the absence of other events, the share price of the dividend-paying stock should fall by exactly the amount of the dividend on the ex- date; in actuality, the price drop is only approximately the dividend amount, due to the effects of taxes, transactions costs, and other market imperfections.

II. DOES DIVIDEND POLICY MATTER? (p. 506)

"Dividend policy" determines the pattern of dividend payments over time. A firm can pay a large percentage of earnings to stockholders as dividends, or pay out a small percentage of earnings and reinvest the remainder with the expectation that larger dividends will be paid in the future.

The central issue of dividend policy is whether either approach is more advantageous to the stockholders. In the absence of complicating factors (such as different tax rates on dividend income and capital gains income) it can be shown that dividend policy is irrelevant, since a dividend increase at some point in time will be exactly offset by a decrease somewhere else.

Homemade Dividends (p. 507) A second explanation of dividend policy irrelevance relies on the fact that individuals may be able to create any policy they want, regardless of the firm's policy. As noted above, if a higher current dividend is desired, the individual can sell some shares; if a lower dividend is desired, the individual can reinvest dividends received. The ability to create a "homemade dividend" suggests that no corporate dividend policy is better than another - it is therefore irrelevant.

III. REAL-WORLD FACTORS FAVORING A LOW PAYOUT (p. 508)

The irrelevance of dividend policy is based on the assumptions that there are no taxes or flotation costs.

Taxes (p. 509) Tax laws impact dividend policy in at least two ways. First, effective tax rates are lower for capital gains than for dividend income. Since a low dividend payout means that earnings are reinvested in the firm, firm value and share prices increase, resulting in capital gains for stockholders. The lower effective tax rate for capital gains thus encourages a low dividend payout.

The second consideration is the relationship between corporate and personal tax rates. All else equal, when personal tax rates are higher than corporate tax rates, a firm will have an incentive to reduce dividend payout, in order to reduce total taxes paid. If personal tax rates are lower than corporate tax rates, however, a firm will have an incentive to pay out any excess cash in dividends. Thus, when we consider the impact of taxes, one dividend policy may be better than another.

Expected Return, Dividends, and Personal Taxes (p. 510) Since rational shareholders are concerned with their aftertax returns, they will require higher returns from firms which pay higher dividends to offset the higher tax burden which results.

Flotation Costs (p. 510) Earlier we noted that a firm could issue common stock to pay dividends. However, we ignored the fact that this would require the firm to incur flotation costs. The existence of flotation costs provides an additional incentive for firms to adopt a policy of low dividend payout.

Dividend Restrictions (p. 510) The ability to pay dividends is limited by legal restrictions. For example, some states do not allow the payment of dividends in an amount that exceeds book retained earnings. And, bond indentures often limit a corporation's dividend payout to some fraction of net income.

IV. REAL-WORLD FACTORS FAVORING A HIGH PAYOUT (p. 511)

Some have argued that stockholders prefer a high dividend payout policy because of the desire for current income and the resolution of uncertainty.

Desire for Current Income (p. 511) Some investors undoubtedly desire current income. They might pay a premium for stocks with high dividends. Selling a portion of one's stock each period to produce current income may be undesirable because of brokerage fees, among other reasons. However, a mutual fund could very easily provide this service by regularly selling its holdings of low-dividend stocks in order to pay dividends to its stockholders. Therefore, a high dividend payout is not necessarily preferable, even for stockholders who desire current income.

Uncertainty Resolution (p. 512) A dollar received in the form of a dividend has a known value today, while a dollar reinvested by the firm has an uncertain future value. Thus, it has been argued that cash dividends reduce the risk of owning the stock. However, this conclusion is erroneous because one can accomplish the same result by selling shares to create homemade dividends, as noted earlier.

Tax and Legal Benefits from High Dividends (p. 512) Tax considerations which reduce the effective tax rate for capital gains generally lead individual investors to prefer common stocks with low dividend payout. However, other investors (such as corporations) are not subject to higher tax rates on dividends. Consequently, these investors often prefer to own common or preferred stocks with high dividend payouts, rather than either common stocks with low dividend payouts or corporate bonds.

V. A RESOLUTION OF REAL-WORLD FACTORS? (p. 513)

A general consensus exists regarding those factors which are important in establishing dividend policy. Tax effects and flotation costs lead some investors to favor a low payout, whereas the desire for current income influences others to favor a high payout. Although the issue has been studied extensively, empirical researchers have not found it possible to determine which factor dominates, so the policy question remains unresolved. As explained below, the evidence is not easy to interpret.

Information Content of Dividends (p. 513) Financial actions by the firm are sometimes regarded as a way for managers to **signal** the future prospects of the firm to the financial markets. An announcement of an increase in dividends indicates that the firm expects future cash flow to be sufficient to support a higher level of dividends. This positive signal causes stock price to increase. Unfortunately, it is difficult to separate this **information content** of the announcement from the dividend itself.

The Clientele Effect (p. 513) Some investors prefer high dividend payouts while others prefer low payouts. Different firms may cater to one group of investors (or *clientele*) or another. As long as both groups are satisfied, the corporation does not benefit from a change in its dividend policy: doing so simply attracts a different clientele. This **clientele effect** implies that dividend policy is irrelevant.

VI. ESTABLISHING A DIVIDEND POLICY (p. 516)

In this section, we discuss alternative approaches to establishing a dividend policy. We also consider the stock repurchase as an alternative to the payment of cash dividends.

Residual Dividend Approach (p. 516) A firm which adopts the **residual dividend approach** relies primarily on internally generated funds to finance positive NPV projects. After allocating these funds to all positive NPV projects, the firm pays dividends *only* if any residual funds remain.

Dividend Stability (p. 518) Under the residual dividend approach, quarterly dividends depend on both the firm's earnings and its investment opportunities. Since these quantities can vary significantly over time, the actual dividend paid can be very unstable. Since investors seem to value stability, alternative policies which lead to more stable dividends might be preferred. One such policy is a **cyclical dividend policy**: it sets each quarter's dividend equal to a fixed fraction of quarterly earnings. This policy is cyclical because earnings (and consequently dividends) may vary throughout the year although total annual dividends remain relatively stable.

A Compromise Dividend Policy (p. 518) Many firms seem to follow a compromise dividend policy based on the following goals:

1. Avoid the rejection of positive NPV projects.
2. Avoid reducing dividends.
3. Avoid issuing new equity.
4. Maintain a target debt/equity ratio.
5. Maintain a target dividend payout ratio.

For this kind of compromise policy, both the target debt/equity ratio and the target dividend payout ratio are regarded as long-term goals, rather than strict requirements. The long-run **target payout ratio** is the fraction of earnings the firm normally expects to pay as dividends; if earnings are unusually low in a given quarter, the firm might temporarily increase the payout ratio to avoid reducing dividends.

VII. STOCK REPURCHASE: AN ALTERNATIVE TO CASH DIVIDENDS (p. 521)

Cash Dividends versus Repurchase (p. 521) In the absence of taxes and transactions costs, a share repurchase has the same effect on stockholders as a cash dividend of the same amount. This is another example of dividend irrelevance.

Real-World Considerations in a Repurchase (p. 522) In the absence of taxes or transaction costs, stockholders are indifferent between a cash dividend payment and a stock repurchase. However, existing tax laws lead stockholders to favor a stock repurchase because they may participate (and pay taxes on the sale of their shares) or do nothing and incur no current tax liability.

Share Repurchase and EPS (p. 523) Share repurchases increase EPS; however, in the absence of other events or of market imperfections, firm (and share) value should be unaffected.

VIII. STOCK DIVIDENDS AND STOCK SPLITS (p. 523)

A **stock dividend** is paid in the form of additional shares of stock. By itself, it is not a true dividend since neither the shareholder's proportional ownership nor wealth change when it is declared. A **stock split** is similar to a stock dividend, except that it is expressed as a ratio rather than as a percentage.

Some Details on Stock Splits and Stock Dividends (p. 523) For accounting purposes, stock splits and stock dividends are classified as (1) small stock dividends; (2) large stock dividends; and, (3) stock splits. Stock dividends of less than 20% to 25 % are classified as small stock dividends. For each category accountants adjust the firm's balance sheet somewhat differently; however, in all three cases, the total owner's equity is unaffected by the distribution.

Value of Stock Splits and Stock Dividends (p. 525) Those who contend that stock splits and stock dividends have value to stockholders often argue that the value of a stock is enhanced if its price is within a certain **trading range**. There is little empirical evidence to support this contention.

Reverse Splits (p. 526) A reverse split decreases the number of shares outstanding and increases the price of the remaining shares accordingly. Reverse splits are implemented to (1) lower stockholder transactions costs, (2) increase the liquidity and marketability of the firm's shares, (3) raise share price to meet minimum listing requirements on an exchange, and (4) induce small shareholders to sell out.

KEY TERMS AND CONCEPTS

Clientele effect - that stocks attract particular groups based on dividend yield and tax effects. (p. 514)

Date of payment - date that the dividend checks are mailed. (p. 504)

Date of record - date on which holders of record are designated to receive a dividend. (p. 504)

Declaration date - date on which the board of directors passes a resolution to pay a dividend. (p. 504)

Distribution - payments to owners from sources other than current or accumulated earnings. (p. 503)

Dividend - payment from earnings to owners, either in the form of cash or stock. (p. 503)

Ex-dividend date - 4 business days before the record date; establishes those entitled to dividend. (p. 504)

Homemade dividends - idea that individual investors can undo corporate dividend policy by reinvesting dividends or selling shares of stock. (p. 507)

Information content effect - the market's reaction to a change in corporate dividend payout. (p. 514)

Regular cash dividend - cash payment made by a firm to its owners in the normal course of business, usually made four times a year. (p. 503)

Repurchase - another method used to pay out a firm's earnings to its owners, which provides more preferable tax treatment than dividends. (p. 521)

Residual dividend approach - policy where a firm pays dividends only after meeting its investment needs while maintaining a desired debt-to-equity ratio. (p. 516)

Reverse split - procedure where the number of a firm's shares outstanding is reduced. (p. 526)

Stock dividend - payment to owners in the form of stock. (p. 523)

Stock split - an increase in a firm's shares outstanding without any change in owner's equity. (p. 523)

Target payout ratio - a firm's long-term desired dividend-to-earnings ratio. (p. 520)

Trading range - price range between highest and lowest prices at which a stock is traded. (p. 526)

CONCEPT TEST

1. If a cash dividend is from sources other than current earnings, it is called a(n)_____ or a(n)_____ dividend. Types of cash dividends: A dividend typically paid four times a year is a(n)_____ cash dividend. A dividend which is paid periodically, but which may not continue in the future is a(n)_____ dividend. A dividend which is regarded as a unique event is a(n)_____ dividend. A dividend paid subsequent to the liquidation of the firm is a(n)_____ dividend. When the size of a cash dividend is expressed as dollars per share, it is identified in terms of _____ . When the size of the dividend is stated as a percentage of market price, it is called the _____ . When the dividend is expressed as a percentage of EPS, it is called the _____ . (p. 503)

2. The date on which the directors announce the dividend amount is the _____. Dividends are paid to holders of record on the _____. Dividend checks are mailed to these owners on the _____. The _____ date is four business days before the record date. Anyone purchasing a share on or after the ex-dividend date (does/does not) receive the dividend. Prior to the ex-dividend date, the stock is said to be trading _____; subsequently, it trades _____ . Prior to the ex-dividend date, stock price declines overnight by about _____ . (p. 504)

3. A stock dividend takes the form of _____ . A stock dividend (is/is not) a true dividend. Firm value (does/does not) change when a stock dividend is declared, and the total value of a stockholder's shares (does/does not) change. A stock split (is/is not) similar to a stock dividend. A split is expressed as a _____, while a stock dividend is expressed as a _____ . When a 20% stock dividend is declared, a stockholder who owns 100 shares of stock receives _____ new shares, so the total number of shares owned after the stock dividend is _____ . When a three-for-two stock split is declared, a stockholder who owns 100 shares receives _____ new shares, so the total number of shares owned after the split is _____ . A three-for-two stock split is equivalent to a _____% stock dividend. A 20% stock dividend is equivalent to a _____ -for-_____ stock split. Those who feel that stock splits and stock dividends are valuable argue that the value of a stock is enhanced if its price is within a certain _____ . (p. 524)

4. The argument for the dividend policy irrelevance assumes that an investor can create _____ dividends if the firm's pattern of dividend payments does not match his preferences. Irrelevance requires that there are no _____ or _____ . Under current U.S. tax laws dividend income and capital gains (are/are not) both taxed as ordinary income and (are/are not) subject to the same tax rates. Capital gains taxes are deferred until the stock is sold, so effective tax rates are (lower/higher) for capital gains. A policy of (low/high) dividend payout means earnings are reinvested in the firm, so firm value (increases/decreases), resulting in capital gains for stockholders. So taxation of capital gains has implications for the firm's dividend policy. The lower effective tax rate for capital gains encourages (low/high) dividend payout. Flotation costs provide an incentive for firms to adopt a policy of (low/high) dividend payout. (p. 506)

5. Some argue that a (low/high) dividend payout policy is preferable due to the desire for current income and the resolution of uncertainty; e.g., a cash dividend payment (increases/decreases) the risk of owning a stock. However, a stockholder can accomplish the same result by _____ in order to create _____ dividends. (p. 508)

6. Some investors are not subject to taxes on dividends; for them, _____% of dividend income is excluded from taxable income. Pension funds, endowment funds, and trust funds favor stocks with (low/high) dividend payouts because they are _____. (p. 511)

7. Some investors prefer high dividend payouts while others prefer low payouts. Different firms may end up catering to one group or the other; this is the _____. Evidence suggests that investors in low tax brackets tend to hold (low/high) payout stocks, and investors in high tax brackets tend to hold (low/high) payout stocks. (p. 511)

8. Firms with low dividend payout ratios require (less/more) external financing than firms with high payout ratios. Since external financing requires that the firm incur flotation costs, it is cheaper to obtain financing by retaining earnings and adopt a (low/high) dividend payout ratio. A firm which adopts the _____ approach relies primarily on internally generated funds to finance positive NPV projects. After allocating these funds to positive NPV projects, the firm pays dividends only from any _____ funds which remain. (p. 516)

9. Under the residual dividend approach, the dividend paid to stockholders each quarter depends on the firm's _____ and its _____; so the actual dividend paid can be very unstable. A stable dividend policy which sets quarterly dividends equal to a fixed fraction of quarterly earnings is a _____ policy. Another policy sets quarterly dividends equal to a specified fraction of annual earnings; this is a _____ dividend policy if earnings are relatively stable from one year to the next. (p. 516)

10. Many firms follow a compromise dividend policy with the following goals: (a) Avoid rejecting _____ NPV projects to pay a dividend; (b) Avoid reducing _____; (c) Avoid issuing _____; (d) Maintain a target _____; (e) Maintain a target _____. For this kind of policy both target _____ and target _____ are regarded as long-term goals, rather than strict requirements. (p. 519)

11. A firm can pay cash to shareholders by repurchasing stock from them. In the absence of _____ and _____, stockholders are indifferent between a dividend payment and a stock repurchase. Existing tax laws lead stockholders to favor a _____ . (p. 521)

ANSWERS TO CONCEPT TEXT

1. distribution; liquidating; regular; extra; special; liquidating; dividends per share; dividend yield; dividend payout
2. declaration date; date of record; date of payment; ex-dividend; does not; cum dividend; ex dividend; the after-tax value of the dividend
3. additional shares of stock; is not; does not; does not; is; ratio; percentage; 20; 120; 50; 150; 50; six; five; trading range
4. homemade; taxes; flotation costs; are; are; lower; low; increase; low; low
5. high; decreases; selling shares of stock; homemade
6. 100; high; tax-exempt
7. clientele effect; high; low
8. less; low; residual dividend; residual
9. earnings for the quarter; investment opportunities; cyclical; stable
10. positive; dividends; new equity; debt/equity ratio, dividend payout ratio; debt/equity ratio; dividend payout ratio
11. taxes; transaction costs; stock repurchase

PROBLEMS

1. The market value balance sheet for Agee Jones Associates, Inc., is shown below:

Market value balance sheet for Agee Jones

Cash	$ 20,000	Debt	$ 10,000
Fixed assets	$ 30,000	Equity	$ 40,000
Total	$ 50,000		$ 50,000

The firm has 1,000 shares outstanding and has declared a 25% stock dividend. T. Agee owns 400 shares of the firm's common stock. What is the effect of the stock dividend on the firm's market value? How does the stock dividend affect the value of a share of stock? How does the stock dividend affect the value of T. Agee's holdings?

2. Suppose that, for the data in Problem 1, Agee Jones declares a two-for-one stock split. What is the effect of the stock split on the firm value? How does the stock split affect the value of a share of stock? How does the stock split affect the value of T. Agee's holdings?

3. Krane Pools Company is an all-equity firm with 1,000 shares outstanding. The firm expects to pay total dividends of $6,000 one year from now and total liquidating dividends of $72,000 two years from now. The required return is 20%. What is the value of the firm? Of a share of common stock?

4. Suppose the stockholders of Krane Pools prefer total dividend payments of $30,000 at the end of one year, rather than the dividend payments in Problem 3. What payment will the firm make at the end of the second year? What is the value of the firm if it adopts the new dividend payment schedule? What is the value of a share of stock?

5. E. Charles owns 100 shares of Krane Pools common stock. The firm plans to pay dividends as described in Problem 3, but Charles would like to receive the payments he would receive if the firm paid dividends as described in Problem 4. How can he use homemade dividends to duplicate his desired dividend payments?

6. A firm which adopted a residual dividend approach has $30,000 in earnings and a debt/equity ratio of 1/3. What is the maximum amount of capital spending possible if the firm does not obtain any new equity financing and maintains the current debt/equity ratio?

7. Suppose the firm described in Problem 6 has positive NPV projects available which require the investment of $24,000. How will these projects be financed? How much will the firm pay in dividends?

8. Suppose the firm described in Problem 6 has $60,000 of positive NPV projects available. How will these projects be financed? How much will the firm pay in dividends?

9. An all-equity firm has the following market value balance sheet:

Market value balance sheet

Excess cash	$ 10,000	Debt	$	0
Other assets	$ 90,000	Equity	$100,000	
Total	$100,000		$100,000	

The firm has 2,000 shares outstanding and is considering paying dividends with the excess cash. What is the impact on the firm's market value balance sheet? How does the dividend payment affect a stockholder who owns 500 shares of stock?

10. Suppose the firm described above is considering a stock repurchase rather than the dividend payment. What is the impact on the firm's market value balance sheet? How does the stock repurchase affect the stockholder who owns 500 shares of stock?

Use the following information to solve Problems 11 through 15. The balance sheet for Reebop Corporation is shown. Reebop has 1,000 shares outstanding.

<u>Market value balance sheet</u>

Cash	$ 10,000	Debt	$ 0
Other assets	$ 50,000	Equity	$ 60,000
Total	$ 60,000		$ 60,000

11. Reebop has declared a dividend of $3.00 per share. The stock goes ex-dividend tomorrow. What is the price of the stock today? What will its price be tomorrow? (Assume no taxes.)

12. Reebop has declared a 20% stock dividend, rather than the cash dividend described in Problem 11. The stock goes ex-dividend tomorrow. What is the ex-dividend price?

13. Instead of paying a cash dividend, Reebop has announced a $3,000 repurchase of stock. What is the effect of this repurchase? Ignoring taxes, show how this repurchase is the same as a $3.00 dividend.

14. Suppose capital gains are not taxed, but dividends are taxed at a 40% rate, and taxes are withheld when the dividend is paid. If Reebop is going to pay a $4.00 dividend, what is the ex-dividend price?

15. Suppose that, in Problem 14, capital gains are taxed at a 20% rate. What is the ex-dividend price?

16. Dadadas Company is in the same risk class os Old Balance Company. Dadadas has an expected dividend yield over the next year of 10%, while Old Balance pays no dividends. The required return on Old Balance is 20%. Capital gains are not taxed, but dividends are taxed at 40%. What is the required pre-tax return on Dadadas?

17. You own 20 shares of stock in Boing Aircraft. You are certain you will receive a $.50 dividend at date 1. At date 2, Boing will pay a liquidating dividend of $13.80 per share. The required return is 20%. Assuming no taxes, what is the price per share of the common stock? Suppose you would rather have equal dividends in each of the next two years; how can you accomplish this using homemade dividends?

18. Try this one on your own. Suppose that, in Problem 17, you wanted only $5 at date 1. What is your homemade dividend at date 2?

CHAPTER 18

SHORT-TERM FINANCE AND PLANNING

CONCEPTS FOR REVIEW

Previous chapters have dealt with the lower left-hand side of the balance sheet (capital budgeting) and the lower right-hand side (long-term financing). With this chapter, we move to the top half of the balance sheet. Analysis of current asset and liability decisions is called *working capital management.*

CHAPTER HIGHLIGHTS

This chapter introduces the fundamentals of **short-term financial management** - the analysis of decisions involving cash flows which occur within a year or less. These decisions affect current assets and/or current liabilities. Examples of short-term financial decisions are questions such as: How much inventory should be held? How much cash? Should goods be sold on credit? On what terms?

I. TRACING CASH AND NET WORKING CAPITAL (p. 537)

Current assets are assets expected to be converted to cash within one year. The four major categories of current assets are: cash, marketable securities, accounts receivable, and inventory. Current assets appear on the balance sheet in order of **liquidity** - the ease and time involved in converting assets into cash. Current liabilities are short-term obligations which require payment within one year. The three major categories current liabilities are: accounts payable; accrued wages and taxes, and other expenses; and notes payable. In order to trace the flow of cash we identify those activities which:

Increase cash
- Increase long-term debt (e.g., issue bonds);
- Increase equity (sell stock);
- Increase current liabilities (borrow short-term);
- Decrease current assets other than cash;
- Decrease fixed assets (sell fixed assets).

Decrease Cash
- Decrease long-term debt;
- Decrease equity (repurchase stock);
- Decrease current liabilities;
- Increase current assets other than cash;
- Increase fixed assets (buy fixed assets).

II. THE OPERATING CYCLE AND THE CASH CYCLE (p. 538)

A manufacturer's short-run operating and financing activities might include the following:

EVENTS	DECISIONS
1. Buying raw materials	1. How much inventory to order?
2. Paying cash for purchases	2. To borrow, or draw down cash balance?
3. Manufacturing the product	3. What choice of production technology?
4. Selling the product	4. To offer cash terms or credit?
5. Collecting cash	5. How to collect cash?

158

Defining Operating and Cash Cycles (p. 539) Short-term operating activities and cash flows are represented by the **operating** and **cash cycles**. The length of the **operating cycle** equals the inventory period plus the accounts receivable period. The **inventory period** is the time required to order, produce, and sell a product. The **accounts receivable period** is the time required to collect cash from a sale.

The **cash cycle** is the difference between the operating cycle and the accounts payable period. The **accounts payable period** is the time the firm can delay payment on its purchases. A cash cycle of 30 days means that inflows occur 30 days after outflows. This mismatch suggests the need for short-term financing, which can be provided either by borrowing or by maintaining a reserve of marketable securities. Or, the cash cycle can be shortened by changing the inventory, accounts receivable or accounts payable periods.

The Operating Cycle and the Firm's Organizational Chart (p. 540) Several people within the firm make financial decisions. Table 18.1 details those involved in short-term financial management decisions.

Calculating the Operating and Cash Cycles (p. 541) Formulas to remember:

The operating cycle:
    (1) Inventory turnover = cost of goods sold/average inventory
    (2) Inventory period = 365/inventory turnover
    (3) Receivables turnover = credit sales/average accounts receivable
    (4) Receivables period = 365/receivables turnover
    (5) Operating cycle = Inventory period + receivables period

The cash cycle:
    (1) Payables turnover = cost of goods sold/average payables
    (2) Payables period = 365/payables turnover
    (3) Cash cycle = Operating cycle - accounts payable period.

Interpreting the Cash Cycle (p. 543) The cash cycle is influenced by the firm's inventory, receivables, and payables balances, among other things. Further, the cash cycle is related to profitability as measured by ROA and ROE, since both include total asset turnover as a component.

III. SOME ASPECTS OF SHORT-TERM FINANCIAL POLICY (p. 544)

Short-term financial policy concerns the size of the investment in, and the financing of, current assets.

The Size of the Firm's Investment in Current Assets (p. 544) A *flexible* current asset policy implies that the firm maintains relatively high levels of cash, marketable securities and inventories, and grants liberal credit terms which result in relatively high levels of accounts receivable; *restrictive* policies mean that the firm maintains relatively low levels of current assets.

A flexible policy requires greater initial cash outflows to purchase inventory, finance credit sales, and maintain high levels of cash and marketable securities. Future cash inflows, however, should be higher for a flexible policy. This higher inventory reduces the likelihood of inventory 'stockouts,' so sales are stimulated. Liberal credit policies also stimulate sales. Larger cash balances ensure that bills can be paid promptly, increasing discounts taken on payables and reducing borrowing costs.

The costs associated with managing current assets are: **carrying costs**, which increase with the level of investment in current assets; and **shortage costs**, which decrease with increases in the level of investment in current assets. Carrying costs are the opportunity costs of investment in current assets. The two kinds of shortage costs are trading (or order) costs and costs related to safety reserves. Trading costs arise when the firm runs out of cash or inventory and must consequently incur the cost of restocking. Costs related to safety reserves include loss of sales or customer goodwill, or production time when a stock out (or "cash out") occurs. **The optimal investment in current assets is that which minimizes the sum of carrying and shortage costs.**

Alternative Financing Policies for Current Assets (p. 546) Many financing policies are feasible. Ideally, short-term assets are financed by short-term debts and net working capital would be zero. In reality, firms employ a permanent investment in current assets - i.e., levels never fall to zero. To finance the permanent component of working capital, a firm could use long-term debt in an amount which always exceeds the firm's total asset requirement; as a result, the firm has excess cash available for investment in marketable securities. Alternatively, a restrictive strategy uses permanent short-term borrowing to finance any deficit between long-term financing and total assets.

Which Financing Policy is Best? (p. 549) There is no definitive answer to the question: "How much short-term borrowing is optimal?" Several factors must be considered. First, firms with flexible policies are generally less likely to experience financial distress since this policy implies less difficulty in meeting short-term obligations. Second, most firms hedge interest-rate risk by matching debt maturities with asset maturities; a policy of financing long-term assets with short-term debt, for example, is inherently risky since frequent refinancing is needed, and short-term interest rates are more volatile than long-term rates. Finally, short-term interest rates tend to be lower than long-term rates, so borrowing long-term is costly.

Current Assets and Liabilities in Practice (p. 550) Current assets make up about 40 percent of the average firm's total assets. Current liabilities make up approximately 30 percent of the average firm's total liabilities and equity. These figures differ over time and across industries, as well as across firms.

IV. THE CASH BUDGET (p. 551)

The **cash budget** is a forecast of estimated cash inflows and outflows over a period of time; it is the primary tool of short-run financial planning. We illustrate its preparation with an example.

Example. C. Erskine & Company has estimated sales for the next four quarters as follows:

	Qtr. 1	Qtr. 2	Qtr. 3	Qtr. 4
Sales	$150	$200	$300	$250

Beginning accounts receivable are $100. Erskine has a 54-day collection period. Cash outflows consist of: (1) payments to suppliers, (2) wages, taxes, and other expenses, (3) capital expenditures, and (4) long-term financing payments (dividends, interest, and principal paid). Erskine's purchases during a quarter equal 50% of next quarter's forecasted sales. Erskine's payments equal the previous period's purchases. In the most recent quarter, Erskine's purchases are $(.50 \times \$150) = \$75$, which will be paid during the first quarter. Wages, taxes, and other expenses are 30% of sales. Interest and dividends are $20 per

160

quarter. Capital expenditures of $100 are planned in the second quarter. Erskine maintains a $10 minimum cash balance.

Sales and Cash Collections (p. 551) We compute cash collections for Erskine for each quarter. The 54-day collection period implies that $[(90 - 54)/90] = 40\%$ of the sales in a given quarter will be collected during the current quarter and $(54/90) = 60\%$ during the following quarter; that is, sales made during the first $(90 - 54) = 36$ days of the quarter will be collected before the end of the quarter, while sales during the remaining 54 days will be collected during the following quarter. So ending receivables for a given quarter are 60% of sales during that quarter. In the first quarter,

$$\text{Cash collections} = \text{Beginning accounts receivable} + (40\% \times \text{Sales})$$
$$= \$100 + (.40 \times \$150) = \$100 + \$60 = \$160$$

	Qtr. 1	Qtr. 2	Qtr. 3	Qtr. 4
Beginning Receivables	$100	$ 40	$120	$180
Sales	150	200	300	250
Cash Collections	160	160	240	280
Ending Receivables	40	120	180	150

Cash Outflows (p. 552) The cash outflows for Erskine are:

	Qtr. 1	Qtr. 2	Qtr. 3	Qtr. 4
Payment of Accounts	$ 75	$100	$150	$125
Wages, taxes, other expenses	45	60	90	75
Capital Expenditures	0	100	0	0
Long-term financing expenses (interest and dividends)	20	20	20	20
Total	$140	$280	$260	$220

The Cash Balance (p. 553) The **net cash inflow** is the difference between cash collections and cash outflows.

	Qtr. 1	Qtr. 2	Qtr. 3	Qtr. 4
Total cash collections	$160	$160	$240	$280
-Total cash disbursements	140	280	260	220
Net cash inflow	$ 20	-$120	-$ 20	$ 60

Assuming that Erskine maintains their $10 minimum balance at the beginning of the first quarter, we compute the cumulative surplus or deficit for Erskine at the end of each quarter:

	Qtr. 1	Qtr. 2	Qtr. 3	Qtr. 4
Beginning cash balance	$ 10	$ 30	-$ 90	-$110
+ Net cash inflow	20	- 120	- 20	60
Ending Cash balance	$ 30	-$ 90	-$110	-$ 50
- Minimum cash balance	10	10	10	10
Cumulative surplus (deficit)	$ 20	-$100	-$120	-$ 60

Beginning in the second quarter, Erskine has a cash shortfall. It occurs because of the seasonal pattern of sales, the delay in collections, and the planned capital expenditure.

V. SHORT-TERM BORROWING (p. 554)

Erskine must finance the cash shortfall beginning in the second quarter. Options include unsecured and secured short-term financing.

Unsecured Loans (p. 554) Short-term borrowing used to cover a temporary cash deficit often takes the form of an unsecured short-term bank loan. Such loans are usually arranged as either a noncommitted or a committed line of credit. The former is an informal agreement allowing the firm to borrow without submitting the usual paperwork. The latter is a formal legal agreement specifying that the bank will lend up to a specified amount to the firm in return for a fee based on the committed funds. The interest rate is usually stated as a number of percentage points above the prime rate.

A line of credit arrangement requires that the firm keep some amount of money on deposit in a low-interest (or zero-interest) account. This **compensating balance** increases the effective rate on the loan.

Secured Loans (p. 556) Secured short-term loans require either accounts receivable or inventories as security for the loan. With **accounts receivable financing**, accounts are either "assigned" or "factored." If factored, they are sold to a lender who assumes the risk of customer default. Under assignment, the lender has a lien on receivables, and the borrower is responsible for bad accounts.

Inventory loans are secured by inventory. A *blanket lien* is a lien against all inventory. **Trust receipt** arrangements identify specific inventory items as collateral. **Field warehousing** arrangements segregate inventory for use as security and place it under the control of an independent third party.

Other Sources (p. 557) **Commercial paper** consists of short-term notes issued by large, highly-rated firms; maturities are short, generally less than 270 days. Another source of financing is **trade credit**, which is equivalent to borrowing from suppliers. Trade credit is discussed in Chapter 19.

VI. A SHORT-TERM FINANCIAL PLAN (p. 557)

Example Erskine will borrow needed funds at 12 percent APR, or $(.12/4) = .03 = 3\%$ per quarter. Assume Erskine begins the year with no short-term debt and will repay any short-term borrowings as soon as possible. Ignore taxes, and assume that the cash surplus during the first quarter does not earn interest. The complete short-term financial plan is presented in the following table:

	Qtr. 1	Qtr. 2	Qtr. 3	Qtr. 4
Beginning cash balance	$ 10	$ 30	$ 10	$ 10.00
+Net cash inflow	20	- 120	- 20	60.00
+New short-term borrowing	--	100	23	--
-Interest on short-term borrowing	--	--	3	3.69
-Short-term borrowing repaid	--	--	--	56.31
Ending cash balance	$ 30	$ 10	$ 10	$ 10.00
-Minimum cash balance	10	10	10	10.00
Cumulative surplus (deficit)	$ 20	$ 0	$ 0	$ 0.00
Beginning short-term borrowing	0	0	$100	$123.00
+Change in short-term debt	0	100	23	- 56.31
Ending short-term debt	$ 0	$100	$123	$ 66.69

With no borrowing, the cumulative deficit at the end of quarter 2 is $100. Consequently, short-term borrowing of $100 is required in quarter 2. Interest of $(.03 \times \$100) = \$3$ must be paid during quarter 3, which increases the cumulative deficit for the quarter from $120 to $123. Thus, additional short-term borrowing of $23 is required during the quarter; ending short-term debt is $(\$100 + \$23) = \$123$, which covers the cumulative deficit of $123. Interest paid during quarter 4 is $(.03 \times \$123) = \$3.69$, so that $(\$60 - \$3.69) = \$56.31$ of the $60 cash inflow is available to repay short-term debt.

KEY TERMS AND CONCEPTS

Accounts payable period - the time between receipt of inventory and payment for it. (p. 539)
Accounts receivable financing - secured short-term loan involving assignment or factoring of receivables. (p. 556)
Accounts receivable period - time between sale of inventory and collection of receivable. (p. 539)
Carrying cost - costs that rise with increases in the level of investment in current assets. (p. 545)
Cash budget - a forecast of cash receipts and disbursements for the next planning period. (p. 551)
Cash cycle - the time between cash disbursement and cash collection. (p. 539)
Cash flow time line - graphical representation of the operating cycle and the cash cycle. (p. 540)
Compensating balance - money kept by the firm with a bank in low-interest or non-interest-bearing accounts as part of a loan agreement. (p. 555)
Inventory loan - a secured short-term loan to purchase inventory. (p. 557)
Inventory period - the time it takes to acquire and sell inventory. (p. 539)
Line of credit - formal (committed) or informal (noncommitted) short-term bank loan. (p. 554)
Operating cycle - time period between acquisition of inventory and collection of receivables. (p. 539)
Shortage costs - costs that fall with increases in the level of investment in current assets. (p. 545)

CONCEPT TEST

1. Current assets are expected to be converted to _____ within _____. The categories are: _____, _____, _____, and _____. Current assets are on the balance sheet in order of _____. Short-term obligations are _____. Categories are _____, _____, and _____. (p. 536)

2. Activities which increase cash are: (increases/decreases) in long-term debt; (increases/decreases) in equity; (increases/decreases) in current liabilities; (increases/decreases) in current assets other than cash; and (increases/decreases) in fixed assets. Activities which decrease cash are: (increases/decreases) in long-term debt; (increases/decreases) in equity; (increases/decreases) in current liabilities; (increases/decreases) in current assets other than cash; and (increases/decreases) in fixed assets. (p. 537)

3. The length of the operating cycle equals the _____ period plus the _____ period. The cash cycle is the _____ minus the _____ period. A cash cycle of 30 days means that _____ occur 30 days after _____ . (p. 539)

4. A flexible current asset policy implies that the firm maintains relatively (high/low) levels of cash, marketable securities and inventories, and grants (liberal/restrictive) credit terms which result in relatively (high/low) levels of accounts receivable; a restrictive policy means the firm maintains relatively (high/low) levels of current assets. A flexible policy requires (larger/smaller) initial cash outflows, and future cash inflows should be (larger/smaller). The (higher/lower) level of inventory associated with a flexible policy (reduces/increases) the likelihood of inventory stockouts, so sales are (increased/decreased). Similarly, the (liberal/restrictive) credit policies associated with a flexible policy result in (increased/decreased) sales. Also, the (larger/smaller) cash balances associated with a flexible policy result in (increased/decreased) discounts taken on accounts payable and (reduced/increased) borrowing costs. (p. 545)

5. The costs of managing current assets include: carrying costs, which are costs that (increase/decrease) with increases in current assets; and, shortage costs, which (increase/decrease) with increases in current assets. Carrying costs are the _____ costs of investment in current assets. The two kinds of shortage costs are: (1) _____ or _____ costs; and, (2) costs related to _____. The optimal investment in current assets is the level that _____ the sum of carrying and shortage costs. (p. 545)

6. Firms often require a permanent investment in current assets because _____. To finance the permanent component of working capital, a firm could use a (flexible/restrictive) strategy for which the amount of long-term debt exceeds the total asset requirement. The alternative is a (flexible/restrictive) strategy which involves the use of permanent short-term borrowing to finance any deficit between long-term financing and total assets. Firms with (flexible/restrictive) policies are generally less likely to experience financial distress. Most firms hedge interest-rate risk by matching _____ and _____. A policy of financing long-term assets with short-term debt is inherently risky since frequent refinancing is needed and short-term interest rates are (more/less) volatile than long-term rates. Short-term interest rates tend to be (higher/lower) than long-term rates so borrowing long-term is (more/less) costly. (p. 545)

164

7. The _____ is a forecast of estimated cash inflows and outflows over a period of time. Net cash inflow is cash _____ minus cash _____. (p. 558)

8. Short-term borrowing to cover a temporary cash deficit often takes the form of _____ loan. A _____ is an informal agreement allowing the firm to borrow without submitting the usual paperwork. A _____ is a formal legal agreement specifying that the bank will lend up to a specified amount to the firm. The interest rate is usually stated as a percent above the _____. (p. 551)

9. A line of credit arrangement often requires that the firm keep some money on deposit in a low-interest (or zero-interest) account; this arrangement is called a _____, which serves to (increase/decrease) the effective rate on the loan. (p. 554)

10. Loans which usually require either accounts receivable or inventories as security for the loan are _____ loans. When accounts receivable are sold to the lender, they are said to be _____; in this case, the (lender/borrower) assumes the risk of default on the part of the borrower's customer. Under the arrangement referred to as _____ of accounts receivable, the lender has a lien on receivables, and the (lender/borrower) assumes the risk of default on the part of the borrower's customer. (p. 556)

11. When an inventory loan involves a lien on all of the borrower's inventory, the arrangement is referred to as _____. Inventory loans for which the borrower holds inventory "in trust" for the lender involve the use of a _____. When a warehouse company controls inventory, this arrangement is a _____. (p. 557)

ANSWERS TO CONCEPT TEST

1. cash; one year; cash; marketable securities; accounts receivable; inventory; liquidity; current liabilities; accounts payable; accrued wages, taxes, and other expenses payable; notes payable
2. increases; increases; increases; decreases; decreases; decreases; decreases; decreases; increases; increases
3. inventory; accounts receivable; operating cycle; accounts payable; inflows; outflows
4. high; liberal; high; low; larger; larger; higher; reduces; increased; liberal; increased; larger; increased; reduced; less; more; more; less
5. increase; decrease; opportunity; trading; order; safety reserves; minimizes
6. current assets never decline to zero; flexible; restrictive; flexible; debt maturities; asset maturities; more; lower; more
7. cash budget; collections; outflows
8. an unsecured short-term bank; noncommitted line of credit; committed line of credit; prime rate
9. compensating balance; increase
10. secured short-term; factored; lender; assignment; borrower
11. a blanket inventory lien; trust receipt; field warehouse financing

PROBLEMS

1. The following data for the Bleys Company apply to the year just ended:

1. Accounts payable increased by $20
2. A $10 dividend was paid
3. Inventories were increased by $120
4. Short-term bank borrowing increased by $80
5. Accounts receivable increased by $30

Identify each of the above as either a **source (S)** or a **use (U)** of cash.

Selected items from Oberon Corporation's balance sheets for the beginning and ending of 1991, and income statement are shown below. Use this information to solve Problems 2-6:

BALANCE SHEET ITEM	Beginning	Ending	Average
Inventory	$1,000	$1,400	$1,200
Accounts Receivable	1,800	2,100	1,950
Accounts Payable	900	1,100	1,000

INCOME STATEMENT ITEM	Annual
Net Sales (all credit)	$30,000
Cost of Goods Sold	16,000

2. Calculate the inventory period.

3. Calculate the accounts receivable period.

4. Calculate the accounts payable period.

5. Calculate the operating cycle.

6. Calculate the cash cycle.

Use the following information on Osiris Company to solve Problems 7-14. Osiris has estimated sales for the next four quarters as:

	Qtr. 1	Qtr. 2	Qtr. 3	Qtr. 4
Sales	$510	$870	$450	$600

Accounts receivable at the beginning of the year were $210. Osiris has a 60-day accounts receivable collection period. Osiris's purchases from suppliers during a quarter are equal to 50% of the next quarter's forecast sales. Projected sales for each quarter of the year following the current one are uniformly 10% higher than the corresponding quarter's forecast sales during the current year. The accounts payable period is 45 days. Wages, taxes, and other expenses are one-third of sales, and interest and dividends are $10 per quarter. No capital expenditures are planned. Osiris is required to maintain a $10 minimum compensating balance, but currently has a cash balance of $0.

7. Calculate Osiris's projected cash collections.

8. Calculate Osiris's projected cash outflows.

9. Calculate net cash inflow and cumulative financing surplus (or deficit) for Osiris.

10. Osiris will borrow needed funds at an interest rate of 16 percent APR, or (.16/4) = .04 = 4% per quarter. Assume that Osiris begins the year with no short-term debt, and repays short-term debt as soon as possible. Ignore taxes, and assume that any cash surplus does not earn interest. Prepare a short-term financial plan for Osiris for the year.

11. Suppose the receivable collection period decreases from 60 days to 30, and the accounts payable period increases from 45 days to 72. Calculate projected cash collections.

12. Calculate Osiris's projected cash outflows, based on the changes described in Problem 11.

13. Calculate the net cash inflow and cumulative financing surplus (or deficit) for Osiris.

14. Prepare a complete short-term financial plan for Osiris for the year.

Selected items from Isis Company's balance sheets for the beginning and ending of the year, and income statement for the year are shown below. Use this information to solve Problems 15 - 20.

BALANCE SHEET ITEM	Beginning	Ending	Average
Inventory	$600	$700	$650
Accounts Receivable	800	900	850
Accounts Payable	200	250	225
INCOME STATEMENT ITEM	Annual		
Net Sales (all credit)	$10,000		
Cost of Goods Sold	6,000		

15. Calculate the inventory turnover period, accounts receivable turnover period and operating cycle.

16. Calculate the accounts payable period and the cash cycle for Isis.

17. Suppose that Isis is able to reduce its inventory period from 39.54 days to 30 days. How will this affect the firm's short-term financing requirements?

18. Suppose that Isis is able to reduce its accounts receivable turnover period from 31.04 days to 25 days. How will this affect its short-term financing requirements?

19. Suppose that Isis is able to extend its accounts payable period to 18 days, from the current 13.69 days. How will this affect the firm's short-term financing requirements?

20. Given the changes in Problems 17 - 19, what is the new operating cycle? The new cash cycle?

21. A bank offers a line of credit with a 13% annual interest rate and a 6% compensating balance. How much interest is paid on a $400,000, one-year loan? What is the compensating balance requirement? What is the effective interest rate?

22. Refer to the loan terms described in Problem 21: What size loan is necessary if the borrower requires net proceeds of $500,000? What is the compensating balance requirement? How much interest is paid on the loan for one year? What is the effective interest rate?

23. Kristy Konstruction Inc. factors its receivables at a 2.5 percent discount. The firm's average collection period is 40 days. What is the effective annual interest rate? (Assume 360 days in a year.)

CHAPTER 19

CASH AND LIQUIDITY MANAGEMENT

CONCEPTS FOR REVIEW

Previous chapters dealt with the measurement of liquidity via the analysis of firm financial statements. This chapter examines more closely the determinants of the firm's liquid asset holdings, and describes many of the factors financial decision-makers must contemplate in managing liquidity.

CHAPTER HIGHLIGHTS

Cash management involves evaluating the tradeoff between the benefits of liquidity and the opportunity cost of foregone interest. Effective cash management requires that managers consider (1) how much cash to hold, (2) how to manage cash collections and disbursements, and (3) how to invest excess cash.

I. REASONS FOR HOLDING CASH (p. 567)

The three reasons for holding cash are: precautionary, speculative, and transactions motives. We discuss each as they apply to corporate cash management, and the role of compensating balance requirements.

The Speculative and Precautionary Motives (p. 567) The **speculative motive** is the desire to take advantage of investment opportunities which might arise in the future. The **precautionary motive** is the need to hold cash as a financial reserve in the event of unanticipated cash outflows or unanticipated decreases in cash inflows. Both can be satisfied by reserve borrowing ability and by holding marketable securities, as well as holding cash.

The Transaction Motive (p. 568) Cash also is held to satisfy the **transaction motive** - i.e., for regular disbursements and collections.

Compensating Balances (p. 568) A compensating balance is a minimum deposit in an account earning little or no interest, which is required by a commercial bank as compensation for services. Compensating balance requirements plus the minimum transactions balance establish a minimum total cash requirement.

Costs of Holding Cash (p. 568) A firm which holds cash in excess of the minimum balance required for transactions and compensating balances incurs an opportunity cost in the form of the interest income foregone by holding cash rather than securities. A firm whose cash balance is too low is subject to the risk of being unable to meet funds needs. The optimal cash balance minimizes the sum of these costs.

Cash Management versus Liquidity Management (p. 569) **Liquidity management** is a fairly broad area which concerns the optimal quantity of liquid assets a firm should have on hand. **Cash management** deals with the mechanisms for optimizing the collection and disbursement of cash.

II. UNDERSTANDING FLOAT (p. 569)

The amount of cash on a firm's financial statements (i.e., the 'book' or 'ledger' balance) is not the same as the firm's bank balance (i.e., the firm's 'available' or 'collected' balance). The difference is the **float**.

Disbursement Float (p. 569) Checks written by the firm reduce the book balance immediately, but do not affect the available balance until the check is presented to the firm's bank for payment. The difference in the balances is **disbursement float**.

Collection Float and Net Float (p. 570) Checks *received* increase your book balance but do not increase your available balance until payment is actually received by the bank. The difference is **collection float**. **Net float** is the sum of collection and disbursement floats.

Float Management (p. 571) Float management involves speeding collections and delaying disbursements. Float has three parts: mail float (the time during which a check is in the mail), processing float (the time between the receipt and deposit of a check), and availability float (the time required to clear the check through the banking system). The *size* of the float depends on both the dollar amount and the time delay involved. Larger dollar amounts and/or longer delays increase the size of the float. The *cost* of float is the opportunity cost resulting from not being able to use the money.

A reduction in float has value to the firm, but there is generally a cost to reduce it. Procedures for reducing float are described next - adopting a technique is appropriate only if the decision has a positive NPV; i.e., the benefit derived from the reduction in float exceeds the cost of implementing the change.

Electronic Data Interchange: The End of Float? (p. 575) Electronic data interchange (EDI) is the electronic exchange of information between businesses. Financial electronic data interchange (FEDI) involves the electronic transfer of bills, paychecks, invoices, and deposits, among other things.

III. CASH COLLECTION AND CONCENTRATION (p. 575)

Components of Collection Time (p. 576) The cash collection process entails three components: **mailing time**, **processing delays**, and **availability delays**. Because each increases the float costs incurred by the collecting firm, techniques have been developed to reduce collection delays. Lockboxes and cash concentration procedures are popular among treasurers.

Cash Collection (p. 576) Optimal cash collection procedures are designed to collect cash from customers in the most timely and cost-efficient manner.

Lockboxes (p. 576) In a **lockbox** arrangement, a firm arranges for customers to mail payments to a strategically located post office box maintained by a local bank. The bank collects the checks several times a day and deposits them in the firm's account. Lockboxes reduce mailing time as well as the time the firm would spend processing checks prior to making the deposit.

Cash Concentration (p. 577) **Concentration banking** systems operate similarly, but in this case the firm's sales offices are used to receive and process checks. Surplus funds are subsequently transferred to the firm's main bank (the "concentration bank"). The process of collecting cash in this manner is called **cash concentration**.

IV. MANAGING CASH DISBURSEMENTS (p. 580)

Collecting firms seek to minimize the amount of float time, *paying* firms seek to maximize it. Doing so reduces required cash balances and the opportunity costs of liquidity.

Increasing Disbursement Float (p. 581) The goal is to slow payments as much as possible without damaging the firm's credit rating or reputation.

Controlling Disbursements (p. 581) Controlling disbursements can be accomplished by the utilization of a system of **zero-balance accounts** under which a safety stock of cash is held in a master account, while various sub-accounts are monitored to maintain a net zero balance. Alternatively, the firm may maintain a **controlled disbursement account** into which funds are transferred on a daily basis and only in the amount needed in order to meet payment requirements on that day.

V. INVESTING IDLE CASH (p. 582)

Temporary Cash Surpluses (p. 582) Temporary cash surpluses arise largely because of seasonal or cyclical activities, as well as for the financing of planned expenditures. Idle cash can be invested in *money-market* securities (i.e., securities with maturity of less than one year). Most large firms do their own investing, while smaller firms often rely on money-market mutual funds, some of which specialize in corporate cash management.

Characteristics of Short-Term Securities (p. 583) The most important characteristics of short-term marketable securities are the maturity, default risk, marketability, and tax status of the securities. Most firms limit their investments in money-market securities to those with maturities of 90 days or less, which reduces **interest-rate risk**. Firms also restrict their short-term investments to highly-rated securities with little or no **default risk**. Firms also prefer to invest in securities which are highly **liquid**.

Some Different Types of Money-Market Securities (p. 584) **Treasury bills** are direct obligations of the U.S. government. They are issued with maturities of 90, 180, 270 and 360 days, via auction. State and local governments and agencies also issue short-term debt, but it has greater default risk and is less marketable than Treasury debt. Since the interest is exempt from federal taxes, the pre-tax yield is lower than for Treasury securities with comparable maturity.

Commercial paper is short-term, unsecured debt issued by businesses, with maturities ranging from a few weeks to 270 days. Since there is no active secondary market for commercial paper, marketability is low. Default risk varies with the issuer's strength. **Certificates of deposit (CDs)** are time deposits in banks. There is an active market for 3-month, 6-month, 9-month and 12-month CDs. **Repurchase agreements** are transactions involving the purchase of an instrument (usually Treasury securities) and a simultaneous agreement to sell it back at a higher price in the future.

KEY TERMS AND CONCEPTS

Cash concentration - practice of moving cash from multiple banks to the firm's main accounts. (p. 577)
Controlled disbursing - disbursement practice under which the firm transfers an amount to a disbursing account that will be sufficient to cover demands for payment along with a safety reserve. (p. 581)
Float - difference between book cash and bank cash - net effect of checks in clearing process. (p. 569)
Lockboxes - special post office boxes set up to speed accounts receivable collections (p. 576)
Precautionary motive - the need to hold cash as a safety margin to act as a financial reserve. (p. 568)
Speculative motive - the need to hold cash to take advantage of investment opportunities (p. 567)
Transaction motive - need to hold cash to satisfy normal disbursement and collection activities (p. 568)

172

Zero-balance account - a disbursement account in which the firm maintains a zero balance, transferring funds in from a master account only as needed to cover checks presented for payment. (p. 581)

CONCEPT TEST

1. The desire to take advantage of investment opportunities which might arise in the future is the _____ motive for holding cash. The need to hold cash as a financial reserve in the event of unanticipated cash outflows or unanticipated decreases in cash inflows is the _____ motive. Both can be satisfied by access to _____ and by holding _____ . The need to hold cash for regular disbursements and collections is the _____ motive. A need to hold cash arises from the need to keep a _____ - a minimum deposit required by a bank as compensation. (p. 567)

2. A firm which holds cash in excess of the minimum balance required for transactions and compensating balances incurs a(n) _____ cost. This is the interest income the firm forgoes by holding cash rather than investing it; as a carrying cost, it (increases/decreases) with the cash balance. The costs of holding too little cash are _____ costs. (p. 568)

3. The level of cash on the firm's statements is the _____ balance or _____ balance. The firm's bank balance is the _____ balance or _____ balance. The difference between the firm's available balance and its book balance is called _____ . Checks written by the firm reduce the _____ balance immediately, but do not affect the _____ balance until the check is actually presented to the firm's bank for payment. The difference in the balances is called _____ float. Checks received increase the _____ balance but do not increase the _____ balance until payment is actually received by the bank. The difference is called _____ float. Net float is the sum of _____ float and _____ float. Float management involves speeding up _____ and delaying _____ . Float has three parts: _____ float is the time a check is in the mail; _____ float is the time between receipt and deposit of a check; and _____ float is the time required to clear the check through the banking system. (p. 569)

4. Total float equals _____ × _____ . Average daily float equals _____ ÷ _____ , or _____ × _____ . The cost of float is the _____ cost of being unable to use the money. (p. 572)

5. A common approach to accelerate collections is the _____ . This reduces _____ float and eliminates _____ float. (p. 575)

6. Idle cash can be invested in _____ or _____ securities, which have maturities less than one year. The market for these securities is the _____ market. Most firms limit their investments in money-market securities to those with maturity of _____ which virtually eliminates _____ risk. Firms restrict their short-term investments to highly-rated securities with little or no _____ risk. Firms also prefer to invest in securities which are highly _____ or _____ , meaning that they can be quickly sold without loss of value. (p. 582)

7. Treasury bills are direct obligations of _____ . Debt of state and local governments and agencies debt has (more/less) default risk, and is (more/less) marketable than Treasury debt. Since the interest is exempt from federal taxes, the pre-tax yield is (higher/lower) than for Treasury securities with comparable maturity. _____ is short-term unsecured debt, issued by firms, with maturities ranging from a few weeks to 270 days. _____ are time deposits in banks. _____ are transactions involving the purchase of an instrument and a simultaneous agreement to sell it back at a higher price in the future. (p. 584)

ANSWERS TO CONCEPT TEST

1. speculative; precautionary; reserve borrowing ability; marketable securities; transaction; compensating balance
2. opportunity; increases; shortage
3. book; ledger; available; collected; float; book; available; disbursement; book; available; collection; disbursement; collection; collections; disbursements; mail; processing; availability
4. number of days delay; dollar amount of check; total float; total days; average daily receipts; weighted average delay; opportunity
5. lockbox; mail; processing
6. short-term; marketable; money; 90 days or less; interest-rate; default; marketable; liquid;
7. U.S. government; more; less; lower; commercial paper; Certificates of deposit; Repurchase agreements

PROBLEMS

1. On a typical business day, a firm writes checks totalling $5,000. On average, these checks clear in 8 days. Simultaneously, the firm receives checks totalling $7,000. On average, the cash is available in 4 days. Calculate the disbursement float, the collection float, and the net float. Interpret your answer.

2. A real estate firm receives 100 rental checks a month. Of these, 70 are for $300 and 30 are for $200. The $300 checks are delayed 4 days on average; the $200 checks are delayed 5 days on average. Calculate the average daily collection float, and interpret your answer.

3. Using data from Problem 2, calculate the weighted average delay and average daily float.

4. Suppose that, for the data of Problem 2, a bank has offered to operate a lockbox system which will reduce float by two days. The bank's fee is $200 per year, payable at the end of the year, and the annual interest rate is 9%. Calculate the NPV of this system.

5. Consider the data for Problems 2-4; what is the most the firm would pay to reduce float by two days?

6. Your firm's average receipt is $100. A bank has approached you concerning a lockbox service that will decrease collection float by three days. Your firm receives 10,000 checks per day. The daily interest rate is .02%. If the bank's fee for the service is $.05 per check, should the lockbox service be adopted?

7. Suppose the bank in Problem 6 charges an annual fee of $5,000, payable at the end of the year, in addition to the variable fee; is the lockbox service still acceptable?

8. Suppose that, in addition to the fixed and variable fees described in Problems 6 and 7, the bank requires that the firm maintain a compensating balance of $500,000. Should the service be adopted?

9. Given the bank fees identified in Problems 6 and 7, what compensating balance would leave the firm indifferent as to whether it adopts the lockbox service?

175

10. A company has its collections handled by a bank located in the same city as its home office. The bank requires a compensating balance of $100,000 and handles collections of $750,000 per day. The firm is considering a concentration banking system which would require total compensating balances of $450,000, but would accelerate collections by two days. The T-bill rate is 6%. Should the firm implement the new system?

11. Your firm mails out 15,000 checks, with a total value of $500,000 on a typical day. You have determined that if the checks were mailed from Outer Mongolia, mail time would be increased by 3 days, on average. However, it would cost an extra $.10 per check in postage and handling. The daily interest rate is .00015. Should you adopt this method of delaying disbursements?

APPENDIX 19A: DETERMINING THE TARGET CASH BALANCE

The Basic Idea (p. 590) A firm with a flexible working capital policy holds marketable securities to satisfy transaction and precautionary motives, while a firm with a restrictive policy relies on short-term borrowing to meet unanticipated cash requirements. **Adjustment costs** for the firm with a restrictive policy are comprised of interest expenses and other expenses associated with short-term debt. A firm with a flexible policy incurs shortage costs associated with buying and selling marketable securities; these costs are referred to as trading costs. In the discussion of this section, we assume that the firm has a flexible working capital policy, so that we refer to shortage costs as **trading costs**.

A firm that holds an extremely low cash balance incurs high trading costs but few opportunity costs because it sells marketable securities to meet a cash shortage and buys marketable securities with excess cash balances. With extremely high cash balances, opportunity costs are very high, but trading costs are very low; cash shortages are infrequent, so that sales and purchases of securities are infrequent. The optimal (or *target*) cash balance which minimizes the sum of opportunity costs and trading costs.

The BAT Model (p. 590) The Baumol-Allais-Tobin (BAT) model determines the target cash balance by minimizing total costs. To illustrate the use of the model, consider the following example:

T	=	$240	=	the total cash needed for transactions over a period (e.g., a year);
F	=	$1	=	the fixed cost of making a securities trade to replenish cash balances;
r	=	10%	=	the interest rate on marketable securities (i.e., the opportunity cost);
C	=	$10	=	the beginning cash balance.

Assume the cash balance is initially at C and declines to zero; when it reaches zero, it is replenished to C by the sale of marketable securities. The average cash balance over the period is $[(C+0)/2] = (\$10/2) = \$5$. Total opportunity cost is the average cash balance times the interest rate on marketable securities:

$$\text{Opportunity costs} = (C/2) \times r = \$5 \times .10 = \$.50.$$

The number of times the cash balance is replenished during the year is $(T/C) = (\$240/\$10) = 24$ times. The total trading cost for the year is: $(T/C) \times F = 24 \times \$1 = \$24$.

The BAT model identifies the cash balance (C^*) which minimizes the total cost.

$$\text{Total cost} = \text{Opportunity costs} + \text{Trading costs} = [(C/2) \times r] + [(T/C) \times F], \text{ and } C^*:$$
$$C^* = \sqrt{(2T \times F)/r}$$

For our example, the target cash balance is
$$C^* = \sqrt{(2 \times \$240 \times \$1)/.10} = \sqrt{4800} = \$69.28$$

The BAT model is simple to apply, but has some deficiencies. It assumes that cash disbursements are the same every day, and are known with certainty; to the extent that these assumptions are inconsistent with reality, the model may not be applicable for a particular firm.

The Miller-Orr Model: A More General Approach (p. 594) The Miller-Orr model allows for cash-flow variability. The essence of the model is that the firm sets a lower limit (L) on cash holdings, based on the likelihood of a cash shortfall and the firm's willingness to tolerate the risk of a shortfall; then an upper limit (U*) and a target cash balance (C*) are determined. When the cash balance reaches U*, the firm returns to its target balance C* by investing (U* - C*) dollars in marketable securities. When the balance declines to L, the firm sells (C* - L) dollars of marketable securities in order to increase the cash balance to C*. As long as the firm's cash balance is between L and U*, no transactions are made.

Given L, the values of C* and U* which minimize expected total cost are determined as follows:

$$C^* = L + [(\tfrac{3}{4} \times F \times \sigma^2)/r]^{\frac{1}{3}}$$
$$U^* = (3 \times C^*) - (2 \times L)$$

where F is the cost per transaction of buying and selling marketable securities, σ^2 is the variance of the firm's net cash flows per period, and r is the interest rate, per period, on marketable securities. The average cash balance equals = $[(4 \times C^*) - L]/3$.

Suppose the daily variance of cash flows is $4, the daily interest rate is .02% (.0002), and management has determined that a lower limit of $10 is desirable. Using the other data from the BAT model example we calculate C*, U*, and the average cash balance:

$$C^* = \$10 + [(\tfrac{3}{4} \times \$1 \times \$4)/.0002]^{\frac{1}{3}} = \$34.66$$
$$U^* = (3 \times \$34.66) - (2 \times \$10) = \$83.99$$

$$\text{Average cash balance} = [(4 \times \$34.66) - \$10]/3 = \$42.88$$

Implications of the BAT and Miller-Orr Models (p. 596) Both models considered in this section specify an inverse relationship between the interest rate and the cash balance, and a direct relationship between the transaction cost and the cash balance. The Miller-Orr model establishes the relationship between risk, as measured by the variance of the firm's cash flows, and the cash balance; the greater the uncertainty of the firm's cash flows, the higher the target cash balance, the upper limit and the average cash balance.

Other Factors Influencing the Target Cash Balance (p. 597) An alternative to selling securities in order to raise cash is to borrow. The interest rate at which the firm borrows is generally higher than the foregone interest on marketable securities. Also, a firm maintaining a low cash balance is more likely to have to borrow the greater its cash flow variability and the lower its investment in marketable securities.

For large firms, the transaction cost of buying and selling T-bills is almost certainly less than the interest that can be earned on T-bills, even for an overnight investment. As a result, the primary reasons for such firms to hold cash relate to compensating balance requirements. A large firm may have thousands of accounts so that it may not be worthwhile to manage them all on a daily basis.

KEY TERMS AND CONCEPTS

Adjustment costs - the costs associated with holding too little cash. Also *shortage costs*. (p. 590)
Target cash balance - firm's desired cash level as determined by the trade-off between carrying costs and shortage costs. (p. 590)

CONCEPT TEST

1. A firm that holds a low cash balance incurs (high/low) shortage costs and (high/low) opportunity costs. As the balance increases, opportunity costs (increase/decrease) while shortage costs (increase/decrease). With high cash balances, opportunity costs are (high/low) and shortage costs are (high/low). The optimal (or target) cash balance is the balance which minimizes the sum of _____ and _____ . (p. 590)

2. A firm with a (restrictive/flexible) working capital policy holds marketable securities to satisfy transaction and precautionary motives, and one with a (restrictive/flexible) policy relies on short-term borrowing to meet unanticipated cash requirements. In the former case, shortage costs are _____ costs; in the latter, shortage costs are _____ expenses. (p. 591)

3. The BAT model assumes the cash balance is initially at C and declines to _____, at which time it is replenished to _____ by the sale of marketable securities. The average cash balance over the period is _____ . The opportunity cost is the _____ times the _____, or, expressed algebraically, _____ . The number of times the cash balance is replenished during the year equals _____ . The total trading cost for the year equals _____ . The BAT model identifies the cash balance (C*) which minimizes the total cost, which is the sum of the _____ cost and the _____ cost. (p. 591)

4. In applying the Miller-Orr model, the firm sets a(n) _____ limit (L) on cash holdings, an upper limit (U*), and a target cash balance (C*), which minimize _____ . C* = _____ and U* = _____ . The average cash balance equals _____ . When the cash balance reaches U*, the firm returns to its target balance C* by investing _____ dollars in _____ . When it declines to L, the firm sells _____ dollars of _____ obtain C*. (p. 594)

ANSWERS TO CONCEPT TEST

1. high; low; increase; decrease; high; low; opportunity; shortage
2. flexible; restrictive; trading; interest
3. zero; C; $[(C+0)/2]$; average cash balance; interest rate on marketable securities; $[(C/2) \times r]$; (T/C); $[(T/C) \times F]$; opportunity; trading
4. lower; expected total cost; $\{L+[(\frac{3}{4} \times F \times \sigma^2)/r]^{\frac{1}{3}}\}$; $[(3 \times C^*)-(2 \times L)]$; $\{[(4 \times C^*)-L]/3\}$; (U*-C*); marketable securities; (C*-L); marketable securities

PROBLEMS

1. Given the following information, use the BAT model to calculate the target cash balance:

Annual interest rate	10%
Fixed order cost	$ 50
Total cash needed	$2,500,000

2. Calculate the opportunity cost, the trading costs, and the total cost for holding the target cash balance determined in Problem 1.

3. Using the data given in Problem 1, calculate the opportunity cost, the trading costs and the total cost assuming that a $50,000 cash balance is held. Calculate the costs if a $100,000 cash balance is held.

4. Suppose that, for the data in Problem 1, the fixed order cost increased from $50 to $200; how does this affect the target cash balance, and the costs computed in the solution to Problem 2?

5. Suppose that, for the data in Problem 1, the interest rate decreased from 10% to 5%; how does this affect the target cash balance?

6. Suppose that the fixed cost per transaction to buy and sell marketable securities is $100, the daily interest rate is .03%, and the standard deviation of daily net cash flows is $50. Management has set a lower limit of $200 on cash holdings. Calculate the target cash balance, upper limit, and the average cash balance using the Miller-Orr model.

CHAPTER 20

CREDIT AND INVENTORY MANAGEMENT

CONCEPTS FOR REVIEW

Surveys indicate that management of the *least* liquid of the firm's current assets - accounts receivable and inventory - occupies a great deal of managerial time. As with the management of long-term investment and financing decisions, we describe several influences on the firm's decision-makers, and several models with which to analyze decisions.

CHAPTER HIGHLIGHTS

A firm may require cash on or before delivery in payment for its products, or it may decide to extend credit to its customers. If credit is extended, the firm must establish a **credit policy,** which involves three components: **terms of the sale, credit analysis,** and **collection policy**. These decisions impact the level and composition of receivables. Similarly, the amount and types of inventory held reflect managerial decisions regarding the costs of ordering and holding inventory. Accordingly, we consider several techniques for managing inventory.

I. CREDIT AND RECEIVABLES (p. 600)

Granting credit results in the creation of an account receivable for the seller and an account payable for the buyer. Credit management is an important aspect of a firm's short-term financial policy.

<u>Components of Credit Policy</u> (p. 601) Credit policy entails terms of sale, credit analysis, and collection policy. **Terms of sale** consist of: the credit period, the cash discount and the discount period, and the type of credit instrument used. **Credit analysis** is the process of attempting to distinguish between customers who are likely to make payment on an account and those who are not. **Collection policy** is the set of procedures the firm uses to collect payment on accounts.

<u>The Cash Flows from Granting Credit</u> (p. 601) The accounts receivable period is the time required to collect payment on a credit sale. Credit policy is a primary determinant of the accounts receivable period via its relationship to the average collection period and sales. Previously 5 we computed the average collection period (ACP) as follows:

$$ACP = \text{Accounts receivable/Average daily sales.}$$

As such,

$$\text{Accounts receivable} = \text{Average daily sales} \times ACP$$

<u>The Investment in Receivables</u> (p. 602) It is evident from the above that a firm's credit policy has an impact on both average daily sales and on the average collection period; consequently, credit policy affects the level of the firm's investment in accounts receivable.

II. TERMS OF THE SALE (p. 602)

Terms of sale involve the credit period, the cash discount, discount period, and type of credit instrument.

The Basic Form (p. 602) The general form of credit terms is as follows:

(take this discount off the invoice price)/(if you pay in this many days),
(else pay the full invoice amount in this many days)

Credit Period (p. 603) The credit period is the length of time during which the customer must make payment. When a discount is offered, the credit period has two components: the **net credit period**, which is the total amount of time the customer has to make payment; and the **cash discount period**, which is the time the discount is available to the customer. Factors to consider when setting the length of the credit period include the buyer's inventory period and operating cycle, perishability and collateral value of the goods, product demand, the buyer's credit risk, size of the account, and the level of industry competition.

Cash Discounts (p. 605) Cash discounts speed collections of receivables because they provide customers an incentive to pay earlier. Additionally, a discount is a way to charge higher prices to credit customers.

Credit Instruments (p. 606) A credit instrument is evidence of indebtedness. Most trade credit is offered on **open account**, which means that the credit instrument is the invoice. The customer signs the invoice when goods are received. Or, the selling firm may require a **promissory note**, which is a basic IOU. A **commercial draft** is a demand for payment sent to a customer's bank, along with the shipping invoices. The buyer signs the draft before goods are shipped. If the draft requires immediate payment, it is called a **sight draft**. If the bank 'accepts' the draft for future payment, it is a **banker's acceptance** and the bank accepts responsibility for making payment. A firm can also use a **conditional sales contract**; in this case, the firm retains title to the goods until payment is completed, and payment is often made in installments.

III. ANALYZING CREDIT POLICY (p. 607)

Credit Policy Effects (p. 607) The credit decision depends on the following:

1. *Revenue effects.* Granting credit results in a delay in collections and an increase in total revenue.
2. *Cost effects.* Granting credit results in increased costs directly associated with the credit process and, if sales increase, increased variable costs.
3. *The cost of debt.* The cost of financing receivables must be considered in analyzing credit policy.
4. *The probability of nonpayment.* Some buyers granted will default on their obligation to pay.
5. *The cash discount.* Some customers will pay during the discount period to take the discount.

Evaluating a Proposed Credit Policy (p. 608) To assess the impact of a change in credit policy, we compute the NPV of the change. The relevant variables are:

P = Price per unit
v = Variable cost per unit
Q = Current quantity sold per month
Q' = Quantity sold under new policy
r = Monthly required return

Example. Suppose a firm is considering granting credit terms of net 30 days. Assume the following:

P	= $11	v	= $5	r	=1%
Q	= 100	Q'	=120		

Should the firm grant credit terms of net 30 days to its customers? If it does not, monthly sales are:

$P \times Q = (\$11 \times 100) = \$1100$, and monthly variable costs are: $v \times Q = (\$5 \times 100) = \$500$. Cash flow under the old policy equals: $(P - v) \times Q = (\$11 - \$5) \times 100 = \$600$

If credit is granted, then cash flow under the new policy equals:

$$(P - v) \times Q' = (\$11 - \$5) \times 120 = \$720$$

The incremental cash flow is: Cash flow (new policy) - Cash flow (old policy) = $\$720 - 600 = \$120$. This incremental cash flow constitutes a perpetual monthly annuity whose present value is:

$$PV = [(P - v) \times (Q' - Q)]/r = \$120/.01 = \$12,000$$

The cost of the change in credit policy is the sum of two components. First, the variable cost of producing the additional units:

$$v(Q' - Q) = \$5 \times (120 - 100) = \$100$$

Second, the first month's sales which would be collected under the old policy are not collected until thirty days later under the new policy. Since collections are permanently delayed by thirty days, this cost is:

$$PQ = \$11 \times 100 = \$1100$$

The sum of these costs is: $PQ + v(Q' - Q) = \$1100 + \$100 = \$1200$. Finally, the NPV of the change in credit policy is:

$$NPV = -[PQ + v(Q' - Q)] + [(P - v) \times (Q' - Q)]/r = -\$1,200 + \$12,000 = \$10,800.$$

Since the NPV is positive, the change in credit policy to terms of net 30 days is beneficial.

IV. OPTIMAL CREDIT POLICY (p. 610)

The Total Credit Cost Curve (p. 610) The discussion to this point has focused on whether a firm should grant or deny credit. However, an additional issue to be considered is the determination of the optimal *amount* of credit to be granted. The firm must consider two categories of costs: **carrying costs** associated with granting credit and making the corresponding investment in receivables, and **opportunity costs** which result from a refusal to grant credit. Carrying costs include the required return on the investment in receivables, losses from bad debts, and costs of managing credit and collections. Opportunity costs are foregone profits from the lost sales which result if we refuse to grant credit. The optimal amount of credit minimizes the sum of the carrying and opportunity costs.

Organizing the Credit Function (p. 611) Firms that extend credit either bear the expense of running their own credit and collections department, or contract out ("outsource") all or part of the credit department's responsibilities.

V. CREDIT ANALYSIS (p. 612)

Credit analysis is the process of estimating the probability that a customer will not pay, and deciding whether to extend credit to that customer.

When Should Credit Be Granted? (p. 612) We analyze the credit decision for two special cases. The first is the case of a one-time sale, as illustrated by the following example.

Example A new customer plans to purchase one unit on credit at a price of P' = $100 per unit. The variable cost is v = $70 per unit and the monthly required return is r = 1%. Assume the firm has no repeat customers, so this is a one-time sale. Also assume that, at the end of sixty days, the customer will either pay the full amount due or will default. The probability of default is π = 25%, because 25% of new credit customers do not pay. Should the firm grant credit to the new customer?

The cost of granting credit is the variable cost (v = $70) of the product, which must be expended this month. The cash inflow in two months is:

$$(1 - \pi) \times P' = .75 \times \$100 = \$75,$$

so the NPV = -v + [(1 - π) ×P']/(1 + r)^2 = -$70 + $75/(1.01)^2 = $3.52. Since the NPV is positive, the firm should extend credit to the new customer.

In the next example, we analyze the credit decision under the assumption that a new customer who does not default on his first purchase will remain a customer indefinitely and will never default.

Example Assume the following data from the previous example: P' = $100, v = $70, and π = 25%. Also, the firm's required return for a two-month period is 2%. Assuming that a customer who does not default will purchase one unit every other month forever, should the firm extend credit?

The cost to the firm is the variable cost v = $70. In two months, the customer will either default, or will pay P' = $100 and purchase another unit. The probability that he will not default is (1 - π) = 75% and the expected net cash inflow in two months is:

$$(1 - \pi) \times (P' - v) = .75 \times \$30 = \$22.50$$

The NPV = -v + [(1 - π) × (P' - v)]/r = -$70 + $22.50/.02 = $1,055, so we should extend credit.

Credit Information (p. 614) Information used to assess creditworthiness can be obtained from financial statements, credit reports, banks, and the customer's payment history. Also, credit reports can be purchased from several sources.

Credit Evaluation and Scoring (p. 615) The traditional guidelines for assessing the probability of default are the **five Cs** of credit: character, capacity, capital, collateral, and conditions. **Credit scoring** is the process of computing a numerical rating as a guideline for assessing creditworthiness.

VI. COLLECTION POLICY (p. 615)

Collection policy is the process of monitoring receivables and obtaining payment of overdue accounts.

184

Monitoring Receivables (p. 615) Two tools used to monitor outstanding accounts are the **average collection period** (ACP) and the **aging schedule**. The relationship between the ACP and the firm's credit terms indicates whether customers are generally paying accounts when due.

Collection Effort (p. 617) Collection effort generally involves a series of steps such as: (1) sending a delinquency letter, (2) calling the customer, (3) hiring a collection agency, and (4) initiating legal action.

VII. INVENTORY MANAGEMENT (p. 618)

The Financial Manager and Inventory Policy (p. 618) The management of inventory is an optimization decision. Too much inventory ties up funds and reduces asset turnover (indicating inefficient use of resources). Too little inventory increases the risk of lost sales due to stockouts. The following techniques are designed to balance these costs.

Inventory Types (p. 618) We define three categories of inventories: raw materials, work-in-progress, and finished goods. The relative levels of each held are a function of expected sales, holding costs, and the length of the productions process, among other things.

Inventory Costs (p. 619) **Carrying costs** include costs of storing and insuring inventory as well as losses due to obsolescence and theft, and the opportunity cost of the funds invested. **Shortage costs** are incurred when the firm must continually restock, or when the firm loses sales due to inability to fill orders.

VIII. INVENTORY MANAGEMENT TECHNIQUES (p. 620)

The following techniques seek to either reduce the cost of holding a given amount of inventory, or to reduce the amount of inventory held, thereby reducing costs.

The ABC Approach (p. 620) This techniques requires the categorization of inventory into three (or more) categories, based on the value of inventory represented. High-value inventory items are monitored more closely than low-value items.

The Economic Order Quantity (EOQ) Model (p. 620) The EOQ model is a cost-minimization approach to inventory management. Define total costs:

$$\text{Total costs} = \text{carrying costs} + \text{shortage costs}$$

$$= (\text{Average inventory} \times \text{Carrying costs per unit}) + (\text{Fixed cost per order} \times \text{Number of orders})$$

$$= [(Q/2) \times CC] + [F \times (T/Q)].$$

The economic order quantity is that level of Q which minimizes total costs and is defined as

$$Q^* = [(2T \times F)/CC]^{1/2}$$

The EOQ model can be extended to include such factors as the holding of safety stocks and the existence of lags in the time between order placement and the receipt of goods.

Extensions to the EOQ Model (p. 625) The standard EOQ model can be extended to include **safety stocks** (which is the value below which inventory levels will not be allowed to fall) and **reorder points** (which are the times at which the firm will actually place orders).

Managing Derived-Demand Inventories (p. 625) Inventory levels based on "derived-demand" inventory management techniques such as **MRP (Materials Requirements Planning)** are determined by anticipated finished goods requirements. Once a finished goods forecast is in hand, we estimate the level of work-in-progress and then raw materials necessary to meet the firm's needs.

Just-in-Time inventory (JIT) is another derived-demand technique in which the firm orders inventory only to meet immediate production needs. As a result, inventory holdings are minimized.

KEY TERMS AND CONCEPTS

Aging schedule - a compilation of accounts receivable by the age of each account. (p. 617)
Cash discount - a discount given for a cash purchase. (p. 605)
Collection policy - procedures followed by a firm in collecting accounts receivable. (p. 601)
Credit analysis - the process of determining the probability that customers will or will not pay. (p. 601)
Credit cost curve - graph of the sum of the carrying and opportunity costs of credit policy. (p. 611)
Credit instrument - evidence of indebtedness. (p. 606)
Credit period - the length of time that credit is granted. (p. 603)
Credit scoring - process of quantifying the probability of default when granting consumer credit. (p. 615)
Economic order quantity (EOQ) - the restocking quantity that minimizes total inventory costs. (p. 620)
Five Cs of credit - character, capacity, capital, collateral, and conditions. (p. 615)
Just-in-time inventory (JIT) - system that minimizes inventory holdings. (p. 627)
Material requirements planning (MRP) - a set of procedures used to determine inventory levels for demand-dependent inventory types such as work-in-progress and raw materials. (p. 625)
Terms of sale - conditions on which a firm sells its goods and services for cash or credit. (p. 601)

CONCEPT TEST

1. Granting credit results in the creation of a(n) _____ for the seller, and a(n) _____ for the buyer. Collectively, the credit period, the cash discount and discount period, and the type of credit instrument are the _____ . Attempting to distinguish between customers who are likely to make payment and those who are not is _____ . The procedures to collect payments constitute the firm's _____ . (p. 600)

2. The time required to collect payment on a credit sale is the firm's _____ or _____ . The firm's level of accounts receivable equals the product of the firm's _____ and the _____ . That is: Accounts receivable = _____ × _____ . (p. 603)

3. The time during which the customer is obligated to make payment is the _____ period. When a discount is offered, this period consists of the _____ period, which is the total amount of time the customer has to make his payment, and the _____ period, which is the period during which the discount is available. The beginning of the credit period is the _____ date. (p. 603)

4. Most trade credit is offered on open account; i.e., the credit instrument is the _____.
Or the seller may require a(n) _____ , a basic IOU. A(n) _____
draft is a demand for payment sent to a customer's bank. If the draft requires immediate payment, it
is a(n) _____ draft. If the bank 'accepts' the draft for future payment, it is a(n)
_____. A firm can also use a(n) _____ contract as a credit
instrument; the firm retains title to the goods until payment is completed. (p. 606)

5. When deciding whether to extend credit, the financial manager must compute the _____
of a change in credit terms. Assuming no discount period and a thirty-day credit period, the
incremental cash flow for a change in credit terms equals _____ . Since this cash
flow is an annuity, its PV equals _____ . The cost of the change in credit policy
is the sum of (1) the variable cost of producing the additional units which will be sold with the new
credit policy, which equals _____ , and (2) the first month's sales which would be
collected under the old policy but are not collected until thirty days later under the new policy. Since
collections are permanently delayed by thirty days, this cost is _____ . The sum of
these costs is _____ . The NPV of the change in policy equals
_____ . (p. 607)

6. To determine the optimal amount of credit granted, firm must consider two categories: the
_____ costs associated with granting credit and making the corresponding investment
in accounts receivables, and _____ costs which result from a refusal to grant credit.
The optimal amount of credit minimizes the _____ of the _____ costs
and _____ costs. (p. 611)

7. Traditional guidelines for assessing the probability that a customer will not pay are the 'five Cs' of
credit: (1) willingness to pay (i.e., _____); (2) ability to pay (i.e.,
_____); (3) financial reserves (i.e., _____); (4) business
conditions (i.e., _____); and (5) _____ . Computing a numerical
rating as a guideline for assessing creditworthiness is called _____. Statistical
procedures, called _____, are used by some firms to forecast the probability that
a customer will default. (p. 612)

8. The process of monitoring receivables and obtaining payment of overdue accounts is referred to as
_____ . Two tools used to monitor outstanding accounts are the
_____ period and the _____ schedule. (p. 617)

9. The _____ model is a cost-minimization approach to inventory management. The optimal
order quantity minimizes the sum of _____ costs and _____ costs. (p. 620)

10. _____ inventory management techniques employ anticipated finished goods needs
in order to estimate work-in-progress and raw materials needs. (p. 625)

ANSWERS TO CONCEPT TEST

1. account receivable; account payable; terms of sale; credit analysis; collection policy
2. accounts receivable period; average collection period (ACP); average daily sales; average collection
period; average daily sales; ACP
3. credit; net credit; discount; invoice;

4. invoice; promissory note; commercial; sight; banker's acceptance; conditional sales
5. net present value; $[(P-v)\times(Q'-Q)]$; $[(P-v)\times(Q'-Q)]/r$; $v(Q'-Q)$; $P\times Q$; $PQ+v(Q'-Q)$; $-[PQ+v(Q'-Q)]+[(P-v)\times(Q'-Q)]/r$
6. carrying; opportunity; sum; carrying; opportunity
7. character; capacity; capital; conditions; collateral; credit scoring; credit-scoring models
8. collection; average collection; aging
9. economic order quantity (EOQ); carrying; restocking
10. Derived-demand

PROBLEMS

1. Icarus Company (a well-known 'high flyer') manufactures suntan lotion. Its credit terms are 2/20, net 40. Suppose a retailer purchases 10 cases of suntan lotion for $200 per case. If the retailer takes the full credit period to pay, how much should the retailer remit to Icarus? When should payment be made?

2. For the data of Problem 1, when must the retailer pay in order to receive the discount offered by Icarus? If the retailer takes the discount, how much should she remit to Icarus? If the retailer does not take advantage of the discount, how many days' credit does she receive?

3. If the retailer in Problem 1 does not take the discount, what is the effective interest rate paid?

4. Suppose the Icarus Company in Problem 1 finds that, historically, 80% of its customers take the discount. What is the firm's average collection period (ACP)?

5. Suppose that the Icarus Company described in Problem 1 sells 600 cases of suntan lotion each month, at a price of $200 per case. What is its average balance sheet amount in accounts receivable? (Assume the ACP from Problem 4.)

6. Suppose the Icarus Company in Problem 1 has production costs equal to 80% of selling price. What is the firm's average investment (i.e., its actual cost) in receivables?

7. Daedulus Company has an ACP of 30 days and an average level of accounts receivable of $600,000. What are the firm's annual credit sales? What is the receivables turnover ratio?

8. A firm offers credit terms of 3/15, net 60. What effective annual interest rate does the firm earn when a customer does not take the discount?

9. For the following credit terms, compute the effective annual rate: 1.5/20, net 45; 1/10, net 40.

10. For each of the credit terms identified in Problems 8 and 9, determine whether a firm should take the discount or pay the net amount of the invoice. Assume the firm would have to borrow from a bank at a 15% annual interest rate to take the discount.

11. Krishna, Inc., is considering a new credit policy. The current policy requires cash payment, while the new policy would extend credit for one month. The following information has been collected:

	Current policy	New policy
Price per unit	$ 50	$ 50
Cost per unit	$ 40	$ 40
Unit sales per period	300	345

The required return is 1.5% per month, and there will be no defaults. Should Krishna make the change?

12. Verify the calculation for Problem 11 by computing the NPV of the change in credit policy using the following alternative approach: first compute the NPV of the change under the assumption that the change is in effect for one time period only, and then treat the one-period NPV as a perpetuity.

13. Verify the calculation for Problem 11 by computing the NPV of the change in credit policy using the following approach: compare the opportunity cost of the investment in receivables to the monthly net benefit resulting from the change in credit policy.

14. Brahma Company is considering a change in its credit policy. Current policy requires cash payment, while the new policy would extend credit for one month. The following information has been collected:

	Current policy	New policy
Price per unit	$195	$200
Cost per unit	$150	$150
Unit sales per period	1,000	1,000

The required return is 1% per month, the cash discount is 2.5%, and all customers will buy on credit. Brahma expects 2% of its customers to default. Should Brahma make the change in credit policy?

15. A new customer, Mr. Hernandez, intends to purchase 200 units of a product from the Gooden-Carter Company, Inc. The price of the product is $500 per unit and the variable cost of producing the product is $350. Mr. Gooden must decide whether to extend credit to Mr. Hernandez for one month. Mr. Gooden has concluded that the probability of default is 30%, and the required return is 1% per month. Should Gooden-Carter extend credit to Mr. Hernandez? (Assume this is a one-time sale and Mr. Hernandez will not buy from Gooden-Carter if credit is not extended.)

16. Consider the following additional information for problem 15: If Mr. Hernandez does not default, then he will continue to purchase 200 units each month for the foreseeable future. Should Gooden-Carter extend credit to Mr. Hernandez?

APPENDIX 20A MORE ON CREDIT POLICY ANALYSIS

In this appendix we elaborate on our previous discussion of the analysis of a change in credit policy.

Two Alternative Approaches (p. 633) The **one-shot approach** requires that we compute the one-time increase in cash flows associated with the decision, and subtract from that value the incremental investment. If the process is repeated every period, the PV of the decision is equal to the PV of the perpetuity represented by the net cash inflow, discounted at the appropriate required rate of return.

More widely used is the **accounts receivable approach,** in which we compute the incremental gross profit per unit, then subtract the carrying cost of the incremental receivables balance. The difference is assumed to represent a perpetual cash flow and is discounted at the appropriate required rate of return to obtain a present value.

Discounts and Default Risk (p. 635) It is unlikely that all of the firms to which we grant credit will pay us back. The cost of defaults can be accounted for in the NPV analysis by including an estimate of the percentage of sales which must be written off due to nonpayment. It can be shown that, whenever this default proportion exceeds the percentage discount offered, granting credit decreases firm value.

RISK MANAGEMENT: AN INTRODUCTION TO FINANCIAL ENGINEERING

CONCEPTS FOR REVIEW

Previous chapters dealt with the quantification of risk and its effect on required return. This chapter describes methods which allow firms to reduce some of the risks to which they are exposed.

CHAPTER HIGHLIGHTS

Hedging is the process by which a firm attempts to shield itself from the effects of unexpected changes in interest rates, commodity prices, or exchange rates. Increasing volatility in these prices and rates has focused attention on the creation and use of instruments designed to facilitate hedging or "risk management". Risk management is one of the "frontier" areas of finance, and brings together topics related to microeconomics, valuation, time value, and, of course, risk and return.

I. HEDGING AND PRICE VOLATILITY (p. 642)

In broad terms, reducing a firm's exposure to price, foreign exchange, or interest rate fluctuations is **hedging** (or **"immunization"**). The financial manager's job is to find a way, either by using existing financial instruments or by creating new ones, to reduce the firm's risk related to such fluctuations. The process of designing new financial instruments is **financial engineering**, and has become popular due to increased volatility in prices, interest rates, and foreign exchange rates since the 1970s.

Price Volatility: A Historical Perspective (p. 643) Time series data suggest that many commodity prices, along with market interest rates and foreign exchange rates, have grown more volatile. As such, the ability to hedge against unanticipated changes has become increasingly important.

Interest Rate Volatility (p. 644) In October, 1979 the Fed abandoned interest rate stability as a policy objective in favor of targeting money supply growth. Interest rates have been allowed to "float", and, as a result, volatility has increased sharply. A major implication of the Fed's policy change is that financial managers find it more difficult to forecast borrowing rates.

Exchange Rate Volatility (p. 644) A firm involved in international trade must engage in financial transactions in foreign currency. Thus, the rate of exchange between dollars and, say, yen, becomes an important consideration. Since the collapse of the Bretton Woods accord in 1971, exchange rates have been allowed to "float", so firms engaging in foreign trade are exposed to exchange rate risk.

Commodity Price Volatility (p. 646) The prices of some commodities (particularly oil) have also become more volatile in the last two decades. Those firms which utilize these commodities in the production of goods and services are therefore exposed to a third source of volatility.

The Impact of Financial Risk: The U.S. Savings and Loan Industry (p. 646) The S&L debacle was due, at least in part, to the adverse effects of unanticipated interest rate changes. S&L managers were essentially caught holding the wrong mix of assets and liabilities, and were generally unable (or unwilling) to adjust their portfolios in a timely manner.

II. MANAGING FINANCIAL RISK (p. 648)

The first step in managing risk is to identify the types of price fluctuations that have the greatest impact on firm value. For example, managers of firms with large amounts of debt should be more concerned with interest rate volatility than managers in unlevered firms, and managers of import-export firms should be more concerned about exchange rate changes than those of firms whose business is largely domestic.

The Risk Profile (p. 648) The basic tool for identifying and measuring a firm's exposure to financial risk is the **risk profile**, which graphs the relationship between changes in the price of some good or service and changes in the value of the firm.

Learning Tip: The risk profile is a variation on the NPV profile described previously. The direction of the slope reflects the direction of the relationship between firm value and the price of the good or service, while the slope gradient indicates how sensitive firm value is to changes in the price of the good or service. This sensitivity measures the firm's **risk exposure** *to fluctuations.*

Reducing Risk Exposure (p. 649) The essence of reducing risk exposure is to find a way to insulate the firm from price or rate changes. For example, the farmer with 400 acres of corn in the field is exposed to the risk of a drop in corn prices before he can bring his crop to market. By contracting with a cannery today to sell his crop at a specified price in the future, he eliminates the risk of a drop in price. Put another way, his risk profile is now flat. (It should also be pointed out that he forgoes profits which would have been earned had the price of corn risen before he brought his crop to market.)

Hedging Short-Run Exposure (p. 651) Price fluctuations have two components: short-run (temporary) changes, and long-run (permanent) changes. These fluctuations have different implications for the firm.

Short-run changes in prices result from unforeseen events or shocks. These are often called *transitory* changes. Short-run price changes can drive a businesses into financial distress even though, long-run, the business is fundamentally sound. This happens when a firm finds itself with sudden cost increases that it cannot pass on immediately, which may lead to financial distress. Short-run financial exposure is often called **transactions exposure** because short-term financial exposure typically arises because a firm must make transactions in the near future at uncertain prices or rates.

Cash Flow Hedging: A Cautionary Note (p. 651) So far, we have talked about hedging firm value, what is usually being hedged is the firm's near-term cash flow. Generally speaking, hedging short-term financial exposure, hedging transactions exposure, and hedging near-term cash flows are the same thing.

Hedging Long-Term Exposure (p. 652) Price fluctuations also have longer-run, more permanent components which are the result of fundamental shifts in the underlying economics of a business. A firm's exposure to long-run financial risks is often called its **economic exposure**, and is more difficult to hedge against. No amount of hedging can affect the economic fundamentals (e.g., the product market structure) faced by the firm's managers. However, by hedging management may be able, over the short run, to buy itself time to figure out how it might adapt the firm to changing economic fundamentals. Thus, by successful hedging, managers can (1) insulate the firm from transitory price fluctuations, and (2) give the firm some time to adapt to fundamental changes in market conditions.

III. HEDGING WITH FORWARD CONTRACTS (p. 653)

Forward Contracts: The Basics (p. 653) A **forward contract** is an agreement between two parties calling for the sale of an asset or product in the future at a price agreed upon today. The terms of the contract call for one party to deliver the goods to the other on a certain date in the future, called the **settlement date**. The other party pays the previously agreed-upon **forward price** and takes delivery of the goods. Forward contracts allow buyers and sellers to lock in today the prices at which transactions will occur, whether those prices take the form of commodity prices, interest rates, or exchange rates. The ability to reduce the potential losses from unanticipated price changes makes forward contracts useful hedging tools for both producers and users.

Forward contracts can be bought and sold. The **buyer** of a forward contract has the obligation to take delivery and pay for the goods; the **seller** has the obligation to make delivery and accept payment. The buyer of a forward contract benefits if prices increase because the buyer will have locked in a lower price. And the seller wins if prices fall because a higher selling price has been locked in. *Notice: one party to the contract can win only at expense of the other, so a forward contract is a zero-sum game.*

Learning Tip: In theory, neither party to the contract need lose. If the parties contract at today's price, and the price on the settlement date is the same, neither party has gained at the expense of the other.

The Payoff Profile (p. 653) The **payoff profile** is a graph of the gains and losses on a forward contract due to unexpected price changes in the asset or product being contracted for. The contract buyer benefits if market prices rise, because he has locked in a price that is lower than market price. (At this point, the contract buyer could gain either by taking delivery of the asset, or by selling the contract at a price higher than it was purchased for.) And the seller of the forward contract benefits when prices subsequently fall.

Hedging With Forwards (p. 653) The essence of managing risk is to use a hedging instrument such as a forward contract which has a payoff profile opposite to the one we already have. We first identify the firm's exposure to financial risk using a risk profile. We then try to find a financial arrangement such as a forward contract that has an offsetting payoff profile. Combining the two payoff profiles results in a flat (or nearly flat) profile, which reflects the fact that risk has been hedged away.

Another characteristic of forward contracting is that no money changes hands when the contract is signed, since it is simply an agreement to transact in the future at a specified price. However, because a forward contract is a financial obligation, there is *credit risk*. When the settlement date arrives, the losing party has a significant incentive to default. **Futures contracts** reduce this risk.

IV. HEDGING WITH FUTURES CONTRACTS (p. 656)

A **futures contract** obligates the contract buyer (seller) to take (make) delivery of a specified asset at a specified price on a specified date. A crucial distinction between a forward contract and futures contract, however, is that in the case of the latter, gains and losses are realized on a *daily* basis, rather than only on the settlement date. This procedure is called **marking-to-market** and reduces the likelihood of default by the person on the losing end of the contract.

Trading in Futures (p. 656) Commodity futures contracts have been used by producers and users of agricultural products for many centuries. Financial futures contracts (for which the underlying goods are financial assets such as stocks, bonds, or currencies) are a more recent innovation, but have grown in importance rapidly in the last two decades. This growth is due largely to the increased interest and foreign exchange rate volatility described earlier in the chapter.

Futures Exchanges (p. 657) Futures contracts are traded on exchanges across the globe. Table 21.1 provides a group of actual exchange prices as reported in *The Wall Street Journal*.

Hedging with Futures (p. 657) Hedging with futures contracts is conceptually identical to hedging with forward contracts, and the payoff profile on a futures contract is drawn just like the profile for a forward. And, as with forward contracts, hedging is a zero-sum game: when prices change, what one party to the futures contract wins, the other loses. However, gains and losses are realized on a daily basis. *Cross-hedging* is the practice of using a contract on a related, but not identical asset, to hedge. Cross-hedging is required when there exists no futures contract on precisely the asset the firm wishes to hedge. The resulting hedge is *imperfect*, because the risk is usually not completely eliminated by the hedge.

V. HEDGING WITH SWAP CONTRACTS (p. 659)

A **swap contract** is an agreement by two parties to exchange or swap specified cash flows at specified intervals. A swap contract can be thought of as a portfolio of forward contracts because the contract parties exchange assets several times over the life of the contract, rather than just on the settlement date. Most swaps contracts fall into one of three categories: currency, interest rate, and commodity swaps.

Currency Swaps (p. 660) A **currency swap** involves the exchange of one currency for another at specified dates in the future. An import-export firm headquartered in the U.S., for example, must routinely collect receivables denominated in one currency and make payments in another. One way to reduce the risk of exchange rate fluctuations is to contract with another firm engaged in international trade to swap foreign currencies at specified rates on specified future dates.

Interest Rate Swaps (p. 660) **Interest rate swaps** are used to modify the pattern of payments made, to modify the index used in a floating-rate arrangement, or even to convert a fixed-rate loan to a floating-rate loan (or vice-versa).

Commodity Swaps (p. 660) A **commodity swap** is an agreement to exchange a fixed quantity of a commodity at fixed times in the future.

The Swap Dealer (p. 661) Swap contracts are not currently traded on organized exchanges. Instead, *swap dealers* act as intermediaries, bringing together firms wishing to enter swap agreements on either side of the contract. Because it may take some time to find the second party, the swap dealer may take the other side of the agreement and then seek an offsetting transaction with another party. The dealer's objective is to facilitate the transaction for his customers while limiting his net exposure.

VI. HEDGING WITH OPTION CONTRACTS (p. 662)

Forward, futures, and swap contracts *obligate* the contracting parties to transact on a future date on specified terms. An **option contract** gives the owner the right, but not the obligation, to buy or sell a asset at a specified price for a specified period.

Option Terminology (p. 663) Options are classified as either puts or calls. The owner of a **call option** has the right, but not the obligation, to *buy* an underlying asset at a fixed price, called the *strike price* or **exercise price** from the seller of the option. Thus, the holder of a call option profits when prices rise. The owner of a **put option** has the right, but not the obligation, to *sell* an underlying asset for a specified time to the seller of the option at the **strike price,** so puts increase in value when prices fall. The act of buying or selling the underlying asset using the option contract is called *exercising* the option. **"American"** options can be exercised at any time up to and including the **expiration date**; **"European"** options can only be exercised on the expiration date. Most options are American.

Learning Tip: An easy way to keep puts and calls straight is to remember the following ditty.

"Buy call or sell a put when you think the price is going up.
Buy a put or sell a call when you think the price is going to fall."

Source: "A Fool and His Money," by John Rothchild.

Options Versus Forwards (p. 663) Two features distinguish options from forwards. Forward contracts obligate the contracting parties to transact in the future; options obligate only the option seller, and only if the contract buyer chooses to exercise. Second, no money changes hands when a forward contract is created, but the option buyer pays the **option premium** immediately to enter into the contract.

Option Payoff Profiles (p. 663) Payoff profiles for options depict the difference between the asset's value and the strike price on the option. If the price of the underlying asset rises above the strike price, the owner of the option will exercise it and profit. If the value of the asset falls, the owner of the option will not exercise. The payoff profile does not consider the premium paid for the option, so as before, options represent a zero-sum game, because the seller's payoff profile is exactly the opposite of the buyer's.

Option Hedging (p. 664) Hedgers seek to reduce the risk associated with a position currently held by using a hedging instrument to take an offsetting position. Thus, a corporate treasurer whose firm holds stock in another firm may buy puts on that stock. Then any losses suffered if the price of the stock falls are offset by gains in the value of the puts.

Hedging Commodity Price Risk with Options (p. 665) A relatively recent development is the introduction of options contracts for which the underlying asset is a futures contract. These "futures options" work in a manner analogous to a standard option. Exercise of a call option provides the option holder with a futures contract which can be closed immediately, and with an amount equal to the difference between the strike price on the option and the current futures price. Options on commodity futures contracts provide the opportunity to hedge against commodity price changes.

Hedging Exchange Rate Risk with Options (p. 666) Firms can hedge *exchange risk* with options for which the underlying asset is a foreign currency, or for which the underlying asset is a futures contract for which, in turn, the underlying asset is a foreign currency. Which vehicle is chosen depends largely on such factors as the amount of exposure to be hedged, the relevant time frame, and the relative prices of the currency available at a point in time.

Hedging Interest Rate Risk with Options (p. 666) One can use options to hedge against **interest rate risk**. These options may take the form of options on futures or options on interest-bearing assets themselves. An **interest rate cap** is a call option on an interest rate, usually sold in conjunction with a floating-rate loan. Exercise of the call allows the borrower/option holder to "acquire" a prespecified interest rate. A **floor** is a put option on an interest rate. If a floating-rate borrower sells a floor, then the loan rate can never fall below that specified in the option contract. The simultaneous purchase of a cap and sale of a floor is a **collar**. It ensures that the borrowing rate will always be between the floor and the cap (or "ceiling"), regardless of what happens to market rates.

Since we can buy an option on a futures contract, it stands to reason that we should be able to buy one on a swap contract. Options on swaps are called **swaptions**. *Compound options* are options on options. And so it goes. **Financial engineering** is the business of combining existing financial instruments in order to create new ones with the desired characteristics.

KEY TERMS AND CONCEPTS

Call option - An option that gives the owner the right, but not the obligation, to buy an asset. (p. 663)
Cross-hedging - Hedging with futures contracts written on related, but not identical, assets. (p. 659)
Derivative security - A financial asset that represents a claim to another financial asset. (p. 643)
Economic exposure - Long-term financial risk arising from permanent changes in prices or other economic fundamentals. (p. 652)
Forward contract - A legally binding agreement between two parties calling for the sale of an asset or product in the future at a price agreed upon today. (p. 653)
Futures contract - A forward contract with the feature that gains and losses are realized each day rather than only on the settlement date. (p. 656)
Hedging - Reducing a firm's exposure to price or rate fluctuations. (p. 642)
Option contract - An agreement that gives the owner the right, but not the obligation, to buy or sell a specific asset at a specific price for a set period of time. (p. 662)
Payoff profile - plot of contract gains and losses resulting from unexpected price changes. (p. 653)
Put option - An option that gives the owner the right, but not the obligation, to sell an asset. (p. 663)
Risk profile - A plot showing how the value of the firm is affected by changes in prices or rates. (p. 648)
Swap contract - two-party contract to exchange or swap specified cash flows at future intervals. (p. 659)
Transactions exposure - Short-run financial exposure arising from the need to buy or sell at uncertain prices or rates in the near future. (p. 651)

CONCEPT TEST

1. The use of financial instruments to reduce a firm's exposure to price or rate fluctuations is
    _____ . Using available financial instruments to create new ones with desired
    characteristics is _____ . Substantial increases have been observed in
    _____, _____, and _____ . (p. 642)

2. The _____ graphs the relationship between changes in the price of some good
    or service and changes in firm value. It depicts the firm's exposure to _____ .
    The sensitivity of firm value to price or rate changes is reflected in the _____ .
    Hedging results in a graph that is relatively _____ . (p. 648)

3. Short-run or temporary changes in prices are called _____. Short-run financial exposure is called _____. Exposure to long-run financial risks is called _____ . (p. 651)

4. A(n) _____ is a legally binding agreement between two parties calling for the sale of an asset or product in the future at a price agreed upon today. The contract terms call for one party to deliver goods to the other on a certain date in the future, called the _____ . The other party pays the previously agreed-upon _____ and takes the goods. (p. 653)

5. A _____ is similar to a forward contract except gains and losses are realized daily rather than only on the settlement date. This is called _____ and reduces the likelihood that one of the parties will _____ at the settlement date. (p. 656)

6. A _____ is an agreement by two parties to exchange specified cash flows at specified future intervals. A _____ involves the exchange of one currency for another at specified future dates. _____ can be used to modify the pattern of payments made, to modify the index used in a floating-rate arrangement, or even to convert a fixed-rate loan to a floating-rate loan (or vice-versa). A _____ is an agreement to exchange a fixed quantity of a commodity at fixed times in the future. (p. 659)

7. A(n) _____ gives the owner the right, but not the obligation, to buy or sell an asset at a specified price for a specified time. The owner of a _____ has the right to *buy* an underlying asset at a fixed price, called the *strike price* or *exercise price* from the seller of the option. The owner of a _____ has the right to *sell* an underlying asset for a specified time to the option seller. (p. 662)

8. _____ obligate contracting parties to transact in the future; _____ obligate only the seller, and then only if the contract buyer exercises. No money changes hands when a _____ is created, but the buyer of an _____ pays the _____ immediately to enter into the contract. Exercise of a _____ provides the option holder with a futures contract which can be closed immediately, and with an amount equal to the difference between the strike price and the current futures price. (p. 663)

9. A(n) _____ is a call option on an interest rate, usually sold in conjunction with a floating-rate loan. Exercise of the option allows the borrower/option holder to "acquire" a prespecified interest rate. A _____ is a put option on an interest rate. The simultaneous purchase of a cap and sale of a floor is called a _____ . (p. 667)

ANSWERS TO CONCEPT TEST

1. hedging; financial engineering; commodity prices; foreign exchange rates; interest rates
2. risk profile; financial risk; slope gradient; flat
3. transitory changes; transaction exposure; economic exposure
4. forward contract; settlement date; forward price
5. futures contract; marking-to-market; default

6.   swap; currency swap; Interest rate swap; commodity swaps
7.   option; call; put
8.   Forward contracts; options; forward contract; option contract; option premium; futures option
9.   interest rate cap; floor; collar

PROBLEMS

1. Compare and contrast (1) forward contracts, (2) futures contracts, and (3) options contracts. Which do you believe is the most liquid? Least liquid? Why?

2. Rob Petrie owns 1000 shares of Calvada Productions common stock. The price has increased from $10 to $30 per share in the last six months. Rob is unsure about what the future holds for the stock and is trying to decide what action to take. If he sells the stock now, and the price subsequently rises farther, he will have foregone the additional gain. On the other hand, if he hangs on and the price subsequently falls, he will suffer a loss. Describe how Rob could use options to hedge his current position.

3. Suppose Rob buys call on 100 shares of IBM stock. The strike price is $50. Construct a payoff table given future market prices of $70, $60, $50, $40, and $30.

4. Referring again to Problem 3, suppose Rob had purchased a *put* rather than a call. (The put also has a $50 exercise price.) Now draw his payoff table.

5. Why is a convertible bond equivalent to the combination of a "straight" bond and an option? How would you value a convertible bond? <u>Ex ante</u>, who "wins" when investors purchase convertible bonds?

6. Herb Tarlek is obligated to deliver 1,000 barrels of heating oil to a customer six months from today. He believes that the price of heating oil will be rising in the next six months and would like to use futures contracts to lock in the futures price. Should he buy or sell contracts? Are there any advantages to using futures rather than forward contracts?

7. Refer to the previous problem. Suppose Herb is not obligated to deliver any oil, but just wishes to make some quick money. He still believes the price of heating oil will be rising in the next six months and would like to use futures contracts to profit from his forecasting prowess. Should he buy or sell contracts? How will Herb eliminate his position when the maturity date nears?

CHAPTER 22

OPTIONS AND CORPORATE SECURITIES

CONCEPTS FOR REVIEW

Previous chapters described the characteristics of securities such as stocks and bonds, which have value because they represent claims on future cash flows. In this chapter we examine securities which represent claims on other securities or assets.

CHAPTER HIGHLIGHTS

Specific options (such as the call provision on corporate debt) have been encountered previously. This chapter concerns the valuation of options in general. We also discuss the fact that stocks and bonds are themselves options; thus we gain new insights into many financial decisions.

I. OPTIONS: THE BASICS (p. 673)

An **option** gives its owner the right, but not the obligation, to buy or sell a certain asset at a fixed price (called the **striking price** or **exercise price**) during a specified period of time. The act of purchasing or selling the underlying asset is called **exercising** the option. The option matures on the **expiration date**. An **American option** can be exercised at any time up to the expiration date. A **European option** can be exercised only on the expiration date. Options on stocks and bonds are traded on several exchanges, the largest of which is the Chicago Board Options Exchange (CBOE).

Puts and Calls (p. 674) A **call option** gives its owner the right to *buy* a specified asset, while **put option** gives its owner the right to *sell* the underlying asset. You might purchase a call (put) option if you expect the value of the underlying stock to increase (decrease).

One who sells an option contract is the *writer* of the option. The writer of a call is obligated to *sell* the stock at the striking price if the call buyer chooses to exercise. Similarly, the writer of a put is obligated to *buy* the stock at the exercise price should the put buyer exercise the option.

Stock Option Quotations (p. 674) Table 22.1 in the text provides a set of stock option quotations from *The Wall Street Journal*.

Option Payoffs (p. 675) Suppose that, on October 1, an investor purchases a call option to buy 100 shares of Times Mirror common stock: the expiration date is the third Friday in December; the exercise price is $30; the price of the option is quoted as $1½; the current market price of Times Mirror stock is $27½. How much does the investor pay for the option? What is his gain (or loss) if the price of the stock declines between October 1 and the third Friday in December? What if the stock price increases?

Since the option price is $1½ per share, the total cost is ($1½ × 100) = $150. If the price of Times Mirror stock declines to, say $25, the investor would not exercise the option; he would not purchase shares for $30 when the market price of the stock is $25. When the market price of the stock is less than the exercise price of the option, the option is **out of the money**. If the option is out of the money on the expiration date, the option expires worthless and the investor has lost the purchase price of the option.

If the stock price exceeds the exercise price, the option is **in the money**. Suppose the stock price is $32¾ on the expiration date. The investor can exercise the option [i.e., purchase 100 shares of stock for ($30 × 100) = $3,000], and then immediately sell the shares for ($32.75 × 100) = $3,275. His profit is ($3,275 - $3,000) = $275, less the $150 option purchase price, for a net profit of ($275 - $150) = $125.

Consider these transactions from the perspective of the option seller (writer). Recall that the call writer must sell shares at the exercise price if the call buyer exercises. If the option expires out of the money (and is therefore not exercised) the option writer does not sell the underlying stock, but keeps the option purchase price. In the Times Mirror example above, if the option expires out of the money, the option writer has a $150 profit. Since the buyer's $150 loss is the seller's $150 profit, options are a *zero-sum game*, because the profit earned by one party is a loss to the other. This conclusion also holds if the option expires in the money.

II. FUNDAMENTALS OF OPTION VALUATION (p. 677)

Value of a Call Option At Expiration (p. 677) Let:

S_1 = Stock price at expiration (in one period)
S_0 = Stock price today
C_1 = Value of the call option on the expiration date (in one period)
C_0 = Value of the call option today
E = Exercise price on the option

The example above demonstrates that the value of a call option on the expiration date (C_1) is zero if the stock price (S_1) is less than the exercise price (E) is out of the money). This statement can be written:

$$C_1 = 0 \text{ if } S_1 \leq E \text{ or } C_1 = 0 \text{ if } (S_1 - E) \leq 0.$$

Or, a call option is in the money if $S_1 > E$. The value of an in-the-money call at expiration is ($S_1 - E$). This relationship can be stated in either of the following equivalent ways:

$$C_1 = (S_1 - E) \text{ if } S_1 > E \text{ or } C_1 = (S_1 - E) \text{ if } (S_1 - E) > 0$$

Suppose the exercise price is $100. At expiration, the option is in the money if $S_1 > \$100$, and its value is ($S_1 - \$100$). If S_1 is $120, the option owner can acquire the stock for $100 by exercising the option and then immediately sell the stock for $120, for a $20 gain. If $S_1 < \$100$ at expiration, the option is out of the money and has no value. A call cannot have a negative value because its owner need not exercise.

The Upper and Lower Bounds on a Call Option's Value (p. 678) We have established the value of a call option on the expiration date. Now we seek to determine the value of a call prior to expiration. Since a call option is a right to buy the stock, the option cannot be worth more than the stock. Thus, the upper bound on the value of a call option can be expressed as: $C_0 \leq S_0$. The lower bound on the value of a call option depends on whether the option is out of the money or in the money. Previously we established that the value of a call option at expiration is zero if it is out of the money. However, prior to expiration, an out-of-the-money option is valuable if the investor believes the price of the stock might increase sufficiently so that, at some time prior to expiration, the option will be in the money. So the lower bound for the value of an out-of-the-money call option, prior to the expiration date, can be written as follows:

$$C_0 \geq 0 \text{ if } (S_0 - E) < 0.$$

A call that is in-the-money prior to expiration is worth at least the difference between the value of the stock and the exercise price. In reality, the option price generally exceeds the difference between the stock price and the exercise price due to the opportunity for additional profit should the stock price increase further prior to the expiration date of the call. This relationship can be summarized as follows:

$$C_0 \geq (S_0 - E) \text{ if } (S_0 - E) \geq 0$$

The lower bound on the value of a call option is referred to as the **intrinsic value** of the option.

A Simple Model: Part I (p. 680) Assume initially that future stock prices have only two possible values.

Example Suppose a share of stock sells now for $100, and the risk-free rate (R_f) is 10%. Also assume that one year from now, the stock price will be either $105 or $120. A call option with expiration in one year has an exercise price of $100. How much is the call worth today?

If you buy a share of stock today, then, one year from now, you will have a share of stock whose value is either $105 or $120. If you buy the option today, you will have either ($105 - $100) = $5 or ($120 - $100) = $20 one year from now. Suppose that, in addition to buying the option today, you also lend an amount equal to the present value of the exercise price: ($100/1.10) = $90.91. At the end of the year, you have $100 from the repayment of the loan and either $5 or $20 from the exercise of the option; the total return is either ($100 + $5) = $105 or ($100 + $20) = $120. Notice that the strategy of buying the option and lending $90.91 has the same possible future returns as does the strategy of simply buying the stock. Since the two strategies have the same future returns, they must have the same value today. The call value plus the PV of the exercise price must equal the stock price: C_0 + $90.91 = $100. The value of the call is $9.09. This result can be written as: $C_0 + E/(1 + R_f) = S_0$ or $C_0 = S_0 - E/(1 + R_f)$.

Although this result is based on the unrealistic assumption that the stock price will be one of only two possible values at the expiration date, it can be generalized to the case where the stock price at the expiration date will be any value greater than or equal to the exercise price of the option. Further, it the option expires in t time periods, then the value of the call option is: $C_0 = S_0 - E/(1 + R_f)^t$.

Four Factors Determining Option Values (p. 682) If we assume a call is certain to expire in-the-money, then four factors determine the its value. (If the option can expire out-of-the-money, a fifth factor influences the option's price; this fifth factor is discussed in the next section.) The four factors are:

1. *Stock price.* As the price of the stock (S_0) increases, the value of the option increases.
2. *Exercise price.* A higher exercise price (E) makes the option less valuable.
3. *Time to expiration.* The option value decreases as time to expiration (t) decreases.
4. *The risk-free rate.* The value of the call increases as the risk-free rate (R_f) increases.

III. VALUING A CALL OPTION (p. 682)

Now we value a call under the more realistic assumption that the option might expire out-of-the-money.

A Simple Model: Part II (p. 683) To identify the factors which determine the value of an option which might expire out of the money, consider a modification of the example of the previous section.

Example Assume again that the current price of the stock is $100, that the possible stock prices at the expiration of the option are $105 and $120, and that the risk-free rate is 10%; a call option with an exercise price of $115 expires out of the money if the stock price is $105, and is in the money if the stock price is $120. What is the value of the call option with an exercise price of $105?

To establish the option value, we again develop a strategy of investing in the risk-free asset and purchasing calls to duplicate the possible returns from owning the stock.

*Learning Tip: This is the key to option pricing; it is **always** possible to identify a combination of buying the option and either lending or borrowing which has exactly the same payoff as simply buying the stock.*

For this example, the strategy which duplicates the payoff on the stock is: invest ($105/1.10) = $95.45 in the risk-free asset, and buy three call options. In one year, the value of the investment in the risk-free asset is $105, which is the lower of the two possible stock prices. If the stock price in one year is $105, the three calls are out-of-the-money, and the position's total value is [$105 + (3 × $0)] = $105. Or, if the stock price is $120, the calls are in-the-money and the value of each call is ($120 - $115) = $5. The position's total value is then [$105 + (3 × $5)] = $120. Thus investing $95.45 in the risk-free asset and buying three calls has the same future returns as the stock. The value of the two strategies must be the same: (3 × C_0) + $105/(1.10) = $100. Solving for C_0, the call value is $1.52.

The Fifth Factor (p. 684) The fifth factor influencing the value of the option is the variability in the price of the underlying asset. The more variable the price of the underlying asset, the greater the value of the option, because there is a greater chance that the asset's price will exceed the exercise price.

A Closer Look (p. 685) Two other results come from our analysis:

1.   The number of options needed to replicate the value of the stock is always equal to $\Delta S/\Delta C$, where ΔS is the difference in the possible stock prices, and ΔC is the difference in the possible option values.
2.   Unless the option is certain to finish in the money, $\Delta S/\Delta C$ is always greater than one.

IV. EQUITY AS A CALL OPTION ON THE FIRM'S ASSETS (p. 686)

Suppose a firm has a single debt issue coming due in one year. If the value of the firm (V_1) exceeds the face value of the debt (B_1), then the stockholders will pay off the debt and the stock will be worth $S_1 = (V_1 - B_1)$. By doing so, they retain their claim on the firm's assets. But if V_1 is less than B_1, stockholders will not exercise their option and the bondholders will own the firm. The stock is worthless. Thus the equity of a levered firm can be viewed as a call on the firm's assets. The bondholders own the firm and have written a call against firm value with an exercise price equal to the value of the debt. The value of the bonds is then equal to the value of the firm's assets less the value of the call held by the stockholders.

V. WARRANTS (p. 688)

A **warrant** gives the holder the right to buy common stock *directly from the company* at a fixed price during a specified period. To the holder, a warrant is a call option, although warrants usually have longer maturities. Warrants are generally issued in combination with privately placed debt, but are sometimes issued with public debt or new common stock issues. Typically, warrants are attached to the bond with which they are issued; some warrants are *detachable*, i.e., they can be sold separately from the bond.

The Difference Between Warrants and Call Options (p. 689)

1. Call options are issued by individuals; warrants are issued by firms.
2. When a warrant is exercised, the number of a firm's outstanding shares rises; there is no change in the number of outstanding shares associated with the exercise of a call that was written by an individual.
3. When a warrant is exercised, cash flows into the firm. An option exercise has no effect on the firm's cash.

Warrants and the Value of the Firm (p. 690) Since calls are not issued by the firm and result in the issuance of no new shares upon exercise, firm value is unaffected by their existence. Warrants, however, are issued by the firm and, upon exercise, the firm issues new shares to the warrant holder. Thus, the number of shares increases when warrants are exercised. Firm value (and total shareholder wealth) increases; however, since there are more shares outstanding, market value per share remains unchanged.

Warrant exercise increases the number of outstanding shares, so EPS will be diluted. Firms with many warrants outstanding report EPS in two ways: *primary* (earnings divided by outstanding shares) and *fully-diluted* (earnings divided by shares that would be outstanding if all warrants are converted to stock).

VI. CONVERTIBLE BONDS (p. 692)

A **convertible bond** can be exchanged for a fixed number of shares of the firm's common stock at the holder's option any time prior to maturity. **Convertible preferred stock** is similar but has no maturity date.

Features of a Convertible Bond (p. 692) Consider a convertible subordinated debenture with a face value of $1000 and a $50 **conversion price**. The bondholder can exchange this bond for ($1000/$50) = 20 shares of stock; the **conversion ratio** is 20. When a convertible bond is issued, the conversion price typically exceeds the stock price - the difference is the **conversion premium**.

Value of a Convertible Bond. (p. 693) The value of a convertible bond can be thought of in terms of its value as a straight bond and the value of the conversion feature. The **straight bond value** is the price at which the bond would sell if it were not convertible. A convertible sells at a price only slightly above its straight bond value when the conversion price greatly exceeds the stock price. The straight bond value is the PV of the coupon payments and maturity value, and is dependent on the discount rate.

The **conversion value** is the value of the bond if it were immediately converted into common stock - it equals the conversion ratio times the current stock price. The bond cannot sell for less than its conversion value. If the stock price exceeds the conversion value, the value of the convertible bond depends primarily on the conversion value, because that value is significantly greater than the straight bond value. *The value of a convertible bond exceeds both the straight bond value and the conversion value because the holder has the right to convert; the bondholder holds a call, which increases the value of the bond.*

VII. REASONS FOR ISSUING WARRANTS AND CONVERTIBLES (p. 695)

A convertible bond or one with warrants attached pays a lower coupon rate than an identical straight bond. This interest saving is an apparent advantage to the issuing firm. However, it must be recognized that the firm is also issuing an option to the security purchaser. In an efficient market, any security issuance is a zero-NPV proposition.

VIII. OTHER OPTIONS (p. 697)

If one looks closely, options are embedded in many places in corporate finance. The call provision on a bond is an obvious example. "Puttable" bonds, which can be sold back to the issuer at the bondholder's option are another. The key point is that, once we recognize an embedded option, we can use our knowledge of option valuation to determine its worth.

APPENDIX 22A THE BLACK-SCHOLES OPTION PRICING MODEL

Previously we derived the value of a call option prior to expiration under the assumption that the future price of the underlying asset could only take one of two known values. In reality, of course, the future value of a share of stock can range from zero to infinity. The Black-Scholes model allows us to compute the equilibrium value of a call option under this more realistic assumption. According to the model,

$$C_0 = S_0 \times N(d_1) - E/(1+R_f)^t \times N(d_2)$$

where

$$d_1 = [\ln(S_0/E) + (R_f + \tfrac{1}{2} \times \sigma^2) \times t]/(\sigma \times \sqrt{t})$$

and

$$d_2 = d_1 - \sigma \times \sqrt{t}$$

In the model, $N(d_*)$ is the probability that a standardized, normally distributed, random variable is less than or equal to d_*.

KEY TERMS AND CONCEPTS

American option - an option that can be exercised at any time until its expiration date. (p. 674)
Call option - the right to buy an asset at a fixed price during a particular period of time. (p. 674)
Conversion premium - difference between conversion price and current stock price, divided by the current stock price. (p. 693)
Conversion price - dollar amount of bond's par value that is exchangeable for a share of stock. (p. 693)
Conversion ratio - the number of shares per $1,000 bond received for conversion into stock. (p. 693)
Conversion value - value of a convertible bond if immediately converted into common stock. (p. 693)
Convertible bond - bond exchangeable for a fixed number of shares for a specified period (p. 692)
European option - an option that can only be exercised on the expiration date. (p. 674)
Exercise price - see *striking price*. (p. 674)
Exercising the option - the act of buying or selling the underlying asset via the option contract. (p. 674)
Expiration date - the last day on which an option can be exercised. (p. 674)
Intrinsic value - lower bound of an option's value - the option's value at expiration. (p. 679)

206

Option - contract giving owner the right to buy/sell asset at a fixed price on/before a given date. (p. 673)
Put option - the right to *sell* an asset at a fixed price during a particular period of time. (p. 674)
Striking price - fixed price in contract at which holder can buy or sell the underlying asset. (p. 674)
Straight bond value - value of a convertible bond if not convertible into common stock. (p. 693)
Warrant - security giving holder the right to buy stock at a fixed price for a given period. (p. 688)

CONCEPT TEST

1. An option gives the owner of the option the right to buy or sell a certain asset at a fixed price during a specified period. The asset specified in the contract is the _____ asset. The specified price is the _____ price or _____ price. Buying or selling the underlying asset is called _____ the option. The maturity date of the option is called the _____ date. A call gives the owner of the option the right to (buy/sell) a specified asset; a put gives its owner the right to (buy/sell) a specified asset. The option writer is one who (buys/sells) an option. The call writer must (buy/sell) the stock if the option buyer exercises. The put writer must (buy/sell) the stock if put buyer exercises the option. (p. 673)

2. A call is out-of-the-money when the stock price is (less/greater) than the exercise price. At expiration, a call is worthless if the stock price is (less/greater) than the exercise price. A call is in-the-money when the stock price is (less/greater) than the exercise price. A put is out-of-the-money when the stock price is (less/greater) than the exercise price and is in-the-money when the market price is (less/greater) than the exercise price. The put owner will not exercise the option if the market price is (less/greater) than the exercise price. Because the profit earned by one party to an options contract is a loss to the other party, options represent a _____ . (p. 674)

3. If, at expiration, the stock price (S_1) is less than the exercise price (E) of a call option, then the call value (C_1) is _____ . Or: $C_1 = $ _____ if _____ . The value of a call that is in-the-money at expiration is _____ . That is: $C_1 = $ _____ if _____ . The upper bound on the value of a call option prior to expiration (C_0) is _____ . Prior to expiration, an out-of-the-money call has a value (less/greater) than _____ if the investor believes that the price of the stock might increase sufficiently so that, at some time prior to expiration, the option is in the money. The lower bound for the value of an out-of-the money call option, prior to the expiration date, can be written as: C_0 _____ if _____ < 0. A call in the money prior to expiration is worth at least the difference between the _____ and the _____ . Or: $C_0 \geq$ _____ if _____ ≥ 0. (p.677)

4. We can duplicate a stock's possible future returns with a combination of options and lending or borrowing. For a call certain to expire in-the-money, the value prior to expiration (C_0) equals _____ minus the PV of the _____ . Or: $C_0 = $ _____ . So for a call certain to expire in-the-money, the following factors determine its value: (1) _____ ; (2) _____ ; (3) _____ ; (4) _____ . (p. 680)

5. To establish the value of a call which might expire out-of-the-money, a strategy is developed which duplicates the possible _____ which result from owning _____. This strategy consists of investing in _____ and purchasing _____. The value of the call prior to expiration (C_0) is determined by equating the _____ of the two strategies; total value of the _____ plus the PV of the _____ equals the _____. For an option which might expire out-of-the-money, the fifth factor influencing its value is _____ in the price of the _____. The greater the _____, the greater the value of the option. (p. 680)

6. Equity in a levered firm can be viewed as a _____ option on _____. Bondholders own the firm and have written a _____ option against the _____ with an exercise price equal to _____. The value of the bonds equals the value of _____ less the value of _____ held by the stockholders. (p. 686)

7. A warrant holder can buy _____ from the issuer at a fixed price during a specified period. To the holder, a warrant is a _____ option. Warrants are generally issued in combination with _____. A _____ on the firm's stock is a transaction between investors, while a _____ is issued by the firm. Existing stock changes hands when a _____ is exercised, but the firm issues new stock when a _____ is exercised. In the case of the _____, firm value and share values are unaffected by option exercise. Both firm and share value are affected by exercise of a _____; firm value (increases/decreases) and share value (increases/decreases). (p. 688)

8. A convertible bond can be exchanged for a fixed number of _____ any time prior to _____. The conversion ratio specifies the _____ into which the bond can be converted. The face value of the convertible bond divided by the conversion ratio equals the _____. When a convertible bond is issued, the conversion price is typically (less/greater) than the price of the firm's common stock. The difference between the conversion price and the stock price is the _____. (p. 692)

9. The value of a convertible bond can be thought of in terms of its value as a _____ and the value of the _____ feature. The straight bond value is the price at which the bond would sell if it were _____; it is the _____ of the coupon payments and maturity value; it is dependent on the _____. The conversion value is the bond value if it were _____. It equals _____ times _____. (p. 693)

ANSWERS TO CONCEPT TEST

1. underlying; striking; exercise; exercising; expiration; buy; sell; sells; sell; buy
2. less; less; greater; greater; less; greater; zero-sum game
3. zero; zero; $S_1 \leq E$ or $(S_1\text{-}E) \leq 0$; $(S_1\text{-}E)$; $(S_1\text{-}E)$; $S_1 > E$ or $(S_1\text{-}E) > 0$; the stock price; greater; zero; greater than or equal to 0; $(S_0\text{-}E)$; value of the stock; exercise price; $(S_0\text{-}E)$; $(S_0\text{-}E)$
4. current stock price; exercise price; $S_0\text{-}[E/(1+R_f)^t]$; stock price; exercise price; time to expiration; the risk-free rate
5. future returns; the stock; risk-free asset; call options; current value; call options; exercise price; price of the stock; variability; stock; variability
6. call; firm assets; call; firm value; the value of the firm's debt; the firm's assets; the call option

208

7. common stock; call; privately placed debt; call option; warrant; call option; warrant; call option; warrant; increases; decreases
8. shares of the firm's common stock; maturity; number of shares; conversion price; greater; conversion premium;
9. straight bond; convertibility; not convertible; present value; discount rate; converted into common stock; conversion ratio; current stock price

PROBLEMS

Use the following information about the Walden Corporation to solve Problems 1-5:

The price of Walden Corporation common stock will be either $60 or $80 at year-end. A call option for the purchase of 100 shares of Walden stock has an expiration date in one year. The risk-free rate is 8%.

1. Suppose the current price of Walden stock is $65 and that the exercise price of the call is $70. What are the possible values of the call contract on the expiration date?

2. For the data in Problem 1, what is the current value of the call contract?

3. Suppose the option in Problem 1 has an exercise price of $50. What is the value of the call contract?

4. Suppose a call for 100 shares of Walden common stock, with an exercise price of $65, sells for $1,000. What is the current value of the stock?

5. Calculate the value of the call if the current stock price is $50 and the exercise price is $70.

6. The common stock of Hanna Corporation sells for $50 per share. Assume the *continuously compounded* interest rate is 10% and the price of Hanna stock is certain to increase at that rate. What is the value of a call option to buy one share for $40, if the expiration date is one year from today?

7. Calls on Barbera Corporation common stock are currently selling for $10; puts are selling for $8. The exercise price is $80 and the expiration date of both options is in one year. Barbera common stock is currently selling for $73⅝ per share. Suppose that an investor buys a put and holds the put until the expiration date. What is the investor's profit (or loss) if the price of the stock, on the expiration date, is $65? $75? $80? $85? $95? What is the maximum return the investor can earn?

8. For the data in Problem 7, compute the gain (or loss) to the writer of the put if the price of the stock, on the expiration date, is $65? $75? $80? $85? $95? What is the maximum return the writer of the put can earn? What is the maximum possible loss for the writer of the put option?

9. For the Barbera Corporation stock in Problem 7, assume that an investor buys a call and holds the call until the expiration date. What is his profit (or loss) if the stock price on the expiration date is $65? $75? $80? $85? $95? What is the maximum return the investor can earn?

10. For the data in Problems 7 and 9, compute the gain (or loss) to the writer of the call if the price of the stock, on the expiration date, is $65? $75? $80? $85? $95? What is the maximum return the writer of the call can earn? What is the maximum possible loss for the writer of the call option?

11. A firm has a pure-discount debt issue due in one year with a maturity value of $5,000. The risk-free rate is 11%, and the market value of the firm's assets is $4,600. In one year the value of the assets will be either $5,100 or $5,500. What is the value today of the firm's equity? What is the value of the debt?

12. For the data in Problem 11, suppose the possible values of the firm's assets one year from now are $4,500 or $5,500. What is the value of the firm's equity? The value of the firm's debt? What is the interest rate on the firm's debt?

13. A convertible bond issued by Erving Manufacturing, Inc. has a face value of $1,000, a coupon interest rate of 12%, and matures in 18 years. Interest is paid annually. The bond is rated BB; non-convertible, BB-rated corporate bonds currently yield 13%. The bond can be exchanged for 16 shares of Erving common stock, which currently sells for $45 per share. What is the conversion ratio? What is the conversion price? What is the conversion premium?

14. Compute the straight bond value for the Erving bond described in problem 13.

15. Compute the conversion value for the Erving bond in Problem 13. What is its floor value?

16. A bond with ten detachable warrants has been offered for sale for $1,000. It matures in 30 years and has an annual coupon payment of $100. Each warrant gives the owner the right to purchase five shares of stock at $15 per share. Similar bonds without warrants yield 14%. What is the value of a warrant?

17. Using the data from Problem 16, determine the maximum current price of the firm's stock.

CHAPTER 23

MERGERS AND ACQUISITIONS

CONCEPTS FOR REVIEW

The valuation and acquisition of assets (both physical and financial) is the essence of finance. This chapter examines the process by which *firms* are valued and acquired.

CHAPTER HIGHLIGHTS

The decision to acquire another firm is a capital budgeting decision much like any other. Since the NPV of an acquisition is difficult to measure, the subject of mergers and acquisitions warrants specific attention. Mergers differ from ordinary investment decisions in four ways. First, the value of a merger may depend on benefits (or *synergies*) arising from the combination. Second, the accounting, tax, and legal aspects of a merger are frequently complex. Third, mergers often involve issues of *corporate control*. Finally, some mergers are 'unfriendly' - target managers may not want the acquisition to occur.

I. THE LEGAL FORMS OF ACQUISITIONS (p. 711)

Merger or Consolidation (p. 711) A **merger** is the absorption of one firm by another - the acquiring firm retains its identity while the acquired firm ceases to exist. In a **consolidation**, an entirely new firm is created. Since the differences between the two are insignificant for our purposes, we will use the general term 'merger' to refer to both of these forms of reorganization.

Acquisition of Stock (p. 712) Another way to acquire a firm is to buy the target firm's voting stock directly from stockholders. This is accomplished through a **tender offer**, in which the acquiring firm makes an offer, directly to the shareholders of a firm, to buy the firm's common stock. This approach bypasses the board of directors, and does not require a stockholder vote for approval. Tender offers are often used when target firm management is opposed to the acquisition.

Acquisition of Assets (p. 713) A firm can acquire another firm by purchasing its assets; this involves a costly legal transfer of title to the assets and must be approved by the shareholders of the selling firm.

Acquisition Classifications (p. 711) A **horizontal** acquisition occurs if the two firms compete in the same product market. A **vertical** acquisition is a reorganization of firms at different stages of the production process. **Conglomerate** acquisitions involve the combination of firms in unrelated lines of business.

A Note on Takeovers (p. 713) A **takeover** is the transfer of control of a firm from one group to another. The acquirer or **bidder** makes an **offer** to pay cash or securities to acquire the target firm. A takeover can occur by **acquisition, proxy contest**, or a **going-private transaction**. In a proxy contest, dissident shareholders seek proxies from existing shareholders to gain control of the board of directors. In a going-private transaction, a small group of investors buys all of the firm's common stock, which is then delisted and no longer trades publicly. When financing is obtained primarily by borrowing, going-private transactions are called **leveraged buyouts (LBOs)**.

II. TAXES AND ACQUISITIONS (p. 714)

Determinants of Tax Status (p. 715) The acquisition of one firm by another may or may not be a

212

taxable transaction. The primary issue in determining the tax status of an acquisition is whether the shareholders of the acquired firm have sold their shares, resulting in a realized, taxable capital gain, or exchanged their shares for new shares of equal value. The former is a **taxable acquisition**, while the latter is a **tax-free acquisition**.

<u>Taxable versus Tax-Free Acquisitions</u> (p. 715) Under some circumstances, shareholders of the acquired firm may have to pay capital gains taxes in the event of an acquisition. This is the **capital gains effect** and may increase the cost of the acquisition. The **write-up effect** allows the purchasing firm to increase the depreciation expense on the acquired firm's assets and reduce the acquirer's taxes.

III. ACCOUNTING FOR ACQUISITIONS (p. 715)

<u>The Purchase Method</u> (p. 715) The **purchase accounting method** for an acquisition requires that the assets of the acquired firm are reported at fair market value on the acquirer's financial statements. The difference between the purchase price and fair market value of the acquired assets is 'goodwill' on the acquirer's balance sheet.

<u>Pooling of Interests</u> (p. 716) With a **pooling of interests**, the balance sheets of two firms are combined but no goodwill is created. The pooling method is used when at least 90 percent of the voting common stock of the acquired firm is exchanged for voting stock in the combined firm; else the purchase method is used.

<u>Which is Better: Purchase or Pooling of Interests?</u> (p. 716) The pooling method does not involve goodwill. The purchase method does, and may reduce reported (accounting) income. Most importantly, the alternative accounting treatments have no consequences for cash flow or NPV determinations.

IV. GAINS FROM ACQUISITION (p. 717)

<u>Synergy</u> (p. 718) If Firm A (with value V_A) acquires Firm B (with value V_B), the acquisition is beneficial to the stockholders of Firm A if: $V_{AB} > V_A + V_B$, where V_{AB} is the value of the combined firm. The incremental net gain derived from the acquisition (ΔV) is: $\Delta V = V_{AB} - (V_A + V_B)$. If ΔV is positive, the acquisition is said to generate **synergy**. Synergy exists when the cash flow for the combined firm is greater than the sum of the cash flows for the two firms as separate entities. The gain from the merger is the PV of this difference in cash flows. Synergy results from one or more of the following: (1) revenue enhancement, (2) cost reduction, (3) lower taxes, or (4) lower capital requirements.

<u>Revenue Enhancement</u> (p. 719) Increased revenues may result from marketing gains, strategic benefits, and increases in market power. **Marketing gains** are produced by more effective advertising, an improved distribution network, and a more balanced product mix. **Strategic benefits** are the opportunities presented by options to enter and exploit new lines of business. Finally, a merger may reduce competition, and thereby increase **market power**, allowing the company to increase prices and to obtain monopoly profits.

<u>Cost Reductions</u> (p. 720) Under some circumstances, a larger firm operates more efficiently than two smaller firms; this is the principle of 'economies of scale'. Economies may also be achieved when firms have complementary resources. And, some acquisitions serve to eliminate inefficient management.

Lower Taxes (p. 721) Tax gains from a merger may arise because of unused tax losses, unused debt capacity, surplus funds, or the ability to write up the value of depreciable assets. A profitable firm may acquire a firm that has net operating losses (NOL), and use these losses to reduce taxes on current income. Acquisition of a firm with little debt can be beneficial to the acquirer since the combined firm can then obtain additional debt financing. The additional interest provides a tax shield. A firm with surplus funds may acquire another firm rather than pay dividends or repurchase shares, since the latter two actions may increase the tax liabilities of the shareholders of the acquiring firm.

Reductions in Capital Needs (p. 722) Reduced capital requirements might result from an acquisition if one of the merged firms has excess capacity while the other requires additional capacity to expand.

Avoiding Mistakes (p. 723) Guidelines for evaluating mergers parallel those for evaluating capital budgeting projects: (1) don't ignore market values, (2) estimate incremental cash flows, (3) use the correct discount rate, (4) be aware of transactions costs.

A Note on Inefficient Management (p. 723) One potential benefit of an acquisition is that the existing management team may be replaced by another that is more skilled. Of course, there are numerous examples in which the new management turns out to be no better (and is sometimes far worse) than the existing management.

V. SOME FINANCIAL SIDE EFFECTS OF ACQUISITIONS (p. 723)

Two important financial side effects of an acquisition are EPS growth and diversification. Surprisingly, neither has any impact on the value of the combined firm.

EPS Growth (p. 723) In some circumstances the combination of two firms can result in a higher EPS for the remaining firm. Unless the merger *creates value* (through synergy or other means) the market should not be fooled into paying more than the true value for the remaining shares.

Diversification (p. 724) Diversification is often cited as a benefit in mergers. But diversification by itself does not create value because the shareholders of the acquiring firm can accomplish the same result by purchasing stock in the target firm. (Remember that diversification reduces only unsystematic risk.)

VI. THE COST OF AN ACQUISITION (p. 725)

Earlier we observed that the gain from a merger is: $\Delta V = V_{AB} - (V_A + V_B)$. If we define the value of Firm B to Firm A as: $V^*_B = \Delta V + V_B$, the NPV of a merger is: V^*_B - Cost to Firm A of the acquisition. We illustrate the calculation of the NPV with the following information for Firms A and B.

	Firm A	Firm B
Price per share	$ 10	$ 5
Number of shares	20	20
Total market value	$200	$100

Both firms are all-equity firms. The incremental gain (ΔV) is $80, and Firm B will agree to the acquisition at a price of $150. The difference between the acquisition price and V_B is the *merger premium*; here it is ($150 - $100) = $50.

To compute the NPV of the acquisition, we first compute the value of Firm B to Firm A:

$$V^*_B = \Delta V + V_B = \$80 + \$100 = \$180$$

Next, we determine the cost to Firm A of the acquisition. Although Firm B agrees to be acquired for $150, the cost of the acquisition to Firm A varies with the means of payment from Firm A to Firm B. The two methods of payment are a cash acquisition and a stock acquisition.

Case I: Cash Acquisition (p. 726) If the acquisition is paid in cash, the NPV is: V^*_B - Cost = $180 - $150 = $30. Since the NPV is positive, the acquisition is beneficial to the stockholders of Firm A. The value of the merged firm after the acquisition equals the value of the combined firm less the cash paid for Firm B: $V_{AB} = V_A + V^*_B$ - Cost = $200 + $180 - $150 = $230. After the merger, the value of the merged firm's stock will increase to [($380 - $150)/20] = $11.50. The increase of $1.50 per share above the price of Firm A stock is the NPV of $30, or ($30/20) = $1.50 per share gain.

Case II: Stock Acquisition (p. 726) Suppose that Firm A pays the $150 acquisition cost by giving 15 shares of stock to the stockholders of Firm B. The cost appears to be $150 in this case, because each share of Firm A is worth $10 prior to the merger; however, this is an underestimate of the actual cost. After the merger, the value of the firm is: $V_{AB} = V_A + V_B + \Delta V = \$200 + \$100 + \$80 = \$380$. The merged firm has (20 + 15) = 35 shares outstanding, the price per share is ($380/35) = $10.857. So the actual cost of the acquisition is (15 × $10.857) = $162.86, and the NPV of the merger is V^*_B - Cost = $180 - $162.86 = $17.14. Note that the $10.857 per share case is less than the $11.50 value for a cash acquisition. The difference arises from the fact that a portion of the $30 NPV for the cash acquisition now goes to the new stockholders. The 15 new shares are each worth ($10.857 - $10) = $.857 more than the pre-merger value of Firm A stock, for a total of (15 × $.857) = $12.86 to the former stockholders of Firm B. So the stockholders of Firm B actually receive $162.86 in this merger.

Cash versus Common Stock (p. 727) The decision to finance an acquisition with cash or stock depends on three factors. First, the use of stock means that the shareholders of the acquirer will share in any gains from the merger; on the other hand, if the merger is unsuccessful, then the acquirer's shareholders will share in the loss. Second, a cash acquisition is usually a taxable transaction; this may result in a higher price for the target firm. Third, a cash acquisition does not affect control of the acquiring firm.

VII. DEFENSIVE TACTICS (p. 728)

Target firm managers frequently resist takeover attempts. This may enable stockholders to subsequently receive a higher price for their shares, or it may stem from management's desire to protect its own interests. Defensive tactics to resist takeovers are described below.

The Corporate Charter (p. 728) The *corporate charter* consists of the firm's articles of incorporation and the corporate bylaws, which documents specify the firm's governance rules. The charter can be amended to make acquisition difficult for the acquiring firm.

Repurchase/Standstill Agreements (p. 728) A **standstill agreement** specifies that the bidding firm will limit its holdings in the target. Such agreements often precede a **targeted repurchase** in which the target firm buys back its own stock from the bidder. Since this repurchase is usually at a premium above market price, the premium is viewed by critics as a bribe, and is frequently termed **greenmail**.

Exclusionary Self-Tenders (p. 729) In an **exclusionary self-tender** the target firm offers to buy back its own stock, at a premium, from all stockholders except the bidder. By excluding the bidder, the firm effectively transfers wealth to other stockholders by reducing the value of the bidder's stock.

Poison Pills and Share Rights Plans (p. 729) A **poison pill** is forces a bidder to negotiate with target firm management rather than acquire the firm in a tender offer. Such procedures are sometimes called **share rights plans (SRPs)** because the target firm's stockholders receive share rights which entitle them to purchase shares of stock at a specified ('exercise') price below the current market price of the firm's stock. Rights are 'triggered' when a tender offer is announced, or when a stockholder acquires 20 percent of the target's stock. Another provision triggered by a takeover attempt is that shareholders are able to purchase, at the exercise price, stock in a merged firm worth twice the exercise price. Since this provision would be disastrous for the merged firm, it forces the bidder to negotiate with management.

Going Private and Leveraged Buyouts (p. 731) A privately-owned firm is not subject to unfriendly takeovers. So a management buyout (MBO) might be regarded as a takeover defense by the target firm's management, while the target firm's stockholders view the MBO as a takeover itself.

Other Devices and Jargon of Corporate Takeovers (p. 731) A **golden parachute** pays top managers if their firm is acquired. A **poison put** forces the acquirer to buy securities at a specified price. A **crown jewel** is a desirable asset owned by the target, which may be sold off when threatened with a takeover. A **white knight** is a friendly acquirer. A **lockup** is an option granted to a friendly acquirer giving it the right to purchase stock or some asset of the target in the event of a takeover bid. **Shark repellent** is any tactic designed to discourage unwanted takeover bids. A **bear hug** is an unfriendly takeover bid that is so attractive that target management has little choice but to take it.

VIII. SOME EVIDENCE ON ACQUISITIONS (p. 732)

Shareholders of acquired firms benefit substantially from acquisitions, earning excess returns of approximately 20% in the case of mergers and 30% for tender offers. Gains to shareholders of acquiring firms are difficult to measure. Evidence suggests that these shareholders gain little from an acquisition, and value losses subsequent to merger announcements are not unusual. These results suggest that overvaluation of the target by the bidder is common.

KEY TERMS AND CONCEPTS

Consolidation - merger in which new firm is created; acquired and acquiring firms disappear. (p. 711)
Going-private transactions - transactions in which all publicly owned stock in a firm is replaced with complete equity ownership by a private group. (p. 714)
Greenmail - a targeted stock purchase where payments are made to potential bidders to eliminate unfriendly takeover attempts. (p. 728)
Leveraged buyouts (LBOs) - going-private transactions in which a large percentage of the money used to buy the stock is borrowed. Oftentimes, incumbent management is involved. (p. 714)
Merger - the complete absorption of one company by another, where the acquiring firm retains its identity and the acquired firm ceases to exist as a separate entity. (p. 711)
Poison pill - a financial device designed to make unfriendly takeover attempts unappealing. (p. 729)
Proxy contests - an attempt to gain control of a firm by soliciting a sufficient number of stockholder votes to replace existing management. (p. 714)

216

Share rights plans - provisions allowing existing stockholders to purchase stock at some fixed price should an outside takeover bid take place, discouraging a hostile takeover. (p. 729)
Synergy - incremental gain associated the combination of two firms via merger or acquisition. (p. 718)
Tender offer - a public offer by one firm to directly buy the shares from another firm. (p. 712)

CONCEPT TEST

1. The acquiring firm in a merger is the _____; the firm being sought is the _____; and the payment offered is the _____ . (p. 711)

2. The absorption of one firm by another, such that the acquirer retains its identity while the acquired firm ceases to exist, is called a(n) _____ . In a(n) _____, a new firm is created. Another way to acquire a firm is to buy the target firm's voting stock directly from stockholders; this is accomplished through a(n) _____ . A firm can also buy another firm by purchasing its _____ . (p. 712)

3. If the two firms compete in the same product market, the acquisition is a(n) _____ acquisition. A reorganization of firms at different stages of the production process is a(n) _____ acquisition. Acquisitions involving firms in unrelated lines of business are _____ acquisitions. (p. 713)

4. The transfer of control of a firm from one group to another is a(n) _____ . A proxy authorizes another party to _____ . In a(n) _____ contest, dissident shareholders seeks to obtain enough proxies from the existing shareholders to gain control of the board of directors. In a(n) _____ transaction, a small group of investors buys all of the firm's common stock; since much of the financing transactions is generally obtained by borrowing, they are often called _____ . (p. 714)

5. The key issue in determining the tax status of an acquisition is whether acquired firm shareholders have sold their shares, resulting in a realized _____, or exchanged for new shares of equal value. The former (is/is not) a taxable acquisition, while the latter (is/is not). (p. 714)

6. The _____ method requires that assets of the acquired firm are reported at fair market value on the financial statements of the acquirer; the difference between the purchase price and the fair market value of these assets is _____ on the balance sheet of the acquirer. The second treatment is a(n) _____; in this case, the balance sheets of the two firms are simply combined and asset values are not adjusted to market value. (p. 715)

7. If Firm A (with value V_A) is acquiring Firm B (with value V_B), then the acquisition is beneficial to the stockholders of Firm A if $V_{AB} >$ _____, where V_{AB} is the value of the combined firm. The gain from the acquisition (ΔV) is: $\Delta V =$ _____ . If ΔV is positive, the acquisition is said to generate _____ . (p. 717)

8. Synergy from an acquisition results from the following: (1) increase in _____, (2) decrease in _____, (3) decrease in _____, or (4) decrease in _____ . (p. 718)

9. The NPV of a merger equals _____ - _____. The difference between the acquisition price and V_A is the _____. The two methods of payment are a(n) _____ acquisition and a(n) _____ acquisition. For a cash acquisition, NPV equals _____ - _____. The value of the merged firm after the cash acquisition is _____ + _____ - _____ . (p. 726)

10. Defensive tactics are used by target managers to resist takeovers. The articles of incorporation and corporate bylaws constitute the _____; these documents can be amended to make acquisition difficult. An agreement which specifies that the bidder firm will limit its holdings in the target is a(n) _____ agreement. These often precede a _____; under this arrangement, the target firm buys back its own stock from the bidder. The premium paid in such arrangements is viewed by critics as a bribe, and is frequently termed _____. In a(n) _____, the target firm offers to buy back its own stock at a premium, from all stockholders except the bidder. A(n) _____ forces a bidder to negotiate with target management; such procedures are sometimes called _____ . (p. 728)

ANSWERS TO CONCEPT TEST

1. bidder; target firm; consideration
2. merger; consolidation; tender offer; assets
3. horizontal; vertical; conglomerate
4. takeover; cast a stockholder's votes; proxy; going-private; leveraged buyouts
5. capital gain; is; is not
6. purchase accounting; goodwill; pooling of interests
7. (V_A+V_B); $[V_{AB}-(V_A+V_B)]$; synergy
8. revenues; cost; taxes; capital requirements
9. V^*_B; Cost to Firm A of the acquisition; merger premium; cash; stock; V^*_B; Cost; V_A; V^*_B; Cost
10. corporate charter; standstill; targeted repurchase; greenmail; exclusionary self-tender; poison pill; share rights plans

PROBLEMS

Use the following information for Problems 1-9. Assume that Firms A and B have no debt outstanding.

	Firm A	Firm B
Total earnings	$3,500	$1,400
Shares outstanding	700	350
Price per share	$ 50	$ 20

1. Firm A is considering the acquisition of Firm B. Firm A has estimated that the value of the combined firm will be $43,000. Firm B has indicated it would accept a cash purchase offer of $22 per share. Should Firm A proceed with the acquisition?

2. For the data of Problem 1, what is the synergy from the merger? What is the merger premium? Use the synergy and the premium to determine the net present value of the acquisition.

3. For the data of Problem 1, what is the price of Firm A's stock after the merger?

4. For the data of Problem 1, what is the NPV of the merger if Firm A pays for the acquisition with common stock, based on the current market prices? What is the post-merger price of the stock?

5. For the data of Problem 4, what is the synergy from the merger? What is the merger premium? Use the synergy and the premium to determine the NPV. Why is the NPV lower for the acquisition through exchange of stock in Problem 4 compared to the acquisition for cash in Problem 1?

6. Problem 1 indicates that Firm B shareholders will accept $7,700 for the acquisition. How many shares of Firm A stock should Firm B stockholders receive so they actually receive the $7,700 price?

7. Suppose that, for the data in Problem 1, Firm A acquires Firm B in exchange for stock valued at $21 per share. How will this affect earnings per share for Firm A?

8. For the data of Problem 7, what is the new firm's share price if the market is 'fooled' by this earnings growth (i.e., if the P/E ratio does not change)? What will the P/E ratio be if the market is not 'fooled?'

9. Blizzard Mfg. is analyzing the possible acquisition of Max Motors. Blizzard forecasts that the purchase would result in incremental after-tax cash flows of $10,000 per year for the foreseeable future. The current market values of Blizzard and Max are $500,000 and $200,000, respectively. The relevant cost of capital for the incremental cash flows is 20 percent. What is the synergy from the merger?

10. Suppose that, for the data of Problem 9, Blizzard is considering an offer of $220,000 cash for the acquisition of Max. What is the merger premium? What is the net present value of the merger?

11. As an alternative to the $220,000 offer described in Problem 10, Blizzard is considering offering 25 percent of its stock to the stockholders of Max. What is the net present value of this offer?

Use the following information to solve Problems 12 and 13:

M. Wilson Company, Inc. ($ in thousands)

Current assets	$ 2,000	Current liabilities	$ 600
Fixed assets	$ 8,000	Long-term debt	$ 3,400
		Equity	$ 6,000
Total	$10,000		$10,000

B. Buckner Company, Inc. ($ in thousands)

Current assets	$ 1,500	Current liabilities	$ 750
Fixed assets	$ 3,500	Long-term debt	$ 1,000
		Equity	$ 3,250
Total	$ 5,000		$ 5,000

12. Assume that the above are **book value** balance sheets. Construct the balance sheet for M. Wilson Company, assuming M. Wilson purchases B. Buckner, and the pooling of interests method is used.

13. Suppose the fair market value of Buckner's fixed assets is $5,000. Wilson pays $7,500 for Buckner and raises the needed funds by issuing long-term debt. Construct the balance sheet for M. Wilson Company, assuming that the purchase method of accounting is used.

CHAPTER 24

LEASING

CONCEPTS FOR REVIEW

In previous chapters we examined the acquisition of assets using various capital budgeting techniques in an attempt to answer the following question: Should we acquire this asset? This chapter extends the analysis by asking, Given the financial need for an asset, *how* should we finance its acquisition?

CHAPTER HIGHLIGHTS

For most firms, physical assets are acquired because they can be used; ownership per se is irrelevant. Leasing is an alternative method for obtaining the use of an asset (as opposed to its ownership); this chapter frames leasing as another type of financing decision to be made by the firm's financial managers.

I. LEASES AND LEASE TYPES (p. 740)

A **lease** is a contractual agreement between two parties: the lessee and the lessor. The **lessee** is the *user* of the equipment; the **lessor** is the *owner*. Lessees make payments to lessors in order to purchase the *use* of the leased equipment rather than ownership of the equipment itself. As owners, lessors obtain the financial benefits (primarily the depreciation tax shields) associated with ownership.

If the lessor purchases equipment from the manufacturer and leases it to another firm, the lease is called *direct lease*. If the manufacturer acts as a lessor of its own equipment, it will do so by setting up a wholly-owned subsidiary called a *captive finance company* to lease its products.

Leasing versus Buying (p. 741) To obtain the use of equipment, lessees may borrow and buy it, or may to lease it. As such, the decision to lease or buy amounts to a comparison of alternative financing arrangements for the use of an asset, and the analysis of the decision compares the net costs of each.

Operating Leases (p. 741) **Operating leases** have the following characteristics.

1. Payments received by the lessor are usually not enough to fully recover the cost of the asset.
2. Operating leases are often relatively short-term - sometimes significantly of the asset.
3. Operating leases frequently require that the lessor take responsibility for maintenance of the asset, as well as for any taxes or insurance.
4. Operating leases are frequently cancelable at the option of the lessee. This option is particularly valuable when technological and/or economic conditions are likely to make the value of the asset to the lessee less than the value of the future lease payments under the lease.

Financial Leases (p. 742) **Financial leases** are the focus of our analysis in this chapter. Financial leases have the following distinguishing characteristics.

1. The total of the payments are sufficient to cover the lessor's cost of purchasing the asset and pay the lessor a return on the investment.
2. The lessee is usually responsible for insurance, maintenance, and taxes.
3. Financial leases are generally noncancellable by the lessee, unless the lessee is willing to pay a significant financial penalty.

Financial leases come in many forms. **Tax-oriented leases** are financial leases in which the lessor is the owner for tax purposes. **Leveraged leases** are financial leases in which the lessor borrows a large portion of the equipment's purchase price on a nonrecourse basis. In the event of default by the lessee, the lessor makes no more loan payments and the lender seeks redress against the lessee. In a *sale and leaseback* arrangement, the lessees sells a previously owned asset to the lessor and then leases it back. Doing so provides immediate cash to the lessee, plus providing for continued use of the asset.

II. ACCOUNTING AND LEASING (p. 743)

Accounting for leasing on the firm's financial statements is governed by Statement of Financial Accounting Standards No. 13 (FAS 13), "Accounting for Leases", which requires that financial leases must be "capitalized." The present value of the lease payments must be reported on the right-hand side of the lessee's balance sheet, while an equivalent amount is shown as an asset on the left-hand side. For the purposes of FAS 13, a lease is a financial lease if at least one of the following criteria holds:

1.   The lease transfers ownership of the property to the lessee by the end of the term of the lease.
2.   The lessee can purchase the asset at a price below fair market value (bargain purchase price option) when the lease expires.
3.   The lease term is 75 percent or more of the estimated economic life of the asset.
4.   The present value of the lease payments is at least 90 percent of the fair market value of the asset at the start of the lease.

III. TAXES, THE IRS, AND LEASES (p. 745)

Lease payments are deductible as operating expenses as long as the IRS is convinced that a bona fide lease exists. A valid lease from the IRS's perspective will meet the following standards:

1.   The term of the lease must be less than 80% of the asset's life.
2.   The lease should not include a "bargain purchase option"; i.e., an option to acquire the asset at a price below its fair market value at the end of the lease's life.
3.   The lease should not have a schedule of payments that is very high at the start of the lease term and thereafter very low.
4.   The lease payments must provide the lessor with a fair market rate of return.
5.   The lease should not limit the lessee's right to issue debt or pay dividends.
6.   Renewal options must be reasonable and reflect the fair market value of the asset.

IV. THE CASH FLOWS FROM LEASING (p. 746)

Quantitative analysis of the leasing decision proceeds in three steps: identification of the relevant cash flows associated with leasing and buying, respectively; compute the implicit after-tax cost of leasing; and, compare that rate to the after-tax cost of borrowing (and buying).

The Incremental Cash Flows (p. 746) We identify the following incremental cash flows from the viewpoint of the lessee.

1.   Since lease payments are fully deductible, each payment is an after-tax **outflow** equal to (lease payment) $\times$ $(1 - T_c)$.

2.   Since the lessee forgoes the depreciation tax shield, he incurs an opportunity cost equal to depreciation $\times$ (T_c) each year. Consider this cost an additional **outflow**.

3.   Finally, if the machine is leased, the lessee is spared the initial outlay necessary to buy it today. We designate this amount a cash **inflow** associated with the decision to lease rather than buy.

Two points should be raised here. First, we now have a stream of cash flows in which the first cash flow is an inflow, while the remaining cash flows are outflows; this pattern is the opposite of that described in typical capital budgeting projects. Also, notice that the anticipated benefits from the use of the machine, e.g., cost savings, are ignored, since the lessee will obtain the use of the machine (and the attendant benefits) regardless of how the financing is structured.

V. LEASE OR BUY? (p. 747)

The lease/buy decision is a cost-minimization problem: calculate the cost of each alternative and select the lowest.

A Preliminary Analysis (p. 747) Upon identifying relevant cash flows, we compute the after-tax cost of leasing, and compare it to the firm's after-tax cost of borrowing. To obtain the after-tax cost of leasing, we equate the incremental benefits (item 3) and the present values of the incremental costs (items 1 and 2), and solve for the discount rate. This is the after-tax cost of leasing, and is mathematically equivalent to the IRR, except that since it signifies a cost, rather than a benefit, the lessee prefers it to be lower than higher. The after-tax cost of borrowing is equal to $R(1 - T_c)$, where R is the rate at which the firm can borrow. Call this rate R^*.

Three Potential Pitfalls (p. 748) Consider the following when calculating the implicit lease rate.

1. Cash flows are not conventional since the first cash flow is positive, so the IRR represents the rate we pay. The *lower* the IRR the better.
2. Advantage to leasing over borrowing—prefer the lower IRR. If we determine the advantage to borrowing over leasing, the cash flow signs would be reversed—prefer the higher IRR.
3. The implicit rate is based on the *net* cash flows of leasing instead of borrowing.

NPV Analysis (p. 748) We stated that leasing is an alternative to borrowing and buying. Thus, the relevant discount rate is the after-tax cost of debt. The NPV of the lease/buy decision, therefore, equals:

$$NPV = \text{(outlay if purchased)} - [\text{(lease payment)} \times (1 - T_c) + \text{(depreciation)} \times (T_c)][1 - 1/(1 + R^*)^t/R^*.$$

The NPV is the **net advantage to leasing (NAL)**, a very popular means of analysis in the real world.

VI. A LEASING PARADOX (p. 749)

Given equal tax rates and borrowing costs, the NPV of the transaction for the lessor will be equal but opposite in sign to the NPV of the transaction for the lessee. Why then, would both firms willingly engage in the transaction when one firm's losses must be equal to the other firm's gains?

VII. REASONS FOR LEASING (p. 751)

Good Reasons for Leasing (p. 751) Leasing rather than buying makes financial sense when (1) the tax rates of the lessor and the lessee differ, (2) when the ability of the lessee and the lessor to utilize tax shields differ, (3) when leasing reduces the transactions costs the lessee would incur in obtaining the use of the asset, and (4) when leasing reduces uncertainty about the asset's residual value to the lessee.

Bad Reasons for Leasing (p. 753) On the other hand, the following are dubious reasons for leasing.

1. Using leasing to distort the firm's financial statements. If leased assets are somehow kept off the books, some financial ratios (e.g., those measuring asset utilization) will be inflated.
2. Leasing is sometimes said to represent "100 percent financing". However, many leases require a "down payment" in the form of an advance lease payment and/or a security deposit.
3. Leasing may also be used to circumvent capital expenditure control systems set up by the firm. Assuming that the control system is rational, this too may decrease firm value.

KEY TERMS AND CONCEPTS

Financial lease - long-term, fully-amortized lease under which the lessee is responsible for upkeep. Usually not cancelable without penalty. (p. 742)

Lessee - The user of an asset in a leasing agreement. Lessee makes payments to lessor. (p. 740)

Lessor - owner of an asset in a leasing agreement. Lessor receives payments from the lessee. (p. 740)

Leveraged lease - A financial lease in which the lessor borrows a substantial fraction of the cost of the leased asset on a nonrecourse basis. (p. 743)

Net advantage to leasing (NAL) - NPV of the decision to lease an asset instead of buying it. (p. 749)

Operating lease - Usually a shorter-term lease where the lessor is responsible for insurance, taxes, and upkeep. Often cancelable on short notice. (p. 741)

Sale and leaseback - financial lease in which the lessee sells an asset and then leases it back. (p. 743)

Tax-oriented lease - a financial lease in which the lessor is the owner for tax purposes. (p. 742)

CONCEPT TEST

1. Leases can be separated into two types: _____ and _____.
   _____ leases are long-term, fully-amortized, and not cancelable.
   _____ leases are usually shorter-term, partially-amortized, and cancelable.
   _____ leases must be reported on the balance sheet. (p. 741)

2. The user of the leased asset is the _____ . The user makes payments to the _____ , who is the owner of the asset in a leasing agreement. (p. 740)

3. _____ are the focus of this chapter; this type of lease fully covers the lessor's cost of purchasing the asset and pays him a return on the investment. Because of this, this type of lease is often called a _____ or a _____ lease. A _____ is a financial lease transaction in which the lessee sells an asset and then leases it back. (p. 742)

4.   FASB 13 requires that certain financial leases must be capitalized and appear on the firm's financial statements. For accounting purposes, a least must be disclosed on the firm's balance sheet if at least one of the following is true: a. _____, b. _____, c. _____, d. _____ . (p. 743)

5.   The NAL is the NPV of a lease/buy analysis where the NPV is computed using the following equation:
_____ - [_____ + _____] / [_____]. The discount rate is _____, because leasing is a substitute for borrowing and buying. (p. 749)

6.   The following are *good financial reasons* for a firm to engage in a leasing contract.
a. _____ b. _____ c. _____ d. _____ (p. 751)

7.   A number of dubious justifications for leasing are also often proposed. For example, leasing may wrongly be chosen as an alternative to buying if:
a. _____ b. _____ c. _____ (p. 753)

SOLUTIONS TO CONCEPT TEST

1.   financial or capital leases; operating leases; Financial; Operating; Capital
2.   lessee; lessor
3.   Financial lease; fully amortized; full payout; sale and leaseback
4.   ownership transfers to the lessee at the end of the lease term; the lease contains a bargain purchase option; the lease term is 75% or more of the asset's economic life; the present value of the lease payments is at least 90% of the fair market value of the asset
5.   (outlay if purchased)-[(lease payment)x$(1-T_c)$+(depreciation)x(T_c)][1-1/$(1 + R^*)^t$/R^*; R$(1- T_c)$
6.   the tax rates of the lessor and the lessee differ; the ability of the lessee and the lessor to utilize tax shields differ; leasing reduces the transactions costs the lessee would incur in obtaining the use of the asset; leasing reduces uncertainty about the asset's residual value to the lessee.
7.   leasing is to be used to distort the firm's financial statements; leasing is believed to constitute "100 percent financing"; leasing is used to circumvent capital expenditure control systems

PROBLEMS

Use the following information to solve problems 1 through 6.

Andy wishes to obtain a new squad car for the Mayberry Sheriff's Department. A new car can be purchased for $25,000; funds can be borrowed at a rate of 8%. Assume a marginal tax rate of 34%. If purchased, the car will be depreciated on straight-line basis over four years. (Assume the salvage value is zero.) Barney has determined that a similar car can be leased for four years from Mount Pilot Leasing - the firm requires an annual lease payment of $6,000.

1. What is the annual net cash outflow required if the Sheriff's Department leases the car?

2. What is the net advantage to leasing (NAL) for the Mayberry Sheriff's Department?

3. Consider the transaction from the viewpoint of Mount Pilot Leasing. What is the NPV for them if we assume that borrowing and tax rates are the same as those for the Mayberry Sheriff's Department?

4. All else equal, leasing is zero-sum game. That is, a positive NPV for the lessee is a negative NPV for the lessor. In reality, however, all else usually isn't equal. Suppose the borrowing and tax rates for Mount Pilot Leasing are 6% and 50%, respectively. Now what is the NAL for Mount Pilot Leasing?

5. Suppose that, because Mount Pilot Leasing has more bargaining power with auto dealers, they can purchase the car for $20,000. Recompute the NPV, given the tax and borrowing rates in problem 4.

6. Here's a problem that's a bit more difficult. Refer back to the basic information which precedes problem 1. Now suppose the residual value of the car at the end of the lease term is $8000. Recompute the NAL for the Mayberry Sheriff's Department.

7. Finally, suppose the original information from Problem 1, except that the residual value is uncertain at the inception of the lease. Should the firm apply a higher or lower discount rate to the residual value in obtaining the NAL? Recompute the NAL assuming the firm believes a 2% differential is called for.

CHAPTER 25

INTERNATIONAL CORPORATE FINANCE

CONCEPTS FOR REVIEW

As we move increasingly toward a global economy, it is important to develop tools with which to analyze financial decisions in an international context. This chapter introduces several important concepts related to the application of financial techniques when cash flows cross one or more borders.

CHAPTER HIGHLIGHTS

The basic principles of corporate finance apply to international corporations just as they do to domestic corporations - international firms seek positive NPV projects and arrange financing that creates value for shareholders. However, application of these principles is complicated by differences in foreign exchange, interest rates, accounting methods, tax rates and government intervention.

I. TERMINOLOGY (p. 758)

Because the terminology is defined both in the text and in the "Key Terms" section of this chapter, we do not repeat it here. If you would like to review these terms, please turn to the end of this chapter.

II. FOREIGN EXCHANGE MARKETS AND EXCHANGE RATES (p. 759)

The **foreign exchange market** is the world's largest financial market. It is an over-the-counter market, consisting of a telecommunications network among traders in major commercial and investment banks worldwide. Most trading takes place in a small number of major currencies, including the U.S. dollar, West German deutsche mark (DM), British pound sterling (£), Japanese yen (¥), Swiss franc (SF), and French franc (FF).

Exchange Rates (p. 759) An **exchange rate** is the price of one country's currency in terms of the currency of another. A quote stating units of foreign currency per dollar is an **indirect** or **European quote**. A rate can also be quoted in terms of the number of dollars required to buy one unit of foreign currency; this is a **direct** or **American quote**. Most exchange rates are quoted in terms of U.S. dollars.

Suppose the following exchange rates existed:

French francs/German D-marks:	5
French francs/U.S. dollars:	10
German D-marks/U.S. dollars:	3

You could convert $1 into three marks. Next, convert three marks to 15 francs and then convert francs to dollars: at the exchange rate of 10 francs to the dollar, you will have $1.50, or a 50% risk-free return! This outcome is impossible in an efficient market. This activity is **triangle arbitrage**. Arbitrage is the simultaneous purchase and sale of the same asset at different prices. Since arbitrage opportunities cannot exist in an efficient market, the above rates cannot exist simultaneously. If $1 buys DM 3, and $1 buys FF 10, the cross rate must be: (DM 3/$1)/(FF 10/$1) = DM 3/FF 10 = DM .3/FF 1.

Types of Transactions (p. 763) Two basic kinds of transactions exist in the foreign exchange market. **Spot trades** involve agreement on the exchange rate today, (the **spot exchange rate**), for settlement in two business days. **Forward trades** involve agreement today on an exchange rate for future settlement. This is the **forward exchange rate**, and settlement is typically one to fifty-two weeks in the future.

When a foreign currency is more expensive in the forward market than in the spot market, it is said to be selling at a **premium** to the dollar. For example, if the Japanese yen costs $.0075 in the spot market and $.0080 in the forward market, the Japanese yen is selling at a premium to the dollar. Equivalently, the dollar is selling at a **discount** relative to the Japanese yen.

III. PURCHASING POWER PARITY (p. 764)

In this section, we address the following questions: (1) What factors determine the level of the spot exchange rate? (2) What determines the rate of change in exchange rates? The concepts of **absolute purchasing power parity** and **relative purchasing power parity** provide part of the answer.

Absolute Purchasing Power Parity (p. 764) **Absolute purchasing power parity** is based on the concept that a particular commodity must have the same price regardless of the currency used to purchase it, or where it is purchased. Absolute purchasing power parity must hold in the absence of arbitrage opportunities. It implies that both prices and exchange rates adjust to eliminate arbitrage opportunities. The argument is strictly accurate only if there are no shipping or other transactions costs, no barriers to trade, and commodities are identical in both countries. These conditions are rarely met, so we do not expect absolute purchasing power parity to hold precisely.

Relative Purchasing Power Parity (RPP) (p. 765) The concept of *relative purchasing power parity* addresses the rate of change in an exchange rate; it is determined by relative inflation rates in two countries. To summarize this concept, we will use the following notation.

Let:
S_o	=	Current spot exchange rate
$E[S_t]$	=	Expected exchange rate in t periods
h_{US}	=	Inflation rate in the United States
h_{FC}	=	Inflation rate in foreign country

The expected percentage change in the exchange rate during the next year is: $(E[S_1] - S_0)/S_0$. RPP states that the expected change in the exchange rate is equal to the difference in the inflation rates:

$$(E[S_1] - S_0)/S_0 = h_{fc} - h_{US}.$$

Rearranging, RPP can be expressed as: $E[S_1] = S_0 \times [1 + (h_{FC} - h_{US})]$. If the inflation rate remains constant for the next two years, the relationship for year 2 is: $E[S_2] = E[S_1] \times [1 + (h_{FC} - h_{US})]$. Using the above relationship, $E[S_2]$ can be computed as follows:

$$
\begin{aligned}
E[S_2] &= E[S_1] \times [1 + (h_{FC} - h_{US})] \\
&= (FF\ 10.4) \times [1 + (.09 - .05)] = (FF\ 10.4) \times 1.04 = FF\ 10.816.
\end{aligned}
$$

Alternatively, $E[S_2]$ can be computed as follows: $E[S_2] = S_0 \times [1 + (h_{FC} - h_{US})]^2$. In general, for any time period t, relative purchasing power parity is: $E[S_t] = S_0 \times [1 + (h_{FC} - h_{US})]^t$.

IV. INTEREST RATE PARITY, UNBIASED FORWARD RATES, AND THE INTERNATIONAL FISHER EFFECT (p. 767)

In this section, we investigate the relationship among spot exchange rates, forward exchange rates, and interest rates. The additional notation required in this section is:

F_t = Forward exchange rate for settlement at time t
R_{US} = Nominal risk-free interest rate in the U.S.
R_{FC} = Nominal risk-free interest rate in foreign country

Covered Interest Arbitrage. (p. 768) An investor who makes an investment in a risk-free asset (e.g., T-bills) in the U.S. earns a return on the investment equal to R_{US}. One who invests at the risk-free rate in a foreign country must first convert dollars to that foreign currency, invest in the risk-free asset, and then convert the foreign currency to dollars. Thus, the return on this investment depends on both the nominal risk-free rate in the foreign country (i.e., R_{FC}) and the spot exchange rate (S_0) and the forward exchange rate (F_t). If the future exchange rate could not be established today, the investment in the foreign country would not be risk-free; the actual return would depend on the spot exchange rate at time t. Since the forward rate can be established today, the investment is risk-free, but the rate of return is not the same as R_{FC}. If the actual rate on this investment differs from R_{US}, an arbitrage opportunity exists.

S_0 = FF 10.0
F_1 = FF 9.6
R_{US} = 9%
R_{FF} = 6%

At the end of one year, an investor who invests $1 in T-bills will have ($1 × 1.09) = $1.09. One who invests at the risk-free rate available in France proceeds as follows:

1. Convert $1 to ($1 × S_0) = [$1 × (FF 10/$1)] = FF 10.
2. Simultaneously, the investor enters into a forward agreement to convert dollars to francs at the forward rate $1 = FF 9.6.
3. Invest FF 10 at the rate R_{FF} = 6%, so that, at year-end, he has [(FF 10) x 1.06] = FF 10.6.
4. Convert FF 10.6 to dollars at the rate in (2), so he has [(FF 10.6)/(FF 9.6/$1)] = $1.10417.

The investor prefers the latter investment; the actual return is 10.417%, compared to R_{US} = 9%. The existence of the discrepancy in rates of return on risk-free investments gives rise to an arbitrage opportunity, referred to as **covered interest arbitrage.** Suppose an American investor can borrow $100,000 at R_{US} = 9%, and invest the $100,000 at the French risk-free rate, as described above. At year-end, the investor would repay ($100,000 × 1.09) = $109,000 on the loan. On the other hand, the investor would have ($100,000 × 1.10417) = $110,417 from the investment at the French risk-free rate. The arbitrage profit is ($110,417 - $109,000) = $1,417.

Interest Rate Parity (IRP) (p. 769) In an efficient market, arbitrage opportunities cannot exist, so the return for each of the risk-free investments above must be the same. The return per dollar for the investment at the risk-free rate R_{US} is [$1 × (1 + R_{US})]. The return per dollar for the investment in the foreign risk-free investment is [$1 × S_0 × (1 + R_{FC})]/F_1. The **interest rate parity** condition states that these two returns must be equal: (1 + R_{US}) = [S_0 × (1 + R_{FC})]/F_1. Rearranging:

$$F_1/S_0 = (1 + R_{FC})/(1 + R_{US})$$

IRP indicates that the relationship between the forward and spot exchange rates is a function of the relationship between foreign and domestic interest rates. An approximation to this statement of IRP can further clarify the relationship. This approximation states that the percentage forward premium or discount is equal to the difference between the foreign and domestic interest rates:

$$(F_1 - S_0)/S_0 = R_{FC} - R_{US}$$

Rearranging, $F_1 = S_0 \times [1 + (R_{FC} - R_{US})]$. This statement can be extended to any number of time periods, t, as follows: $F_1 = S_0 \times [1 + (R_{FC} - R_{US})]^t$.

Forward Rates and Future Spot Rates (p. 770) The **unbiased forward rates (UFR)** condition is the statement that the forward rate (F_1) equals the expected future spot rate $(E[S_1])$: $F_1 = E[S_1]$. UFR can also be stated for any number of time periods: $F_t = E[S_t]$. Thus, the forward rate must equal the market consensus expectation regarding the future spot rate. UFR can also be thought of as long-run average; i.e., on average, the one-period forward rate for a particular currency equals the spot rate one period from now. Equivalent statements apply to the forward rate for any time period t.

Putting It All Together (p. 770) We have developed three basic relationships of international finance: absolute purchasing power parity (PPP), interest rate parity (IRP), and unbiased forward rates (UFR). In this section, we use these to develop two additional important concepts. To reiterate:

PPP: $E[S_1] = S_0 \times [1 + (h_{FC} - h_{US})]$
IRP: $F_1 = S_0 \times [1 + (R_{FC} - R_{US})]$
UFR: $F_1 = E[S_1]$

F_1 is on the left side of both IRP and UFR. Thus, the right-hand sides of these equations must be equal: $E[S_1] = S_0 \times [1 + (R_{FC} - R_{US})]$. This is **uncovered interest parity (UIP)**, which can be stated for t time periods as follows: $E[S_t] = S_0 \times [1 + (h_{FC} - h_{US})]^t$.

The right-hand sides of PPP and UIP must be equal: $S_0 \times [1 + (h_{FC} - h_{US})] = S_0 \times [1 + (R_{FC} - R_{US})]$. This statement can be simplified as: $h_{FC} - h_{US} = R_{FC} - R_{US}$. That is, the difference in foreign and domestic inflation rates is equal to the difference in foreign and domestic interest rates. Rearranging:

$$R_{US} - h_{US} = R_{FC} - h_{FC}.$$

This is the **international Fisher effect (IFE)**: *real* interest rates in different countries are equal. In the absence of differences in attitudes toward risk from one country to another and barriers to the movement of money, the IFE is another implication of efficient markets. If the IFE did not apply to two countries, money would flow to the country with the higher real rate; this would increase asset values, and lower returns in that country, with the opposite effect in the country with the lower real rate.

V. INTERNATIONAL CAPITAL BUDGETING (p. 772)

International capital budgeting decisions are made using the same NPV criterion as is used for domestic capital budgeting. The difference is that we must compute the NPV in *dollars* even though cash flows are in another currency. Two equivalent approaches to accomplishing this objective are considered in this section: the **home currency approach** and the **foreign currency approach**.

A firm is considering building a factory in Slobovia. It is a 3-year project, which will cost 100 slobs (SL 100) to build and will produce after-tax cash inflows of SL 40 per year. The current spot exchange rate is SL 2 = \$1. The one-year risk-free rates for the U.S. and Slobovia are 5% and 3%, respectively, and the appropriate cost of capital for *dollar* cash flows is 10%.

Method 1: The Home Currency Approach (p. 772) To calculate the NPV using the home currency approach, first convert the SL cash flows to dollar flows, and then discount the dollar cash flows at the 10% cost of capital. To convert the foreign currency cash flows to dollar cash flows, we compute the expected future exchange rates using the uncovered interest parity (UIP) relationship:

$$
\begin{aligned}
E\,[S_t] &= S_0 \times [1 + (R_{FC} - R_{US})]^t \\
&= (SL\ 2) \times [1 + (0.3 - .05)]^t \\
&= (SL\ 2) \times [1 + (-.02)]^t \\
&= (SL\ 2) \times (.98)^t.
\end{aligned}
$$

The expected spot exchange rates for years 1, 2 and 3 are presented in the following table:

Year	Expected exchange rate
1	$(SL\ 2) \times (.98)^1 = SL\ 1.9600$
2	$(SL\ 2) \times (.98)^2 = SL\ 1.9208$
3	$(SL\ 2) \times (.98)^3 = SL\ 1.8824$

These exchange rates are then used to convert cash flows to dollars:

Year	Cash Flow (in SL)	Expected exchange rate	Cash flow (in $)
0	-SL 100	SL 2.0000	-$50.0000
1	SL 40	SL 1.9600	$20.4082
2	SL 40	SL 1.9208	$20.8247
3	SL 40	SL 1.8824	$21.2495

Using the 10% opportunity cost, the net present value of the investment in the new factory is +\$1.7285.

Method 2: The Foreign Currency Approach (p. 773) This approach requires that we discount the cash flows measured in the foreign currency; the resulting NPV measured in the foreign currency is then converted to a dollar NPV. The foreign currency cash flows are not discounted at the firm's cost of capital. Rather, the cost of capital is converted to an appropriate rate for the foreign currency, using the IFE before computing the NPV of the foreign currency cash flows. The difference in nominal rates is:

$$h_{FC} - h_{US} = R_{FC} - R_{US} = .03 - .05 = -.02$$

So the firm's 10% cost of capital is reduced by 2%, to 8%. The NPV of the cash flows for the project measured in the foreign currency and discounted at 8%, is SL 3.0839. Using the spot exchange rate, this NPV is converted to dollars: (SL 3.0839)/(SL 2/$1) = $1.5420. (Note that this NPV differs from that obtained using the home currency approach. The reason for the difference is the approximation used in the previous section in deriving the international Fisher effect.)

Unremitted Cash Flows (p. 774) The example above assumes that the cash flows from the project are remitted to the United States as they are earned. In reality, this assumption is frequently inappropriate. First, foreign countries often place limitations on the ability of international firms to remit cash flows. Second, the issue of remittance is affected by foreign taxes. (For example, tax incentives may make it advantageous for an international firm to reinvest foreign cash flows in the foreign country.) Third, total taxes paid by a multinational firm may be affected by the timing of remittances. Thus, the timing of remittances may alter the NPV of a foreign investment.

VI. EXCHANGE RATE RISK (p. 774)

Exchange rate risk is the risk of loss from fluctuations in exchange rates over time. The three categories of exchange rate risk, or exposure, are: short-run exposure, long-run exposure, and translation exposure.

Short-Run Exposure (p. 774) Firms dealing in international trade are subject to exchange rate risk because they both make payments in foreign currencies and receive foreign currencies in payments. Suppose the spot exchange rate for the Japanese yen is ¥ 125, and that a company has receivables of ¥ 1,500,000 to be collected in ninety days. At the current exchange rate, the firm will be able to exchange ¥ 1,500,000 for [(¥ 1,500,000)/(¥ 125/$1)] = $12,000. If, however, the exchange rate in 90 days is ¥ 150, then the firm will actually receive only [(¥ 1,500,000)/(¥ 150/$1)] = $10,000. Of course, it is also possible that the exchange rate will decrease during the next ninety days; this would result in an increase in the dollar value of the future payment. *The firm's exchange rate risk is the uncertainty associated with the dollar-value of the future payment in the foreign currency.*

The forward market provides a means for hedging exchange rate risk. Suppose that, in the receivables example above, the ninety-day forward rate is ¥ 140. The firm can eliminate exchange rate risk by purchasing a forward contract and promising to deliver yen for dollars. At the ¥ 140 forward exchange rate, the firm is certain to receive [(¥ 1,500,000)/(¥ 140/$1)] = $10,714.29 ninety days from now. Hedging in the forward contract means that, when the firm receives the payment of ¥ 1,500,000 ninety days from now, it will be able to exchange this sum for $10,714.29, eliminating the risk associated with fluctuations in the exchange rate over the next ninety days.

Hedging is generally considered advantageous because, in an efficient market, exchange rate speculation is a zero-NPV activity; that is, the UFR condition indicates that the forward rate is equal to the expected future spot rate so that, on average, there is no gain from speculating in the direction of the exchange rate. In addition, the costs of hedging are generally quite low.

Long-Run Exposure (p. 775) Long-run exposure to exchange rate risk arises from, for example, a long-term commitment to purchase resources, such as labor or materials, in a foreign country. Since such commitments are denominated in the foreign currency, the dollar value of future payments is subject to exchange rate risk. Such long-run exposures to exchange rate risk can be hedged in the forward markets only to a limited extent, because forward contracts have maturities of one year or less. Protection against long-run exposures is generally accomplished by matching inflows and outflows in the foreign currency; then when changes in the exchange rate result in a decrease in the dollar value of the firm's inflows, these changes are offset by a decrease in the dollar value of the outflows. Exchange rate risk can also be hedged by obtaining financing in the country where the investment is to be made. Risk reduction occurs because changes in the value of the investment will be partially offset by changes in the liabilities.

Translation Exposure (p. 776) When a U.S. firm prepares its financial statements, the data for foreign operations must be translated into dollars. The major issues which arise from this process are: (1) determination of the appropriate exchange rate; and, (2) accounting for gains and losses from foreign currency translation. Financial Accounting Standards Board Statement 52 requires that all assets and liabilities are translated at current, rather than historical, exchange rates. Gains and losses from exchange rate fluctuations are carried as a separate item in the shareholder's equity portion of the balance sheet, but are not recognized on the income statement.

VII. POLITICAL RISK (p. 777)

Political risk is the risk of loss associated with political actions in foreign countries and arises from events such as changes in the foreign government, as well as changes in foreign tax laws and regulations.

KEY TERMS AND CONCEPTS

American Depository Receipt (ADR) - security issued in the United States representing shares of a foreign stock and allowing that stock to be traded in the United States. (p. 758)
Cross-rate - the implicit exchange rate between two currencies (usually non-U.S.) quoted in some third currency (usually the U.S. dollar). (p. 758)
Eurobonds - international bonds issued in multiple countries but denominated in a single currency (usually the issuer's currency). (p.758)
Eurocurrency - money in a financial center outside of the country whose currency is involved. (p. 758)
European Currency Unit (ECU) - index of 10 European currencies intended to serve as a monetary unit for the European Monetary System (EMS). (p. 758)
Exchange rate - the price of one country's currency expressed in terms of another currency. (p. 759)
Exchange rate risk - risk of having international operations when relative currency values vary. (p. 774)
Foreign bonds - international bonds issued in one country, denominated in that currency. (p. 759)
Foreign exchange market - the market where one country's currency is traded for another's. (p. 759)
Gilts - British and Irish government securities, including issues of local British authorities and some overseas public-sector offerings. (p. 759)
London Interbank Offer Rate (LIBOR) - the rate most international banks charge one another for overnight Eurodollar loans. (p. 759)
Forward exchange rate - the agreed-upon exchange rate to be used in a forward trade. (p. 763)
Forward trade - agreement to exchange currency at some time in the future. (p. 763)
International Fisher effect (IFE) - the theory that real interest rates are equal across countries. (p. 771)
Interest rate parity - condition stating that the interest rate differential between two countries is equal

to the percentage difference between the forward exchange rate and the spot exchange rate. (p. 769)

Political risk - risk related to changes in value that arise because of political actions. (p. 777)

Purchasing power parity (PPP) - exchange rates adjust to keep purchasing power constant across currencies. (p. 764)

Spot exchange rate - the exchange rate on a spot trade. (p. 763)

Spot trade - agreement to trade currencies based on the exchange rate today. (p. 763)

Swaps - agreements to the exchange of two securities or currencies. (p. 759)

Unbiased forward rates (UFR) - the condition stating that the current forward rate is an unbiased predictor of the future exchange rate. (p. 770)

Uncovered interest parity (UIP) - the condition stating that the expected percentage change in the exchange rate is equal to the difference in interest rates. (p. 771)

CONCEPT TEST

1. A security issued in the United States, representing a share of a foreign company's stock is a(n) _____. When the exchange rates for two currencies are quoted in a third currency, the exchange rate is a(n) _____. A basket of ten European currencies intended to serve as the monetary unit for the European Monetary System is the _____. A bearer bond issue denominated in one currency and sold simultaneously in several European countries is a(n)_____. Money in financial institutions outside the country whose currency is involved is _____. Dollars in banks outside the U.S. are _____. Bonds issued by foreign borrowers in another country and denominated in the currency of the country where issued are _____. The rate on overnight Eurodollar loans between major international banks is the _____. An agreement to exchange currencies is a(n) _____. An exchange of a debt with a floating-rate payment for a debt with a fixed-rate payment (or vice versa) is a(n) _____. (p. 758)

2. The price of one country's currency expressed in terms of another currency is a(n) _____. A quote of units of foreign currency per dollar is called a(n)_____ or _____ quote. (p. 759)

3. The simultaneous purchase and sale of the same asset at different prices is _____. Conversions among three currencies, to profit from discrepancies in spot exchange rates, is _____. Such opportunities cannot exist in a(n) _____ market. (p. 761)

4. Spot trades involve agreement on the exchange rate today, called the _____ rate, for settlement in _____ business days. Forward trades involve agreement today on an exchange rate for settlement in the future; this exchange rate case is the _____ rate. When a foreign currency is more expensive in the forward market than in the spot market, it is selling at a _____ to the dollar; equivalently, the dollar is selling at a _____ to the foreign currency. (p. 763)

5. If a commodity has different prices in with different currencies, this is a violation of _____; it would create opportunities for _____ profits if the following three conditions are also met: (1) no _____ costs; (2) no barriers to _____; and, (3) the commodities are _____ in both countries. In efficient markets, p_{FC} = _____ × _____ . In an efficient market, any deviation from this condition results in adjustments in both _____ and _____ . (p. 764)

6. Relative purchasing power parity states that the rate of change in an exchange rate is determined by _____ in the two countries. The expected change in the exchange rate is equal to _____, as indicated in the equation: _____ = _____ . Rearranging, $E[S_1]$ = _____ . For any period t, $E[S_t]$ = _____ . (p. 765)

7. The return on a risk-free investment in a foreign country depends on both the nominal risk-free rate in the foreign country, and the _____ exchange rate. If the actual rate on this investment differs from the risk-free rate in the U.S., an opportunity exists for a(n) _____ profit; the process of taking advantage of this opportunity is _____ . The statement that these two returns must be equal is the _____ condition. Stated mathematically, _____ = _____ . Algebraically: F_1/S_0 = _____ . An approximation to this equation states that the percentage forward premium or discount is equal to the difference between foreign and domestic interest rates: _____ = _____ . So F_1 = _____ . For t periods: F_t = _____ . (p. 769)

8. The statement that the forward rate equals the expected future spot rate is the _____ condition; i.e., _____ = _____ . This indicates that the forward rate equals the _____ the _____ rate. (p. 769)

9. UIP states: $E[S_1]$ = _____ . For t periods: $E[S_t]$ = _____ (p. 771)

10. The IFE is derived by equating the right-hand sides of the PPP and UIP relationship: _____ = _____ . Or: $h_{FC} - h_{US}$ = _____ . That is, the difference in foreign and domestic inflation rates is equal to the difference in foreign and domestic _____ . Rearranging, $R_{US} - h_{US}$ = _____ . This is the IFE; it indicates that _____ in different countries are equal. In the absence of differences in attitudes toward risk from one country to another, and barriers to the movement of money, the IFE is an implication of _____ markets. (p. 771)

11. International capital budgeting decisions are made using the _____ criterion. The _____ approach requires that foreign currency cash flows are converted to dollar cash flows. This conversion requires the calculation of _____ exchange rates, using the _____ relationship, as follows: $E[S_t]$ = _____ . Dollar cash flows are then discounted using the required return for dollar cash flows. (p. 772)

12. The _____ approach to international capital budgeting requires that we discount the cash flows measured in terms of _____; the resulting NPV is then converted to a NPV measured in _____. The foreign currency cash flows are not discounted at the firm's cost of capital. Rather, the cost of capital is converted to an appropriate rate for the foreign currency, using the _____ relationship. This NPV is converted to dollars using the _____ exchange rate. (p. 773)

13. The risk of loss from fluctuations in exchange rates over time is _____ risk. Firms dealing in international trade are subject to exchange rate risk because they both make payments in foreign currencies and receive foreign currencies in payments. Consequently, changes in exchange rates can result in losses; this is considered a _____ exposure. For example, a firm which has receivables denominated in a foreign currency, experiences a(n) (increase/decrease) in the dollar value of the receivables when the exchange rate increases; the firm experiences a(n) (increase/decrease) in the dollar value of the receivables when the exchange rate decreases. Similarly, a firm which has payables denominated in a foreign currency, experiences a(n) (increase/decrease) in the dollar value of the payables when the exchange rate increases. The _____ risk is the uncertainty associated with the dollar-value of the future payment in the foreign currency. A means of hedging exchange rate risk is provided by the _____ market. The firm can eliminate exchange rate risk by _____ a forward contract and promising to deliver the foreign currency in exchange for dollars. (p. 774)

14. A long-term commitment to purchase resources in a foreign country results in a _____ exposure to exchange rate risk. Protection against such exposures is generally accomplished by _____ in the foreign currency. When a U.S. firm prepares its financial statements, the information on foreign operations must be translated into dollars; this results in _____ exposure. FASB Statement 52 requires that all assets and liabilities are translated at _____ exchange rates. Gains and losses from exchange rate fluctuations are carried as a separate item in the _____ portion of the balance sheet, but are not recognized on the income statement. (p. 775)

ANSWERS TO CONCEPT TEST

1. American depository receipt; cross rate; European currency unity; Eurobond; Eurocurrency; Eurodollars; foreign bonds; London interbank offered rate; currency swap; interest rate swap
2. indirect; direct; American
3. arbitrage; triangle arbitrage; efficient
4. spot; two; forward; premium; discount
5. absolute PPP; arbitrage; transactions; trade; identical; S_0; P_{US}; prices; exchange rates
6. inflation rates; difference in the inflation rates; $[E(S_1) - S_0)/S_0]$; $(h_{FC} - h_{US})$; $S_0 \times [1 + (h_{FC} - h_{US})]$; $S_0 \times [1 + (h_{FC} - h_{US})]$
7. spot; forward; arbitrage; covered interest arbitrage; IRP; $(1 + R_{US})$; $[S_0 \times (1 + R_{FC})]/F_1$; $(1 + R_{FC})/(1 + R_{US})$; $(F_1 - S_0)/S_0$; $(R_{FC} - R_{US})$; $S_0 \times [1 + (R_{FC} - R_{US})]$; $S_0 \times [1 + (R_{FC} - R_{US})]^t$
8. unbiased forward rates; F_t; $E[S_t]$; market consensus; future spot
9. $S_0 \times [1 + (R_{FC} - R_{US})]$; $\{S_0 \times [1 + (R_{FC} - R_{US})]^t$
10. $S_0 \times [1 + (h_{FC} - h_{US})]$; $S_0 \times [1 + (R_{FC} - R_{US})]$; inflation rates; $(R_{FC} - R_{US})$; $(R_{FC} - h_{FC})$; real rates; efficient

11.   NPV; home currency; expected future; uncovered interest parity; $S_0 \times [1 + (R_{FC}-R_{US})]^t$
12.   foreign currency; foreign currency; dollars; international Fisher effect; spot
13.   exchange rate; short-run; decrease; increase; decrease; exchange rate; forward; purchasing
14.   long-run; matching inflows and outflows; translation; current; shareholders' equity

PROBLEMS

1. The direct exchange rate for German deutsche marks is $.50/DM 1. The direct exchange rate for British pounds is $1.50/£ 1. If you have 1 DM, how many pounds can you buy? (What is the cross rate?)

2. Suppose that, for the data in Problem 1, the cross rate is DM 3.3/£ 1, rather than the calculated result of DM 3/£ 1. Describe the triangle arbitrage opportunity which would exist under these circumstances.

3. Suppose, for Problem 1, the cross rate is DM 2.7/ £ 1. Describe the triangle arbitrage opportunity.

Use the following data to solve Problems 4 through 7:

The spot exchange rate for the British pound is $1.80/£ 1, and the ninety-day forward rate is $1.75/£ 1. The spot and 90 day forward rate for the Swiss franc are $.80/SF 1, and the $.75/SF 1; respectively. The spot and 90-day forward rate for the deutsche mark are $.65/DM 1, and $.70/DM 1, respectively.

4. Compute the indirect exchange rate for each of the exchange rates quoted above. Which currencies are selling at a premium to the dollar? For which currencies is the dollar selling at a premium?

5. What is the cross-rate in the spot market, for pounds in terms of deutsche marks? What is the cross-rate, in the spot market, for deutsche marks in terms of pounds?

6. Suppose that the cross-rate for pounds in terms of deutsche marks is actually £ .35/DM 1, rather than the result computed in the solution to Problem 5. Describe the triangle arbitrage opportunity.

7. Suppose that the cross-rate for pounds in terms of deutsche marks is actually £ .75/DM 1, rather than the result computed in the solution to Problem 5. Describe the triangle arbitrage opportunity.

8. An ounce of silver costs $5 in the U.S. and 800 yen in Japan. Assume ¥ 150 = $1. Is this an equilibrium situation? Suppose that a trader has $500 available; can the trader earn an arbitrage profit?

9. Suppose that, for Problem 8, the price of silver in the U.S. and Japan does not change. What is the equilibrium exchange rate which is consistent with absolute purchasing power parity?

10. Suppose that, for the data in Problem 8, the price of silver in Japan is ¥ 700 per ounce. Describe the arbitrage profit opportunity for a trader with $500 available.

11. The direct spot exchange rate for marks is $.50/DM 1 and the 90-day forward rate is $.51/DM 1. Is the mark selling at a premium or discount? Compute the indirect spot and forward rates.

12. If, in Problem 11, the U.S. 90-day risk-free rate, $R_{US} = 3\%$. What is the German risk-free rate, R_G?

13. Suppose the Swiss inflation rate is forecast to be 2% during the coming year and the United States rate over the same period will be 5%. The current exchange rate is $1.50 = SF 1. What is the expected spot exchange rate in one year?

14. The current yen/dollar exchange rate is ¥ 150/$1. The risk-free interest rate in Japan is 6% and in the United States is 8%. What is the expected spot exchange rate in one year?

15. Suppose that, for the data in problem 14, the U.S. inflation rate is expected to be 4%.' What is the expected spot exchange rate in five years?

Use the following information to solve Problems 16 and 17:

You must evaluate a proposed investment in the country of Westfield, whose home currency is the Sar, abbreviated SA. The current exchange rate is SA 2/$1. The inflation rate in Westfield is expected to be 10% higher than in the U.S. The project will cost SA 1000 and is expected to generate SA 300 per year for three years. The project will then be sold for SA 400. The discount rate for dollar flows is 12%.

16. What is the expected spot exchange rate at the end of the project's life?

17. Use the home currency approach to compute the NPV of the proposed investment in dollars.

SOLUTIONS TO
CHAPTER PROBLEMS

CHAPTER 2

1.

TERRI-YUNG COMPANY, INC.
1997 Income Statement

Net Sales		$1,000
Cost of goods sold	400	
Depreciation	100	
Earnings before interest and taxes		$ 500
Interest paid	150	
Taxable income		$ 350
Taxes (34%)		119
Net income		$ 231

2. EPS = ($231/100) = $2.31. Dividends per share equals ($120/100) = $1.20.

3.

TERRI-YUNG COMPANY, INC.
Balance sheets as of December 31, 1996 and 1997

	1996	1997		1996	1997
Assets			*Liabilities and Owners' Equity*		
Current assets			Current liabilities		
Cash	$ 800	$ 500	Accounts payable	$2,400	$ 2,000
Mkt. sec.	400	300	Notes payable	1,200	1,600
Accts. rec.	900	800	Total	$3,600	$ 3,600
Inventory	1,800	2,000			
Total	$3,900	$3,600	Long-term debt	3,000	2,800
Fixed assets			Owners' equity	3,300	5,200
Net PP&E	$6,000	$ 8,000			
Total Assets	$9,900	$11,600	Total Lia. & OE	$9,900	$11,600

4. OCF = EBIT + Depreciation - Taxes = $500 + 100 - 119 = $481.

5. Net fixed assets increased by $2,000. The income statement in Problem 1 indicates that the old assets depreciated by $100. If no assets were bought or sold during the year, fixed assets would have been ($6000 - $100) = $5,900 at the end of 1996. However, the 1997 balance sheet shows $8,000 in fixed assets. So net capital spending was ($8,000 - $5,900) = $2,100 during 1997. Note that this result is derived without using the data for sales of fixed assets ($300) or acquisition of fixed assets ($2,400). The figures confirm net capital spending of ($2,400 - $300) = $2,100 for 1997.

6. Net working capital in 1996 was ($3,900 - $3,600) = $300. In 1997 it was ($3,600 - $3,600) = $0. So the addition to net working capital was ($0 - $300) = -$300; since this is negative, it reflects a reduction in net working capital of $300. This figure can also be computed as the change in current assets minus the change in current liabilities. Current assets decrease from $3900 to $3600 for a change of - $300. The change in current liabilities is zero, so the change in net working capital is (-$300) - $0 = - $300, as computed previously.

7. Total cash flow to the firm can be calculated as:

OCF - Net Capital Spending + Addition to Net Working Capital = $481 - 2,100 + 300 = -$1,319

Note from Problem 1 net income is positive, but cash flow is negative. This is because the calculation of net income does not include capital spending. In general, net income is **not** equal to cash flow.

8. Cash flow to creditors is interest paid ($150) plus repayment of long-term debt ($200), less new borrowing ($0), or $350 total.

9. From Problem 7, total cash flow is -$1319. Since cash flow to creditors is $350, cash flow to stockholders is -$1669 (= -$1319 - 350). Since dividends paid is $120, the firm sold stock of $1789.

10.

.15($ 50,000)	=	$ 7,500
.25($ 75,000 - 50,000)	=	6,250
.34($100,000 - 75,000)	=	8,500
.39($200,000 - 100,000)	=	39,000
		$61,250

The average tax rate is ($61,250/$200,000) = .30625 = 30.625%. An additional dollar of income would be taxed at the 39% rate so K&M's marginal tax rate is 39%.

11.

.15($ 50,000)	=	$ 7,500
.25($ 75,000 - 50,000)	=	6,250
.34($100,000 - 75,000)	=	8,500
.39($335,000 - 100,000)	=	91,650
.34($1,000,000 - 335,000)	=	226,100
		$340,000

The average tax rate is ($340,000/$1,000,000) = .34 = 34%. Since K&M earned more than $335,000 (but less than $10 million), an additional dollar of income is taxed at 34%; the marginal tax rate is 34%.

CHAPTER 3

1.

COOGAN DEVELOPMENT CO., INC.

Balance Sheets as of December 31, 1996 and 1997

	1996	1997	Change
Assets			
Current Assets			
Cash	$ 4,000	$ 3,000	-$ 1,000
Accts. rec.	9,000	11,000	+ 2,000
Inventory	5,000	4,500	- 500
Total	$18,000	$18,500	+$ 500
Fixed assets			
Net PP&E	30,000	31,500	+ 1,500
Total assets	$48,000	$50,000	+$2,000
Liabilities and Owners' Equity			
Current liabilities			
Accts. payable	$3,000	$2,500	-$ 500
Notes payable	6,000	6,416	+ 416
Total	$9,000	$8,916	-$ 84
Long-term debt	5,000	$13,000	-$ 2,000
Owners' equity			
Common stock and			
paid-in surplus	14,000	6,500	+ 2,500
Retained earnings	10,000	11,584	+ 1,584
Total	$24,000	$28,084	+$4,084
Total liabilities and			
owners' equity	$48,000	$50,000	+$2,000

Sources of cash:	
Decrease in inventory	$ 500
Increase in notes payable	416
Increase in common stock	2,500
Increase in retained earnings	1,584
Total sources	$5,000

Uses of cash:	
Increase in accounts receivable	$2,000
Decrease in accounts payable	500
Decrease in long-term debt	2,000
Net fixed asset acquisitions	1,500
Total uses	$6,000
Net decrease in cash	$1,000

2.

COOGAN DEVELOPMENT CO., INC.
1997 Statement of Cash Flows

Cash, beginning of year	$4,000
Operating activities	
Net income	$2,640
Plus: Depreciation	3,000
Decrease in inventory	500
Less: Increase in accounts receivable	-2,000
Decrease in accounts payable	- 500
Net cash from operating activity	$3,640
Investment activities	
Fixed asset acquisitions	-$4,500
Net cash from investment activity	-$4,500
Financing activities	
Increase in notes payable	+$ 416
Decrease in long-term debt	- 2,000
Dividends paid	- 1,056
Increase in common stock	+2,500
Net cash from financing activity	-$ 140
Net decrease in cash	$1,000
Cash, end of year	$3,000

3.

COOGAN DEVELOPMENT CO., INC.
1997 Sources and Uses of Cash

Cash, beginning of year	$4,000
Sources of cash	
Operations	
Net income	2,640
Depreciation	3,000
Working capital:	
Decrease in inventory	$ 500
Increase in notes payable	416
Long-term financing:	
Increase in common stock	2,500
Total sources of cash	$9,056
Uses of cash	
Working capital:	
Increase in accounts receivable	$2,000
Decrease in accounts payable	500
Long-term financing:	
Decrease in long-term debt	2,000
Fixed asset acquisitions	4,500
Dividends paid	1,056
Total uses of cash	$10,056
Cash, end of year	$ 3,000

4.

COOGAN DEVELOPMENT CO., INC.
Common-Size Balance Sheets as of December 31

	1996	1997	Change
Assets			
Current assets			
Cash	8.3%	6.0%	-2.3%
Accounts receivable	18.8	22.0	+3.2
Inventory	10.4	9.0	-1.4
Total	37.5	37.0	- .5
Fixed assets			
Net PP&E	62.5	63.0	+ .5
Total assets	100.0%	100.0%	+ 0. 0%
Liabilities and Owners' Equity			
Current liabilities			
Accounts payable	6.3%	5.0%	-1.3%
Notes payable	12.5	12.8	+ .3
Total	18.8	17.8	-1.0
Long-term debt	31.3	26.0	-5.3
Owners' equity			
Common stock and paid-in surplus	29.2	33.0	+3.8
Retained earnings	20.8	23.2	+2.4
Total	50.0	56.2	+6.2
Total liabilities and owners' equity	100.0%	100.0%	+ 0.0%

5.

COOGAN DEVELOPMENT CO., INC.
Common-Size Income Statement 1997

Sales	100.0%
Cost of goods sold	64.0
Depreciation	12.0
Earnings before interest and taxes	24.0
Interest paid	8.0
Taxable income	16.0
Taxes (34%)	5.4
Net income	10.6%
Retained earnings	6.3
Dividends	4.2%

6. Current ratio = $18,500/$8,916 =2.07
Quick ratio = ($18,500 - $4,500)/$8,916 = 1.57
Cash ratio = $3,000/$8,916 = .34

7. Total debt ratio = ($50,000 - $28,084)/$50,000 =.44
Debt/equity ratio = $21,916/$28,084 =.78
Equity multiplier = $50,000/$28,084 = 1.78
Times interest earned = $6,000/$2,000 = 3.00 times
Cash coverage ratio = ($6,000 + $3,000)/$2,000 = 4.5 times

8. Inventory turnover = $16,000/$4,500 = 3.56 times
Days sales in inventory = 365 days/3.56 = 103 days
Receivables turnover = $25,000/$11,000 = 2.27 times
Days sales in receivables = 365 days/2.27 = 161 days
Total asset turnover = $25,000/$50,000 = .50 times

9. Profit margin = $2,640/$25,000 = 10.56%
Return on assets = $2,640/$50,000 = 5.28%
Return on equity = $2,640/$28,084 = 9.40%

10. ROA = Profit margin × Total asset turnover = .1056 × .5 = .0528 = 5.28%
ROE = Return on assets × Equity multiplier = .0528 × 1.78 = .0940 = 9.40%

11. EPS = $2,640/1,000 = $2.64.
P/E ratio = $40/$2.64 = 15.2
Book value per share is ($28,084/1,000) = $28.08, so market-to-book = $40/$28.08 = 1.42 times.

12. The debt/equity ratio can be computed from the total debt ratio. The new total debt ratio indicates that Coogan Development would have $0.20 of debt and $0.80 of equity financing for each dollar of assets. Therefore, the debt/equity ratio is ($0.20/$0.80) = 0.25. Since Coogan has $0.80 of equity for each $1.00 of assets, the equity multiplier equals $1.00/$0.80 = 1.25. The new ROE can be computed using the Du Pont identity: ROE = Profit margin × Total asset turnover × Equity multiplier

$$= .1056 \times .50 \times 1.25 = .0660 = 6.60\%$$

To determine the amount of new equity financing required, use the new total debt ratio to determine total equity for Coogan Development once new financing is obtained. This is X below:

Total debt ratio = (Total assets - Total equity)/Total assets = ($50,000 - X)/$50,000 = .20

Solving for X, total equity is $40,000. So additional equity financing is ($40,000 - $28,084) = $11,916.

13. The debt/equity ratio can be computed from the new total debt ratio. Coogan Development would have $0.80 of debt and $0.20 of equity financing for each dollar of assets. Therefore, the debt/equity ratio is ($0.80/$0.20) = 4.00. The equity multiplier equals (1 + debt/equity ratio) = (1 + 4.00) = 5.00. The new ROE equals .1056 × .50 × 5.00 =.2640 = 26.40%

Total equity after the new financing is the value of X in the following equation:

Total debt ratio = (Total assets - Total equity)/Total assets = ($50,000 - X)/$50,000 = .80

Solving for X, total equity is $10,000 and the additional long-term debt is ($18,084 - $10,000) = $8,084.

14. The average collection period (ACP) is another name for the days' sales in receivables ratio. To determine the required reduction in accounts receivable, we first determine the receivables turnover required in order to accomplish the reduction in ACP by solving for X in the following equation:

(365 days)/Receivables turnover = 365/X = 120 days

Solving for X, the receivables turnover is 3.04 times. Next, solve for Y in the following equation to determine the required level of accounts receivable:

Sales/Accounts receivable = $25,000/Y = 3.04 times.

The required level of accounts receivable is $8,223.68. So the firm would have to collect ($11,000 - $8,223.68) = $2,776.32 of its accounts receivable.

If collected funds were held as cash, it would not affect either the current ratio or the quick ratio, because total current assets and total current liabilities would not be changed. However, if the collected funds were used to pay outstanding notes payable, both current assets and current liabilities would be reduced by $2,776.32, so both the numerator and denominator of these ratios would be reduced. The current ratio would increase from 2.07 to 2.56 and the quick ratio would increase from 1.57 to 1.82.

CHAPTER 4

1. Increasing income statement and balance sheet items by 15% results in the following statements:

G. T. SEAVER CORPORATION
Pro Forma Income Statement

Sales	$92,000
Costs	64,400
Net Income	$27,600

Pro Forma Balance Sheet

Current assets	$ 17,250	(+$ 2,250)	Current liabilities	$ 11,500	(+$ 1,500)
Fixed assets	97,750	(+$12,750)	Long-term debt	28,750	(+$ 3,750)
				74,750	(+$ 9,750)
Total	$115,000	(+$15,000)	Total	$115,000	(+$15,000)

The figures in parentheses indicate the increase in the respective balance sheet items. The increase of $9,750 in equity is inconsistent with the net income of $27,600 from the pro forma income statement.

If these figures are reconciled using dividends as the "plug" figure, then total cash dividends for the year must be ($27,600 - $9,750) = $17,850.

2. If dividends are zero, then retained earnings are $27,600 and equity on the pro forma balance sheet is equal to ($65,000 + $27,600) = $92,600. Equity plus current liabilities equals ($92,600 + $11,500) = $104,100, so long-term debt is ($115,000 - $104,100) = $10,900. Seaver must pay off ($25,000 - $10,900) = $14,100 of long-term debt. The pro forma balance sheet appears as follows:

G. T. SEAVER CORPORATION
Pro Forma Balance Sheet

Current assets	$17,250	(+$ 2,250)	Current liabilities	$11,500	(+$ 1,500)
Fixed assets	97,750	(+$12,750)	Long-term debt	10,900	(-$14,100)
			Equity	92,600	(+$27,600)
Total	$115,000	(+$15,000)	Total	$115,000	(+$15,000)

3. Dividends are ($27,600 x .80) = $22,080, and retained earnings are ($27,600 - $22,080) = $5,520. Equity on the pro forma balance sheet is ($65,000 + $5,520) = $70,520. Equity plus current liabilities is ($70,520 + $11,500) = $82,020. Long-term debt must be ($115,000 - $82,020) = $32,980, so Seaver must borrow ($32,980 - $25,000) = $7,980. The pro forma balance sheet appears below:

G. T. SEAVER CORPORATION
Pro Forma Balance Sheet

Current assets	$ 17,250	(+$ 2,250)	Current liabilities	$11,500	(+$ 1,500)
Fixed assets	97,750	(+$12,750)	Long-term debt	32,980	(+$ 7,980)
			Equity	70,520	(+$ 5,520)
Total	$115,000	(+$15,000)	Total	$115,000	(+$15,000)

4. The pro forma income statement is based on the assumption that costs, as percentage of sales, remain constant; that is, (costs/sales) = ($17,000/$20,000) = 85%. Consequently, the profit margin also remains constant at ($1,980/$20,000) = 9.9%. The dividend payout ratio is ($990/$2,475) = 40%.

GROTE & CO., INC.
Pro forma Income Statement

Sales	$25,000
-Costs	21,250
Taxable income	$ 3,750
-Taxes (34%)	1,275
Net income	$ 2,475
Retained earnings	$ 1,485
Dividends	$ 990

The pro forma balance sheet is derived by applying the respective percentages of sales to the projected sales levels for those items which are expected to increase proportionately with sales. Retained earnings on the pro forma balance sheet is computed by adding the retained earnings figure from the pro forma income statement to the current balance sheet retained earnings figure. All other balance sheet accounts remain constant, and the "plug" figure is external financing needed (EFN). The figures in parentheses on the partial pro forma balance sheet represent the respective increases from the current balance sheet.

GROTE & CO., INC.
Partial Pro Forma Balance Sheet

Current assets			Current liabilities		
Cash	$ 3,750	($ 750)	Accounts payable	$ 7,500	($1,500)
Accts. rec.	6,250	(1,250)	Notes payable	3,000	(0)
Inventory	8,750	(1,750)			
Total	$18,750	(3,750)	Total	$10,500	($1,500)
			Long-term debt	$15,000	(0)
Fixed assets			Owners' equity		
			Common stock and		
Net PP&E	$37,500	($7,500)	paid-in surplus	$13,000	($ 0)
			Retained earnings	9,485	(1,485)
			Total	$22,485	($1,485)
Total assets	$56,250	($11,250)	Total liabilities & OE	$47,985	($2,985)
			External financing needed		$ 8,265

The balance sheet is considered a partial pro forma balance sheet because the firm must determine how the external financing of $8,265 is to be obtained. The pro forma balance sheet is completed when the source (or sources) of external financing are determined and indicated appropriately on the balance sheet. If, for example, all of the external financing is obtained in the form of additional long-term debt, then the pro forma balance sheet would indicate long-term debt equal to ($15,000 + $8,265) = $23,265.

250

5. PM   = $1,650/$10,000 = 16.5\%$
    R   = $660/$1,650 = 40\%$
    ROA = $1,650/$15,000 = 11\%$
    ROE = $1,650/$9,000 = 18.333\%$
    D/E = $6,000/$9,000 = 66.667\%$

6. The increase in assets to be financed is: $15,000 \times .20 = 3,000$. To compute the financing available in the form of retained earnings, we first compute projected sales:

$$\text{Sales} \times (1 + g) = \$10,000 \times 1.20 = \$12,000$$

Projected net income equals profit margin times projected sales: $.165 \times \$12,000 = \$1,980$. The projected addition to retained earnings is the retention ratio times projected net income:

$$.40 \times \$1,980 = \$792$$

Therefore, the external financing needed is: EFN = $3,000 - $792 = $2,208.

7. The pro forma statements appear in the problem and are therefore not repeated here.

8. From the solution to Problem 6, EFN = -$660 + ($14,340 × g). Now we determine the growth rate the firm can achieve without external financing, by setting EFN equal to zero and solving for g:

$$\text{EFN} = -\$660 + (\$14,340 \times g)$$

$$g = \$660/\$14,340 = .04603 = 4.603\%$$

9. The sustainable growth rate, g^*, equals $(ROE \times b)/(1 - ROE \times b)$, or

$$g^* = [(.18333)(.40)]/[1 - (.18333)(.40)] = .07914 = 7.914\%.$$

Therefore, T. McGraw Corporation can grow at a rate of 7.914% without issuing new equity.

10. According to the Du Pont identity, ROE equals Profit margin × Total asset turnover × Equity multiplier, substituting the data for T. McGraw from Problem 5:

$$\text{ROE} = .165 \times (\$10,000/\$15,000) \times [1 + (\$6,000/\$9,000)] = .18333$$

The sustainable growth rate equals $(.1833 \times .4)/(1 - (.1833 \times .4)) = .07914$.

11. The pro forma statements for McGraw, assuming a growth rate of 7.914%, are as follows:

T. MC GRAW CORPORATION
Pro Forma Income Statement

Sales	$10,791.40
-Costs	8,093.55
Taxable income	$ 2,697.85
-Taxes (34%)	917.27
Net income	$ 1,780.58
Retained earnings	$ 712.23
Dividends	$ 1,068.35

Pro Forma Balance Sheet

Current assets	$ 5,395.70	Total debt	$ 6,000.00
Fixed assets	10,791.40	Owner's equity	9,712.00
Total	$16,187.10	Total	$15,712.23
		External funds needed	$ 474.87

Since the external financing is all debt, the debt/equity ratio is ($46,474.87/$9,712.23) = 66.667%; the debt/equity ratio is unchanged from the calculation in the solution to Problem 5.

12. The retention ratio is ($88/$132) = ⅔, and the growth rate for sales is ($200/$2,000) = 10%. Applying this rate, the pro forma income statement and partial pro forma balance sheet are as follows:

RYAN & CO., INC.
Pro Forma Income Statement

Sales	$2,200.00
-Costs	1,980.00
Taxable income	$ 220.00
-Taxes (34%)	74.80
Net income	$ 145.20
Retained earnings	$ 96.80
Dividends	$ 48.40

RYAN & CO., INC.
Partial Pro Forma Balance Sheet

Current assets	$ 550.00	Current liabilities	$ 181.50
Fixed assets	1,265.00	Long-term debt	535.00
		Equity	1,046.80
Total	$1,815.00	Total	$1,763.30
		External funds needed	$ 51.70

CHAPTER 5

1. If you deposit $10,000 today, the balance at the year-end will be $10,000 × 1.1038 = $11,038. If you need $12,000 in one year, you must deposit $12,000/1.1038 = $10,871.53 today.

2. If the collector invests $2 million in the certificates of deposit (CDs), their value one year from now will be: FV_1 = $2,000,000 × 1.10 = $2.2 million. Thus, the investment in the paintings is not a good investment; the collector will have a greater cash flow one year from now if he purchases the CDs.

3. The rate of return for the investment is computed by solving the following equation for r:

$$FV_1 = PV \times (1 + r)^1 = \$2.18 \text{ million} = \$2.00 \text{ million} \times (1 + r)^1 \text{ so } r = .09 = 9\%.$$

Since the rate of return for the investment in paintings is less than that available on the bank certificates of deposit, it is clear that the paintings are an unacceptable investment.

4. PV = $2.18 million/1.10 = $1.982 million. The PV is the amount the collector would have to invest today in the alternative investment (i.e., the bank certificates) to duplicate the cash flow he would receive by selling the paintings in one year. Since the collector can duplicate the $2.18 million cash flow for only $1.982 million, he would be unwilling to pay more than $1.982 million for the paintings today.

5.

Future cash flow	Interest rate	Present value
$ 10,000	10%	$ 9,090.91
153,200	13%	135,575.22
153,200	10%	139,272.73
2,567,450	5%	2,445,190.48
120,600	9%	110,642.20

6. This year you need a total of ($28,320 + $3,248 + $34,000) = $65,568. So you must borrow ($65,568 - $42,000) = $23,568 this year. The amount you will have to repay next year is:

$$FV_1 = 23,568 \times 1.14 = \$26,867.52$$

Therefore, you will have ($46,000 - $26,867.52) = $19,132.48 of next year's income left to spend.

7. Substitute the relevant values (PV = $1,000; FV = $1,200) into either the future value formula or the present value formula, and then solve for the interest rate r. Using the future value formula:

$$FV = PV \times (1 + r)$$

$$\$1200 = \$1000 \times (1 + r)$$

$$r = .20 = 20\%$$

Therefore, the rate of return for the investment is 20%. If the rate of return available on alternative investments is less than 20%, then the investment opportunity described above is acceptable. If the rate of return available elsewhere is greater than 20%, then the investment described above is unacceptable.

8. The PV of the investment is $195. The investor can duplicate the cash flows for the investment described above (i.e., $114 one year from today and $144 two years from today) by investing $195 at the 20% market rate of interest. Since $195 is the cost of the investment described above, the investor is indifferent between the investment opportunity described here and an investment at the market rate of interest. Consequently, the return for the investment is the same as the market rate of interest, 20%.

9. The present value of the future cash inflow is PV = $300,000/1.20 = $250,000. Therefore, each of the 1,000 shares is worth $250. An individual who owns one share is entitled to 1/1000 of the future cash inflow or, [(1/1,000) × $300,000] = $300. The present value of the $300 is ($300/1.20) = $250.

Alternatively, an individual who owns one share is the owner of 1/1,000 of the present value of the asset, or [(1/1,000) × $250,000] = $250. Furthermore, an individual who buys a share for $250 today and receives $300 one year from today earns a rate of return equal to 20%. Since this is the same as the rate of return available on alternative investments, an investor would be willing to pay $250 for a share. If the entrepreneur chose to issue all 1,000 shares to the general public, he would realize a gain of ($300,000 - $250,000) = $50,000. By selling 900 shares, he has realized a gain of $45,000; the remaining $5,000 is an unrealized gain, unless he also chooses to sell the additional 100 shares.

10. PV = $145/(1.08)^5 = $98.685. This means that an investor would have to deposit $98.69 today, at an 8% interest rate, in order to be able to withdraw $145 five years from today.

11. FV$_4$ = $235 × (1.12)^4 = $369.777. This means that an investor who deposits $235 today in an account paying 12% interest will have a balance of $369.78 in his account four years from today.

12.

Future value	Years	Interest rate (%)	Present value
$ 498	7	13	$ 211.680
1,033	13	6	4.311
14,784	23	4	5,998.258
898,156	4	31	304,976.653

13.

Present value	Years	Interest rate (%)	Future value
$ 123	13	13	$ 602.45
4,555	8	8	8,430.98
74,484	5	10	119,957.22
167,332	9	1	183,008.54

14.

Present value	Future Value	Interest rate (%)	Time (years)
$ 100	348	12	11
123	351	10	11
4,100	8,523	5	15
10,543	26,783	6	16

15.

Present value	Future Value	Interest rate (%)	Time (years)
$ 100	466	8	20
123	218	10	6
4,100	9,064	12	7
10,543	21,215	6	12

CHAPTER 6

1.

Payment	Years	Interest rate (%)	Present Value
$ 678.09	7	13	$ 2,998.93
7,968.26	13	6	70,540.48
20,322.93	23	4	301,934.55
69,712.54	4	31	148,519.49

2.

Payment	Years	Interest rate (%)	Future Value
$ 123	13	13	$ 3,688.12
4,555	8	8	48,449.84
74,484	5	10	454,732.07
167,332	9	1	1,567,654.90

3. The interest rate is actually $(.09/12) = .0075 = .75\%$ per month. Since there are 24 months in two years, the future value factor is: $(1.0075)^{24} = 1.1964$. Multiply the FV factor times the $700 deposit; you will have $837.489 after 2 years. Similarly, after 2.5 years (30 months), you will have $(1.0075)^{30} \times \$700 = \$875.89$.

4.

Stated rate	Number of times compounded	Effective rate
5%	semiannually	5.063%
11%	quarterly	11.462%
16%	daily	17.347%

5. We compare the two alternatives by computing the PV of each series of payments. Since PVIFA(16%,3) = 2.24588, the PV of the 3 year $50,000 annuity equals $50,000 \times 2.245888 = \$112,249.40$. The PV of the annuity of $25,000 per year for 3 years is half as much, or $56,147.20. The total value of the second option is $106,147.20. You should select the $50,000 per year option.

6. Solve the following equation for q:

$$[1 + (q/12)]^{12} - 1 = .08$$
$$1 + (q/12) = (1.08)^{1/12}$$
$$(1.08)^{1/12} = 1.006434$$

Thus, $q/12 = 1.006434 - 1 = .006434$ and $q = 7.7208\%$.

7. The interest rate is $[(5/4) - 1] = 25\%$ for 6 days. There are about $(365/6) = 60.8333$ periods in a year. The effective rate is 1.25 to the power 60.8333, minus 1. This works out to be a nice round 785,826 percent. This is high, but it beats having your legs broken.

8. The most you can spend at the end of the next 5 years is the future value of the annuity:

$$AFV = \$1,000(FVIFA_{12,5}) = \$6,352.85.$$

The most you can spend today is what someone would lend you in return for the 5 expected payments; this is the present value of the annuity: $APV = \$1,000(PVIFA_{12,5}) = \$3,604.78$.

9. Solve the following equation for r (where PV is the beginning amount):

$$PV \times (1 + r/4)^{68} = PV \times (1 + 2.70) = 3.70C$$
$$r/4 = (3.70)^{1/68} - 1 = .019426$$
$$r = .07770 = 7.770\%.$$

10. $PV = C/r = \$100/.10 = \$1,000$. Three years from now (or n years from now) the value of the perpetuity is still $1,000. The value of the perpetuity changes only if the market rate of interest changes.

11. Solve for r: $\$1,000,000/r = \$4,500,000$. The solution is $r = .2222 = 22.22\%$. For values of r less than 22.22%, the present value of the project is greater than $4,500,000.

CHAPTER 7

1. $PV = [\$120 \times PVIFA(14\%,10)] + \$1,000 \times (1.14)^{10} = (\$120 \times 5.2161) + (\$1,000 \times .26974) = \$895.68$. The bond is selling at a discount because the yield (the market's required return) is greater than the coupon rate.

2. $PV = [\$120 \times PVIFA(12\%,10)] + \$1,000 \times (1.12)^{10} = (\$120 \times 5.6502) + (\$1,000 \times .3219) = \$1,000$. The bond is selling at par because the coupon rate is the same as the market's required return.

3. $PV = [\$120 \times PVIFA(9\%,10)] + \$1,000 \times (1.09)^{10} = (\$120 \times 6.4176) + (\$1000 \times .4224) = \$1,192.53$. Now the bond is a premium bond, because the bond's yield is less than its coupon rate.

4. Coupon payments are now $60 per period for 20 time periods; the relevant discount rate is 7%.

$PV = [\$60 \times PVIFA(7\%,20)] + \$1,000 \times (1.07)^{20} = (\$60 \times 10.5940) + (\$1,000 \times .2584) = \$894.06$. Notice that this value differs somewhat from the result obtained in Problem 1; this difference results from the assumption of *annual* interest payments in the earlier problem.

5. This problem can be solved by calculating the PV of each coupon interest payment, plus the PV of the face value. However, an easier approach is to first calculate the PV of the bond under the assumption that all the coupon interest is paid; then deduct the PV of the payments that are skipped and add the PV of the payments made at maturity. The bond's value, ignoring skipped and repaid coupons, is $1,211.88.

The PV of skipped coupons is:

$$PV = \$90/(1.07)^8 + \$90/(1.07)^9 + \$90/(1.07)^{10} = \$147.09.$$

At maturity, an extra $(3 \times \$90) = \$270$ will be paid. The PV of this $270 is $69.77. Thus the value of the bond is $(\$1,211.88 - \$147.09 + \$69.77) = \$1,134.56$.

6. The yield to maturity is 8%; that is, when $r = .08$, the PV of the future payments is exactly $1,000. However, this problem can be solved directly by realizing that the $80 coupon interest payment is 8%

of the face value of the bond. The result is true regardless of the time period: an investor who buys a bond for its $1,000 face value earns a yield to maturity equal to the coupon interest rate.

7. The yield to maturity is 9.01969%.

8. The yield to maturity is 7.05224%.

9. $R = 1.04 \times 1.10 - 1 = 1.144 - 1 = .144 = 14.4\%$.

10. $R = .02 + .05 + (.02 \times .05) = .071 = 7.1\%$.

11. The real rate of return, r, equals .04854 = 4.854%.

12. The real return is determined by substituting R=.08 and h=.10 in the following equation:

$$1 + r = (1 + R)/(1 + h) = 1.08/1.10 = .98182$$

Therefore, $r = .98182 - 1 = -.01818 = -1.818\%$. In real terms, the investor has lost almost 2% on the Treasury bill investment because the inflation rate was higher than the nominal rate of return.

13. The current market price is 110.5% of $1,000 = $1,105. The annual coupon payment is 9% of $1,000 = $90. The YTM is 7.94%.

CHAPTER 8

1. $P_0 = PV = \$1.50/(1.14)^1 + \$1.75/(1.14)^2 + \$2.20/(1.14)^3 + \$48.50/(1.14)^3 = \$36.88$

2. $P_0 = PV = D/r = \$10/.08 = \$125$. If the opportunity cost is 11%, then $P_0 = (\$10/.11) = \$90.91$.

3. Since $D = \$12$ and $P_0 = \$75$, and $P_0 = D/r$; $\$75 = \$12/r$. Therefore, $r = .16 = 16\%$.

4. Hilliard is a constant growth stock with $D_0 = \$2.00$. $D_1 = \$2.00 \times 1.08 = \$2.16$, so

$$P_0 = PV = D_1/(r - g) = \$2.16/(.16 - .08) = \$27.00.$$

5.
$$P_0 = D_1/(r - g) = [\$10(1.05)]/(.10 - .05) = \$210.$$
$$P_{-1} = D_0/(r - g) = \$10/(.10 - .05) = \$200$$
$$P_1 = D_2/(r - g) = [\$10(1.05)^2]/(r - g) = \$220.50$$

6. Since $r = D_1/P_0 + g$, and $P_0 = \$20$, we can determine the values of g and D_1. The growth rate for dividends is the same as that for the stock price. Solve for g:

$$P_0 = P_{-1} \times (1 + g)$$
$$\$20 = \$18.87 \times (1 + g)$$
$$(1 + g) = \$20/\$18.87 = 1.05988$$

Therefore, g is approximately 6%. Applying the growth rate to dividends, $D_1 = \$2 \times 1.06 = \$2.12$.

Substituting these values into the above equation for r, we find that $r = .166 = 16.6\%$.

7. Substitute $P_0 = \$30$, $D_0 = \$2$, $g = .05$ into the following equation and solve for r:

$$P_0 = D_1/(r - g) = [\$2(1.05)]/(r - .05) = \$30.$$

The rate of return, r, equals $.12 = 12\%$.

8. P_0 equals the PV of the dividends from the high-growth phase, plus the PV of the stock price when that phase ends. The *next* dividend (D_1) is forecasted at \$4. To calculate the stock price at year 4, we first determine the year 5 dividend (D_5): $D_5 = D_1 \times (1.15)^3 \times (1.05) = \$6.39$. So $P_4 = D_5/(r - g) = \$6.39/(.18 - .05) = \$49.16$. The PV of this is $[\$49.16/(1.18^4)] = \$25.36$. The PVs of the first four dividends are:

Year	Growth Rate (g)	Expected Dividend	Present Value
1	15%	\$4.000	\$3.3898
2	15%	\$4.600	\$3.3036
3	15%	\$5.290	\$3.2197
4	15%	\$6.084	\$3.1381

The total PV of the first four dividend payments is \$13.0512. P_0 is (\$25.34 + \$13.05) = \$38.39.

9. $\quad D_1 = \$1.20 \times (1.03) = \$1.24$
$\quad D_2 = \$1.20 \times (1.03) \times (1.04) = \$1.29$
$\quad D_3 = \$1.20 \, (1.03) \times (1.04) \times (1.05) = \$1.35$
$\quad P_3 = D_4/(r - g) = [\$1.35(1.06)]/(.12 - .06) = \$23.83$

The current price (P_0) is the PV of the next three year's dividends plus the PV of P_3, discounted at 12%. The PV of the former is \$3.10; the PV of the latter is \$16.98. Therefore, P_0 is \$20.08.

CHAPTER 9

1. The payback period for project A is 3.25 years. The payback period for project B is 2.5 years.

2. Project A's discounted cash flows sum to \$1931.41, so A does not pay back its initial cost. For B, the payback period is almost exactly four years.

3. Project A's IRR is 10.4845%. Project B's IRR is 12.0351%.

4. Given a 5%, the NPV for A is \$283.26 and the NPV for B is \$268.08. So A is preferred even though it has the lower IRR.

5. A has a negative NPV at a 12% discount rate (-\$68.59). B has an NPV of \$1.20, so it is preferred.

6. At a discount rate of 6.0654%, both A and B have an NPV of \$223.51.

7. Since the cash flows for each of these investments change sign more than once, each investment has more than one IRR. The two solutions here are r_1 = .25 = 25% and r_2 = .3333 = 33.33%. These values are also the two solutions for the second investment. To interpret these results, compute the NPV at a rate between the two IRRs. At a discount rate of 30%, for example, the NPV is +$.06 for the first investment and -$.06 for the second. The first investment is acceptable only if the required rate of return is between 25% and 33.33%; the second investment is acceptable only is the required return is outside the range 25% to 33.33%. This conclusion derives from the fact that a quadratic equation, when graphed, has the shape of a parabola, so the NPV must be either exclusively negative or exclusively positive between the two solutions identified here, and has the opposite sign outside the range of the two solutions.

8. This is a problem designed to keep students out of trouble by keeping them busy. There is *no* IRR! That is, there is no real number for which the NPV is zero. At any discount rate, the NPV is negative, so the required return is irrelevant.

9. The average net income is [($11 + $10 + $16 + $15)/4] = $13. The average book value is $80, so the AAR is ($13/$80) = .1625 = 16.25%.

10. Cash flows are $51, $50, $56, and $55, respectively over the four-year period. The initial investment is $160. The IRR is 12.0608%.

11. The sign of the cash flows changes twice, so there are two IRRs: 11.1111% and 13.6364%.

12. Calculate the NPV for the investment at each required return. The NPVs are $.26, -$.09, and $.06, respectively, for the three required rates. The investment is acceptable if the required return is either 10% or 14%, but it is unacceptable if the required rate of return is 12%.

13. The IRR is of the loan cash flows represents the lender's return and is 11.6488%. Borrowing at the market rate of 11.5% is preferable.

14. The NPV for project A is $84.20 and the NPV for project B is $117.58, so B is preferred alternative. (Note that we ignore the difference in the lives of the two assets.)

15. The IRRs are 14.9500% and 10.9162% for projects A and B, respectively. Despite the fact that project A has the higher IRR, the solution to Problem 13 indicates that project B is preferable.

16. For project A, the profitability index (PI) is ($584.21/$500) = 1.1684. For project B, the PI is ($5117.58/$5000) = 1.0235. If these two projects were independent of each other, both would be acceptable according to the PI criterion because each PI is greater than 1. This conclusion is consistent with that implied by the NPV and IRR rules for independent projects. However, the projects are mutually exclusive, so the PI criterion cannot be used to select the preferred alternative.

CHAPTER 10

1.

Year	ACRS Percentage		Depreciation	Ending book value
1	20.00%	.2000 × $500,000 = $100,000		$400,000
2	32.00	.3200 × 500,000 =	160,000	240,000
3	19.20	.1920 × 500,000 =	96,000	144,000
4	11.52	.1152 × 500,000 =	57,600	86,400
5	11.52	.1152 × 500,000 =	57,600	28,800
6	5.76	.0576 × 500,000 =	28,800	0

2.

	Year 1	Year 2	Year 3	Year 4	Year 5	Year 6
Sales Revenue	$650,000	$650,000	$650,000	$650,000	$650,000	$650,000
-Variable Costs	-390,000	-390,000	-390,000	-390,000	-390,000	-390,000
-Fixed Costs	- 80,000	- 80,000	- 80,000	- 80,000	- 80,000	- 80,000
-Depreciation	-100,000	-160,000	- 96,000	- 57,600	- 57,600	- 28,800
EBIT	80,000	20,000	84,000	122,400	122,400	151,200
-Taxes (at 34%)	- 27,200	- 6,800	- 28,560	- 41,616	- 41,616	- 51,408
Net Income	$ 52,800	$ 13,200	$ 55,440	$ 80,784	$ 80,784	$ 99,792

3.

	Year 1	Year 2	Year 3	Year 4	Year 5	Year 6
EBIT	$ 80,000	$ 20,000	$ 84,000	$122,400	$122,400	$151,200
+Depreciation	100,000	160,000	96,000	57,600	57,600	28,800
-Taxes (at 34%)	- 27,200	- 6,800	- 28,560	- 41,616	- 41,616	- 51,408
OCF	$152,800	$173,200	$151,440	$138,384	$138,384	$128,592

4. Initial cash outflow is $575,000 (= $500,000 + 75,000). For year 6, recovery of net working capital results in a cash inflow of $75,000. Fixed assets are fully depreciated at the end of year 6 and have zero market value, so there are no consequences for cash flows from disposal of fixed assets at the end of the project's life. Total inflow for year 6 is $203,592 (= $128,592 + $75,000).

5. PV = $152,800/(1.16) + $173,200/(1.16)^2 + $151,440/(1.16)^3 + $138,384/(1.16)^4

$$+ \$138,384/(1.16)^5 + \$203,592/(1.16)^6 = \$583,338.58.$$

The NPV is ($583,338.58 - $575,000) = $8,338.58, so the new product line is an acceptable investment. The cost of the $50,000 marketing studying is a sunk cost and irrelevant. The IRR is 16.539%.

6.

	Year 1	Year 2	Year 3	Year 4	Year 5	Year 6
Sales Revenue (S)	$650,000	$650,000	$650,000	$650,000	$650,000	$650,000
-Total Costs (C)	-470,000	-470,000	-470,000	-470,000	-470,000	-470,000
(S - C)	180,000	180,000	180,000	180,000	180,000	180,000
(S - C) × (1 - TC)	118,800	118,800	118,800	118,800	118,800	118,800
Depreciation (D)	100,000	160,000	96,000	57,600	57,600	28,800
(D × T_C)	34,000	54,400	32,640	19,584	19,584	9,792
OCF	$152,800	$173,200	$151,440	$138,384	$138,384	$128,592

7.

	Year 1	Year 2	Year 3	Year 4	Year 5	Year 6
Net Income	$52,800	$13,200	$55,440	$80,784	$80,784	$99,792
+Depreciation	100,000	160,000	96,000	57,600	57,600	28,800
OCF	$152,800	$173,200	$151,440	$138,384	$138,384	$128,592

8.

	Year 1	Year 2	Year 3	Year 4	Year 5	Year 6
Sales Revenue	$650,000	$650,000	$650,000	$650,000	$650,000	$650,000
-Total Cost s	-470,000	-470,000	-470,000	- 470,000	-470,000	-470,000
-Taxes	- 27,200	- 6,800	- 28,560	- 41,616	- 41,616	- 51,408
OCF	$152,800	$173,200	$151,440	$138,384	$138,384	$128,592

9.

	Year 1	Year 2	Year 3	Year 4	Year 5
Sales Revenue	$ 0	$ 0	$ 0	$ 0	$ 0
-Operating Costs	+ 30,000	+ 35,000	+ 40,000	+ 45,000	+35,000
-Depreciation	- 25,000	- 25,000	- 25,000	- 25,000	0
EBIT	5,000	10,000	15,000	20,000	35,000
-Taxes (at 34%)	- 1,700	- 3,400	- 5,100	- 6,800	- 11,900
Net Income	$ 3,300	$ 6,600	$ 9,900	$13,200	$23,100

Sales revenue doesn't change; since we are concerned with incremental cash flows for the capital budgeting project, we enter zero for sales revenue. The decrease in operating costs results in an increase in EBIT and net income. OCFs are computed using data from the pro forma income statements:

	Year 1	Year 2	Year 3	Year 4	Year 5
EBIT	$ 5,000	$10,000	$15,000	$20,000	$35,000
+Depreciation	25,000	25,000	25,000	25,000	0
-Taxes (at 34%)	- 1,700	- 3,400	- 5,100	- 6,800	-11,900
OCF	$28,300	$31,600	$34,900	$38,200	$23,100

10. For years 1 through 4, total cash flow is the same as OCF. For year zero, net working capital is reduced by $5,000 and capital expenditures are $100,000. The reduction in net working capital is a cash inflow, so year zero cash outflow is ($100,000 - $5,000) = $95,000. We assume the termination of the project stops the reduction in net working capital, so that, at the end of year 5, we return to the previous level of net working capital; consequently, the resulting increase in net working capital at the end of year 5 is a cash outflow. Also at the end of year 5, fixed assets have a salvage value of $20,000 and a book value of zero. So the after-tax cash inflow from the sale of fixed assets equals ($20,000 - $0) $\times$ (1 - .34) = $13,200. Total cash inflow for year 5 is $23,100 - $5,000 + $13,200 = $31,300.

11. NPV = [$28,300/(1.16) + $31,600/(1.16)^2 + $34,900/(1.16)^3 + $38,200/(1.16)^4

   + $31,300/(1.16)^5 = $106,239.31] - $95,000 = $11,239.31. The IRR is 20.794%.

12. At a 12% discount rate, the PVs of the costs for A and B are $7,883.82 and $7,644.82, respectively. For Machine A, the EAC is $2,187.05; the EAC for Machine B is $2,516.94. The EAC for A is less than the EAC for B, so A has the lower cost and is therefore preferable.

13. For machine A, annual OCF is -$528 + 340 = -$188. The present value of the OCFs is -$677.70 and the EAC is $1,575.05. For Machine B, the OCF is -$452, the PV of the cash outflows is $5,372.88, and the EAC is $1,768.96 , so Machine A is the preferable alternative.

14. At a 15% discount rate, the PVs of the costs for X and Y are $1,228.25 and $1,056.65, respectively. For Machine X, the EAC is $430.21; the EAC for Machine Y is $462.79. The EAC for X is less than the EAC for Y, so X has the lower annual cost and is therefore preferable.

15. The cash outflow in year zero is the sum of the additional net working capital and the capital expenditure: ($25,000 + $150,000) = $175,000. The total cash flow in year 3 is the sum of the OCF, the recovery of net working capital, and the inflow from the sale of the equipment. The latter has tax implications because the book value of the asset differs from the market value. The book value is ($150,000 - $90,000) = $60,000. The difference between the market value ($50,000) and the book value ($60,000) is a tax deduction because the firm has under-depreciated the asset by $10,000. The tax deduction results in a tax savings of $3,400, so that the inflow from the sale of the equipment at the end of year 3 is ($50,000 + $3,400) = $53,400. The total cash inflow at the end of year 3 is OCF + $25,000 + $53,400 = OCF + $78,400. The PV of the $78,400 inflow at the end of year 3 is [$78,400/(1.18)^3] = $47,716.66. Solving for OCF,

   OCF = $127,283.34/PVIFA(18%,3) = ($127,283.34/2.174273) = $58,540.64.

If the firm's OCF for the project is $58,540.64 per year, then the NPV would be zero. Consequently,

262

the return on the firm's investment in equipment and working capital would be 18%, the required return. Next we determine net income (then price per unit) for the project which will provide the necessary OCF.

$$OCF = [(S - C - D) \times (1 - T_c)] + D, \text{ so}$$

$$OCF = \$58,540.64 \text{ and } D = (\$150,000/5) = \$30,000, \text{ and}$$

$$\text{Net income} = OCF - D = \$58,540.64 - \$30,000 = \$28,540.64.$$

Solve for S:

$$\text{Net income} = [(S - C - D) \times (1 - T_c)]$$

$$\$28,540.64 = (S - \$40,000 - \$30,000) \times (1 - .34)$$

$$S = \$113,243.39$$

The value of C is the sum of variable and fixed costs for the project. Fixed costs are $38,000 per year and variable costs are ($2 × 1000) = $2000, so C = ($38,000 + $2,000) = $40,000. The solution for S represents total sales required to generate the required OCF. Since the bid is for 1000 hammers, the price per unit is ($113,243.39/1000) = $113.24. This price will provide the firm with annual OCF of $58,540.64 and NPV equal to zero, so the firm would earn the required 18% return.

CHAPTER 11

1.

Sales	$110,000
-Variable Costs	44,000
-Fixed Costs	10,000
-Depreciation	28,000
EBIT	$ 28,000
-Taxes (34%)	9,520
Net income	$ 18,480

EBIT	28,000
+Depreciation	28,000
-Taxes	9,520
Operating Cash Flow	$ 46,480

2. The NPV of the project is $155,808 - $140,000 = $15,808.

3. The worst-case scenario comprises the least favorable outcome for each of the four forecasted variables, while the best-case scenario is comprised of the most favorable outcome for each. These scenarios are described in the following table:

263

	Worst case	Best case
Unit sales	1,800	2,200
Price per unit	$ 50	$ 60
Variable costs per unit	$ 23	$ 21
Fixed costs per year	$10,500	$ 9,500

Scenario	Net income	Cash flow	Net present value	Internal rate of return
Base case	$18,480	$46,480	$15,808	19.68%
Worst case	6,666	34,666	-23,794	7.57
Best case	31,878	59,878	60,720	32.16

The base-case NPV indicates that the project is acceptable. But the negative NPV for the worst-case scenario indicates further analysis is necessary. Sensitivity analysis might be useful so Newcombe can identify those variables which most clearly contribute to the possibility that the NPV is negative.

4. The solution is provided in the following table:

Scenario	Unit sales	Cash flow	Net present value	Internal rate of return
Base case	2,000	$46,480	$15,808	19.68%
Worst case	1,800	42,124	1,206	15.36
Best case	2,200	50,836	30,410	23.85

For both the worst case and best case scenarios here, we assume that price, variable costs and fixed costs take on their base case values. The results indicate that NPV is sensitive to unit sales forecasts; however, even assuming the lower bound sales level, NPV is still positive. This is encouraging, but Newcombe's optimism must be tempered by the fact that we assume base case levels for all variables other than sales; if any additional variable takes on its 'worst case' value, it is likely that NPV would become negative.

5. Sensitivity analysis of **unit price** is performed in the following table:

Scenario	Price per unit	Cash flow	Net present value	Internal rate of return
Base case	$55	$46,480	$15,808	19.68%
Worst case	50	39,880	- 6,316	13.08
Best case	60	53,080	37,932	25.95

The results suggest that the NPV of the project is more sensitive to changes in unit price than it is to changes in sales level; when unit price is at its lower bound, the NPV of the project is negative. This sensitivity to price changes may seem surprising, especially since the change from the base case to the worst case is somewhat larger, on a percentage basis, for sales (10%) than for unit price (9%); however, in the case of the sales forecast, the 10% reduction in sales also results in a 10% reduction in total variable costs, somewhat ameliorating the effect on net income and cash flow. Newcombe must further assess the sensitivity of NPV to both sales level and unit price.

6. Sensitivity analysis of **variable costs** is performed in the following table:

Scenario	Variable costs	Cash flow	Net present value	Internal rate of return
Base case	$22	$46,480	$15,808	19.68%
Worst case	23	45,160	11,383	18.39
Best case	21	47,800	20,233	20.95

NPV is relatively insensitive to changes in variable costs. Therefore, in assessing the acceptability of the project, it may not be particularly important for Newcombe to further evaluate this forecast.

7. Sensitivity analysis of **fixed costs** is presented in the following table:

Scenario	Fixed costs	Cash flow	Net present value	Internal rate of return
Base case	$10,000	$46,480	$15,808	19.68%
Worst case	10,500	46,150	14,702	19.35
Best case	9,500	46,810	16,914	20.00

NPV is not particularly sensitive to changes in fixed costs because the percentage change in fixed costs from the base case to the upper bound is relatively small, and because fixed costs are a relatively small portion of the total costs for the project.

8. The accounting break-even point is ($10,000 + $28,000)/($55 - 22) = 1,151.52. Net income (and EBIT) will be zero if Newcombe produces and sells 1,151.52 units.

9. The cash break-even point for Newcombe is $10,000/($55 - 22) = 303.03 units.

10. The OCF for the project is a five-year annuity. At the financial break-even point, the NPV is zero, which is equivalent to stating that the PV of the annuity is equal to the $140,000 cash outflow.

$$\$140,000 = OCF \times PVIFA(15\%,5)$$

Since $140,000 = OCF $\times$ 3.352155, OCF = $140,000/3.352155 = $41,764.18. The financial BEP is:

$$Q = (FC + OCF)/(P - v) = (\$10,000 + \$41,764.18)/(\$55 - 22) = 1,568.61$$

Therefore, sales must be 1569 units in order for the project to have a NPV greater than zero.

11. The DOL = Percentage change in OCF/Percentage change in Q. OCF for output of 2000 units equals

$$OCF = [(P - v) \times Q] - FC = [(\$55 - \$22) \times 2,000] - \$10,000 = \$56,000.$$

OCF for output of 2,200 units is $62,600. The percentage change in OCF is:

$$(\$62,600 - \$56,000)/\$56,000 = .11786 = 11.786\%.$$

The percentage change in output is $(2,200 - 2,000)/2,000 = .10\%$. DOL is $(11.786\%/10\%) = 1.1786$. Or,

$$DOL = 1 + FC/OCF = 1 + \$10,000/\$56,000 = 1.1786.$$

12. OCF for output of 2,000 units is $56,000. OCF for output of 1,600 units is:

$$OCF = [(P - v) \times Q] - FC = [(\$55 - \$22) \times 1,600] - \$10,000 = \$42,800.$$

The percentage change in OCF is $(\$42,800 - \$56,000)/\$56,00 = -.23571 = -23.571\%$. The percentage change in output is $(1,600 - 2,000)/2,000 = -.20 = -20\%$. The DOL $= -23.571\%/-20\% = 1.1786$.

13. When $Q = 1,600$, OCF $= \$42,800$; when $Q = 2,000$, OCF $= \$56,000$. The percentage change in OCF is $(\$56,000 - \$42,800)/\$42,800 = .30841 = 30.841\%$. The percentage change in output is $(2,000 - 1,600)/1,600 = .25 = 25\%$. The DOL $= 30.841\%/25\% = 1.2336$. Alternatively,

$$DOL = 1 + FC/OCF = 1 + (\$10,000/\$42,800) = 1.2336$$

14. The percentage change in output is $(23,000 - 20,000)/20,000 = .15 = 15\%$. Substituting this value and the DOL value into the definition of DOL, we can solve for the percentage change in OCF:

$$DOL = \text{Percentage change in OCF/Percentage change in Q}$$
$$2.5 = \text{Percentage change in OCF}/.15$$

The percentage change in OCF $= (2.5 \times .15) = .375 = 37.5\%$. OCF increases by 37.5%, so the new level of OCF is $(1.375 \times \$50,000) = \$68,750$.

15. The alternative formula for computing DOL is: $1 + FC/OCF$. Substituting DOL $= 2.5$ and OCF $= \$50,000$. Since $2.5 = 1 + FC/\$50,000$, FC $= \$75,000$.

16. Sales are $(\$3 \times 6,000) = \$18,000$ and net income is $(\$18,000 - \$16,000) = \$2,000$. Since depreciation and taxes are zero, OCF is also $2,000. Treating this cash flow as a perpetuity, the present value is $(\$2,000/.25) = \$8,000$; the NPV is $(\$8,000 - \$10,000) = -\$2,000$, so the project is unacceptable.

17. If sales volume is 5,500 cars per year, sales will be $(\$3 \times 5,500) = \$16,500$; net income and OCF will be $(\$16,500 - \$16,000) = \$500$. At 6,500 cars per year, net income and OCF are $3,500. If the two are equally likely, the expected value of first year OCF is $[(.5 \times \$500) + (.5 \times \$3,500)] = \$2,000$.

If sales volume the first year is 5,500 cars, then OCF will be $500 for all subsequent years; the value of this perpetuity, as of the end of the first year, is ($500/.25) = $2,000. Since the property can be sold for $10,000, the investor would sell the property at the end of the first year. On the other hand, at 6500 cars per year, OCF will be $3,500 and the value of the business would be ($3,500/.25) = $14,000; under these circumstances, the investor will continue to operate the business. Therefore, at the end of the first year, the investor will have an expected cash flow of $2,000, plus either $10,000 in cash or a business worth $14,000. The expected value at the end of the first year is $2,000 + [(.5 × $10,000) + (.5 × $14,000)] = $14,000. The PV of this $14,000 is ($14,000/1.25) = $11,200, and the NPV of the investment is ($11,200 - $10,000) = $1,120. The investment is acceptable. The option to abandon at the end of the first year has added value to the project.

CHAPTER 12

1. Total dividend income is ($2.50 × 100) = $250. Capital gains are [($33.50 - $32) × 100] = $150 and total dollar return is ($250 + $150) = $400.

2. Dividend yield is: D_{t+1}/P_t = $2.50/$32 = .0781 = 7.81%. Capital gains yield is ($33.50 - $32)/$32 = .0469 = 4.69%. Total return is dividend yield plus capital gains yield: 7.81% + 4.69% = 12.50%

3. Total dividend income expected is ($2 × 100) = $200. Expected capital gains equal [($33 - $33.50) × 100] = -$50; this is a capital loss of $50. The total dollar return expected is ($200 - $50) = $150.

4. Dividend yield is $2.00/$33.50 = .0597 = 5.97%. The capital gains yield is ($33 - $33.50)/$33.50 = -.0149 = -1.49%. The total percentage return is 5.97% - 1.49% = 4.48%.

5. The mean returns are $\overline{R}$ = (.30/5) = .06 = 6% for GM common stock and $\overline{R}$ = (.35/5) = .07 = 7% for ATT common stock.

6.

Year	Rate of Return R		Deviation from Average Return $(R - \overline{R})$		Squared value of Deviations $(R - \overline{R})^2$	
	GM	ATT	GM	ATT	GM	ATT
1	.10	.12	.04	.05	.0016	.0025
2	.04	.06	-.02	-.01	.0004	.0001
3	-.09	-.10	-.15	-.17	.0225	.0289
4	.20	.22	.14	.15	.0196	.0225
5	.05	.05	-.01	-.02	.0001	.0004
Totals	.30	.35	.00	.00	.0442	.0544

Thus Var(R) = σ^2 = (.0442/4) = .01105 for GM and Var(R) = σ^2 = .0136 for ATT.

7. The standard deviation for GM is SD(R) = σ = $(.01105)^{.5}$ = .10512 = 10.512%, and for ATT SD(R) = σ = $(.0136)^{.5}$ = .11662 = 11.662%.

8. For GM, the range of returns within one SD of the mean is from [.06 - (1 × .10512)] to [.06 + (1 × .10512)], or -4.512% to 16.512%. The range within two SDs of the mean is from [.06 - (2 × .10512)] to [.06 + (2 × .10512)], or -15.024% to 27.024%. There is a 68% probability that, in a given year, the return for GM stock will be between -4.512% and 16.512%, and a 95% probability that the return will be between -15.024% and 27.024%. For ATT, the probability is 68% that the return will be between -4.662% and 18.662%, and 95% that the return will be from -16.324% and 30.324%.

9. To solve this problem, we first determine the relevant value of z, which is the number of standard deviation units between $R = 0$ and $R = \overline{R} = 6\%$. For GM, $z = [(0 - .06)/.10512] = -.57$. A table of the normal distribution indicates the probability that a value of z is between 0 (i.e., the mean of a distribution) and $z = -.57$; this probability is .2157. Since the probability of a z value less than 0 is .50, then the probability of a z value less than -.57 is $(.50 - .2157) = .2843$ or 28.43%. Therefore, the probability is 28.43% that the return for GM common stock is negative. For ATT common stock, $z = [(0 - .07/.11662] = -.60$. So the probability of a negative return is $(.50 - .2257) = .2743 = 27.43\%$.

CHAPTER 13

1.
$$E(R_{ATT}) = (Pr_1 \times R_1) + (Pr_2 \times R_2) + (Pr_3 \times R_3) + (Pr_4 \times R_4) + (Pr_5 \times R_5)$$
$$= (.2 \times .12) + (.2 \times .06) + [.2 \times (-.10)] + (.2 \times .22) + (.2 \times .05)$$
$$= .024 + .012 + (-.020) + .044 + .010 = .07 = 7\%$$

2.

State of economy	Rate of return if state occurs R	Deviation of return from expected return $(R - \overline{R})$	Squared deviation of return from expected return $(R - \overline{R})^2$
1	.12	.05	.0025
2	.06	-.01	.0001
3	-.10	-.17	.0289
4	.22	.15	.0225
5	.05	-.02	.0004
Totals	.35	.00	.0544

Thus, computing the variance as a strict average, $Var(R) = \sigma^2 = (.0544/5) = .01088$. Alternatively, we can compute the variance as a weighted average as follows:
$$Var(R) = [Pr_1 \times (R_1 - \overline{R})^2] + [Pr_2 \times (R_2 - \overline{R})^2] + \cdots + [Pr_T \times (R_T - \overline{R})^2]$$
$$= (.2 \times .0025) + (.2 \times .0001) + (.2 \times .0289) + (.2 \times .0225) + (.2 \times .0004)$$
$$= .00050 + .00002 + .00578 + .00450 + .00008 = .01088.$$

3. The standard deviation equals $(.01088)^{.5} = .10431 = 10.431\%$.

4. The expected returns for Firm A and for Firm B are, respectively:

$$\overline{R}_A = E(R_A) = (Pr_1 \times R_1) + (Pr_2 \times R_2) + (Pr_3 \times R_3)$$
$$= (.3 \times .05) + (.5 \times .15) + (.2 \times .20) = .13 = 13\%$$
$$\overline{R}_B = E(R_B) = (Pr_1 \times R_1) + (Pr_2 \times R_2) + (Pr_3 \times R_3)$$
$$= (.3 \times .00) + (.5 \times .16) + (.2 \times .30) = .14 = 14\%$$

5.

State of economy	Rate of return if state occurs R		Deviation of return from expected return $(R - \bar{R})$		Squared deviation of return from expected return $(R - \bar{R})^2$	
	A	B	A	B	A	B
Recession	.05	.00	-.08	-.14	.0064	.0196
Moderate Growth	.15	.16	.02	.02	.0004	.0004
Rapid Expansion	.20	.30	.07	.16	.0049	.0256

The variance of Firm A is $(.3 \times .0064) + (.5 \times .0004) + (.2 \times .0049) = .0031$. That of firm B is $(.3 \times .0196) + (.5 \times .0004) + (.2 \times .0256) = .01120$.

6. For firm A, $\sigma = (.00310)^{.5} = .05568$. For Firm B, $\sigma = (.01120)^{.5} = .10583$.

7.

State of economy	Probability of state of economy (Pr)	Rate of return if state occurs (R_K)	(R_M)	$(Pr \times R_K)$	$(Pr \times R_M)$
Boom	.10	.25	.18	.025	.018
Growth	.20	.10	.20	.020	.040
Normal	.50	.15	.04	.075	.020
Recession	.20	-.12	.00	-.024	.000
Totals	1.00			.096	.078

Thus the expected returns are $E(R_K) = \bar{R}_K = 9.6\%$ and $E(R_M) = \bar{R}_M = 7.8\%$.

8.

State of economy	Probability of state of economy (Pr)	Deviation of return from expected return $(R_K - \bar{R}_K)$	$(R_K - \bar{R}_K)^2$	$[Pr \times (R_K - \bar{R}_K)^2]$
Boom	.10	.154	.023716	.0023716
Growth	.20	.004	.000016	.0000032
Normal	.50	.054	.002916	.0014580
Recession	.20	-.216	.046656	.0093312
Totals	1.00			.0131640

The variance for Stock K is: $\sigma^2 = .013164$. Similarly, we compute the variance for Stock M as follows:

State of economy	Probability of state of economy (Pr)	Deviation of return from expected return $(R_K - \bar{R}_K)$	$(R_K - \bar{R}_K)^2$	$[Pr \times (R_K - \bar{R}_K)^2]$
Boom	.10	.102	.010404	.0010404
Growth	.20	.122	.014884	.0029768
Normal	.50	-.038	.001444	.0007220
Recession	.20	-.078	.006084	.0012168
Totals	1.00			.0059560

The variance for Stock M is: $\sigma^2 = .005956$.

9. For Stock K, the standard deviation is the square root of $\sigma^2 = .013164$: $\sigma = .11473 = 11.473\%$. For Stock M, the standard deviation is the square root of $\sigma^2 = .005956$: $\sigma = .07718 = 7.718\%$.

10. The portfolio weights are: $x_K = (\$3,000/\$5,000) = .60 = 60\%$ invested in Stock K, and $x_M = (\$2,000/\$5,000) = .40 = 40\%$ invested in Stock M.

11. For the portfolio of Stocks K and M:

$$E(R_P) = [x_1 \times E(R_1)] + [x_2 \times E(R_2)] = [x_K \times E(R_K)] + [x_M \times E(R_M)]$$
$$= (.60 \times .096) + (.40 \times .078) = .0888 = 8.88\%$$

12.

State of economy	Probability of state of economy (Pr)	Rate of return if state occurs (R_P)	$(R_P - \bar{R}_P)^2$	Squared deviation of return from expected return $[Pr \times (R_P - \bar{R}_P)^2]$
Boom	.10	.222	.01774224	.001774224
Growth	.20	.140	.00262144	.000524298
Normal	.50	.106	.00029584	.000147920
Recession	.20	-.072	.02585664	.005171338
Totals	1.00			.007617760

The portfolio variance is .007617760 and the standard deviation is $(.007617760)^{.5} = .0872798$.

13.
$$E(R_P) = [x_A \times E(R_A)] + [x_B \times E(R_B)] = (.75 \times .09) + (.25 \times .10) = .0925 = 9.25\%.$$
$$\beta_P = (x_A \times \beta_A) + (x_B \times \beta_B) = (.75 \times .95) + (.25 \times 1.25) = 1.025$$

14. Solve for x_A:
$$E(R_P) = [x_A \times E(R_A)] + [x_B \times E(R_B)]$$
$$.095 = [x_A \times .09] + [(1 - x_A) \times .10]$$

where x_A is the proportion of the portfolio invested in Stock A and $(1 - x_A)$ is that invested in Stock B. Thus $x_A = .50 = 50\%$ and $x_B = (1 - x_A) = .50 = 50\%$. $\beta_P = (x_A \times \beta_A) + (x_B \times \beta_B) = (.50 \times .95) + (.50 \times 1.25) = 1.10$.

15. Denote Stock A security 1, Stock B security 2, and the risk-free asset as security 3. Then

$E(R_P) = [x_1 \times E(R_1)] + [x_2 \times E(R_2)] + [x_3 \times E(R_3)] = (.10 \times .09) + (.30 \times .10) + (.60 \times .06) = .075 = 7.5\%$. Since the beta for the risk-free asset is zero, the beta for the portfolio is:

$$\beta_P = (x_1 \times \beta_1) + (x_2 \times \beta_2) + (x_3 \times \beta_3) = (.10 \times .95) + (.30 \times 1.25) + (.60 \times 0) = .470.$$

16. For Stock A, the reward-to-risk ratio equals $[E(R_A) - R_f]/\beta A = (.105 - .06)/.90 = .0500 = 5.00\%$. For Stocks B and C, the reward-to-risk ratios are 6.087% and 7.083%, respectively.

17. The intercept of the CAPM is $R_f = 6\%$, and the slope is $[E(R_M) - R_f] = 14\% - 6\% = 8\%$. The equation for the CAPM is: $E(R_i) = R_f + [E(R_M) - R_f] \times \beta_i = 6\% + (8\% \times \beta_i)$, where $E(R_i)$ and β_i are the expected return and beta, respectively, for any asset i. The market risk premium is the same as the slope of the CAPM: $[E(R_M) - R_f] = 14\% - 8\% = 6\%$.

18. $E(R_i) = 6\% + (8\% \times \beta_i) = .06 + (.08 \times 2) = .22 = 22\%$

19. Denote the risk-free asset security 1 and Speiss common stock security 2. The portfolio weights are:

$$x_1 = (\$1200/\$4000) = .30 = 30\% \text{ and } x_2 = (\$2800/\$4000) = .70 = 70\%.$$
$$E(R_P) = [x_1 \times E(R_1)] + [x_2 \times E(R_2)] = (.30 \times .06) + (.70 \times .22) = .172 = 17.2\%.$$

Since the $\beta_{Rf} = 0$, $\beta_P = (x_1 \times \beta_1) + (x_2 \times \beta_2) = (.30 \times 0) + (.70 \times 2) = 1.4$.

20. Solve for x_1:
$$\beta_P = (x_1 \times \beta_1) + (x_2 \times \beta_2)$$
$$1.5 = [x_1 \times 0] + [(1 - x_1) \times 2]$$

where x_1 is the proportion of the portfolio invested in the risk-free asset and $(1 - x_1)$ is the proportion invested in Speiss common stock. x_1 is .25 and $x_2 = (1 - x_1) = .75$, so $E(R_P) = 6\% + (8\% \times \beta_i) = .06 + (.08 \times 1.5) = .18 = 18\%$.

21. $E(R_i) = 6\% + (8\% \times \beta_i) = .06 + (.08 \times 1.45) = .176 = 17.6\%$. By the CAPM, a security with $\beta = 1.45$ should have $E(R_i)$ equal to 17.6%. Dorigan Corp. common stock has an expected return of only 15%. Dorigan stock is over-priced; demand for Dorigan will be low, resulting in a lower price and higher expected return.

22. Security 4 has a 7% expected return and zero variance; thus Security 4 is a risk-free asset and the risk-free rate is 7%. Its beta must be zero. Security 1 also has an expected return of 7%; therefore, it must also be a risk-free asset, and must have beta of zero. Security 2 has beta of 0.8. Consider a portfolio with the following weights: 80% invested in the market portfolio and 20% invested in the risk-free asset. This portfolio's beta is 0.8, because it is a weighted average of the betas of the investments. This portfolio has an expected return of 14%. Since the expected return for the portfolio is a weighted average of the expected return of the securities which comprise it, we can solve for the $E(R_M)$ as follows:

$$E(R_P) = [x_1 \times E(R_1)] + [x_2 \times E(R_2)]$$
$$.14 = [.8 \times E(R_M)] + [.2 \times .07]$$
$$E(R_M) = .1575 = 15.75\%$$

The intercept of the CAPM is $R_f = 7\%$, and the slope is $[E(R_M) - R_f] = 15.75\% - 7\% = 8.75\%$. $E(R_3)$ is 10%. Now solve for β_3 by substituting into the CAPM:

$$.10 = .07 + (.0875 \times \beta_3)$$
$$\beta_3 = (.03/.0875) = .343$$

23.

State of economy	Probability of state of economy (Pr)	Rate of return if state occurs (R_X)	(R_M)	(Pr $\times$ R_X)	(Pr $\times$ R_M)
1	.20	.03	.09	.006	.018
2	.20	.17	.16	.034	.032
3	.30	.28	.10	.084	.030
4	.20	.05	.02	.010	.004
5	.10	-.04	.16	-.004	.016
Totals	1.00			.130	.100

Thus the expected returns are $E(R_X) = \overline{R}_X = 13.0\%$ and $E(R_M) = \overline{R}_M = 10.0\%$.

24.

State of economy	Probability of state of economy (Pr)	Deviation of return from expected return ($R_X - \overline{R}_X$)	($R_X - \overline{R}_X$)^2	[Pr $\times$ ($R_X - \overline{R}_X$)^2]
1	.20	-.10	.0100	.00200
2	.20	.04	.0016	.00032
3	.30	.15	.0225	.00675
4	.20	-.08	.0064	.00128
5	.10	-.17	.0289	.00289
Totals	1.00			.01324

The variance for Asset X is $\sigma^2 = .01324$, and the standard deviation is $(.01324)^{.5} = .11507$. The variance for Asset M is $\sigma^2 = .00238$, and the standard deviation is .04879.

25. The intercept of the CAPM is $R_f = 6\%$, and the slope is $[E(R_M) - R_f] = 10\% - 6\% = 4\%$. Thus,

$$E(R_X) = 6\% + (4\% \times \beta_X) = .06 + (.04 \times 1.25) = .11 = 11\%$$

The required return is 11%. Since Asset X has an expected return of 13%, it is an acceptable investment.

CHAPTER 14

1. The firm's pre-tax cost of debt (R_D) is the YTM for the outstanding bond issue. The relevant time period is the remaining twenty years to maturity. The YTM is the value of r which solves the equation:

$$PV = [C \times PVIFA(r,t) + \$1000/(1+r)^t]$$

$$\$915 = [\$90 \times \text{PVIFA}(r,20)] + \$1000/(1+r)^{20}$$

The YTM is 9.998%; the after-tax cost of debt is: $R_D \times (1 - T_C) = .09998 \times (1 - .34) = .06599 = 6.599\%$.

2. Since the thirty-year bond was issued five years ago, the current maturity of the bond is 25 years. The pre-tax cost of debt is the yield to maturity for the bond, or the value of r which solves the equation:

$$PV = C \times \text{PVIFA}(r,t) + \$1000/(1+r)^t$$
$$\$1000 = \$100 \times \text{PVIFA}(r,25) + \$1000/(1+r)^{25}$$

The YTM is 10% so the after-tax cost of debt is: $R_D \times (1 - T_C) = .10 \times (1 - .34) = .06600 = 6.600\%$.

3. Five years from now, the bond will be a twenty-year bond. The YTM at that time would be the value of r in the following equation:

$$PV = C \times \text{PVIFA}(r,t) + \$1000/(1+r)^t$$
$$\$1100 = [\$100 \times \text{PVIFA}(r,20)] + \$1000/(1+r)^{20}$$

We know that the YTM is less than the coupon rate because the bond is selling at a premium. The YTM is 8.911%. The after-tax cost of debt is: $R_D \times (1 - T_C) = .08911 \times (1 - .34) = .05881 = 5.881\%$.

4. To compute the cost of equity (R_E), first compute D_1: $D_1 = D_0 \times (1 + g) = \$3.50 \times 1.04 = \$3.64$. Using the dividend growth model to compute R_E, we find:

$$R_E = D_1/P_0 + g = \$3.64/\$25 + .04 = .1456 + .04 = .1856 = 18.56\%$$

According to the dividend growth model, the cost of equity capital is 18.56%.

5. The cost of equity is: $R_E = R_f + \beta_E \times [R_M - R_f] = .070 + (1.35 \times .085) = .18475 = 18.475\%$.

6. A debt-equity ratio of 0.50 indicates that the firm has $0.50 of debt for each $1.00 of equity. Therefore, E/V = $1.00/($.50 + $1.00) = ⅔, and D/V = $.50/($1.00 + $.50) = ⅓. From the solutions to Problems 1,2,4, and 5, we know that R_E is approximately 18.5%, R_D is approximately 10%, and the after-tax cost of debt is $[R_D \times (1 - T_C)] = (.10 \times .66) = 6.60\%$. The WACC is therefore:

$$WACC = (E/V) \times R_E + (D/V) \times R_D \times (1 - T_C)$$
$$= (⅔ \times .185) + [⅓ \times .10 \times (1 - .34)] = .14533 = 14.533\%$$

7. The weighted average flotation cost for MAM is: $f_A = (E/V) \times f_E + (D/V) \times f_D$

$$= (⅔ \times .09) + (⅓ \times .06) = .08 = 8\%.$$

Given the 8% weighted-average flotation cost, the total financing required is $690,000/(1 - .08) = $750,000, which is the true cost of the expansion.

8. The yield for the outstanding preferred issue equals $R_P = D/P_0 = \$3.25/\$25 = .1300 = 13.00\%$; so the cost of preferred stock for MAM is 13.00%.

9. The WACC is computed as in Problem 6, with the following changes: first, there are now three terms in the WACC calculation; second, the weights are as specified in Problem 7, and; third, the cost of preferred stock is 13.00%. The WACC $= (E/V) \times R_E + (D/V) \times R_D \times (1 - T_C) + (P/V) \times R_P$, where (P/V) is the proportion of the capital structure represented by preferred stock. So the WACC is

$$\text{WACC} = (.60 \times .185) + (.30 \times .10 \times .66) + (.10 \times .13) = .1438 = 14.38\%$$

10. The return for the first issue is $R_P = D/P_0 = \$4.00/\$39.625 = .10095 = 10.095\%$. The dividend yields for the other preferred stock issues were 10.024% and 10.332%, respectively. Therefore, the cost of preferred stock financing for Illinois Power is between 10.0% and 10.4%.

11. The SML cost of equity is $R_E = R_f + \beta_E \times [R_M - R_f] = .08 + (2.00 \times .090) = .2600 = 26.00\%$.

12. The market value of Margo's equity is $(10.5 \text{ million} \times \$80) = \$840$ million. The market value of Margo's debt is $(.90 \times \$400 \text{ million}) = \$360$ million. Firm value is ($\$840$ million + $\$360$ million) = $\$1.2$ billion. The market value weights are: E/V = $\$840$ million/$\$1.2$ billion = .70 = 70%, and D/V = $\$360$ million/$\$1.2$ billion = .30 = 30%. The WACC equals $(E/V) \times R_E + (D/V) \times R_D \times (1 - T_C)$

$$= (.70 \times .26) + [.30 \times .10 \times (1 - .34)] = .2018 = 20.18\%$$

13. The WACC is the appropriate discount rate for this investment since the expansion is in the same risk class as the firm itself. The PV of the investment is computed as follows:

$$\text{PV} = C \times \text{PVIFA(WACC,t)} = \$350,000 \times 2.978806 = \$1,042,582.10$$

The NPV equals $\$1,042,582.10 - \$1,000,000 = +\$42,582.10$, so it is acceptable.

14. The weighted average flotation cost equals $f_A = (E/V) \times f_E + (D/V) \times f_D$

$$= (.70 \times .05) + (.30 \times .02) = .041 = 4.1\%.$$

Total financing required is $\$1,000,000/(1 - .041) = \$1,042,752.87$. The actual NPV is $\$1,042,582.10 - \$1,042,752.87 = -\$170.77$. When flotation costs are considered, the investment becomes unacceptable.

CHAPTER 15

1. Yul obtained financing of $(\$10 \times 1,000,000) = \$10$ million. The underwriter's spread was $[(\$11 - \$10) \times 1,000,000] = \$1$ million. The direct and indirect costs were $(\$60,000 + \$40,000) = \$100,000$. The stock was underpriced by $\$3$ per share, so the total cost associated with underpricing was $(\$3 \times 1,000,000) = \$3$ million. Total costs were $\$4.1$ million, so flotation costs were $(\$4.1 \text{ million}/\$10 \text{ million}) = 41\%$ of the financing obtained. Notice that the major cost is the opportunity cost to the existing stockholders of the underpricing of the IPO.

274

2. Let X be the issue size. Solving for X: $(1 - .12) \times X = \$15$ million. That is, $(1 - .12) = .88 = 88\%$ of the size of the issue is financing available to the firm. X equals ($15 million/.88) = \$17,045,455. The flotation costs are $(\$17,045,455 - \$15,000,000) = \$2,045,455$.

3. If you are able to purchase all the shares for which you bid, you would earn a profit of $100 on the undervalued stock, while you would lose $50 on the overvalued stock, for a total profit of ($100 - $50) = $50. However, the undervalued issue will be rationed while the overvalued issue will not. You should expect to get 50 shares of the former issue, for a profit of $50, and 100 shares of the latter issue, for a loss of $50; so you expect to earn no profit. Notice that, on average, these new issues are underpriced by $(\$.25/\$10) = 2.5\%$. That you expect to earn zero profit illustrates the winner's curse.

4. BPS is $(\$60,000,000/5,000,000) = \$12$. EPS is $(\$7,500,000/5,000,000) = \$1.50$. The P/E ratio is $(\$9/\$1.50) = 6$. ROE is $(\$1.50/\$12.00) = .125 = 12.5\%$. The market-to-book ratio is $(\$9/\$12) = .75$.

5. Total book value is $(\$60,000,000 + \$4,500,000) = \$64,500,000$. Number of shares issued equals $(\$4,500,000/\$9) = 500,000$. Total shares outstanding equals $(5,000,000 + 500,000) = 5,500,000$. BPS is $(\$64,500,000/5,500,000) = \$11.73$. If ROE remains constant at 12.5% (as computed in Problem 16), then net income is $(.125 \times \$64,500,000) = \$8,062,500$. EPS equals $(\$8,062,500/5,500,000) = \$1.466$. If the P/E ratio remains constant at 6.00, then the market price per share is $(\$1.466 \times 6) = \$8.80$. The market-to-book ratio equals $(\$8.80/\$11.73) = .75$. Notice that both *accounting dilution* and *market value dilution* have taken place. Accounting dilution is the reduction in BPS and EPS from the sale of new common stock at a price below the BPS of the outstanding common stock. BPS decreases because the book value of the new shares is $9, which is less than the book value of the existing shares. Given a constant ROE, EPS for the new shares is $(.125 \times \$9) = \$1.125$; since this is less than the EPS computed above, EPS must decrease. Accounting dilution is not relevant to the shareholder, but market value dilution is. The dilution of market value is not caused by the accounting dilution, but because the expansion under consideration by Ebbets has a negative NPV.

6. The market value of the firm prior to the expansion is $(\$9 \times 5,000,000) = \$45,000,000$. After the expansion, the market value is $(\$8.80 \times 5,500,000) = \$48,400,000$, which represents an increase in market value of $3,400,000. Ebbets proposes spending $4,500,000 on a capital budgeting project which increases the firm's market value by only $3,400,000; this project has a NPV of $(\$3,400,000 - \$4,500,000) = -\$1,100,000$. It is this negative NPV which causes the dilution in the market value of the stock. It is also important to note here that, not only is the expansion detrimental to the firm's existing stockholders, it also results in a loss to the new stockholders. They buy shares for $9 which have a market value of only $8.80; it is unlikely that either group will be receptive to this expansion.

7. Firm value will be $(\$45,000,000 + \$5,500,000) = \$50,500,000$. Share value will be $(\$50,500,000/5,500,000) = \$9.18$. Accounting dilution and market value dilution are independent. Accounting dilution occurs because the new shares are sold for a price below the book value of the existing shares. Market value dilution occurs only if the project being financed has a negative NPV. Here we hypothesize that the project has a positive NPV; the negative NPV above results from assumptions that P/E and ROE remain constant after the expansion. There is no reason to believe that these ratios will necessarily remain constant simply because the firm sells stock for less than book value, so there is no reason to believe that market value dilution occurs whenever accounting dilution occurs.

8. At a subscription price of $20 per share, ($10,000,000/$20) = 500,000 shares must be sold. There are 2 million shares outstanding, so (2,000,000/500,000) = 4 rights are required to buy one new share.

9. An investor could buy four shares of Emery common stock for ($80 × 4) = $320, and then exercise the rights to acquire a fifth for $20. Thus, five shares can be purchased for $340, or ($340/5) = $68 per share. Therefore, the ex-rights price is $68 per share, and the value of one right is ($80 - $68) = $12.

10. Before the rights offering, the 100 shares were worth ($80 × 100) = $8,000. The solution above indicates that the ex-rights price of the Emery stock is $68; so after the offering, the shares are worth ($68 × 100) = $6,800. Since the value of a right is $12, the 100 rights can be sold for ($12 × 100) = $1,200. So after the rights offering the investor has stock whose value is $6,800, plus $1,200 in cash, for a total of $8,000.

11. The solution to Problem 8 indicates that the investor can purchase one additional share for every four shares currently owned. Thus, the holder of 100 shares will be able to purchase 25 new shares for ($20 × 25) = $500. The solution to Problem 9 indicates that the ex-rights price of the stock is $68; after exercising the rights, the value of the investor's stock is ($68 × 125) = $8,500. The investor originally owned $8,000 of Emery stock. She then purchased $500 of additional stock, so the total value of her stock is now $8,500. The rights offering has not affected her wealth.

12. An investor who owns 100 shares of Emery common stock would lose ($2 × 100) = $200 if she chose to sell the rights; i.e., as described in the solution to Problem 10, she would own stock worth ($68 × 100) = $6,800, but the value of the rights would be only ($10 × 100) = $1,000, for a total value of only ($6,800 + $1,000) = $7,800. So it would be preferable for this investor to exercise her rights.

An investor who does not own Emery common stock could purchase four rights for ($10 × 4) = $40, and then exercise the rights to acquire a share for $20. Total cost would be ($40 + $20) = $60 per share; since the ex-rights price of the stock is $68, he could then sell the share for an $8 gain. This transaction could be repeated many times by any investor, whether she owns Emery common stock or not. The demand for the rights at a price of $10 would result in an increase in the price of the rights; furthermore, as described in the first part of this problem, those who own stock would not be willing to sell their rights at the $10 price. The conclusion is that the rights could not have a price of less than $10, because there would be an extremely large demand for, and no supply of, rights at the $10 price.

13. An investor who owns 100 shares of Emery common stock should sell the rights for $13. This would result in a $100 gain, compared to the result described in the solution to Problem 10. That is, the investor would have 100 shares worth ($68 × 100) = $6,800, plus ($13 × 100) = $1,300, for a total of ($6,800 + $1,300) = $8,100. An investor who does not own Emery stock would not be willing to purchase a right for $13. Four rights would cost ($13 × 4) = $52; to exercise the rights, the investor would pay the subscription price of $20, for a total cost of ($52 + $20) = $72 per share. Since the ex-rights price is $68, this would not be a rational. Consequently, Emery stockholders would be willing to sell a right for $13, but a rational investor would not be willing to buy a right for this price; thus, the price of the rights cannot be greater than the $12 value computed above.

CHAPTER 16

1. For a firm with no debt, net income equals EBIT, so EPS for Nolever is net income divided by shares outstanding: ($10,000/2,000) = $5.00. ROE equals ($10,000/$80,000) = .125 = 12.5%. Share price is ($80,000/2,000) = $40.

For Maxlever, net income is EBIT less interest. (Remember: we assume no taxes.) The annual interest payment is (.10 × $40,000) = $4,000, and net income is ($10,000 - $4,000) = $6,000. EPS is ($6,000/1,000) = $6.00. ROE is ($6,000/$40,000) = 15%. Price per share is ($40,000/1,000) = $40.

2. The calculations for Problem 2 and the results from Problem 1 are summarized in the following table:

Nolever: No debt

	Recession	Expected	Expansion
EBIT	$ 5,000	$10,000	$20,000
Interest	0	0	0
Net Income	$ 5,000	$10,000	$20,000
ROE	6.25%	12.50%	25.00%
EPS	$2.50	$5.00	$10.00

Maxlever: Debt = $40,000

	Recession	Expected	Expansion
EBIT	$ 5,000	$10,000	$20,000
Interest	$ 4,000	$ 4,000	$ 4,000
Net Income	$ 1,000	$ 6,000	$16,000
ROE	2.50%	15.00%	40.00%
EPS	$1.00	$6.00	$16.00

3. The level of EBIT such that the two firms have the same EPS is equivalent to the break-even level of EBIT. For Nolever, EPS is equal to (EBIT/2,000); for Maxlever, EPS is (EBIT - $4,000)/1,000. Equating these two expressions and solving for EBIT, we find the break-even level of EBIT as follows:

$$\text{EBIT}/2000 = (\text{EBIT} - \$4,000)/1000$$
$$\text{EBIT} = \$8,000$$

When EBIT is $8,000, EPS is $4.00 for both Maxlever and Nolever.

4. The net cost of this investment is ($40 × 200) = $8,000. In a recession, the total earnings for this investment will be ($1.00 × 200) = $200. Earnings for the expected scenario and the recession scenario are $1,200 and $3,200, respectively.

5. The debt/equity ratio of Maxlever is 1.00. So the investor must purchase $8,000 of the equity of Nolever, and borrow $8,000 and purchase $16,000 of Nolever common stock. The returns for this position, and for the investment described in Problem 4, are summarized in the following table:

	Maxlever		
	Recession	Expected	Expansion
EPS	$ 1.00	$ 6.00	$ 16.00
Earnings for 200 shares	$200.00	$1,200.00	$3,200.00

Net cost = ($40 × 200) = $8,000

	Nolever		
	Recession	Expected	Expansion
EPS	$ 2.50	$ 5.00	$ 10.00
Earnings for 400 shares	$1,000.00	$2,000.00	$4,000.00
Less: Interest on			
$8,000 at 10%	$ 800.00	$ 800.00	$ 800.00
Net earnings	$ 200.00	$1,200.00	$3,200.00

Net cost = ($40 × 400) - Amount borrowed = $16,000 - $8,000 = $8,000.

6. The investor's return is the same for the strategies in Problems 4 and 5. However, if the market value of Maxlever is $90,000 rather than $80,000, the cost of buying 200 shares of Maxlever is now greater than the alternative strategy in Problem 5. The value of Maxlever's equity is now ($90,000 - $40,000) = $50,000, and the share price is ($50,000/1,000) = $50. Consequently, the cost of 200 shares of Maxlever is ($50 × 200) = $10,000. The strategy of Problem 5 duplicates the cash flows from 200 shares of Maxlever, but the cost is only $8,000. As a result, a rational investor would pursue the strategy of Problem 5; this would increase the value of Nolever and decrease the value of Maxlever. Prices will adjust until the values of the two firms are equal. Thus, corporate leverage has no value to the shareholder since he can create the same effect with homemade leverage.

7. The net cost of this investment is ($40 × 200) = $8,000. In the event of a recession, the total earnings for this investment will be ($2.50 × 200) = $500. Earnings for the expected scenario and the expansion scenarios are $1,000 and $2,000, respectively.

8. The investor would purchase 100 shares of Maxlever, and lend $4,000 at 10% interest. The returns for this position, and for the investment described in Problem 7, are summarized in the following table:

	Nolever		
	Recession	Expected	Expansion
EPS	$ 2.50	$ 5.00	$ 10.00
Earnings for 200 shares	$500.00	$1,000.00	$2,000.00

Net cost = ($40 × 200) = $8,000

	Maxlever		
	Recession	Expected	Expansion
EPS	$ 1.00	$ 6.00	$ 16.00
Earnings for 100 shares	$100.00	$ 600.00	$1,600.00
Plus: Interest on $4,000 at 10%	$400.00	$ 400.00	$ 400.00
Net earnings	$500.00	$1,000.00	$2,000.00

Net cost = ($40 × 100) + Amount loaned = $4,000 + $4,000 = $8,000

9. The solutions to Problems 7 and 8 indicate that the investor can earn the same returns from either strategy. The net cost of purchasing 200 shares of Nolever is $8,000. If the market value of Maxlever is $70,000, then the market value of the firm's equity is ($70,000 - $40,000) = $30,000, and the market value of a share is ($30,000/1,000) = $30. So the cost of the strategy of Problem 8 is $7,000. Since the same returns can be earned for a lower cost using the strategy of Problem 8, the investor would purchase the stock of Maxlever, rather than the stock of Nolever. This would result in an adjustment of the values of the two firms, until the values are equal. As in Problem 6, leverage does not affect firm value.

10. Given no taxes, M&M Proposition I (no taxes) applies and North's capital structure is irrelevant; hence, the value of the firm is: $EBIT/R_A = \$200/.16 = \$1250$. A debt/equity ratio of .25 indicates that the firm has $0.25 of debt for each dollar of equity. Therefore, North's capital structure is 80% equity, and the value of the equity is (.80 × $1250) = $1000. The value of the debt is ($1250 - $1000) = $250.

11. Using Proposition II, $R_E = R_A + (R_A - R_D) \times (D/E) = .16 + [(.16 - .12) \times .25] = .17 = 17\%$.

12. M&M Proposition I (with corporate taxes) states that the value of a levered firm, V_L, equals the value of the unlevered firm plus the value of the interest tax shield: $V_L = V_U + (T_C \times D)$. The value of North as an unlevered firm is: $V_U = EBIT(1 - T_C)/R_U = [\$200 \times (1 - .30)]/.20 = \$700$. The PV of the tax shield is $(T_C \times D) = (.30 \times \$400) = \$120$. And $V_L = V_U + (T_C \times D) = \$700 + \$120 = \$820$. The value of the firm's equity is ($820 - $400) = $420.

13. M&M Proposition II (with corporate taxes) indicates that the cost of equity for North is:

$$R_E = R_U + (R_U - R_D) \times (D/E) \times (1 - T_C) = .20 + (.20 - .12) \times (\$400/\$420) \times (1 - .30) = .25333.$$

The cost of equity capital is 25.333%. And $WACC = (E/V) \times R_E + (D/V) \times R_D \times (1 - T_C)$

$$= (\$420/\$820) \times .25333 + (\$400/\$820) \times .12 \times (1 - .30) = .17073$$

Therefore, the WACC for an unlevered firm is 20%, while the WACC for North Company is 17.073%.

14. Firm value is ($450,000/.15) = $3,000,000. Since MM is an all-equity firm, the value of the firm's equity is also $3,000,000. Price per share is ($3,000,000/100,000) = $30.

15. The NPV of the expansion equals -$400,000 + ($150,000/.15) = $600,000, so when the firm announces the expansion, firm value increases to ($3,000,000 + $600,000) = $3,600,000. The value of the firm's assets and the value of the equity each increase to $3,600,000. Price per share increases to ($3,600,000/100,000) = $36. This increase in value occurs immediately following the announcement of the expansion, but before the financing is obtained. To obtain $400,000 in equity financing, the firm sells ($400,000/$36) = 11,111 shares of stock. The proceeds of the stock issue are used to acquire the new assets, so firm value becomes ($3,000,000 + $600,000 + $400,000) = $4,000,000, which is the value of the equity. The price per share is still $36 after the financing; that is, ($4,000,000/111,111) = $36.

16. Firm value increases to $3,600,000 after the announcement of the expansion. When the firm issues $400,000 of new debt, the value of the assets increases to $4,000,000, but the value of the equity remains at $3,600,000. The value of the firm is the same as under the equity financing arrangement, as indicated by M&M Proposition I (no taxes). The price of the firm's stock is $36 after the announcement and before the financing is obtained, and remains at $36 after the financing is obtained.

17. Expected yearly income is: $450,000 + $150,000 - (.10 × $400,000) = $560,000. The expected return for the equityholders is ($560,000/$3,600,000) = 15.556%.

18. By M&M Proposition II (no taxes): $R_E = R_A + (R_A - R_D) \times (D/E) = .15 + (.15 - .10) \times$ ($400,000/$3,600,000) = .15556 = 15.556%.

CHAPTER 17

1. Prior to the stock dividend, the market value of the firm's equity is $40,000 and the share price is ($40,000/1,000) = $40. The stock dividend does not affect the total market value of the firm's equity, so the market value balance sheet does not change. However, since there are now an additional (.25 × 1,000) = 250 shares outstanding, value per share declines. The price per share, after the stock dividend, is ($40,000/1,250) = $32 after the stock dividend. Prior to the stock dividend, the market value of T. Agee's holdings is ($40 × 400) = $16,000. Or, since Agee owns (400/1,000) = 40% of the firm, the market value of his position is (.40 × $40,000) = $16,000. After the dividend, Agee owns (1.25 × 400) = 500 shares, which still represents (500/1,250) = 40% of the firm. The value of his position is: $32 × 500 = .40 × $40,000 = $16,000.

2. As in the case of the stock dividend, the stock split does not affect the total market value of the firm's equity. The stock split results in the distribution of one new share for each existing share; it is equivalent to a 100% stock dividend and results in the distribution of 1,000 new shares. The total number of shares is then (1,000 + 1,000) = 2,000. Market value per share, after the stock split, is ($40,000/2,000) = $20 after the stock dividend. After the stock split, Agee owns (2.00 × 400) = 800 shares. The value of his position is: $20 x 800 = .40 × $40,000 = $16,000.

3. The total value of Krane Pools is: $6,000/(1.20) + $72,000/(1.20)^2 = $55,000. The share price is ($55,000/1,000) = $55. Alternatively, the market value of one share equals the PV of the dividends per share to be paid at the end of each of the next two years: $6.00/(1.20) + $72.00/(1.20)^2$.

4. To pay $30,000 in dividends at the end of one year, Krane Pools could sell ($30,000 - $6,000) = $24,000 of common stock at the end of the year. The holders of this new common stock require a 20% rate of return, so they will require ($24,000 × 1.20) = $28,800 in dividends. The dividend payment to the existing stockholders at the end of the second year will be ($72,000 - $28,800) = $43,200. The value of the firm today is the PV of the future dividends to be paid to the existing stockholders:

$$\$30,000/1.20 + \$43,200/(1.20)^2 = \$55,000.$$

Firm value does not change with the change in dividend payments; furthermore, the value per share remains $55 under the new dividend policy.

5. The dividend payments in Problem 4 imply dividends per share of ($30,000/1,000) = $30 and ($43,200/1,000) = $43.20 at the end of one and two years, respectively. So Charles prefers to receive the following dividend payments at the end of one and two years respectively: ($30 × 100) = $3,000 and ($43.20 × 100) = $4,320. According to the dividend payments in Problem 3, dividends paid to Charles at the end of one year will be ($6 × 100) = $600. So Charles will sell ($3,000 - $600) = $2,400 of common stock at the end of the first year. By doing so, he forfeits ($2,400 × 1.20) = $2,880 at the end of the second year. So his total payment at the end of the second year is ($7,000 - $2,880) = $4,320. This is the same payment he would have received at the end of year two if Krane Pools followed the dividend policy in Problem 4.

6. The debt/equity ratio of 1/3 signifies that the firm has $1.00 of debt for every $3.00 of equity. If the firm retains all of the available $30,000 of equity financing then, to maintain the existing debt/equity ratio, the firm must raise (1/3 × $30,000) = $10,000 of debt financing. Therefore, the total financing available, if the firm does not obtain any new equity financing, is ($30,000 + $10,000) = $40,000.

7. The debt/equity ratio of 1/3 signifies that the firm's capital structure consists of $1.00 of debt and $3.00 of equity for each $4.00 of total financing. The capital structure is therefore ($1.00/$4.00) = 25% debt and ($3.00/$4.00) = 75% equity. To finance expenditures of $24,000 while maintaining the existing capital structure, the firm will use debt financing of (.25 × $24,000) = $6,000, and equity financing of (.75 × $24,000) = $18,000. The firm has $30,000 of internal equity financing available, so dividends are ($30,000 - $18,000) = $12,000.

8. If no external equity financing is obtained, total financing available is $40,000. To maintain the debt/equity ratio of 1/3, any additional financing is obtained as follows: 25% debt financing and 75% equity financing. The firm requires additional financing of ($60,000 - $40,000) = $20,000, which is obtained as follows: (.25 × $20,000) = $5,000 of additional debt financing and (.75 × $20,000) = $15,000 of additional equity financing. Total equity financing consists of $30,000 of internally generated funds and $15,000 of new equity; total debt financing is equal to ($10,000 + $5,000) = $15,000. In this situation, the firm pays no dividends.

9. Prior to the payment of the dividend, the market value per share is ($100,000/2,000) = $50. The owner of 500 shares owns stock with a total market value of ($50 × 500) = $25,000. After the payment of the dividends, the market value balance sheet appears as follows:

Market value balance sheet

Excess cash	$ 0	Debt	$ 0
Other assets	$ 90,000	Equity	$ 90,000
Total	$ 90,000		$ 90,000

Dividends are ($10,000/2,000) = $5 per share. Market value per share is now ($90,000/2,000) = $45. The owner of 500 shares owns stock with a market value of ($45 × 500) = $22,500, and has received dividends of ($5 × 500) = $2,500. So the market value of his position is ($22,500 + $2,500) = $25,000, which is the same as it was prior to the dividend payment.

10. The firm's market value balance sheet is identical to the balance sheet above. At $50 per share, the firm can repurchase ($10,000/$50) = 200 shares. Since there are now (2,000 - 200) = 1,800 shares outstanding, the share value is ($90,000/1,800) = $50. The stockholder who owns 500 shares has a position with a total market value of ($50 × 500) = $25,000. Since this market value is the same as the computed above, the stockholder is unaffected by either the dividend payment or the stock repurchase. However, the advantage of the stock repurchase is that the stockholder's tax payments are less than they would be with a dividend payment. In Problem 9, the stockholder pays income taxes on the total dividend payment of $2,500. With the stock repurchase, the stockholder does not pay any income taxes, unless he chooses to create homemade dividends by selling a portion of his holdings. If, for example, he chooses to sell stock in an amount sufficient to duplicate the $2,500 dividend payment he would have received with the dividend payment, he would sell ($2,500/$50) = 50 shares. However, even in this case, his tax payment is less than it would be in the event of the dividend payment; here, he would pay taxes only on the capital gain resulting from the sale of stock, rather than on the full $2,500.

11. Since the balance sheet shows market values, the stock is worth ($60,000/1,000) = $60 per share today (cum dividend). The ex-dividend price will be ($60 - $3) = $57. Notice that once the dividend is paid, Reebop has $3,000 less cash, so total equity is worth $57,000, or ($57,000/1,000) = $57 per share.

12. After the stock dividend is distributed, (1,000 × 1.20) = 1,200 shares will be outstanding. Total share value is still $60,000; that is, the total market value of the equity is unchanged. Therefore, the per share value is ($60,000/1,200) = $50. Notice that this is not 20% less than the old price; rather the old price is 120% of the new price: ($50 × 1.20) = $60.

13. Reebop will purchase ($3,000/$60) = $50 shares, leaving 950 outstanding. The total equity value will be $57,000, so that the market price is still ($57,000/950) = $60 per share.

Consider an investor who owns 100 shares. With the cash dividend, this investor receives ($3.00 × 100) = $300 in cash and has 100 shares with a total value of ($57 x 100) = $5,700. Using the $300, the investor could purchase ($300/$57) = 5.263 more shares and have 105.263 shares worth $57 each, for a total value of $6,000. With the repurchase, the investor has 100 shares worth $60 each, if she does not sell any shares. Alternatively, she could sell ($300/60) = 5 shares. As a result, she would have 95 shares, with a total value of ($60 × 95) = $5,700, and $300 in cash, for a total of $6,000 again.

14. The price will decrease by the after-tax amount of the dividend, or [$4.00 × (1 - .40)] = $2.40. The ex-dividend price will be ($60.00 - $2.40) = $57.60.

15. Consider the following scenario: you buy a share just before it goes ex-dividend, and sell immediately thereafter. You will have an after-tax dividend of $2.40 and a capital loss of D, the decline in the stock price. Your after-tax loss is [D × (1 - .20)]. You will be indifferent with regard to buying the share with the dividend only if: $2.40 = D × (1 - .20). In this scenario, the price decrease will be D = ($2.40/.80) = $3.00. In reality, the capital gains are not taxed until the gain (or loss) is realized, so the size of the price decline would be more difficult to determine; however, it would probably be less than the amount of the dividend but more than the after-tax value of the dividend.

16. The 10% dividend yield is equivalent to a 6% after-tax return. Since the total expected after-tax return is 20%, the expected capital gain is (20% - 6%) = 14%. The after-tax return is thus "grossed up" to a pre-tax return of (10% + 14%) = 25%.

17. The value of your stock is the PV of the future dividends, discounted at 20%, or $10 per share. The total value of your position is $200. An annuity of $130.91 per year for two years has the same PV. At date 1, your stock will be worth the PV of the liquidating dividend, or $11.50. You will receive $10 in total dividends at date 1. You will have to sell $120.91 worth of stock, or ($120.91/11.5) = 10.514 shares, leaving you with 9.486 shares. At the end of the second year, you will receive (9.486 × $13.80) in dividends, for a total of $130.91, thereby accomplishing your goal.

18. Your liquidating dividend will be $282, which is $6 greater than it would have been.

CHAPTER 18

1.	1. Accounts payable increased by $20; **Source** of cash.
	2. A $10 dividend was paid; **Use** of cash.
	3. Inventories were increased by $120; **Use** of cash.
	4. Short-term bank borrowing increased by $80; **Source** of cash.
	5. Accounts receivable increased by $30; **Use** of cash.

2. To compute the inventory period, we first compute the inventory turnover ratio:

Inventory turnover = Cost of goods sold/Average inventory = $16,000/$1,200 = 13.33 times

Inventory is 'turned over' 13.33 times per year, so the Inventory period = 365/Inventory Turnover = 365/13.33 = 27.38 days. The inventory turnover period is the average length of time required to order, produce and sell a product; inventory turned over every 27.38 days, on average.

3. To compute the accounts receivable period, we first compute the accounts receivable turnover ratio:

Receivables turnover = Credit Sales/Average Receivables = $30,000/$1,950 = 15.38 times
Receivables period = 365/Receivables turnover = 365//15.38 = 23.73 days.

Receivables turned over 15.38 times during the year, or every 23.73 days, on average.

4. To compute the accounts payable period, we first compute the accounts payable turnover ratio:

Payables turnover = Cost of goods sold/Average payables = $16,000/$1,000 = 16.0 times
Payables period = 365/Payables turnover = 365/16.0 = 22.81 days.

5. From Problems 2 and 3, the operating cycle equals Inventory period + Accounts Receivable period

$$= 27.38 \text{ days} + 23.73 \text{ days} = 51.11 \text{ days} \approx 51 \text{ days.}$$

6. From problems 4 and 5, the cash cycle equals Operating cycle - Accounts payable period

$$= 51.11 \text{ days} - 22.81 \text{ days} = 28.30 \text{ days} \approx 28 \text{ days.}$$

7. With a 60-day collection period, Osiris collects (30/90) = ⅓ of sales in the quarter in which they occur; ⅔ of sales are collected the following quarter. Cash collections for the first quarter are:

$$\text{Cash collections} = \text{Beginning accounts receivable} + (\tfrac{1}{3} \times \text{Sales})$$
$$= \$210 + (\tfrac{1}{3} \times \$510) = \$210 + \$170 = \$380$$

Cash collections for each quarter are indicated in the following table:

	Qtr. 1	Qtr. 2	Qtr. 3	Qtr. 4
Beginning Receivables	$210	$340	$580	$300
Sales	510	870	450	600
Cash Collections	380	630	730	500
Ending Receivables	340	580	300	400

8. With a 45-day accounts payable period, half of purchases from suppliers are paid in the quarter in which they are ordered and half are deferred one quarter. Projected sales in the first quarter of the next year are ($510 × 1.10) = $561. Projected cash outflows are:

	Qtr. 1	Qtr. 2	Qtr. 3	Qtr. 4
Payment of Accounts	$345	$330	$263	$290
Wages, taxes, other expenses	170	290	150	200
Long-term financing expenses (interest and dividends)	10	10	10	10
Total	$525	$630	$423	$500

9. The net cash inflows are:

	Qtr. 1	Qtr. 2	Qtr. 3	Qtr. 4
Total cash collections	$380	$630	$730	$500
-Total cash disbursements	525	630	423	500
Net cash inflow	-$145	$ 0	$307	$ 0

284

The cumulative surplus (or deficit) is computed as follows:

	Qtr. 1	Qtr. 2	Qtr. 3	Qtr. 4
Beginning cash balance	$ 0	-$145	-$145	$162
+Net cash inflow	- 145	0	307	0
Ending Cash balance	-$145	-$145	$162	$162
-Minimum cash balance	10	10	10	10
Cumulative surplus (deficit)	-$155	-$155	$152	$152

Osiris has a highly seasonal sales pattern. Because purchases are made in advance and collections are deferred, Osiris will have an ongoing pattern of short-term deficits followed by surpluses.

10. The complete short-term financial plan is presented in the following table:

	Qtr. 1	Qtr. 2	Qtr. 3	Qtr. 4
Beginning cash balance	$ 0	$ 10.0	$ 10.00	$149.35
+Net cash inflow	- 145	0.0	307.00	0.00
+New short-term borrowing	155	6.2	--	--
-Interest on short-term borrowing	--	6.2	6.45	--
-Short-term borrowing repaid	--	--	161.20	--
Ending cash balance	$ 10	$ 10.0	$149.35	$149.35
-Minimum cash balance	10	10.0	10.00	10.00
Cumulative surplus (deficit)	$ 0	$ 0.0	$139.35	$139.35
Beginning short-term borrowing	$ 0	$155.0	$161.20	$ 0.00
+Change in short-term debt	155	6.2	- 161.20	0.00
Ending short-term debt	$155	$161.2	$ 0.00	$ 0.00

With no borrowing, the cumulative deficit at the end of quarter 1 is $155. Consequently, short-term borrowing of $155 is required. Interest of (.04 × $155) = $6.20 must be paid during quarter 2, and additional short-term borrowing of $6.20 is required during the quarter because the net cash inflow is zero; ending short-term debt is ($155 + $6.20) = $161.20. Interest paid during quarter 3 is (.04 × $161.20) = $6.45, and the net cash inflow of $307 is more than sufficient to pay total debt of $161.20.

11. With a 30-day collection period, Osiris collects (60/90) = ⅔ of sales in the quarter in which they occur; ⅓ of sales are collected the following quarter. Cash collections for the first quarter are:

$$\text{Cash collections} = \text{Beginning accounts receivable} + (⅔ \times \text{Sales})$$
$$= \$210 + (⅔ \times \$510) = \$210 + \$340 = \$550$$

Cash collections for each quarter are indicated in the following table:

	Qtr. 1	Qtr. 2	Qtr. 3	Qtr. 4
Beginning Receivables	$210	$170	$290	$150
Sales	510	870	450	600
Cash Collections	550	750	590	550
Ending Receivables	170	290	150	200

12. With a 72-day accounts payable period, 20% of purchases from suppliers are paid in the quarter in which they are ordered and 80% are deferred one quarter. Only payment of accounts and, consequently, total cash outflows are affected by the change in the accounts payable period. Projected cash outflows are:

	Qtr. 1	Qtr. 2	Qtr. 3	Qtr. 4
Payment of Accounts	$291	$393	$240	$296
Wages, taxes, other expenses	170	290	150	200
Long-term financing expenses (interest and dividends)	10	10	10	10
Total	$471	$693	$400	$506

13. The net cash inflows are:

	Qtr. 1	Qtr. 2	Qtr. 3	Qtr. 4
Total cash collections	$550	$750	$590	$550
-Total cash disbursements	471	693	400	506
Net cash inflow	$ 79	$ 57	$190	$ 44

The cumulative surplus (or deficit) is:

	Qtr. 1	Qtr. 2	Qtr. 3	Qtr. 4
Beginning cash balance	$ 0	$ 79	$136	$326
+Net cash inflow	79	57	190	44
Ending Cash balance	$ 79	$136	$326	$370
-Minimum cash balance	10	10	10	10
Cumulative surplus (deficit)	$ 69	$126	$316	$360

In comparing the results of this problem with those of Problem 9, we note that Osiris now expects a positive cash inflow for the first three quarters, and that the firm has a cumulative surplus throughout the year; in the earlier problem, a deficit occurs during the first two quarters due to delays in collections. The differences in this problem result primarily from the earlier collections, although the delayed payments also contribute. It is important to note that total collections and outflows for the year do not change substantially; rather, it is the timing of cash flows which produce the results observed here.

14. The complete short-term financial plan is presented in the following table:

	Qtr. 1	Qtr. 2	Qtr. 3	Qtr. 4
Beginning cash balance	$ 0	$ 79	$136	$326
+Net cash inflow	79	57	190	44
+New short-term borrowing	--	--	--	--
-Interest on short-term borrowing	--	--	--	--
-Short-term borrowing repaid	--	--	--	--
Ending cash balance	$ 79	$136	$326	$370
-Minimum cash balance	10	10	10	10
Cumulative surplus (deficit)	$ 69	$126	$316	$360
Beginning short-term borrowing	$ 0	$ 0	$ 0	$ 0
+Change in short-term debt	0	0	0	0
Ending short-term debt	$ 0	$ 0	$ 0	$ 0

Since there are no deficits, and we have assumed that a surplus does not earn interest, the complete financial plan does not add any information not already apparent from the solution to Problem 13.

15. The inventory period is 39.54 days, the accounts receivable period is 31.04 days and the operating cycle is 70.58 days.

16. The accounts payable period is 13.69 days and the cash cycle is 56.89 days.

17. An inventory period of 30 days is equivalent to inventory turnover of (365/30) = 12.17 times per year. With cost of goods sold equal to $6,000 per year, the average level of inventory which would be required is $6000/12.17 = equals $493.01, which is a reduction of ($650 - $493.01) = $156.99 in the level of inventory; consequently, the firm will require, on average, $156.99 less short-term financing with this reduction in the inventory turnover period.

18. An accounts receivable turnover period of 25 days is equivalent to accounts receivable turnover of 14.60 times per year. The average level of accounts receivable is determined by solving for x in the following equation: $10,000/x = 14.60. Therefore, the new level of accounts receivable is $684.93, which represents a reduction of ($850 - $684.93) = $165.07 in the average level of accounts receivable and, consequently, in the average amount of short-term financing required by the firm.

19. An accounts payable period of 18 days is equivalent to accounts payable turnover of (365/18) = 20.28 times per year. The average level of accounts payable which results from this increase is indicated by the value of x in the following equation: $6000/x = 20.28. The new level of accounts payable increases to $295.86, which is an increase of ($295.86 - $225) = $70.86 in the level of accounts payable and consequently a decrease in the amount of short-term financing required from other sources.

20. The operating cycle is 55 days and the cash cycle is 37 days. We have indicated a reduction in the cash cycle here and a resulting reduction in short-term financing requirements as calculated in Problems 17 - 19; however, it is important to realize that changes such as those suggested above cannot be achieved without incurring related costs. So the benefit associated with reductions in financing requirements must be weighed against costs such as potential loss of sales due to reduction in credit period.

21. Assuming a single payment at the end of the year, with no compounding of interest, we have the following calculations:

$$\text{Interest paid} = .13 \times \$400,000 = \$52,000$$
$$\text{Compensating balance} = .06 \times \$400,000 = \$24,000$$
$$\text{Effective interest rate} = \text{Interest paid/Amount available} = \$52,000/\$376,000 = .13830$$

The effective rate is 13.830%, rather than the stated 13%, because the interest paid is computed on the basis of a $400,000 loan, whereas the actual proceeds to the borrower are only $376,000.

22. The size of the loan is x in the following equation: (1 - .06) × x = $500,000;

$$x = \$500,000/.94 = \$531,914.89$$

The size of the loan is $531,914.89 and the compensating balance requirement is ($531,914.89 - $500,000) = (.06 × $531,914.89) = $31,914.89. Interest paid = .13 × $531,914.89 = $69,148.94, so the effective rate = Interest paid/Amount available = $69,184.94/$500,000 = .13830.

23. Kristy receives 97.5¢ for each dollar of receivables, but does not have to wait forty days to collect payment; at the end of forty days, Kristy's customers pay the full amount of the receivables to the factor. This is equivalent to paying 2.5¢ to obtain financing of 97.5¢ for 40 days, which is an interest rate of ($.025/$.975) = .025641 = 2.5641% for forty days. Assuming 360 days in a year, and therefore nine forty-day periods in a year, the effective annual rate is: EAR = $(1.025641)^9 - 1 = 25.59\%$.

CHAPTER 19

1. *Float* is the firm's available balance minus the book balance. For *disbursement float*, the available balance is positive and the book balance is zero; so *disbursement float* is $(8 \times \$5,000) = \$40,000$. For *collection float*, the available balance is zero and the book balance is positive; therefore, *collection float* is $[4 \times (-\$7,000)] = -\$28,000$. The *net float* equals $[\$40,000 + (-\$28,000)] = \$12,000$.

At any given time, the firm typically has disbursed checks which have not yet cleared, with a total value of $\$40,000$; that is, $\$40,000$ is the available balance and the book balance is zero. In addition, the firm has received checks with a total value of $\$28,000$, which are not yet available; therefore, the available balance is zero and the book balance is $\$28,000$. For the disbursement float, float = Available balance - Book balance = $\$40,000 - \$0 = \$40,000$. For the collection float: float = Available balance - Book balance = $\$0 - \$28,000 = -\$28,000$. For the net float: Float = Available balance - Book balance = $\$40,000 - \$28,000 = \$12,000$. Thus, the firm's book balance is typically $\$12,000$ less than its bank cash.

2. The total float during the month is: $(70 \times \$300 \times 4) + (30 \times \$200 \times 5) = \$114,000$. Assuming a 30-day month, the average daily float equals Total float/Total days = $\$114,000/30 = \$3,800$. On an average day, the firm has $\$3,800$ in the mail or otherwise uncollected.

3. Total monthly collections are: $(70 \times \$300) + (30 \times \$200) = \$27,000$. The weighted average delay is: $[(\$21,000/\$27,000) \times 4] + [(\$6000/\$27,000) \times 5] = 4.2222$ days. Average daily receipts are $(\$27,000/30) = \$900$. Average daily float = Average daily receipts $\times$ Weighted average delay = $\$900 \times 4.2222 = \$3,800$.

4. If the weighted average delay is reduced from 4.2222 days to 2.2222 days, average daily float = $\$900 \times 2.2222 = \$2,000$, so float is reduced by $(\$3800 - \$2000) = (2 \times \$900) = \$1800$. Since this $\$1,800$ becomes available to the firm at the time that the lockbox system is instituted, the PV of the change is $\$1,800$. This $\$1,800$ is available to the firm as long as the lockbox system is in effect. The cost of maintaining the lockbox is $\$200$ per year. The PV of the perpetuity is $(\$200/.09) = \$2,222.22$. The NPV of the lockbox system is $(\$1,800 - \$2,222.22) = -\$422.22$, so the system is unacceptable.

5. The maximum fee the firm would pay is the amount such that the NPV of the lockbox system is zero. This is the amount such that the PV of the fee equals the PV of the system. To determine the maximum fee, solve for x: $(x/.09) = \$1,800$ and $x = \$1,800 \times .09 = \$162$. If the firm pays $\$162$ per year, the present value of the fee is $(\$162/.09) = \$1,800$, and the NPV is zero.

6. Average daily collections are $(\$100 \times 10,000) = \$1$ million. Accelerating collections by three days would increase the firm's collected bank balance by $(3 \times \$1 \text{ million}) = \$3$ million, so the PV of the lockbox service is $\$3$ million. The daily cost of the variable fee is $(\$.05 \times 10,000) = \$500$. Since this is a perpetuity, the PV is $(\$500/.0002) = \$2,500,000$. The NPV of the service is $(\$3,000,000 - \$2,500,000) = \$500,000$, so the service should be adopted.

7. To compute the PV of the $\$5,000$ fee, first compute the annual interest rate: $(1.0002)^{365} - 1 = .07572 = 7.572\%$. To maintain the benefit of the lockbox system, the $\$5,000$ fee is paid every year; the PV of this perpetuity is $(\$5000/.07572) = \$66,033$. The total PV of the costs is $(\$2,500,000 + \$66,033) = \$2,566,033$. The NPV is $(\$3,000,000 - \$2,566,033) = \$433,967$. The service is still acceptable.

8. The $500,000 can be viewed as a reduction in the $3 million available cash calculated in Problem 12, so the PV of the lockbox system is $2,500,000. Since the PV of the costs (from Problem 13) is $2,566,033, the NPV of the service is -$66,033; the service should not be adopted.

9. The firm will be indifferent if the PV of the cost of the service is exactly equal to the $3,000,000 PV computed in the solution to Problem 12. Since the PV of the costs, without the compensating balance, is $2,566,033, the compensating balance which leaves the firm indifferent is ($3,000,000 - $2,566,033) = $433,967. Given this figure, the firm might then negotiate the size of the compensating balance with the bank. The firm would adopt the lockbox service only if the bank agreed to accept a compensating balance below this figure. Otherwise, the service has little value to the firm.

10. The concentration banking system would increase the firm's collected bank balance by ($750,000 × 2) = $1,500,000, but an additional $350,000 would be required for compensating balances. The net result would be that ($1,500,000 - $350,000) = $1,150,000 can be invested at a 6%, providing net savings of ($1,150,000 × .06) = $69,000. So the concentration banking system should be implemented.

11. The firm could increase its disbursement float by $1.5 million. Investing this amount generates $225 per day. The extra cost would be $1,500 per day. The firm should not adopt the plan.

CHAPTER 19 APPENDIX

1. The target cash balance is:

$$C^* = \sqrt{(2T \times F)/r}$$

$$= \sqrt{(2 \times \$2,500,000 \times \$50)/.10}$$

$$= \$\sqrt{2,500,000,000} = \$50,000$$

2. The average cash balance is: $(C + 0)/2 = \$50,000/2 = \$25,000$. The annual opportunity cost is: $(C/2) \times r = \$25,000 \times .10 = \$2,500$, and the number of orders during the year is $T/C = \$2,500,000/\$50,000 = 50$. The annual trading cost is $(T/C) \times F = 50 \times \$50 = \$2,500$. Total cost is the sum of the opportunity cost and the trading cost: $(\$2,500 + \$2,500) = \$5,000$.

3. If a $50,000 balance is held, the opportunity, trading, and total costs are $5,000, $1,250, and $6,250, respectively. For a $100,000 balance, the costs are $10,000, $625, and $10,625, respectively. Note that the total costs for both the $50,000 and $100,000 balances are higher than the total costs for the $25,000 balance, as derived in Problem 2. This result is to be expected since the BAT model identifies the cash balance which minimizes the sum of these costs.

4. There are two approaches to computing the new target cash balance for this problem. First, we can compute the solution directly by substituting the appropriate values in the equation for C^*. The alternative approach is to note that the value of F in this problem is four times the value in Problem 1. Since F is in the numerator of the fraction, the value of the figure inside the square root sign is now four times its value in Problem 1. Since we take the square root of this figure, the value of C^* is twice the value in Problem 1. Consequently, the target cash balance here is $(2 \times \$50,000) = \$100,000$. Since the target cash balance is double that of Problem 1, the opportunity cost is also double: $(C/2) \times r = (\$100,000/2)$

× .10 = $5000. At this point, it is not necessary to compute the trading costs, because the opportunity costs and the trading costs are equal when the firm holds a cash balance equal to C*; therefore, the trading costs are $5000 and the total costs are $10,000.

This problem demonstrates the fact that there is a direct relationship between the fixed transaction cost of selling marketable securities and the target cash balance. This is an intuitively reasonable result, because the increased cost of selling securities makes it more economical to hold larger cash balances.

5. As in the solution to Problem 4, the result here can be computed directly. Alternatively, we can take note of the fact that, since r is now half of its previous value, the fraction doubles in value. Consequently the target cash balance here is equal to the solution in Problem 1 times the square root of 2:

$$\$50,000 \times \sqrt{2} = \$70,710.68$$

This solution demonstrates the inverse relationship between the interest rate and the target cash balance; as the interest rate decreases, the target cash balance increases because the opportunity cost of holding additional cash decreases. Similarly, as the interest rate increases, the target cash balance decreases because it becomes more expensive to hold larger balances.

6. The variance of the daily cash flows is $\sigma^2 = (50)^2 = 2,500$. The target cash balance is:

$$C^* = L + [(\tfrac{3}{4} \times F \times \sigma^2)/r]^{\tfrac{1}{3}}$$
$$= \$200 + [(\tfrac{3}{4} \times \$100 \times \$2,500)/.0003]^{\tfrac{1}{3}} \$200 + \$855 = \$1,055$$

The upper limit is: $U^* = (3 \times C^*) - (2 \times L) = (3 \times \$1,055) - (2 \times \$200) = \$2765$. The average cash balance equals $[(4 \times C^*) - L]/3 = [(4 \times \$1,055) - \$200]/3 = \$1340$. When the cash balance reaches $U^* = \$2,765$, the firm returns to its target balance $C^* = 1055$ by investing $(U^* - C^*) = \$1710$ in marketable securities. When the balance declines to $L = \$200$, the firm sells $(C^* - L) = \$855$ dollars of marketable securities in order to increase the cash balance to $C^* = \$1055$.

CHAPTER 20

1. If the retailer does not take the discount, then she must pay the net amount: ($200 × 10) = $2,000. Payment must be made within forty days after the invoice date. For a seasonal product such as this, the invoice date might be May 1, for example, irrespective of whether the shipment is made prior to that date; in this case, the $2,000 payment would be due within forty days of the May 1 invoice date.

2. The retailer must pay within 20 days of the invoice date. The discount is 2% so the retailer must remit: (1 - .02) × $200 × 10 = $1,960. If she does not take the discount, she can than pay the net amount within 40 days, rather than 20 days; she receives 20 days credit if she does not take the discount.

3. By not taking the discount, the customer is actually obtaining $1,960 of financing for 20 days, from day 20 to day 40; the cost of financing is the additional $40 which must be paid on day 40. The interest rate for this 20-day period is ($40/$1,960) = .020408 = 2.0408%. Since there are (365/20) = 18.25 20-day periods in a year, the effective rate is: EAR = $(1.020408)^{18.25} - 1 = 1.44585 - 1 = .44585 = 44.585\%$. A customer who does not take the discount is paying an effective annual rate of 44.585% to finance the $1,960 payment.

4. If we assume that all customers who take the discount pay on the twentieth day, while all customers who do not take the discount pay on the fortieth day, then the average collection period (ACP) is:

$$ACP = (.80 \times 20 \text{ days}) + (.20 \times 40 \text{ days}) = 24 \text{ days}$$

5. Icarus has average daily sales of $[(\$200 \times 600)/30] = \$4,000$. The ACP from Problem 4, is 24 days. So the average level of accounts receivable is: Average daily sales $\times$ ACP $= \$4,000 \times 24 = \$96,000$

6. The solution to Problem 5 indicates that average daily sales are $4,000. So the daily investment in accounts receivable is $(.80 \times \$4,000) = \$3,200$. The average collection period is 24 days, as computed in Problem 4. Therefore, the average investment in receivables is $(\$3,200 \times 24) = \$76,800$.

7. To solve this problem, we note: Accounts receivable $=$ Average daily credit sales $\times$ ACP. Let X represent Average daily credit sales; substitute and solve: $\$600,000 = X \times 30$ days. $X = \$600,000/30 = \$20,000$. Therefore, annual credit sales equal $(\$20,000 \times 365) = \$7,300,000$.

8. Suppose the product costs $100. The firm receives $97 if the discount is taken. If it is not, the firm receives $3, or $(\$3/\$97) = 3.0928\%$, more. This 3.0928% is earned by extending $(60 - 15) = 45$ additional days credit. There are approximately $(360/45) = 8$ such periods per year. The effective annual rate is therefore: EAR $= (1.030928)^8 - 1 = .27593 = 27.593\%$. The calculation here does not depend on the cost of the product since the 3.0928% figure would apply regardless of purchase price.

9. For terms of 1.5/20, net 45, the EAR equals $(1.015228)^{14.4} - 1 = .24313 = 24.313\%$. For terms of 1/10, net 40, the EAR is $(1.010101)^{12} - 1 = .12818 = 12.818\%$.

10. For terms of 3/15, net 60, the firm would have to borrow 97% of the invoice amount in order to take advantage of the discount. Interest on the loan would then accumulate at the rate of 1.5% per month, or approximately 2.25% for 45 days, at which time we assume that the firm would repay the bank loan. Let x represent the net amount, so that the bank loan is .97x and interest plus principal of $[(.97x)(1.0225)] = .9918x$ is repaid to the bank after 45 days. Since this is less than the net amount of the invoice, the firm is better off borrowing from the bank than paying the net amount.

In general, if the annualized effective rate exceeds the borrowing rate, the firm is better off borrowing from the bank to take advantage of the discount. Therefore, for terms of 1.5/20, net 45, the firm should borrow in order to take the discount, but for terms of 1/10, net 40, the firm should pay the net amount.

11. $P = \$50$, $v = \$40$, $Q = 300$, $Q' = 345$, and $r = 1.5\%$. For the current policy, monthly sales are: $P \times Q = (\$50 \times 300) = \$15,000$ and monthly variable costs are $v \times Q = (\$40 \times 300) = \$12,000$. The cash flow is: Cash flow (old policy) $= (P - v) \times Q = (\$50 - \$40) \times 300 = \$3000$. If credit is granted, then: Cash flow (new policy) $= (P - v) \times Q' = (\$50 - \$40) \times 345 = \$3450$. The incremental cash flow equals Cash flow (new policy) - Cash flow (old policy)

$$= (P - v) \times (Q' - Q) = (\$50 - \$40) \times (345 - 300) = \$450$$

Since the incremental cash flow is a monthly annuity, the PV $= [(P - v) \times (Q' - Q)]/r = \$450/.015 = \$30,000$. The cost of the change in credit policy is the sum of two components. First, the variable cost of producing the additional units: $v(Q' - Q) = \$40 \times (345 - 300) = \$1,800$. Second, since collections are permanently delayed by thirty days, the following cost is also incurred: PQ = $50 × 300 = $15,000. The sum of these costs is: PQ + v(Q' - Q) = $15,000 + $1,800 = $16,800. The NPV of the change in credit policy equals -[PQ + v(Q' - Q)] + [(P - v) × (Q' - Q)]/r = -$16,800 + $30,000 = $13,200. So the change in credit policy to terms of net 30 days is beneficial.

12. The firm invests the following in production costs today: (v × Q') = ($40 × 345) = $13,800. Also, the firm forgoes the following net cash inflow, which would be received this month under the existing credit policy: (P - v) × Q = ($50 - $40) × 300 = $3,000. Under the new credit policy, the firm then receives the following cash inflow from payments thirty days later:

$$(P \times Q') = (\$50 \times 345) = \$17,250$$

The PV of this inflow is ($17250/1.015) = $16,995.0739. The NPV of this transaction, if we regard this as a one-month change in policy, is: $16,995.0739 - ($13,800 + $3,000) = $195.0739. Since this NPV actually repeats itself each month, the NPV of the change in credit policy is: $195.0739 + ($195.0739/.015) = $13,200; the same as the NPV computed in the solution to Problem 11.

13. The firm's investment in accounts receivable is comprised of two parts. The first is the amount the firm would have received during the current month if the existing credit policy remained unchanged:

$$P \times Q = \$50 \times 300 = \$15,000$$

The second part is the increase in the investment in receivables which results from the increase in sales:

$$v \times (Q' - Q) = \$40 \times (345 - 300)] = \$1800$$

The total incremental investment in receivables is: (PQ) + [v(Q' - Q)] = $15,000 + $1,800 = $16,800. The required return on this investment for one month is: Carrying cost = [(PQ) + v(Q' - Q)] × r = $16,800 × .015 = $252. The monthly benefit derived from the investment in receivables is:

$$(P - v) \times (Q' - Q) = (\$50 - \$40) \times (345 - 300) = \$450$$

The monthly net benefit is ($450 - $252) = $198. The NPV of the change is ($198/.015) = $13,200.

14. Let P = $195, P' = $200, v = $150, Q = 1,000, r = 1.0%, π = 2.0%, and d = 2.5%. The cost of the change is the firm's investment in production costs plus the firm's foregone net cash inflow; since the change in credit policy does not affect Q, this cost can be computed as follows:

$$(v \times Q) + [(P - v) \times Q] = P \times Q = \$195 \times 1000 = \$195,000$$

The monthly inflow for the current policy is (P - v) × Q = ($195 - $150) × 1000 = $45,000. The monthly cash inflow for the proposed policy is: [(1 - π)P' - v] × Q = [(.98 × $200) - $150] × 1000 = $46,000. The net incremental cash flow is therefore ($46,000 - $45,000) = $1,000. The net incremental cash flow can also be computed as follows:

$$P' \times Q \times (d - \pi) = \$200 \times 1000 \times (.025 - .020) = \$1,000$$

The NPV of the change in credit policy equals NPV = -(P × Q) + [P' × Q × (d - π)]/r = -$195,000 + $1000/.01 = -$195,000 + $100,000 = -$95,000. Since the NPV of the change in credit policy is negative, the firm should not make the change.

15. Let P' = $500, Q = 200, v = $350, r = 1.0%, π = 30.0%. The cost of granting credit to Mr. Hernandez is the product variable cost expended this month: v × Q = $350 × 200 = $70,000. The cash inflow to Gooden-Carter in one month is: (1 - π) × P' × Q = .70 × $500 × 200 = $70,000. The NPV = -(v × Q) + [(1 - π) × P' × Q]/(1 + r) = -$70,000 + $70,000/(1.01) = -$693.07. Since the NPV is negative, Gooden-Carter should not extend credit to the new customer.

16. The cost to Gooden-Carter of extending credit is still $70,000, as in the solution to Problem 15. In one month, Mr. Hernandez will either default, or he will pay (P' × Q) = $10,000 and purchase an additional 200 units. The probability that he will not default is (1 - π) = 70% and the expected net cash inflow in one month is: (1 - π) × (P' - v) × Q = .70 × ($500 - $350) × 200 = $21,000. The NPV of the decision to grant credit equals -$70,000 + $21,000/(.01) = $2,030,000. Since the NPV is positive, it is beneficial for the firm to extend credit to the new customer.

CHAPTER 21

1. Comparison of various hedging instruments:

a)   Forward and futures contracts *obligate* the buyer (seller) to take (make) delivery of a specified asset at a specified point in time for a specified price. Options obligate the contract seller to sell to (buy from) the contract the underlying asset only if the contract seller chooses to exercise.

b)   Futures and options contracts are highly standardized with regard to the quality and quantity of the underlying asset, and are therefore more liquid. Forward contracts can be "customized" to meet the needs of the buyer and the seller, but are consequently less liquid.

c)   Money changes hands immediately when an option contract is purchased; more money will change hands if the option is subsequently exercised. With a forward contract, no money changes hands until the transaction occurs on the specified date. The positions of the parties to a futures contract are marked-to-market daily, so money changes hands whenever daily prices change.

2. Rob can hedge his capital gain by buying puts on his stock. If the price of the stock falls, the losses on his stock position will be offset by the gains on his option position. (Remember - calls increase in value when prices rise, and puts increase in value when prices fall.) If the price of the stock continues to rise (or stays the same), Rob is only out the put premium.

3. The values of Rob's calls at expiration appear in the table below, given various stock prices.

Stock Price	Option Value
$70	$20
$60	10
$50	0
$40	0
$30	0

4. The payoff table for the purchase of an ICM put with a $50 strike price is below.

Stock Price	Option Value
$70	$ 0
$60	0
$50	0
$40	10
$30	20

5. The purchaser of a convertible bond always has the option of *not* converting; as such, the bond is valued as an otherwise identical bond without the conversion feature (i.e., as a "straight" bond). The option to convert may have no immediate value at the time is purchased; however, the fact that it remains "alive" for a long period over which the value of the underlying asset's value could rise gives it a positive value. Since a convertible bond is equivalent to a straight bond plus an option, its value must be equal to the sum of the values those two assets would have if valued separately. In an efficient market, the two components will be priced on the basis of their expected values at any point in time. In other words, a convertible bond will, like any other financial asset in an efficient market, constitute a zero-NPV investment, so nobody "wins" <u>ex ante</u>.

6. Since Herb is currently obligated to **make** delivery of 1000 barrels of oil, he can lock in the futures price (i.e. hedge against price increases) by *buying* contracts, which will obligate him to **take** delivery of 1,000 barrels of oil. Assuming futures contracts are currently traded on the underlying asset, Herb will have the added benefit of liquidity, daily price reporting, and lower credit risk by employing futures contracts rather than forward contracts.

7. A person who buys or sells a futures contract without having an offsetting position is **speculating**, rather than hedging. If Herb is correct in his belief that heating oil prices are going to rise, he will profit by buying a contract today. The contract obligates the holder to take delivery of heating oil at, say, $15 per barrel; if the market price of oil rises to, say, $20, a contract for $15 oil clearly has value to the holder. Like most speculators, Herb will "zero out" his position as the contract nears maturity by taking an identical but opposite position, i.e., selling a contract in this case. Thus, his net position will be zero.

CHAPTER 22

1. On the expiration date, Walden stock will be worth either $60 or $80; that is, $S_1 = $60 or $S_1 = $80. If the stock is worth $60, the option to buy at $70 is worthless; that is, $C_1 = 0$ if $S_1 \leq E$. If the stock is worth $80 on the expiration date (i.e., $S_1 > E$), the value of call for one share of Walden stock is: $C_1 = S_1 - E = $80 - $70 = 10. The value of a call option for 100 shares is (10×100) = $1,000.

2. If you buy the call, at the end of the year you will have either $0 or $1,000, as indicated in Problem 1. We must determine a strategy consisting of lending and buying call options that leaves us with the same returns as the stock. The number of options per share that must be purchased is

$$\Delta S / \Delta C = (\$80 - \$60)/\$10 - 0 = 2$$

so 2 call options must be purchased. The strategy which duplicates the returns from one share of stock is as follows: invest [$60/(1 + R_f)] = ($60/1.08) = $55.56 in the risk-free asset, and buy two call options. The current value of these two strategies must be the same:

$$(2 \times C_0) + \$60/(1 + R_f) = S_0$$
$$(2 \times C_0) + \$60/(1.08) = \$65$$

Solving this equation for C_0, we find that the value of a call option for one share is $4.72; the value of the call option contract for 100 shares is ($4.72 \times 100) = $472.

3. If the exercise price is $50, the option is certain to expire in the money. If you buy a call option for one share of stock, then the return at the end of the year will be either ($60 - $50) = $10 or ($80 - $50) = $30. For an option which is certain to expire in the money, the number of options required for the strategy to replicate the returns for the stock is: $\Delta S/\Delta C$ = ($80 - $60)/($30 - $10) = 1. In addition to buying the option today, you also lend an amount equal to the present value of the exercise price: ($50/1.08) = $46.30. the strategy of buying the option and lending $46.30 has the same possible future returns as does the strategy of simply buying the stock. Since the two strategies have the same future returns, they must have the same value today, as indicated in the following equation:

$$C_0 + E/(1 + R_f) = S_0$$
$$C_0 = S_0 - E/(1 + R_f) = \$65 - \$46.30 = \$18.70$$

The cost of the call option contract for 100 shares of Walden stock is ($18.70 \times 100) = $1,870.

4. The possible returns for a share of Walden stock are $80 and $60. The possible returns for a call option for one share of Walden stock are ($80 - $65) = $15 and $0. The number of options required for the strategy to replicate the returns for the stock is: $\Delta S/\Delta C$ = ($80 - $60)/($15 - 0) = $1\frac{1}{3}$. To duplicate the returns for a call option for one share, invest the following amount in the risk-free asset:

$$\$60/(1 + R_f) = \$60/1.08 = \$55.56$$

The strategy of buying the call options and investing at the risk-free rate has the same returns as does the strategy of buying the common stock. The current value of these two strategies must be the same:

$$S_0 = (1\frac{1}{3} \times C_0) + \$60/(1 + R_f) \ (1\frac{1}{3} \times 10) + \$60/1.08$$

Solving this equation for S_0, the current value of the stock is $68.89 per share.

5. The possible returns for a share of Walden stock are $80 and $60. The possible returns for a call option for one share of Walden stock are ($80 - $70) = $10 and $0. The number of options required for the strategy to replicate the returns for the stock is: $\Delta S/\Delta C$ = ($80 - $60)/($10 - 0) = 2. To duplicate the returns for a call option for one share, invest the following amount in the risk-free asset:

$$\$60/(1 + R_f) = \$60/1.08 = \$55.56$$

The current value of the two strategies must be the same:

$$S_0 = (2 \times C_0) + \$60/(1 + R_f) \ (2 \times C_0) + \$60/1.08 = \$50$$

Solving, C_0 equals (-$2.78) per share, or [(-$2.78) × 100] = (-$278). Since an option cannot have a negative value, the call is worthless. How can the option to buy a share of stock, that may be worth $80, for only $70 be worth nothing? This arises from the fact that the current stock price cannot be $50. You can borrow $50 at an 8% interest rate, and buy one share of stock. Under the worst case scenario, the share will be worth $60, but you will have to repay only ($50 × 1.08) = $54 on the loan. So you would earn at least a costless, riskless $6. There is an arbitrage opportunity here because the return on the stock is always greater than the riskless 8% interest rate. So the stock must sell for more than $50 per share.

6. If there is no uncertainty, the value of Hanna stock one year from now will be: $50e^{.10} = 55.26. The payoff on the option at that time is thus ($55.26 - $40) = $15.26. The value of the call is the PV of the future payoff: $15.26e^{-.10} = 13.81.

7. If the price of the stock on the expiration date is $65, the investor will exercise the put, and sell the stock for $80. The gain on exercise is $(E - S_1) = ($80 - $65) = 15 since the investor can purchase a share in the market for $65 and sell it for $80. Since she paid $8 to purchase the put, her net gain is ($15 - $8) = $7. If the price of the stock is $75 on the expiration date, the investor will exercise the put for a gain of $(E - S_1) = ($80 - $75) = 5. The net gain is ($5 - $8) = -$3 (i.e., a net loss). If the price of the stock is the same as the exercise price of the option, the investor will not exercise; if she did exercise the option, she would have no gain or loss on the transaction, which is the same result she would experience if she were to discard the option. Her net loss would be the $8 price of the option.

At a price of $85 or $95 (or at any stock price such that $E < S_1$), the investor will not exercise the option, so that her net loss is the $8 purchase price of the option. The maximum return the investor can earn is $80 per share, less the $8 price of the option; that is, if the market value of the stock declines to zero on the expiration date, the investor can sell, for $80, stock which has a value of $0.

8. If the stock price at expiration is $65, the put buyer will exercise the option, selling the stock for $80. The put writer must purchase for $80 a share of stock with a value of only $65; the gain on this transaction is ($65 - $80) = -$15 (i.e., a loss of $15). The loss to the put writer equals the put buyer's gain. Since the put writer receives the $8 purchase price of the option, the writer's net loss is (-$15 + $8) = -$7; the net loss to the writer is the same as the net gain to the buyer of the option.

If the price of the stock on the expiration date is $75, then the gain to the writer is ($75 - $80) = -$5, or a loss of $5; the net gain is (-$5 + $8) = $3. Since the option will not be exercised if the price of the stock is $80 or more on the expiration date, the gain to the writer of the put is the $8 purchase price of the option. The maximum return to the put writer is the $8 purchase price of the put. If the price of the stock falls to zero on the expiration date, the loss to the writer of the put is (-$80 + $8) = $72.

9. The value of the call option (C_1) is zero if the value of the stock is less than the exercise price of the option (i.e., if $S_1 \leq E$). If S_1 is $85 on the expiration date, the investor will exercise the option for a gain of $(S_1 - E) = ($85 - $80) = 5; her net gain is ($5 - $10) = -$5. If S_1 is $95, the gain on the exercise of the option is $(S_1 - E) = ($95 - $80) = 15, and the net gain is ($15 - $10) = $5. In principle, there is no upper limit to return on the call; the higher the price of the stock on the expiration date, the greater the net gain to the investor.

10. If the stock price on the expiration date is less than or equal to the exercise price (i.e., if $S_1 \leq E$), then the buyer of the call option will not exercise it and the net gain to the writer of the option is the $10

purchase price. This is the same as the loss to the buyer of the option, as indicated in Problem 9, because the writing of a call option is a zero-sum game.

The buyer of the call will exercise the option if the price of the stock is $85 on the expiration date, forcing the writer of the call to sell, for $80, a share of stock whose market value is $85. Therefore, the exercise of the option results in a $5 loss to the writer of the option; the net gain to the writer of the option is ($10 - $5) = $5. If the price of the stock is $95, the exercise of the option results in a $15 loss to the writer of the option, and a net gain of (-$15 + $10) = -$5, or a loss of $5.

The maximum return to the writer of the call is the $10 purchase price of the call; the writer earns this amount if $S_1 \leq E$, so the call is not exercised. The maximum loss to the writer of the call is, theoretically, unlimited; as the price of the stock increases, the loss to the writer of the option increases.

11. The firm's stockholders own a call option on the firm's assets with an exercise price equal to the debt's face value of $5,000. The option is certain to expire in the money, since the value of the firm's assets will exceed the exercise price on the expiration date of the option. Consequently, the value of the option is equal to the current value of the underlying asset (i.e., the firm's total assets) minus the PV of the exercise price: $C_0 = S_0 - E/(1 + R_f) = \$4,600 - \$5,000/(1.11) = \$95.50$. So the firm's equity is worth $95.50. The current value of the debt is ($5,000/1.11) = $4,504.50.

12. If, in one year, the value of the firm's assets is $4,500, the stockholders will elect to default; since the option is out of the money at expiration, it is worthless. On the other hand, if the value of the firm's assets is $5,500, then the value of the call option is $(S_1 - E) = (\$5,500 - \$5,000) = \$500$. The strategy which replicates the possible values of the underlying asset is an investment of ($4500/1.11) = $4,054.05 in the risk free asset and the purchase of an appropriate number of call options, computed as follows: $\Delta S/\Delta C = (\$5,500 - \$4,500)/(\$500 - 0) = 2$. The current value of the firm must equal the value of the two call options plus the PV of the investment in the risk-free asset: $\$4,600 = (2 \times C_0) + \$4,054.05$. Solving for C_0, we find that the value of the firm's equity is $272.97. The value of the firm's debt is the value of firm less the value of the equity: $4,600 - $272.97 = $4,327.03. The debt has a maturity value of $5,000, so the interest rate on the firm's debt is: ($5,000/$4,327.03) - 1 = .15553 = 15.553%.

13. The bond can be converted into 16 shares of common stock, so the conversion ratio is 16. The *conversion price* is the face value of the bond divided by the conversion ratio: $1000/16 = $62.5. The *conversion premium* is the difference between the conversion price and the stock price: ($62.50 - $45) = $17.50. The conversion premium as a percent of the price is: ($17.50/$45.00) = .39 = 39%.

14. The straight bond value of a convertible bond is the price at which it would sell if it were not convertible. The straight bond value is:
   $[\$120 \times PVIFA(13\%,18)] + \$1,000/(1.13)^{18} = (\$120 \times 6.839905) + (\$1,000 \times .11081) = \$931.60$.

15. The conversion value is the conversion ratio times the stock price: $16 \times \$45 = \$720$. The floor value of a convertible bond is the greater of the straight bond and conversion values; for the Erving bond, the floor value is $931.60.

16. With no warrants, the value of the bond would be the PV of the future coupon interest payments plus the PV of the $1,000 maturity value; so the value of the bond is $719.89. The value of the warrants is ($1,000 - $719.89) = $280.11. Since there are ten warrants, each is worth $28.01.

17. The straight bond value is $719.89. Each bond enables the owner to buy a total of 50 shares of stock for $15 per share. The minimum value of the warrants is [50 × (S - $15)]; the solution to Problem 16 indicates that the total value of the warrants is $280.11. Therefore, the current stock price is at most the value of S in the following equation: 50 × (S - $15) = $280.11. Solving for S, we find that the current stock price is at most: S = $15 + ($280.11/50) = $20.60.

CHAPTER 23

1. At $22 per share, Firm A is paying ($22 × 350) = $7,700 to acquire Firm B. The value of Firm A is: V_A = $50 × 700 = $35,000. The value of Firm B is: V_B = $20 × 350 = $7,000. The incremental net gain from the merger is: $\Delta V = V_{AB} - (V_A + V_B)$ = $43,000 - ($35,000 + $7,000) = $1,000. The value of Firm B to Firm A is: $V*_B = \Delta V + V_B$ = $1,000 + $7,000 = $8,000. The NPV of the merger is: $V*_B$ - Cost to Firm A of the acquisition = $8,000 - $7,700 = $300. Since the NPV is positive, the acquisition is beneficial to the stockholders of Firm A. Firm A should proceed with the acquisition.

2. The *synergy* is the value of the combined firm less the total value of the two separate firms:

$$\Delta V = V_{AB} - (V_A + V_B) = \$1,000$$

as computed in the solution to Problem 1. The *merger premium* is the difference between the acquisition price and V_B, the market value of the acquired firm: ($22 × 350) - ($20 × 350) = $700. The NPV can be computed as the synergy minus the merger premium, or ($1,000 - $700) = $300, as in Problem 1.

3. The NPV of the merger is $300, so the stock will increase in value by ($300/700) = $.43 per share; the stock price will be $50.43. Note that, in the case of a cash acquisition, the NPV accrues to the stockholders of the acquiring firm.

4. Firm A must give ($22/$50) = .44 shares of its stock for every share of B, or (.44 × 350) = 154 shares. [This result is also equal to the cash price of the acquisition divided by the current market value of a share of Firm A stock: ($7,700/$50) = 154.] The new firm will have 854 shares outstanding. Post-merger firm value is: $V_{AB} = V_A + V_B + \Delta V$ = $35,000 + $7,000 + $1,000 = $43,000.

So the per share value is ($43,000/854) = $50.3513, and the actual cost of the acquisition is (154 × $50.3513) = $7,754.10. The NPV of the merger is $V*_B$ - Cost = $8,000 - $7,754.10 = $245.90.

5. The synergy is $1,000, as indicated in Problem 2. The merger premium is the difference between the acquisition price and the value of the acquired firm: $7,754.10 - ($20 × 350) = $754.10. The NPV is the synergy minus the merger premium, or ($1,000 - $754.10) = $245.90. This NPV is $54.10 less than the $300 NPV of the acquisition for cash. When the acquisition is paid for with an exchange of stock, the stockholders of Firm B receive a proportionate part of the NPV of the acquisition: (154/854) × $300 = $54.10. This difference can also be viewed as the increment in the value of the shares of Firm A which is given to the stockholders of Firm B: ($50.3513 - $50) × 154 = $54.10.

6. For Firm B stockholders to receive $7,700, they must receive stock with a value of ($7,700/$43,000) = .17907 = 17.907% of the merged firm. So new shares issued must represent 17.907% of the outstanding shares of the merged firm. This value is determined by solving for x: [x/(700 + x)] = .17907. The number of new shares issued to Firm B stockholders B is 152.691, so the number of shares

outstanding will be $(700 + 152.691) = 852.691$. Share price will be ($43,000/852.691) = $50.4286. Firm B stockholders receive 152.691 shares worth $50.4286, or $(152.69 \times \$50.4286) = \$7,700$.

7. The new firm will have earnings of $4,900. At $21 per share, Firm A must give $[(\$21/\$50) \times 350]$ = 147 shares to the shareholders of Firm B, so the new firm will have 847 shares outstanding. EPS will be ($4,900/847) = $5.785, an increase of $.785 from the pre-merger level of $5 per share.

8. Before the merger, Firm A had a P/E ratio of ($50/$5) = 10. If the market *is* fooled, in that this P/E ratio is unchanged after the merger, the stock will rise in value to $(10 \times \$5.785) = \$57.85$. If the market *is not* fooled, the P/E ratio will fall to ($43,000/$4,900) = 8.776, and share price will be $(8.776 \times \$5.785) = \$50.77$. This equals firm value divided by number of shares: ($43,000/847) = $50.77.

9. The synergy is the PV of a $10,000 perpetuity: $\Delta V = V_{AB} - (V_A + V_B) = (\$10,000/.20) = \$50,000$. So Max's value to Blizzard is: $V^*_B = \Delta V + V_B = \$50,000 + \$200,000 = \$250,000$.

10. The merger premium is ($220,000 - $200,000) = $20,000. The NPV is the synergy minus the merger premium, or ($50,000 - $20,000) = $30,000.

11. $V_{AB} = V_A + V_B + \Delta V = \$500,000 + \$200,000 + \$50,000 = \$750,000$. Twenty-five percent of the combined company is worth $.25 \times \$750,000 = \$187,500$. The NPV of this acquisition would be: V^*_B - Cost = $250,000 - $187,500 = $62,500. Blizzard would prefer to acquire Max Motors for 25 percent of the firm's stock rather than the $220,000 cash offer in Problem 10.

12. With a pooling of interests, the balance sheets are summed; the new balance sheet appears as follows:

M. Wilson Company, Inc. ($ in thousands)

Current assets	$ 3,500	Current liabilities	$ 1,350
Fixed assets	$11,500	Long-term debt	$ 4,400
		Equity	$ 9,250
Total	$15,000		$15,000

13. Buckner's fair market value is $5,000 plus $1,500 in current assets, or $6,500 total. The ($7,500 - $6,500) = $1,000 premium paid is goodwill. Wilson's fixed assets would be $8,000 (the book value of Wilson's pre-merger fixed assets) plus $5,000 (the market value of Buckner's assets), or $13,000 total. The balance sheet appears as follows:

M. Wilson Company, Inc. ($ in thousands)

Current assets	$ 3,500	Current liabilities	$ 1,350
Fixed assets	$13,000	Long-term debt	$10,150
Goodwill	$ 1,000	Equity	$ 6,000
Total	$17,500		$17,500

Solution note: Buckner's assets are ($5,000 + $1,500) = $6,500. If the current liabilities and long-term debt are shown at market value, the equity in Buckner is worth ($6,500 - $750 - $1,000) = $4,750. Wilson pays a $1,000 premium, so the total amount of debt that Wilson must raise is ($4,750 + $1,000) = $5,750. The total long-term debt after the merger is ($5,750 + $3,400 + $1,000) = $10,150.

CHAPTER 24

1. The annual net cash outflow is -$6,000 × (1 - .34) + -$6,250 × (.34) = -$6,085.

2. We compute the NAL for the Mayberry Sheriff's Department as follows. First, the after-tax cost of debt is .08 × (1 - .34) = .0528. And the NAL equals -$6,085 × [1 - 1/(1.0528)⁴/.0528] + $25,000 = $ 3,562.50. Since the NAL is positive, the firm should lease the car, rather than buy it.

3. Mount Pilot Leasing's NAL is $6,085 × [1 - 1/(1.0528)⁴/.0528] - $25,000 = $ -3,562.50.

4. Given R = .06 and T_c = .50, Mount Pilot's R* = .06 × (1 - .5) = .03. The revised NPV equals:

$$[-\$6,000 \times (1 - .5) + (-)6,250(.5)] \times [1 - 1/(1.03)^4/.03] - \$ 25,000 = -\$2,232.77$$

The lease is still not a good project for Mount Pilot Leasing.

5. If Mount Pilot Leasing can buy the car for $ 20,000, the deal becomes worthwhile.

$$[-\$6,000 \times (1 - .5) + (-)6,250(.5)] \times [1 - 1/(1.03)^4/.03] - \$20,000 = \$444.04.$$

6. The cost of purchasing the car at the end of the lease's life is an additional cost of leasing. (See footnote 7 in the Leasing Supplement.) If the car had been purchased at day 0 and then sold for $8,000 at the end of 4 years, the firm would owe additional taxes equal to the book "gain" ($6,000) times the firm's marginal tax rate. The net inflow at time 4 would therefore have been $8,000 × (1 - .34) = $5,280. By leasing, the firm gives up this cash flow. Thus, the revised NAL is

$$\$25,000 - \$6,085 \times [1 - 1/(1.0528)^4/.0528] - \$ 5280 \times [1/(1.0528)^4] = \$ -735.34$$

In this case, the advantage to leasing disappears if one considers the residual value foregone.

7. Since the residual value is a cost of leasing, a higher residual value should reduce the NAL. To obtain a higher residual value, however, we must apply a *lower* discount rate (due to the mathematics of present value. In this case, the appropriate discount rate for the residual value is 5.28% - 2% = 3.28%. Thus, the revised NAL equals:

$$\$25,000 - \$6,085 \times [1 - 1/(1.0528)^4/.0528] - \$ 5280 \times [1/(1.0328)^4] = \$ -1,078.05.$$

CHAPTER 25

1. Your one DM will buy $.50. With $.50, you can buy 1/3 of a pound. The cross rate is DM 3/£ 1.

2. Use the one DM to purchase $.50, and exchange the $.50 for £ (1/3). At the cross rate of DM 3.3/£ 1, 1/3 pound can be exchanged for DM 1.1; this results in an arbitrage profit of 10%.

3. Exchange DM 1 for £ (1/2.7) = £ .37037, and then purchase [£ .37037 x ($1.50/£ 1)] = $.55556. At the exchange rate on DM 2/41, $.55556 can be exchanged for [$.55556 x (DM 2/$1)] = 1.1111 marks. This result represents an arbitrage profit of 11.11%.

4. The direct (or American) exchange rate is the number of dollars per unit of foreign currency; the exchange rates given above are quoted as direct exchange rates. The indirect exchange rate is the number of units or the foreign currency per dollar. To convert the direct spot exchange rate for the British pound to the indirect exchange rate, divide both sides of the direct exchange rate quote by 1.80:

$$\$1.80/1.80 = £ \, 1/1.80$$

Therefore, the indirect exchange rate is £ 0.5556. In general, the indirect exchange rate is the reciprocal of the direct exchange rate. For the British pound, the ninety-day direct exchange rate is (£ 1/1.75) = £ 0.5714. For the Swiss franc, the spot and ninety-day forward rates are SF 1.2500 and SF 1.3333, respectively. For the deutsche mark, the respective rates are DM 1.5385 and 1.4286, respectively.

The German deutsche mark is more expensive in the future than it is today (i.e., $.70/DM 1 and $.65/DM 1, respectively), so the deutsche mark is selling at a premium relative to the dollar; equivalently, the dollar is selling at a discount relative to the deutsche mark. On the other hand, the British pound is less expensive in the future than it is today (i.e., $1.75/£ 1 and $1.80/£ 1, respectively), so the pound is selling at a discount relative to the dollar; equivalently, the dollar is selling at a premium relative to the pound. These latter conclusions also apply to the Swiss franc.

5. The spot rate for British pounds is £ 0.5556/$1; the spot rate for the deutsche mark is DM 1.5385/$1. So £ 0.5556 and DM 1.5385 are equivalent, so the cross-rate for pounds in terms of deutsche marks is:

$$£ \, 0.5556/DM \, 1.5385$$
$$= [(£ \, 0.5556)/1.5385]/[(DM \, 1.5385)/1.5385] = £ \, .3611/DM \, 1$$

The cross-rate for pounds in terms of deutsche marks is

$$DM \, 1.5385/£ \, 0.5556$$
$$= [(DM \, 1.5385)/.5556][(£ \, 0.5556)/.5556] = DM \, 2.7691/£ \, 1$$

Note that the cross-rate for pounds in terms of deutsche marks is the reciprocal of the cross-rate for deutsche marks in terms of pounds.

6. Here, the deutsche mark is less expensive in terms of pounds than it is in terms of dollars. So the triangle arbitrage opportunity requires purchasing deutsche marks using pounds, and then selling deutsche marks for dollars; that is, buy deutsche marks at the lower price and then sell deutsche marks at the higher price. Specifically, first convert $1 to £ 0.5556. Next, convert pounds to deutsche marks:

$$£ \, .35 = DM \, 1$$
$$(£ \, 0.5556)/.35 = DM \, 1.5874$$

Then convert DM 1.5874 to dollars: $$DM \, 1.5385 = \$1$$
$$(DM \, 1.5874)/1.5385 = \$1.0318$$

Thus, $1 has been converted to $1.0318, using triangle arbitrage.

302

7. The deutsche mark is less expensive in terms of dollars than it is in terms of pounds. So the triangle arbitrage opportunity requires purchasing deutsche marks using dollars, and selling deutsche marks for pounds, that is, buy deutsche marks at the lower price and then sell deutsche marks at the higher price. Convert $1 to DM 1.5385. Next, convert DM 1.5385 to pounds. The cross-rate for deutsche marks in terms of pounds is the reciprocal of the rate for pounds in terms of deutsche marks:

$$DM\ (1/.37)/£\ 1 = DM\ 2.7027/£\ 1$$

So DM 1.5385 are converted to [£ (1.5385/2.7027)] = £ 0.5692. Pounds are converted to dollars: £ 0.5692 = [$(.5692/.5556] = $1.0245.

8. The trader can purchase ($500/$5) = 100 ounces of silver in the U.S. This can then be sold for (100 × ¥ 800) = ¥ 80,000 in Japan. At the exchange rate of ¥ 150/$1, the trader can exchange ¥ 80,000 for [¥ 80,000/(¥ 150/$1)] = $533.33; the arbitrage profit is ($533.33 - $500) = $33.33. This is not an equilibrium situation; it is a violation of the concept of *absolute purchasing power parity*. Demand for silver in the U.S. will cause the dollar price of silver to increase and the supply of silver will cause the yen price to decrease in Japan. The exchange rate will increase due to the increased demand for dollars and the decreased demand for yen.

9. The condition for absolute purchasing power parity is: $P_{FC} = S_0 \times P_{us}$. So for APP to prevail, S_0 must equal $P_{FC}/P_{US} = ¥\ 800/\$5 = ¥\ 160/\$1$.

10. In this situation, the trader can exchange $500 for [$500 x (¥ 150/$4)] = ¥ 75,000. With ¥ 75,000, the trader can then purchase (75,000/700) = 107.1429 ounces of solver in Japan. He can sell the silver for ($5 x 107.1429) = $535.71, for an arbitrage profit of $35.71.

11. The indirect rates are the reciprocal of the direct rates; therefore, the spot rate is DM (1/.50) = DM 2.0000 and the forward rate is DM 1.9608.

12. From the interest rate parity condition: $F_1/S_0 = (1 + R_G)/(1 + R_{US})$. Substituting,

$$1.9608/2,000 = (1 + R_G)/1.03$$

So: R_G = .009812. The German risk-free rate is .9812%, or approximately 1%.

13. Since the exchange rates here are in terms of units of foreign currency per dollar, the relevant spot rate here is S_0 = SF (1/1.50) = SF ⅔ = SF 0.66667. Substituting into the RPP relationship:

$$(E[S_1] - S_0)/S_0 = h_{FC} - h_{US}$$
$$(E[S_1] - ⅔)/⅔ = .02 - .05$$
$$E[S_1] = .64667$$

Solution note: Be careful here to use the exchange rate expressed as units of foreign currency per dollar. The difference between the Swiss and the U.S. inflation rates is (-3%), so the price of a dollar, measured in terms of Swiss francs will decrease by approximately 3%: [(SF .66667) x .97] = SF .64667.

14. By IRP: $F_1/S_0 = (1 + R_j)/(1 + R_{US}) = F_1/150 = 1.06/1.08$. The forward rate is ¥ 147.22/$1.

15. Using the international Fisher effect, the Japanese inflation rate (h_J) can be determined as follows:

$$R_{US} - h_{US} = R_J - h_J$$
$$= .08 - .04 = .06 - h_J$$
$$h_J = .02 = 2\%$$

The expected spot exchange rate five years from now is determined using the RPP relationship:

$$E\,[S_t] = S_0 \times [1 + (h_{FC} - h_{US})]^t$$
$$E\,[S_5] = S_0 \times [1 + (h_{FC} - h_{US})]^5 = (¥\,147.22) \times [1 + (.02 - .04)]^5 = ¥\,133.08$$

16. The expected spot exchange rate is determined using the relative purchasing power parity relationship:

$$E\,[S_t] = S_0 \times [1 + (h_{FC} - h_{US})]^t$$
$$E\,[S_3] = S_0 \times [1 + (h_{FC} - h_{US})]^3 = (SA\,2) \times [1.10]^3 = SA\,2.662$$

17. The expected spot exchange rates for years 1, 2 and 3 are presented in the following table:

Year	Expected exchange rate
1	$(SA\,2) \times (1.10)^1 = SA\,2.200$
2	$(SA\,2) \times (1.10)^2 = SA\,2.420$
3	$(SA\,2) \times (1.10)^3 = SA\,2.662$

Year	Cash Flow (in SA)	Expected exchange rate	Cash flow (in $)
0	-SA 1000	SA 2.000	$-500.0000
1	SA 300	SA 2.200	$ 136.3636
2	SA 300	SA 2.420	$ 123.9669
3	SA 700	SA 2.662	$ 262.9602

At a 12% discount rate, the NPV in dollars is -$92.25.